Edwards Amasa Park, Austin Phelps

Hymns and Choirs

Or, the matter and the manner of the service of song in the house of the Lord

Edwards Amasa Park, Austin Phelps

Hymns and Choirs

Or, the matter and the manner of the service of song in the house of the Lord

ISBN/EAN: 9783337298067

Printed in Europe, USA, Canada, Australia, Japan

Cover: Foto ©Thomas Meinert / pixelio.de

More available books at **www.hansebooks.com**

HYMNS AND CHOIRS:

OR,

THE MATTER AND THE MANNER

OF THE

Service of Song in the House of the Lord.

BY

AUSTIN PHELPS AND EDWARDS A. PARK,
PROFESSORS AT ANDOVER,

AND DANIEL L. FURBER,
PASTOR AT NEWTON.

ANDOVER:
WARREN F. DRAPER.
BOSTON: GOULD AND LINCOLN; CROSBY, NICHOLS, LEE & CO.
NEW YORK: JOHN WILEY.
PHILADELPHIA: SMITH, ENGLISH & CO.
1860.

Entered according to Act of Congress, in the year 1860, by
WARREN F. DRAPER,
In the Clerk's Office of the District Court of the District of Massachusetts.

ANDOVER:
ELECTROTYPED AND PRINTED
BY W. F. DRAPER.

PREFACE.

THE principles of hymnology are the principles of worship. The criticisms upon hymns have essentially the same character with criticisms upon prayers. The excellences and the faults of hymns are, substantially, the excellences and the faults of all addresses to God. As the Praise of Jehovah is but one variety of Prayer, so a Christian Hymn Book is the most seemly form of a Christian Prayer Book. The discussions in the present volume, therefore, derive their principal, if they have any, worth, from their liturgical references. They relate to the matter and to the manner of all worship. They illustrate the subject and the form of prayer in general, by the subject and the form of that species of prayer which is expressed in song. While, then, the immediate object of the volume is to examine the contents, the proportion, and the style of hymns, and the method of addressing them to God, the ultimate object of the volume is to examine the principles that underlie all modes of Christian worship.

These principles have been suggested to two of the authors of the present volume, during the several years which they have devoted to the Sabbath Hymn Book. It has been, therefore, convenient for them to use that manual freely in illustration and defence of these principles. It has been also convenient to notice various criticisms upon the Sabbath Hymn Book, not merely for the sake of justifying that manual, but chiefly for the sake of giving greater prominence to certain principles of worship with regard to which discordant opinions are expressed by different critics. It was easier to discuss these principles in connection with the criticisms which had become familiar to the writers, than to discuss them in a more abstract and general way.

The first chapter in the volume was written by Professor Phelps; the second, by Professor Park; and nearly one-half of these chapters has been published in the Bibliotheca Sacra. The third chapter was written by Rev. Daniel L. Furber, Pastor of the Congregational Church in Newton Centre, Massachusetts. Having had no connection with the Sabbath Hymn Book Series, he has felt himself at liberty to speak of that Series with a freedom which might have been unbecoming in his colleagues.

The three authors of these three chapters have written independently of each other, and neither of the three is responsible for any thought or word of his associates. Their discussions are grouped together into one volume, with a view rather to the affinity of subjects, than to the absolute unity of details. It is hoped that they may tend to awaken the interest of pious men in one of the most important parts of sacred and public worship.

ANDOVER THEOLOGICAL SEMINARY,
Oct. 8, 1860.

CONTENTS.

CHAPTER I.

HYMNOLOGY AN EXPRESSION OF RELIGIOUS LIFE.

	PAGE
§ 1. Introductory,	5
§ 2. Hymnology Historic,	6
§ 3. Revival of Hymnology at the Reformation,	8
§ 4. Hymnology of the English Reformation,	15
§ 5. Scriptural Foundation of Hymnology,	21
§ 6. Identity of Psalms and Hymns,	28
§ 7. Hymns founded on other portions of the Scriptures than the Book of Psalms,	31
§ 8. Ancient Hymnology,	37
§ 9. Modern Hymnology,	51
§ 10. The Number of Hymns,	66
§ 11. Proportion of Hymns on Prolific Themes,	70
§ 12. Hymns of Worship,	75
§ 13. Hymns of Joy,	78
§ 14. Comminatory Hymns,	81
§ 15. Unity of Worship,	87
§ 16. Occasional Hymns,	91
Hymns on the Lord's Supper,	91
Hymns for Sabbath Schools,	92
Hymns on Civil Freedom,	99
Hymns of Dedication and Installation,	100
§ 17. Necessity of Inferior Hymns,	103

		PAGE
§ 18. Omitted Hymns, ...		107
Hymns Omitted for Want of Symmetry, . . .		108
" " for Want of Unity, ...		113
" " for Want of Character, . . .		114
" " for Relative Inferiority, . . .		115
" " for Comparative Uselessness, . .		117
" " for Excessive License in use of the Scriptures, ...		118
" " for Want of the Forms of Worship, .		122
" " for an Unseemly Tragic Character, .		123
" " for an Excess of Analytic Character, .		123
" " for Theatrical Structure, . .		124
Omissions required by *many* of the laws of Song, . .		126
Omission of "The Dying Christian to his Soul,"		126
" of "Warning to Magistrates," . .		129
Conclusion, ...		136

CHAPTER II.

THE TEXT OF HYMNS.

Introductory Remarks on the Perils and the Necessity of criticizing Hymns, ... 138
§ 1. The Relation of Changes in the Text to the Rights of Authors, 140
§ 2. The Relation of Changes in the Text to the Encouragement of Authors, ... 143
§ 3. The Immodesty of Changing the Text of Hymns, . . 151
§ 4. The Probability that a Poet's Inspiration will surpass a Critic's Amendment, ... 154
§ 5. Changes in the Text, as affecting Old Associations, . . 161
§ 6. Changes in the Text, as affecting the Uniformity of Worship, 172
§ 7. The Principle of Changes in the Text lies at the Basis of Modern English Hymnology, ... 177
§ 8. The Principle of Deviating from another's Text, is substantially the Principle of Quoting another's Words, . . . 186

	PAGE
§ 9. Difficulty of ascertaining the Original Text of some Hymns,	197
§ 10. Changes in the Text, as affecting its Biblical and Evangelical Character,	206
§ 11. Changes in the Text, as affecting its Dignity,	212
§ 12. Changes in the Text, as affecting its Vivacity,	216
§ 13. Changes in the Text, as affecting its Solemnity,	223
§ 14. Changes in the Text, as affecting its Neatness,	230
§ 15. Changes in the Text, as affecting its Vigor,	234
§ 16. Changes in the Text, as affecting its Poetical and Lyrical Character,	237
§ 17. The Adaptation of a Hymn to the State of Mind in Public Worship,	244
§ 18. Changes in the Text, as affecting the Fundamental Qualities of the Style,	250
§ 19. Changes in the Text, as affecting the Service of Song,	256
§ 20. Changes in the Text, as resulting from Changes in the Application of a Hymn.	270
§ 21. The Indispensable Necessity of some Alterations in some Hymns,	277
§ 22. Changes in the Text, as affecting its Consistency with itself,	283
§ 23. Changes in a Hymn as affecting its Availability,	290
§ 24. Concluding Remarks,	294
On the Completeness of a Particular Hymn,	294
On the Symmetry of an Entire Collection,	295
On a Test for Criticisms,	296
The General Rule *for* and *against* Alterations,	297

CHAPTER III.

THE DIGNITY AND THE METHODS OF WORSHIP IN SONG.

§ 1. Existing Feeling and Usage respecting the Service of Praise,	299
§ 2. The Dignity of Praise, as seen in its Nature,	304
§ 3. The Dignity of Praise, as seen in the Divine Appointments respecting it,	306

CONTENTS.

	PAGE
§ 4. The Manner of Praise, as indicated by the Nature of the Service,	312
§ 5. The Manner of Praise, as indicated by the Common Effect of Choir-singing,	316
§ 6. Choir-singing appropriately Jewish,	320
§ 7. The Manner of Praise, as indicated by the Nature of the Christian Dispensation,	323
§ 8. Singing Habits of the Early Christians,	327
§ 9. The Mode of Song adopted by the Reformers,	332
§ 10. Congregational Psalmody in its Moral and Religious Influence,	337
§ 11. Elevated Religious Feeling usually seeks expression in Song,	349
§ 12. Practical Remarks on Congregational Singing,	355
1. Influence of Ministers,	358
2. Children's Singing,	359
3. Choirs,	365
4. Unisonous Singing,	368

Miscellaneous Details.

1. Attitude in Singing,	376
2. Position of the Organ,	377
3. Meetings for Practice,	378
4. The Hymn and its Tune,	379
5. Musical Expression,	380
6. Organ Interludes,	386

Congregational Tunes.

1. Should be Simple,	389
2. Should be Natural,	390
3. Should be Easy to Sing,	393
4. Should be Strong,	397
5. Should be Spirited,	398
6. Should possess Variety,	399
§ 13. Illustrations of the preceding Remarks,	401
§ 14. Brief statement of Rules for Congregational Singing,	424

HYMNS AND CHOIRS.

CHAPTER I.

HYMNOLOGY AN EXPRESSION OF RELIGIOUS LIFE.

§ 1. *Introductory.*

A GOOD Hymn Book must be a good manual of religious experience. The Ideal of a perfect Hymn Book is that of a perfect expression of the real life of the church, in forms perfectly adjusted to the service of song. It excludes, on the one hand, lyric poetry which is *only* poetry, though it be on sacred themes; and, on the other hand, it is equally unfriendly to devotional rhymes which, though truthful, are so unworthy in respect of poetic form as to degrade the truths they embody; and yet again, it rejects, as unbecoming to the sanctuary, those religious poems which are both true to the Christian life and unexceptionable in their poetic spirit, and yet are of such rhythmic structure as to be unfit for expression with the accompaniment of music. Genuineness of religious emotion, refinement of poetic taste, and fitness to musical cadence —these three are essential to a faultless hymn, as the three chief graces to a faultless character. Yet "the greatest of these," that grace which above all else vitalizes a true hymn, is that which *makes* it true—its fidelity to the realities of religious experience. Every true hymn is a "Psalm of Life:" some soul has lived it. A manual of such psalmody is the guide which the church needs in her worship of God in song.

§ 2. *Hymnology Historic.*

Such a manual must therefore be pervaded by a *historic* spirit. We must search for its materials along the track which a living church has trodden; and must expect to find them in the richest profusion, where the life of the church has been most intense. The search cannot disappoint us. It is a signal fact that the history of hymnology and the history of piety are synchronous in their development. Hymnology has not been swayed mainly by the mutations of literature as such, but by those of the religious vitality of the church. The rise and fall of the one have been the invariable exponent of the ebb and flow of the other. Hebrew piety created the Hebrew literature, and that found its chief expression in the Hebrew psalmody. The "Psalms and Hymns and Spiritual Songs" of the apostolic churches, were an out-gushing of the new spirit of Christianity, which does not seem to have restricted itself to the ancient songs of the temple, or of the synagogue. Even the miraculous endowments of the first Christian age, appear to have manifested one class of their phenomena in the inspired improvisation of psalms. The earliest Christian historians agree in affirming, that the Christian communities of their times employed in the worship of the sanctuary, not only the Psalms and other metrical passages of the Old Testament, but also hymns original to the age, and which the religious character of the age demanded for its own expression. Tertullian states that each participant in the ancient *agapæ* was invited, at the close of the feast, to sing as he might prefer "either from the holy Scriptures, or from the dictates of his own spirit, a song of adoration to God." Contemporaneous heathen writers, also, recount in the same breath, the mild virtues of the new sect and their custom of "singing hymns, of antiphonal structure, to Christ as to a God."

In the emergencies of the early church, the spirit of martyrdom found solace in hymns which the sufferers sung in dungeons, and on their way to the cross or the stake. Augustine speaks of the effect he experienced in listening to the psalms and hymns, on his first entrance into the church at Milan after his conversion. He says: "The voices flowed in at my ears, truth was distilled in my heart, and the affection of piety overflowed in sweet tears of joy." He adds that the custom of chanting hymns and psalms had been introduced from the East, among the Milanese Christians, "that the people might not languish and pine away in sorrow," under the Arian persecution by the empress Justina. Others of the Fathers remark that the singing of the ancient churches often attracted "Gentiles" to their worship, who were baptized before their departure.[1]

An evidence of the pious usage, which must already have become general among Christians in the East,

---

[1] Upon this fact, an English writer of the last century observes: "The generality of *our* parochial music is not likely to produce similar effects; being such as would sooner drive Christians with good ears *out* of the church, than draw Pagans *into* it."

appears in the abuse of the usage in the time of Chrysostom, when bands of Orthodox and Arian choristers were organized to perambulate the streets of Constantinople, singing hymns upon the rival doctrines, in imitation of the processional singing of the pagans. Some of the hymns thus claiming for theology an alliance with song, Chrysostom himself composed. During the eclipse of faith which succeeded, the most conclusive token which remained, to come down to our day, in proof that the vitality of the church had not died out, was the voices from the cloisters, here and there, in spiritual songs which the church still welcomes as treasures. One might trace out, correctly, both the corruption and the life of the church, through that whole night of the Middle Ages, by the line of hymnological literature alone. If indeed we must choose between the creeds and the songs of the church, for a test of her growth or decadence in spirituality, we would select her songs, as her most honest utterances.

§ 3. *Revival of Hymnology at the Reformation.*

The most remarkable, because the most sharply defined, illustration of the sympathy of hymnology with the piety of the church, appears in the history of the Reformation. One of the first symptoms of that great awakening, was the revival of a taste and a demand for religious songs in the vernacular tongues. The demand was sudden, and the result of no visible design. It does not seem to have followed the labors of the reformed clergy, so much as to have been simultaneous with them—the working of a hidden force which moved both the clergy and the people. Its first manifestation on a large scale, was attended by one of those anomalies by which the providence of God often attests its secret agency, in the selection of singular and improbable instrumentalities. The history of the phenomenon, already well known as one of the "Curiosities of Literature," is worthy of review. Clement Marot, " a valet of the bedchamber to king Francis the First, and the favorite poet of France, tired of the vanities of profane poetry, or rather privately tinctured with the principles of Lutheranism, attempted with the assistance of his friend Theodore Beza, and by the encouragement of the professor of Hebrew [Vatable] in the University of Paris, a version of David's Psalms into French rhymes." It was about the year 1540. The amorous ditties of the poet had previously been the delight of the French court; and in dedicating his version of the Psalms in part " to the ladies of France," he apologizes to them for the surprise they would experience in receiving from him such an offering to their literary taste. No evidence appears that the " tincture " of Lutheranism which, it is said, Marot had privately imbibed, was such as to give to this literary "coup d'etat" the character of a design to revolutionize the ballads of the nation, or to aid the dissemination of the reformed faith, or even to express his own. It was rather a freak of poetic license, sobered somewhat by the personal influence of Beza, who may have entertained more intelligent hopes respecting the result. But the most sanguine Reformer could scarcely have indulged anticipations equal to the reality. The publication of Marot's Psalms marked an epoch in the history of the times. His previous contributions to the polite literature of the day were forgotten in the enthusiasm with which the court of Francis received the "Sainctes Chansonettes," as the poet termed his versions from the Hebrew Psalter. No suspicion was, at first, awakened of the tendency of the work towards the heresy of Wittenburg and Geneva. The Catholics were among the most eager purchasers of the volume, and the press was overburdened to meet their demands. The doctors of the Sorbonne saw no reason for withholding their sanction from that which they seem to have regarded as only a literary innovation, bold and fascinating to the frivolous, but probably destined to a brief notoriety. The consequence was, that " in the festive and splendid court of Francis, of a sudden," as we are told, " nothing was heard but the Psalms of Clement Marot. They were the common accompaniment of the fiddle; and with a characteristic liveliness of fancy, by each of the royal family and the principal nobility of the court, a psalm was chosen and fitted to the ballad-tune which each liked best. This fashion does not seem, in the least, to have diminished the gayety and good humor of the court of Francis." Such, regarded merely as a literary phenomenon, was the adventure of the ballad-singer into the field of Hebrew Psalmody, for the entertainment of the " ladies of France." But in the providence of God it had a deeper meaning.

The apostles of the Reformation were, just at this time, meditating improvements in their liturgical services. Luther in Germany and Calvin at Geneva, were intent upon abandoning the antiphonal chanting in which the people took no part. Before the publication of Marot's " Chansonettes," Luther, in a letter to Spalatinus, had said : " I am looking out for poets to translate the whole of the Psalms into the German tongue ;" and Calvin had proceeded so far as to project, with the advice of Luther, the translation of portions of the Psalms into the French language, and the adaptation of them to melodies, by which all could share in the public service of song. The juncture of events was most opportune. Calvin, with characteristic promptness, availed himself of Marot's gallantry, and instantly introduced the poet's thirty metrical versions from the Psalter into the reformed church of Geneva. On a certain Sabbath of the year 1540, might have been heard, probably, the noble ladies and lords of the court of his most Catholic majesty, and the humble congregation of the heresiarch of Geneva, singing the same words from the new psalm book!

The fashion of the court was short-lived. Not so the usage introduced by the Genevan worshippers. Marot soon added twenty to the thirty versions of the Psalms which he had first translated, and the whole were published, with a preface written by Calvin, in 1543. The new movement by which the people were to be made participants in the service of song, by means of metrical psalms in their own language, was thus fairly inaugurated. Its effect was electric. The Scriptures, which had long been shut up in a dead language, were thus released, in part, to the understanding and heart of the worshippers, in metrical forms which, however rude, were not so to the taste of the age. They were welcomed with unbounded enthusiasm. That cardinal principle of the Reformation, by which responsibility was individualized, was thus infused into the theory and practice of worship, and the heart of the people opened to receive it, gratefully. The new method of worship struck deep to the supply of wants, of which nothing could have made the popular mind sensible, but a revived spirituality of faith. It spread itself like the light. The golden candlestick at Geneva sent forth its rays far and wide. In the language of Warton, "France and Germany were instantly infatuated with a love of psalm-singing.... The energetic hymns of Geneva exhilarated the convivial assemblies of the Calvinists, were commonly heard in the streets, and accompanied the labors of the artificer.... They found their way to the cities of the Low Countries, and under their inspiration many of the weavers and woollen manufacturers of Flanders left their looms and entered into the ministry of the gospel." German, Dutch, Bohemian, and Polish versions of the Psalms, in metre, and both French and German hymns, were soon multiplied to an almost fabulous extent. The enthusiasm of Luther in the work is well known; and the popularity of his sixty-three hymns may be inferred from the fact that spurious Collections were hawked about the cities of Germany, under his name. Hymns in the vernacular dialects became a power in the Reformation, coördinate with that of the pulpit. Upon the masses of the people they were far more potent than any other uninspired productions of the press. At Augsburg, in 1551, "three or four thousand singing together at a time," was "but a trifle." The youth of the day sung them in place of ribald songs; mothers sung them beside the cradle; journeymen and servants sung them at their labor, and market-men in the streets, and husbandmen in the fields. At length, the "six thousand hymns" of a single poet, Hans Sachs, bore witness to the avidity of the demand and the copiousness of the supply.

Meanwhile the doctors of the Sorbonne had second thoughts respecting the Psalter of Clement Marot. They marvelled to see it published with the *imprimatur* of Calvin and affixed to the Catechism of Geneva. They bethought themselves of the peril of allowing the people to sing the word of God in their mother tongue; they induced the king to forbid Marot to continue his work; and the use of that and all similar versions of the Psalms was interdicted to the Catholics, under severe penalties. The use of metrical psalms, in the vulgar tongue, became a test of Protestantism. "Psalm-singing and heresy were regarded as synonymous terms." Marot himself was apprehended on suspicion of heresy, and thrown into prison, from which he was released only on condition of his renewed adherence to the mother church. Such was the Protestant reputation of his Psalms, however, in their proximity to the Genevan Catechism, that he found it necessary to retire from France, though he said of himself: "I am neither Lutheran nor Zuinglian. I am one whose delight and whose labor it is to exalt my Saviour and his all gracious mother."

The historian of English poetry ingeniously attributes this entire movement, and the rapid propagation of Calvinism consequent upon it, to the address of Calvin in planning a "mode of universal psalmody," the rudeness of which could draw converts "from the meanest of the people," and which should take the place of the Catholic pageantries and pictures, in the indispensable work of "keeping his congregation in good humor by some kind of allurement, which might enliven their attendance on the rigid duties of praying and preaching." But a wiser criticism will discern in it no human strategy. It was the spontaneous uprising of a demand which the Spirit of truth had aroused by the revival of pious faith, and to which the providence of God responded, in such means for its supply as the literature of the times could be made to furnish. The quickened heart of the people awoke to an experience which they could express only in Christian song. They sung it because they must sing it; and as soon as they could find words and measures in which they *could* sing it with the spirit and the understanding, however uncouthly to the taste of a later age, when it required no superior literary discernment in Voltaire to say, that "in proportion as good taste improved, the Psalms of Clement Marot inspired only disgust." A living scholar has observed, more profoundly, that "the Divine Spirit has always employed the ministry of *that* poetry which was the poetry of the age . . . . . as he has hallowed the prevalent dialects of speech." We probably shall not greatly err in believing, that those metrical versions of the Psalms which the Reformers commended to the use of their churches, were the best that could have been created by the taste, and appreciated by the piety, of that generation. They certainly did not offend the one, and they did express the other. All things considered, we may venture to think of them, as an old English critic said of an English metrical Psalter: "Match these verses for their age, and they shall go abreast with the best poems of those times."

§ 4. *Hymnology of the English Reformation.*

Wherever the spirit of the Reformation went, there followed the new system of popular participation in the service of song. It soon passed over from the Continent to England. And here its history is marked by the same sympathy with spiritual piety, that characterized its origin in the reformed churches of Germany and Switzerland. Two centuries before, the prelude of it had been heard in the psalmody of the disciples of Wicklif, and now as then, the quickening of religious life uttered itself in the revival of sacred melodies. Among the dignitaries of the English church and state, the innovation was approved by those who were friendly to the spirit of reform, and opposed by the adherents of Rome. The people generally were jubilant at its introduction. Those refugees from the intolerance of queen Mary, whom the accession of Elizabeth had restored to their benefices, had returned full of zeal for the Genevan modes of worship, and especially psalm-singing, as well as for the Genevan theology. The sympathy of the people with the continental innovations in worship, is described by Thomas Warton as "this infectious frenzy of sacred song." Says bishop Jewel: " As soon as they had commenced singing in public, in one little church in London, immediately not only the churches in the neighborhood, but even towns far distant, began to vie with each other in the practice." At St. Paul's Cross, six thousand persons, of all ages, might be heard singing the new songs; which, in the shrewd judgment of the bishop, was " sadly annoying to the mass-priests and the devil." Puritanism, then in embryo, throbbed with the popular exhilaration. The church of England, with her characteristic spirit of compromise, retained the choral mode of singing in the cathedrals and collegiate churches, and continued the use of the liturgic hymns in her prayer-book; but provided for the popular demand by a metrical version of the Psalms, which were " set forth and *allowed* to be sung in churches of all the people together." Such was the origin of the metrical Psalter which still bears the names of its chief translators: " The whole Booke of Psalmes, collected into English Metre by T. Sternhold, J. Hopkins, and others, conferred with the Ebrue, with apt Notes to sing them withall." The use of metrical psalmody instantly became the badge, and the test, of sympathy with the new life which the Reformation was breathing into the churches of Great Britain. " It was a sign by which men's affections to the work of the Reformation were everywhere measured, whether they used to sing [David's Psalms] or not." As psalm-singing and heresy were synonymes on the Continent, so psalm-singing and Puritanism became synonymes in England. The Psalms in the vulgar tongue were, on the one hand, stigmatized as " Geneva Jiggs " and " Beza's Ballets," and on the other hand, they were numbered among the national ballads, and at length among the war-songs of the people. The proclamation against the Queen of Scots, in London, in 1586, was received with the " ringing of bells, making of bonfires, and *singing of psalms*, in every one of the streets and lanes of the city." The forces of the Parliament " in Marston cornfield, fell to *singing psalms;* " and after the battle of Dunbar, the " republican soldiers, with their general Lambert, halted near Haddington and sung the one hundred and seven-

teenth Psalm." A comedy of the times represents the
" Roundheads" as being "used to sing a Psalm, and
then *fall on.*" They were not only used with " ravishing effect," in the public worship of the sanctuaries,
but were sung at weddings and at funerals and at national festivals.

It was in the public service of song on the Sabbath,
however, that the spirit of the age proclaimed itself
most vigorously on the vexed question of psalm-singing. We cannot more vividly picture it, than by citations (the length of which will be open to no censure,
at least from the advocates of modern congregational
singing) from the pen of George Wither, a poet of the
seventeenth century, and one of its many versifiers on
sacred themes. In 1623, he published a volume of
" Hymns and Songs of the Church," for which he obtained a royal patent that sounds strangely enough to
modern editors of hymnology. It not only gave to the
author " full and free license to imprint said book," but
it also forbade that any *other* English psalm book, in
metre, should be "uttered or sold, unless these hymns
were coupled with it;" and he was at liberty to confiscate any metrical collection of psalmody which was
found destitute of his hymns! In a " Preparation for
the Psalter," which this privileged poet issued not long
before the publication of his hymn book, he defends the
rendering of the Psalms in metre, by argument which
the sturdy convictions of the age appreciated. " The
Divell is not ignorant," he says, " of the power of these
divine *Charmes;* that there lurks in *Poesy* an enchanting sweetness that steals into the hearts of men before
they be aware; and that (the subject being divine) it
can infuse a kind of heavenly *Enthusiasm,* such delight

into the soule, and beget so ardent an affection unto the purity of God's Word, as it will be impossible for the most powerful *Exorcisms* to conjure out of them the love of such delicacies, but they will be unto them (as *David* saith) *sweeter than hony or the hony combe.* And this secret working which verse hath is excellently expressed by our *drad Soveraigne* that now is (James I.) in a *Poem* of his, long since penned: —

> ' For verses power is sike, it softly glides
> Through secret pores, and in the senses hides,
> And makes men have that gude in them imprinted,
> Which by the learned worke is represented.'

By reason of this power, our adversaries feare the operation of the divine Word expressed in *Numbers;* and that hath made them so bitter against our versified *Psalmes;* yea (as I have heard say), they term the singing of them in our vulgar tongues, *the Witch of Heresy.*" Thus were the early psalmists of Britain accustomed to contend for the popular participation in the service of song. The question, in their robust faith, lay between the pope and the "witch of heresy;" between a "heavenly enthusiasm" and "exorcisms" from the nether world; between "divine charmes" and the "Divell."

That the "divine charmes" had the best of the argument practically, will hardly be doubted by one who reads the testimony of Thomas Mace, a practitioner on the lute in the seventeenth century, distinguished among lovers of music in his day by a folio, whose title, for its entertaining egotism, might stand as a model of a modern advertisement: "Music's Monument; or a Remembrancer of the best Practical Music, both Divine and Civil, that has ever been known to have been in the World." This simple hearted musician speaks of the siege of York in 1644, which continued for eleven weeks, and during which, on every Sunday, the old Minster was "even cramming or squeezing full." And "sometimes a cannon bullet has come in at the windows, and bounced about from pillar to pillar, even like some furious fiend or evil spirit." But "now here you must take notice that they had then a custom in that church, which I hear not in any other cathedral; which was, that always before the sermon, the whole congregation sang a Psalm, together with the quire and the organ; and you must also know, that there was then a most excellent, large, plump, lusty, full-speaking organ, which cost, I am credibly informed, a thousand pounds. This organ, I say, when the Psalm was set before sermon, being let out into all its fulness of stops, together with the quire, began the Psalm. But when that vast concording unity of the whole congregational chorus came, as I may say, thundering in, even so as it made the very ground shake under us; oh! the unutterable, ravishing, soul's delight! in the which I was so transported and wrapt up in high contemplations, that there was no room left in my whole man, viz. body, soul, and spirit, for anything below Divine and heavenly raptures; nor could there possibly be anything to which that very singing might be truly compared, except the right apprehension or conceiving of that glorious and miraculous quire, recorded in the Scriptures, at the dedication of the Temple." Turning to II. Chronicles, 5: 13, 14, we read, "It came even to pass, as the trumpeters and singers were as one, to make one sound to be heard in praising and thanking the Lord; and when they lifted up their voice with the trumpets, and cymbals, and instruments of music, and praised the Lord, saying, 'For he is good; for his mercy endureth forever;' that then the house was filled with a cloud, even the house of the Lord: so that the priests could not stand to minister by reason of the cloud; for the glory of the Lord had filled the house of God."

Abating much from the religious character of the psalm-singing of England in the seventeenth century, on account of the political passions of the day, it still admits of no reasonable question, that the religious element prevailed over all others in introducing and *perpetuating* the innovation. For, the innovation has *lived*, as nothing of the kind can, which is not an exponent of religious vitality. The passions of that age have passed away, and with them the excrescenses they created in and around the national psalmody; but that psalmody, improved by a purer taste, has become *popular* literature, to an extent which cannot be affirmed of any other department of English poetry. The ancient English and Scottish ballad can sustain no comparison in point of power over the national character, with the English hymn. Next to king James's version of the Scriptures, it has been the chief power in defining and fixing the English language. It has received the reverent labors of men whom the world delights to honor, — of such as Sir Philip Sydney, lord Bacon, Milton, Henry More, Addison, of bishops and archbishops of the established church, as well as of men, who loved to subscribe their names to their devout effusions, by the title of " sometime minister of the gospel." Wherever the English language has gone, it has carried with it the English hymnology, with the taste to appreciate it, and the heart to use it; and every new baptism of religious life, like that which resulted in the rise of Methodism, has given a new spirit to that hymnology, and enlarged its compass. To this day, in this new world, a "great awakening" never vivifies the churches, without renewing the ancient fervor in the service of song, and extending the range of hymnological literature, because of a new *experience* of evangelical life, which can express itself in no other way.

We illustrate thus, at length, the sympathy of hymnology with the vital condition of the church, because its recognition is elemental to the true theory of a manual of psalmody for the sanctuary. We turn, now, to the consideration of certain features of such a manual, which, if it be true to its aim, are necessitated by the principle we have observed. We employ the "Sabbath Hymn Book" as illustrative of the views we propound.

§ 5. *Scriptural Foundation of Hymnology.*

In the first place, the alliance of hymnology with the real life of the church, suggests the *preëminence* which must be given, in the truthful construction of a hymn book, to the *choicest lyrical versions of passages from the Scriptures.* Divine Wisdom has made the Bible a compilation of human experiences. This feature of its construction is signally exhibited, in the proportion in which inspiration has adopted into its own service the devotional workings of the hearts of the writers, and of others whose experiences they record. Thus, truth is revealed not only through the medium of inspired histories and biographies, but of inspired autobiographies. The profoundest personal life of hearts swayed by divine grace, is expressed in the thoughts and language of minds inspired with divine truth, and speaking only as they are moved by the Holy Ghost. The inspired poems must therefore be the model of every good collection of devotional poetry; still more, of every such collection designed for the service of praise in the sanctuary. No other development of the life of the church has been so expressive of the depths of regenerate experience. No other is so affluent in suggestion of experiences which it does not express. No other penetrates so profoundly the individual soul, and yet no other is so comprehensive of multiform piety. No other could have illustrated so aptly the discipline of its own age; yet no other, as a whole, is so faithful a mirror to the spiritual consciousness of this age; and no other is pervaded by such truthfulness of proportion as to render it, like this, an epitome of regenerate life in every age. And no other has been authoritatively uttered and recorded. The church can never outlive it — it is for all time. Hymnology has thus a foundation and a model such as no other treasures of song, in any literature, can claim.

We affirm but truisms in speaking thus of the devotional poems of the Bible, and especially of the Book of Psalms. We can scarcely exaggerate the worth of these, as the church of Christ has *felt* it in every period of *genuineness* in her history, and has expressed it, saying with Augustine, " they are a kind of epitome of the whole Scripture;" and with Luther, " they are a miniature Bible;" and with Calvin, " they are an anatomy of all the parts of the soul, since there is no emotion of which one can be conscious, that is not imaged here as in a glass;" and with Hooker, " they are the choice and flower of all things profitable in other books ; " and with Watts, " they are the most artful, most devotional and divine collection of poesy, and nothing can be supposed more proper to raise a pious soul to heaven;" and with a living divine, " they are the thousand-voiced heart of the church."

Yet, an intelligent attachment to the devotional poems of the Scriptures, will discriminate in its use of them. Especially should we weigh well the relations of the Hebrew psalmody to hymnology in its restricted sense. We think it the most brilliant service of Dr. Watts, that he established the authority of a *hymn*, in the hearts of the churches, so as fairly to earn the title which Montgomery gives him, of " almost the *inventor* of hymns in our language." A vast advance was made in spirituality of attachment to the Scriptures, when the theory of Watts respecting the proper use of inspired poems in modern worship, obtained a lodgement in the English churches. Before that time, hymnology as distinct from psalmody, can scarcely be said to have existed in English literature ; and psalmody itself changed its character in the hands of Watts, so that the etymological distinction was well nigh obliterated. The " frenzy of sacred song," which Warton lamented as an importation of fanaticism from Geneva, was confined, in England, almost wholly to translations of the Psalms and other portions of the Scriptures. The more literal the version, if it preserved the metrical structure requisite for the mechanism of song, the more faithful it seemed, in the judgment of the time, to the inspired model of worship. No such latitude of usage had been tolerated in England, as that which had flooded Germany and Switzerland with uninspired hymns. The religious temper of the times would have metrical versions of the Psalms, and nothing else. A relic of this feeling still exists in the well-known pertinacity of the Scottish churches, in resisting all inroads of hymnology upon their ancient psalmody.

Watts, as is well known, stoutly contended for the larger liberty. That was an innovation, the boldness of which it is difficult to appreciate now, in which Watts projected the publication of " The Psalms of David," not metrically translated, but "*imitated* in the language of the New Testament, and *adapted* to the *Christian* state and worship;" and bolder still was the previous publication of " Hymns and Spiritual Songs," avowedly for the purpose of meeting necessities of modern worship, which the letter of the Hebrew psalmody could not satisfy. He lamented that his predecessors " in the composure of song," had so generally imprisoned the spirit of Christian worship, in what he regarded as a superstitious reverence for the letter of the Jewish Scriptures. " Though there are many gone before me," he writes, "who have taught the Hebrew Psalmist to speak English, yet I think I may assume this pleasure, of being the first who hath brought down the royal author into the common affairs of the Christian life, and led the Psalmist of Israel into the church of Christ, without anything of a Jew about him." His " Hymns and Spiritual Songs," too, were composed because he could not understand why " we, under the gospel," should " sing nothing else but the joys, hopes, and fears of Asaph and David." He believed that " David would have thought it very hard to have been confined to the words of Moses, and sung nothing else, on all his rejoicing-days, but the drowning of Pharaoh, in the fifteenth of Exodus." The third book of his hymns was the fruit of his pain in having often observed, "to what a hard shift the minister is put to find proper hymns at the celebration of the Lord's supper, where the people will sing nothing but out of David's psalm-book;" and because he believed that even in those "places where the Jewish psalmist seems to mean the gospel, excellent poet as he was, he was not able to speak it plain, by reason of the infancy of that dispensation, and longs for the aid of a Christian writer."

We should be slow to subscribe to all the applications which Watts made of his theory, in the zeal of his honest heart, against its opposite. But the principle which lay at the bottom of his innovation was, beyond all question, true and vital to the spirituality of Christian praise. We state it at length, in the uncompromising language of its author, because it has a broader application than even he attempted to give to it. The principle, reduced to its simplest form, is that the Scriptural Psalmody is not designed as a *restrictive formulary* of the worship of God in song. Not even the Psalms of David have any such office in the plan of inspiration. Watts applied the principle, and in the general we think justly, to a discrimination between the Psalms themselves. They are not all equally worthy of use in public Christian worship. We have no evidence that all of them *were* used in the ancient service of either the temple or the synagogue. The Psalter was the grand collection of Hebrew devotional poems, not the hymn book of the Hebrew sanctuaries. Lightfoot has collected the psalms used in the temple service, adopting as the basis of his calculations, the Scriptural account of that service, and the Rabbinical traditions. The result is as follows, viz: on the several days of the week were sung, or rather cantilated, in the order here specified, Psalms 24, 48, 82, 94, 81, 93, 92. On certain special festivals were used the single Psalms 81, 29, 105, 50, 94, 95, 80, 82. In addition to these were employed the lesser and greater Hallel, the largest estimate of which does not extend them beyond Psalms 113–118, and 105, 120–137 inclusive. The largest number of distinct psalms, of the actual use of which, in the temple service, or in that of the synagogue before the coming of Christ, we have any record either scriptural or traditional, is less than forty. The introduction of the entire Book of Psalms as a book of song, into public worship of the Christian church, occurred at an uncertain period *after* the time of the apostles. The legitimate inference from these facts is, that the use of metrical versions of the Psalms in modern public worship, must depend upon the intrinsic fitness of them, severally, to such a use, and not upon any supposed prerogative appertaining to them in the mass, as an inspired formulary of worship in all times. We have no authoritative example in which any such prerogative is recognized. Watts, and other psalmists who succeeded him, were right therefore in omitting portions of certain psalms, and certain other psalms entire, because they are intrinsically inexpressive of Christian worship.

In vindication of this liberty, Watts puts the case, very forcibly, to the experience of " pious and observing Christians," who have been accustomed to sing the psalms of David indiscriminately: " Have not your spirits taken wing, and mounted up near to God and glory, with the song of David on your tongue ? But, on a sudden, the clerk has proposed the next line to your lips, with 'dark sayings' and 'prophecies,' with 'burnt offerings' or 'hyssop,' with 'new moons,' and 'trumpets,' and 'timbrels' in it, ... with complaints .... such as you never felt, cursing such enemies as you never had, giving thanks for such victories as you never obtained, or leading you to speak, in your own persons, of the things, places, and actions that you never knew. And how have all your souls been discomposed at once, and the strings of harmony all untuned!" Strict *versions* of *all* parts of *all* the Hebrew psalms cannot properly be employed in modern worship. The introduction of them must often depend on the freedom of departure from the original *thought*, as well as the original expression. Such departure may be so great that the poem ceases to be a psalm; it is only an uninspired hymn. In other cases, the admission of a strict version of a psalm, into a modern manual of song, must depend upon the lyrical quality of that version. We may not acquiesce in the severe judgment of the poet Mason, that "a literal [metrical] version of the Psalms may boldly be asserted to be impracticable;" but does not a meditative and didactic poem, like the first Psalm, require for use in English metre, a more mellifluous version, than a precative psalm, like the fifty-first? The poetry of *form* is more indispensable in the one case than in the other, to breathe into a translation the vivacity of song. He is a rare poet who can compose a spirited English hymn on the basis of the first Psalm. He is no poet who can compose any other, on the basis of the fifty-first.

§ 6. *Identity of Psalms and Hymns.*

It is a further inference from the principle of liberty in the use of inspired psalmody, for which the Christian world is indebted to Isaac Watts, though it is an application of his principle which does not seem to have occurred to him, that in the arrangement of a manual of hymnology, *psalms and hymns need not be distinguished from each other.* Aside from the obvious inconveniences of the distinction, it is not true to the facts of hymnology as now existing in the usage of the churches. The English lyrical poems which we call psalms and hymns, have no such uniform difference of character, as this distinction in title implies. The principle of "imitation," rather than of translation, which all our modern psalm books, except that of the Scottish churches, have inherited from Dr. Watts, virtually destroys the truthfulness of the distinction, by destroying its uniformity. On the contrary, certain so-called "Hymns" are more genuine versions of certain of the Psalms of David, than other so-called "Psalms," of the inspired lyrics which they profess to "imitate." The seventy-ninth Hymn of the first book of "Watts's Hymns" ("God of the morning, at whose voice," etc.), is a more accurate expression of certain verses of the Psalmist, than any version we have seen in modern use, of the fifty-ninth Psalm of David. The one hundred and thirty-sixth Hymn of Watts, Book I. ("God is a spirit, just and wise," etc.) approximates more nearly to a version of the one hundred and thirty-ninth of the Hebrew Psalms, than Watts's own version of the seventy-fifth Psalm approaches *its* original. Why should we distinguish as a "Psalm of David," a poem which, as is the case with the seventy-fifth Psalm, Watts applies to "the glorious Revolution by King William, or the happy accession of King George to the throne;" and which Barlow, whose version is still used in some American churches, applies to "the American Revolution?"

The history of this distinction between psalms and hymns is most instructive. Its origin was very natural, almost inevitable. It grew out of a hostility to the use of *anything* in sacred song, but the language of the Scriptures. An indiscriminate reverence for the letter of the Bible, exhibited itself in a most determined opposition to the introduction of uninspired hymns, in the very earliest period of Christian hymnology. "Original hymns," as they were termed, were deemed, by many of the early Christians, a perilous innovation. The conflict for their exclusion, associated them with the introduction, also, of heathen tunes. We find very early evidence of a distinction, in the usages of worship, between the *singing* of hymns and the *chanting* of psalms. The admissibility of hymns, into the liturgy of the church, was contested for several centuries. The first Council of Braga, held A. D. 561, forbade the use, in public worship, of any poetical compositions but the Scriptures; and this decree remained in force for three quarters of a century, till it was revoked by the fourth Council of Toledo. The dispute seems finally to have died away, partly through the triumph of some of the noble hymns of the ancient church, and partly through the gradual exclusion of the people from the public service of praise. But it was vigorously revived, with the revival of popular "psalm singing," which we have sketched. The musical German ear did not long tolerate the controversy. Hymnology, as the correlative of psalmody, was overwhelmingly triumphant. It was not so in England, till the appearance of Dr. Watts; and to this day is not so, north of the Tweed. " Psalm singing " and " hymn singing " were, to the English and Scottish conscience, very different things. It was objected to George Wither, when he published his " Hymnes and Songs of the Church," that he had "indecently obtruded upon the divine calling;" to which he gave, in reply, the substance of the whole argument, when he said: " I wonder what ' divine calling' Hopkins and Sternhold had, more than I have, that their metricall *Psalmes* may be allowed of, rather than my hymnes."

The great achievement of Dr. Watts, was that of establishing the right of a hymn *to be, at all*, in the public worship of God. What, then, could have been more natural, and for the times more expedient, than this distinction between " Psalms" and " Hymns"? By this distinction the Psalms, of which that age had no conception as being any other than *paraphrases* of the inspired original, seemed to receive superior honor; the hymns being tolerated in supplementary collections. Watts himself published his volume of " Imitations of David's Psalms," piously hoping not only that " David [would be] converted into a Christian," but that the Psalms, thus christianized, would escape some of the objections to " Hymns and Spiritual Songs." Yet the principle for which Watts contended in his " imitation" of the Psalms, virtually abrogated the distinction, by destroying its uniformity, and in many cases its reality. The practice of modern churches, under the wing of Watts's muse, has reduced the distinction to a shadow. Why then retain it? We think it an advance in spirituality of reverence for the Scriptures to abandon it. It is virtually conceded, by the sanction the church has given to the innovation of Watts upon the ancient psalmody.

§ 7. *Hymns founded on other portions of the Scriptures than the Book of Psalms.*

Again, it follows from the views we have advanced of the relation of hymnology to the Scriptures, that a Hymn Book should comprise the choicest metrical paraphrases and "imitations" of *other portions of the Bible, than the book of Psalms.* The versification in English, of other than the lyrical compositions of the Scriptures, was a favorite project with many of the early Psalmists of Great Britain. It was often attempted with no regard to the fitness of the materials to poetic form, or to the service of song. Not only the historical but the statistical portions of the Old Testament were brought into subjection to lyric rhymes. One of the varieties in which the popular reverence for the letter of the Scriptures developed itself, was the favorable reception which many gave to the first fourteen chapters of the Acts of the Apostles, when, as Milton described some of his own versifications of the Psalms, they were completely "done into metre," and were sung in the royal chapel of Edward the Sixth. They were commended to other pious uses also by the title of "The Actes of the Apostles, translated into Englyshe metre, and dedicated to the Kynges moste excellent maiestye, by Christofer Tye, doctor in musyke, and one of the Gentylmen of hys graces moste honourable Chappell, with notes to eche chapter to synge and also to play upon the Lute, *very necessarye for studentes after theyr studye to fyle theyr wyttes,* and alsoe for all Christians that cannot synge, to read the good and godlye storyes of the lives of Christ hys apostles." The Books of Kings and Genesis were in like manner reduced to metre. There is still extant in the Bodleian Library, " The summe of every chapter of the Old and New Testaments, set down Alphabetically in English Verse, ... By Simon Wastell, ... Schoole-master of the Free Schoole in Northampton, 1623." We cannot but be amused at the imagination of the scene, in which a grave assembly must have sounded their way resolutely through the thirty-sixth chapter of Genesis — " Now these are the generations of Esau," etc., or through the fourth chapter of the first Book of Kings, " So king Solomon was king over all Israel ; and these were the princes that he had ; Azariah the son of Zadok, etc. ; " — the worshippers grimly resolute, the while, against the profanation of praising God by the singing of such " unauthorized " lyrics, as " Welcome, sweet day of rest " — " There is a land of pure delight," — " Great God ! how infinite art Thou ! " — " My dear Redeemer and my Lord." The inveteracy of this taste for the rhyming of prosaic portions of the Scriptures, is seen in the remains of it existing even in the Olney Hymns, some of which bear titles like the following, viz : " Manna hoarded," " The Golden Calf," " Samson's Lion," " The milch kine bearing the Ark," " The borrowed axe."

But Dr. Watts was not deterred by the " mob of religious rhymers," from appreciating the richness of many portions of the Bible, abounding with the materials of lyric conception, though not inspired in lyric form. On select groups of inspired thoughts, he founded some of the choicest gems of song in the language. What would our modern hymnology have been, without the first Book of Watts's hymns! We might better retain all its excrescences, including its songs from the Canticles, than to part with some of its unequalled strains. Turning to the selection from this source in the Sabbath Hymn Book, our eye falls upon the following:

> "Come, dearest Lord, descend and dwell."
> "Behold the glories of the Lamb."
> "Come let us join our cheerful songs."
> "What equal honors shall we bring."
> "Come hither, all ye weary souls."
> "No more, my God, I boast no more."
> "Oh for an overcoming faith."
> "I'm not ashamed to own my Lord."
> "Let me but hear my Saviour say."
> "Behold what wondrous grace."
> "Lo what a glorious sight appears," —

and upon a multitude of others, which are either paraphrases or imitations of choice paragraphs of the Scriptures, not in the book of Psalms; and which must live, surely, while the language lives. They suggest the inexhaustible Scriptural resources, from which hymnology may yet gain expansion of range through the labors of future lovers of holy song. It is in this direction that we specially desire to see our psalmody improved. We believe that untold affluence of lyric thought yet lies in the word of God, unuttered in lyric verse. Volumes of Scriptural hymns are yet unwritten. Paraphrases, liberal versions, imitations, motto-hymns, replete with Scriptural thought, radiant with Scriptural imagery, and fragrant with Scriptural devotion, are yet to augment the opulence of our hymnological literature. Every new metrical paraphrase of such a passage, for example, as the fifty-third chapter of Isaiah, if it be worthy of its original, we welcome, as an addition to the Songs of Zion. Such a hymn *must* express with some new fidelity, the experience of Christian hearts. Christians will love it; they will sing it. It will become a joy to them in the house of their pilgrimage; it will linger upon their lips in their last hours.

The " Sabbath Hymn Book " is enriched by some such new treasures of Scriptural song. The first Hymn in the volume, is a new version of the Lord's Prayer, in which the very severity of its faithfulness to the original may conceal its poetic merits, till we reflect or rather *feel*, that fidelity to the original *is* the poetry of *such* a prayer. Hymn 245, is a paraphrase of the doxology to the Saviour with which the visions of the Apocalypse open. Hymns 313, and 321, are simple and touching versions of a portion of the fifty-third chapter of Isaiah. Hymn 339, is founded upon the " New Song," in which the four and twenty Elders worshipped the Lamb in the midst of the throne. Hymn 689, we think, is a beautiful expression of communion with Him, whom " having not seen, ye love." Hymn 779, is a versification, which some struggling disciples will welcome, of the prayer of Thomas. Hymn 868, is a faithful version of one of the most compact representations of the dignity of the Saints, found in the Epistle to the Hebrews. Hymns 1273 and 1275, are paraphrases of two very dissimilar passages suggesting the Resurrection. The one is the representative of the old dispensation ; the other, that of the new. We do not know where to find hymns superior to them, on that doctrine. They illustrate so aptly the truthfulness of our faith that *new* paraphrases and imitations of the Scriptures may be expected to increase the wealth of our hymnological literature, that we refrain from naming others which deserve attention in the Sabbath Hymn Book, in order that we may quote these entire. The first (Hymn 1273), is an imitation in Christian song, and as many interpreters would regard it, a paraphrase, of the literal meaning of Job 19: 25, 26, " For I know that my Redeemer liveth, etc."

>My faith shall triumph o'er the grave,
>   And trample on the tomb;
>I know that my Redeemer lives,
>   And on the clouds shall come.
>
>I know that he shall soon appear
>   In power and glory meet;
>And death, the last of all his foes,
>   Lie vanquished at his feet.
>
>Then, though the grave my flesh devour,
>   And hold me for its prey,
>I know my sleeping dust shall rise
>   On the last judgment-day.
>
>I, in my flesh, shall see my God,
>   When he on earth shall stand;
>I shall with all his saints ascend,
>   To dwell at his right hand.
>
>Then shall he wipe all tears away,
>   And hush the rising groan ;
>And pains and sighs and griefs and fears
>   Shall ever be unknown.

The other (Hymn 1275) is a paraphrase of 1 Thes. 4: 14 — 17, in which the apostle announces, in its fulness, the Christian doctrine of the Resurrection of Saints.

> As Jesus died and rose again,
>   Victorious, from the dead ;
> So his disciples rise, and reign
>   With their triumphant Head.
>
> The time draws nigh, when, from the clouds,
>   Christ shall with shouts descend ;
> And the last trumpet's awful voice
>   The heavens and earth shall rend.
>
> Then they who live shall changéd be,
>   And they who sleep shall wake ;
> The graves shall yield their ancient charge,
>   And earth's foundation shake.
>
> The saints of God, from death set free,
>   With joy shall mount on high ;
> The heavenly host, with praises loud,
>   Shall meet them in the sky.
>
> Together to their Father's house
>   With joyful hearts they go ;
> And dwell forever with the Lord,
>   Beyond the reach of woe.

Such hymns, though they do not rise to the rank of the highest style of psalms of *worship*, appear to us to be among the noblest of meditative and didactic hymns. Are they not worthy to receive the apostolic commendation appended to the text on which one of them is founded : " Wherefore, comfort one another with these words ?"

Some approximation to an estimate of the Sabbath Hymn Book as a collection of Biblical Song, may be obtained from the fact, that more than five hundred and fifty of its pieces are composed of either the literal text, or of paraphrases and imitations of the Scriptures; and that nearly the whole number of its Hymns are referred in its Scriptural Index, by no fanciful resemblance, to inspired passages; and that nearly two thousand such passages are thus illustrated in the volume, each being, in many cases, the centre of a cynosure of hymns which radiate the glow it has imparted to them. This is as it should be. The most hearty hymnology of any age, that to which the most genuine religious life will always respond feelingly, and which in return will be most tonic to any living experience in the church, must be that which is most intensely pervaded with Biblical thought. This should be exhaled from it everywhere, with richer than "Sabean odor." It should be like the mist of Eden, which went up from the earth, and watered the *whole* face of the ground.

§ 8. *Ancient Hymnology.*

The sympathy of hymnology with the religious life, suggests further, *the value of those uninspired hymns which time has proved to be truthful to the general experience of Christians.* These may be emphatically entitled the Hymns of the Church; for, they are the production of the church, as distinct from the temple and the synagogue. As the Hebrew faith created the inspired psalmody, so Christianity as we have seen, very early began to create its own hymnology, and has refreshed itself by outbursts of lyric devotion, all the way down the ages of its pilgrimage. Many of these effusions from the heart of one age and country, have stood the test of time, and of migration to other lands. Different nationalities and different generations of Christendom have given their suffrage to the same strains. Some of them are from the very earliest periods of the church, and were first sung by voices which were almost the echo from apostolic lips. The earliest Greek poem on a sacred theme, from any writer whose name and writings have survived to this day, is a song of praise to " Christ the Redeemer." Others are hymns of the Reformation, on which the venerableness of age is fast gathering, and which are still sung affectionately by devout Christians in Europe, after the lapse of three centuries. Some are " voices of the night," from the Middle Ages, breathing a spirit like that of the old prophecies, anticipative of the time of the end. Reasoning *a priori*, one might say 'there surely must be some gems which the church of every age will delight in, in this treasury of old songs.'

Yet English Hymnology has not drawn very largely upon the resources of other lands and tongues. Cranmer expressed faintly the hope, that some future English poet would translate for his countrymen the hymns of the first Christian centuries. A very few, as we have seen, remained in liturgic form, in the English church. The Wesleys translated nearly thirty hymns from the German language, and some of these are among the most spirited that now bear their names. But, aside from this, the Ancient Hymns have but a meagre representation in the manuals of psalmody now used in the churches of Great Britain and America. Comparatively little of our hymnology, as actually used in the public service of the sanctuary, with the exception of the Psalms by Tate and Brady, date back beyond the time of Watts and Doddridge. The bulk of sacred song in our language, is by at least two centuries, less ancient than that of Germany. Two causes have especially contributed to this result. One is the tendency of the English mind to *insular* tastes in literature and theology. The other is the peculiar intensity of the spirit of reform in Great Britain, in the sixteenth century. The religious spirit of the nation sprang with a rebound from the papal church, when once the bonds were loosened. A positive hostility was felt, not only as we have seen, to "uninspired hymns" in the general, but to the ancient hymns of the church in particular, because many of them had become identified with the Roman missal. The fire which inflamed the iconoclasm of the Scottish Reformers, burned out the leaves of the ancient hymnology from their liturgy. It was by dint of royal authority that the "Gloria in Excelsis" and the "Te Deum Laudamus," remained in the English church. The metrical version of the Psalms by Sternhold and Hopkins, met with stout resistance, from one party, *because* it would expurgate the church of many of the old liturgic hymns.

The same conflict over the ancient Breviary was waged on the Continent, but with this difference, that an original hymnological literature was speedily created there; and this was founded to some extent upon the old hymns of the church. Even before the Reformation, the germs of such a literature existed in the hymns of the Albigenses and the Bohemian Brethren, whose *melodies* originated in the chants to which the Latin hymns of the West were sung. The current of Continental Protestantism was early and strongly *set* in the channel of an original hymnology, and that too a hymnology which made the Breviary and other collections of ancient song pay tribute to its own inspiration, long before English hymnology as distinct from psalmody was in existence; and when the religious mind of England and Scotland was agitated with the question whether psalmody had any *right* thus to expand itself beyond the books of Genesis and the Revelation. Luther felt no scruples of this sort. The singing of the Hussite Brethren had fixed his judgment of the value of original hymns, to the reformed faith. He not only set about the composition of hymns with his own pen, but urged his friends to do the same; and engaged the services of poets and the most eminent musicians of the time, to create the staple of Christian song. He would also *take* a good hymn, or a good tune, wherever he found it, though it were from the teeth of the Pope. "I am far from thinking," he says, "that the Gospel is to strike all Art to the Earth; but I would have all Arts .... taken into that service for which they were given." He accordingly enriched the German psalmody with many reprisals, both of text and tune, from the Latin hymnology. He versified thus the "Te Deum," "Veni Redemptor gentium," "Veni Creator Spiritus," "Media Vita," "O lux beata Trinitas," and many others, some of which are still used in German worship. His example was followed by many of the multitude of German hymnologists who followed him in the seventeenth century; and this eclectic spirit has made the Christian song of Germany what it is.

Good reasons may have existed for the temporary insulation of the psalmody of Great Britain within the resources of her native poets. It is seldom that the taste of a nation is perverted, *all* things considered,

under the influence of a quickening of religious faith.
That faith has a certain regulative force, which tends
to tranquillize those passions that lead to distortions of
character, and to forbid the sacrifice of any good, unless the temporary loss be necessary to protection from
a greater. We are not disposed, therefore, to mourn
over the obduracy of our fathers in clinging to their
own national literature, and seeking its growth from
within itself, rather than by foreign accretions. We
are inclined to regard it as one of the many phenomena
which indicate a design of Providence in the tendency
to *seclusion* existing in British character, of which the
insular geography of Great Britain is an emblem and
a cause.

But such reasons for segregation, in respect of religious sympathy, must be temporary. Now that time
has disciplined the mind of the Anglo Saxon churches,
not to the toleration only, but to the enjoyment of
" original hymns " in their worship, and has created a
more discriminative spirit in its judgment of the Past,
the old Hymns of the Church come back to us in their
true dignity, as *representatives* of a religious life which
the Spirit of God never suffered utterly to die out. It
is to be remembered that from the time of the apostles
to that of Ambrose, the Latin language was vernacular to the churches of the west. The hymns of that
period, therefore, which have survived, are relics, not
of an exclusive liturgic worship in an unknown tongue,
but of the living devotion of the people. Those hymns,
and others of later times, are utterances of the experience which " kings and priests unto God," have thought
and felt, and struggled through, and suffered for, and
sung in triumph. They are the hymns of the early

sanctuary, sung by Christians whose fathers had joined with the apostles in psalms and hymns and spiritual songs. They are the hymns of the early morning prayer-meeting, in which the heathen overheard Christians "singing before daylight in praise of Christ as a God." They are the hymns of the early Christian homes, which were sung at marriage feasts, and over the cradles of children, and at the morning and evening fireside. That was a becoming appellation by which some of them were entitled, from the name of their author, 'Ambrosian Hymns.' They are the hymns of the Eucharist and of Baptism, in which the spirit of primitive consecration breathed the fragrance of its piety. They are the early pastoral hymns of the church which "you could not go into the country without hearing," says Jerome, "from the ploughman, the mower, and the vinedresser." They are the early burial hymns, sung beside the graves of the saints, young men and maidens, old men and children, by those who sorrowed not as others. They are the hymns of the Martyrs, sung by hunted worshippers, at midnight, in dens and caves of the earth, amidst armed men in ambush, and by prisoners in dungeons and in the flames. They are the battle-songs of the church, sung in hours of forlorn hope, and as the prelude and thanksgiving of victory. They are the claustral hymns through which Truth gleamed in upon "spirits in prison," who, like Luther at Erfurt, struggled with unseen foes. They are Pentecostal hymns, in which the voice of the church has broken out anew, in different ages and lands, whenever and wherever the place has been "shaken," where men were assembled, and they have been "all filled with the Holy Ghost." They are some of them older than any living language, yet to-day they speak the life of Christian hearts as freshly as when they were first written. Devout men out of every nation under heaven may come together, and every man shall hear them speak in his own language. Some of these ancient hymns have probably been sung by larger numbers of godly men and women and children, embracing wider diversities of nationality, of social rank, and of Christian opinion, and extending over a longer line of ages, than any other uninspired songs. They more than realize the ideal of the " Laus Perennis," originated by the Monks of Antioch, whose discipline obliged them to preserve in their monastery a *perpetual psalmody*, like the vestal fire or the perpetual lamps of mythology. Writers upon mediæval art, have not failed to trace the plastic influence of these Hymns of the Church, upon Painting and Sculpture. It is believed that the " Dies Iræ " lives in Michael Angelo's fresco of " The Last Judgment."

Hymns so necessary as these to the embodiment of its real life in song, the church should not leave buried in dead languages, or secluded in any national literature. They are the rightful inheritance of all future ages, and should be world-wide in their usefulness. It is surely time that they were incorporated with English hymnology. The Sabbath Hymn Book has attempted a beginning of this work, and we hope that future contributors to our hymnological stores will labor in the same mine. Our space will permit us to extract but a few of these hymns, which we present with the Latin originals, and in some examples with the German versions. The first (Hymn 336) is a " Hymn to the Redeemer," the authorship of which has been contested, but is traced satisfactorily to Gregory the Great (A. D. 540 — 604). It was one of the favorite hymns of Luther, who pronounced it to be among the standard songs of the church, for, he said, it contained the very essence of Christianity.

> O Christ! our King, Creator, Lord!
> Saviour of all who trust thy word!
> To them who seek thee ever near,
> Now to our praises bend thine ear.
>
> In thy dear cross a grace is found —
> It flows from every streaming wound —
> Whose power our inbred sin controls,
> Breaks the firm bond, and frees our souls!
>
> Thou didst create the stars of night;
> Yet thou hast veiled in flesh thy light —
> Hast deigned a mortal form to wear,
> A mortal's painful lot to bear.
>
> When thou didst hang upon the tree,
> The quaking earth acknowledged thee;
> When thou didst there yield up thy breath,
> The world grew dark as shades of death.
>
> Now in the Father's glory high,
> Great Conqu'ror, never more to die,
> Us by thy mighty power defend,
> And reign through ages without end.

The following are the Latin original and Luther's translation.

Rex Christe, factor omnium	Christ, König, Schöpfer aller Welt,
Redemptor et credentium	Zum Heil der Gläubigen bestellt:
Placare votis supplicum	O laß Dir gern der Demuth Fall'n,
Te laudibus colentium!	Und unsern Lobgesang gefall'n.

Crucis benigna gratia,	Du hast durch Deiner Gnade Kraft,
Crucis per alma vulnera,	Durch Deinen Tod am Kreuzes-Schaft,
Virtute solvit ardua	Der angeerbten Sündenhaft
Prima parentis vincula.	Der ersten Eltern uns entrafft.
Qui es creator siderum,	Du schuf'st der Sterne gold'ne Reih'n,
Tegmen subisti carneum,	Und kamst mit uns ein Mensch zu seyn,
Dignatus hanc vilissimam	Du duldetest, uns zu befrei'n,
Pati doloris formulam.	Des ird'schen Todes Schmerz und Pein.
Cruci, redemptor, figeris:	Man schläg't an's Kreuz Dich Heiland, an:
Terram sed omnem concutis;	Die Erde wankt in ihrer Bahn;
Tradis potentem spiritum:	Der Geist entflieht; „Es ist vollbracht"!
Nigrescit atque seculum.	Und alle Welt deckt dunkle Nacht.
Mox in paternae gloriae	Bald aber steig'st aus Todesweh'n
Victor resplendens culmine	Du siegend zu des Lichtes Höh'n:
Cum spiritus munime	So sey mit Deinem Geist nun dort
Defende nos, rex optime!	Uns Schutz und Schirm, Du starker Hort!

The ancient and mediæval hymns are often marked by a subdued depth of pathos towards the person of Christ. This is the very life of them. Hence it is, that they are the voices of Christian hearts to Christian hearts, over continents and through ages. The following is a selection from one of this class, from the pen of St. Bernard (A. D. 1091—1153).

>Jesus! the very thought of thee
> With gladness fills my breast;
>But dearer far thy face to see,
> And in thy presence rest.
>
>Nor voice can sing, nor heart can frame,
> Nor can the memory find
>A sweeter sound than thy blest name,
> O Saviour of mankind!

HYMN BY ST. BERNARD.

O Hope of every contrite heart,
  O Joy of all the meek!
To those who fall, how kind thou art,
  How good to those who seek!

And those who find thee, find a bliss
  Nor tongue nor pen can show:
The love of Jesus — what it is,
  None but its loved ones know.

Jesus, our only joy be thou!
  As thou our prize wilt be;
Jesus, be thou our glory now,
  And through eternity!

The original of these stanzas, and their German version are as follows, viz:

Iesu, dulcis memoria,	Dein Denken, Jesus, schon verleiht
Dans vera cordis gaudia,	Dem Herzen wahre Freudigkeit,
Sed super mel et omnia	Doch mehr als jede Lust erfreut
Eius dulcis praesentia.	Ach Deiner Nähe Süßigkeit.
Nil canitur suavius,	Kein Liederstrom so lieblich fließt,
Auditur nil iucundius,	Kein Klang so freundlich uns begrüßt,
Nil cogitatur dulcius,	Und nichts so süß zu denken ist,
Quam Iesus, Dei filius.	Als: Gottes Sohn ist Jesus Christ.
Iesu, spes poenitentibus,	Jesus, der Sünder Hoffnungsstern,
Quam pius es petentibus?	Den Bittenden erhörst Du gern,
Quam bonus te quaerentibus?	Dem Suchenden bist Du nicht fern,
Sed quid invenientibus?!	Was dem erst, der Dich fand, den Herrn?!
Nec lingua valet dicere,	Kein Wort genügend sich erweis't,
Nec litera exprimere,	Und keine Schrift es würdig preis't,
Expertus potest credere,	Nur fühlen kann's ein gläub'ger Geist,
Quid sit Iesum diligere.	Was es, Dich Jesum lieben, heißt.
Iesu, dulcedo cordium,	Dich lieben! süße Herzenspflicht,
Fons vivus, lumen mentium,	Du Lebensquell, Du Seelenlicht!
Excedens omne gaudium,	Das alle Lust, die in uns liegt,
Et omne desiderium.	Und alle Wünsche überwiegt.

HYMN BY THOMAS AQUINAS.

It is refreshing to find in the very midnight of the Middle Ages, a gleam of spiritual light which gives promise of the morning. Such is the sacramental hymn of Thomas Aquinas (A. D. 1224—1274)—a name which we are glad to rescue, in our own minds, from its associations in dogmatic history, by means of so graphic an outburst of communion with Christ, as the following:

> O Bread to pilgrims given,
>   O Food that angels eat,
> O Manna sent from heaven,
>   For heaven-born natures meet!
> Give us, for thee long pining,
>   To eat till richly filled;
> Till, earth's delights resigning,
>   Our every wish is stilled!
>
> O Water, life-bestowing,
>   From out the Saviour's heart,
> A fountain purely flowing,
>   A fount of love thou art!
> Oh let us, freely tasting,
>   Our burning thirst assuage!
> Thy sweetness, never wasting,
>   Avails from age to age.
>
> Jesus, this feast receiving,
>   We thee unseen adore;
> Thy faithful word believing,
>   We take—and doubt no more;
> Give us, thou true and loving,
>   On earth to live in thee;
> Then, death the vail removing,
>   Thy glorious face to see!

The following original of this Hymn, and its German version, are from a collection of the few hymns certainly known as the productions of this author, of which the German Editor expresses the Christian judgment of his countrymen, by saying, that one of them would be sufficient to preserve the name of Aquinas through all time.

O esca viatorum!	Labsal der Pilgerreise!
O panis angelorum!	O Brod, der Engel Speise!
O manna coelitum!	O Manna, Himmelsfrucht!
Esurientes ciba,	Die Hungrigen ernähre
Dulcedine non priva	Und Süßigkeit gewähre
Corda quaerentium.	Dem Herzen, das dich sucht.
Olympha, fons amoris!	O Strom, Urquell der Liebe,
Qui puro Salvatoris	Der rein, und niemals trübe
E corde profluis:	Des Retters Herz entfließt:
Te sitientes pota!	Die nach dir dürsten, tränke!
Haec sola nostra vota,	Dem Wunsch Gewährung schenke,
His una sufficis!	Der alle in sich schließt.
O Iesu, tuum vultum,	O Herr, auf den wir bauen,
Quem colimus occultum	Den wir verborgen schauen
Sub panis specie:	In dieses Brodes Bild:
Fac, ut remoto velo	Laß, wenn dies Band gefallen,
Glorioso in coelo	Uns in des Himmels Hallen
Cernamus acie!	Dich sehen unverhüllt!

The Christology of the ancient hymns often exhibits an intense vividness of conception, in depicting the *individuality* of the relation between the Redeemer and his disciples. It is like that of a personal friendship. Some of the Passion-Hymns of the old hymnology are excessively theopathic, in their expression of this conception. But that hymnology contains also many which are only the natural embodiment in song, of an experience in which the most eminent saints of all ages are "of one mind and one soul." Such is the well known hymn of Francis Xavier (A. D. 1506 — 1552) of which the following are the original, and the English version from the Sabbath Hymn Book:

O Deus! ego amo te,	I love thee, O my God, but not
Nec amo te ut salves me,	For what I hope thereby;
Aut quia non amantes te	Nor yet because who love thee not,
Æterno punis igne.	Must die eternally:
Tu, tu, mi Jesu! totum me	I love thee, O my God, and still
Amplexus es in cruce;	I ever will love thee,
Tulisti clavos, lanceam,	Solely because my God thou art
Multamque ignominiam,	Who first hast lovéd me.
Innumeros dolores,	
Sudores, et angores,	For me, to lowest depths of woe
Ac mortem; et hæc propter me,	Thou didst thyself abase;
Et pro me peccatore.	For me didst bear the cross, the shame,
Cur igitur non amem te,	And manifold disgrace
O Jesu amantissime!	For me didst suffer pains unknown,
Non ut in cœlo salves me,	Blood-sweat and agony
Aut ne æternum damnes me,	Yea, death itself — all, all for me,
Aut præmii ullius spe;	For me, thine enemy.
Sed sicut tu amasti me,	
Sic amo, et amabo te;	Then shall I not, O Saviour mine!
Solum quia rex meus es,	Shall I not love thee well?
Et solum quia Deus es.	Not with the hope of winning heaven,
	Nor of escaping hell;
	Not with the hope of earning aught,
	Nor seeking a reward,
	But freely, fully, as thyself
	Hast lovéd me, O Lord!

Luther surely was right, in his eclecticism towards the "Hymns of the Church," when such strains as these could proceed from the lips of a Jesuit missionary, his own contemporary. The vitality of some relics of the old Latin psalmody is finely illustrated in the history of the Hymn 1203, of this collection:

"The pangs of death are near."

The original of this was a Latin chant by St. Notker, a monk of St. Gall in the ninth century.

> In media vita
> In morte sumus, etc.

It was imitated in a German hymn which formed a part of the burial-service in the thirteenth century, and was then used also as a battle-song. Luther added to it several stanzas. From the Continent it passed over into England, and a remnant of it still exists in the Liturgy of the Church of England, and of the Episcopal Church of America — a remnant the familiarity and the value of which to the English mind are pleasantly illustrated by the fact, that Robert Hall once sought for it in the Bible, as the text of a sermon. So venerable does a Christian hymn become which has lived a thousand years.

Many others of this class of hymns in the Manual before us, have an impressive history. They not only *have been* the utterances of devout men in a remote age — they *are* on the lips of thousands in the living age. They are among the endeared hymns of Protestant Europe. They are sung often with voices which are, as Ambrose described the congregational singing of his day, "like the blending sound of many waters."

> Hymn 263: "All praise to thee, eternal Lord,"

is a version of one of Luther's favorite hymns on a favorite theme, on which he wrote several that are still used and loved by the churches of Germany, and one which is sung from the dome of the Kreuzkirche in Dresden, before daybreak, on every Christmas morning.

Hymn 899: "Fear not, O little flock, the foe,"

was written by Altenburg in 1631, with the title "A heart-cheering Song of comfort on the watchword of the Evangelical Army in the battle of Leipsic, Sept. 7th, 1631, — "God with us." It was the battle-song of Gustavus Adolphus, often sung by him with his army, as the Puritans sung the inspired Psalms. One tradition affirms that he sung it before *every* battle, and for the last time before the battle of Lützen, in which he perished. A similar hymn by Lowenstern,

Hymn 1022: "O Christ, the Leader of that warworn host,"

was called forth by the sufferings of the Reformed Church in the "Thirty years' war." It was a favorite hymn of Niebuhr.

Hymn 1181: "When from my sight all fades away,"

is taken from a hymn written for his children, by Paul Eber, a friend of Melanchthon. It has long been a favorite hymn for the death-bed. Grotius requested that it might be repeated to him in his last moments, and expired before its close.

Such are the rich memories that cluster around these hymns of the Past. Many, the history of which is not minutely known, bear internal evidence of being themselves a history of struggling or triumphant hearts.

§ 9. *Modern Hymnology.*

The affinity of hymnology with the religious experience of the church suggests, still further, *the value of the best modern contributions to the service of song.*

As in literature, art, and social civilization, so in religious life, every age has an individuality of its own. That individuality needs, and will have, in some form, an expression. Its normal development is, to express itself in the psalmody of the church. If it be denied expression there, it will seek expression in a psalmody without the church. It will force itself into the purest lyric forms of thought, wherever it can find them; and these will be used, enjoyed, loved, as the representatives of an *existing* Christian life. That is an unwise restriction of a manual of sacred song, which admits *only* the familiar and tried hymns of the sanctuary. Especially is that a perilous restriction, which is founded exclusively on the taste and the experience of a past age, and is aimed at a retention of all the accumulations of that age, by the force of endearing association. Such a principle must result in the compilation of many hymns which are intrinsically inferior to others of modern origin, and which will be felt to be so by the *heart* of the church, as well as pronounced to be so by the taste of the age. The consequence is conceivable, that certain classes of Christian mind, if not all, should find themselves omitting, or going through by routine, large portions of their Sabbath psalmody, and reverting, on the week day, to "unsanctioned" lyrics, for the invigoration which the 'service of song in the house of the Lord' has not given them.

The same reasons which required the extension of hymnology, by the adventurous labors of Dr. Watts, beyond the letter of inspired poems, and which have again and again expanded its range by the supplementary labors of Wesley, Steele, Doddridge, and Montgomery, require also its further growth by the admission of the best productions of living hymnologists. The question involved is not a question of taste alone; it is a question of the adaptation of sacred song to a various, and a living Christian experience. There must be breadth of range in our hymnology, in order to flexibility in its expression of a diversified religious life. We need hymns for every existing mood of devotion; and for these we must be indebted, in part, to living poets. In no other manner can the *real life* of the church be symmetrically expressed in song.

This view is eminently truthful as applied to *English* hymnology, which, to an extent unparalleled in any hymnological literature but that of the Hebrews, owes its existence and its idiosyncracies to *one* man. The remarks we have already made indicate, we trust, that we yield to none in our reverence for Isaac Watts. Every student of hymnology knows the *refreshment* he experiences, in plodding through thousands of the lyrics of inferior poets, whenever he comes suddenly upon one of the sterling psalms or hymns of this prince of the house of David. How often has his voice been to us like a song in the night!

Still, we cannot but discriminate between the use and the abuse of his productions, in the construction of a modern manual of psalmody. Well-known facts in the history of English psalmody are often forgotten which yet have an important bearing on the position of Watts among the poets of the sanctuary. He was the pioneer of hymnology in our language. He had no models that were worthy of his imitation. He wrote at an age when *anything* from such a pen as his, was superior to the standard psalmody of the churches. We do not marvel at the enthusiasm, with which the humble worshippers at Southampton recoiled from the tasteless lyrics of the day, to welcome such a song of praise to " the Lamb that was slain," as the first hymn which the youthful poet composed for them at the suggestion of his father :

"Behold the glories of the Lamb!"

He wrote in an age when the poetic taste of England was unformed — its taste respecting religious poetry *de*formed. It was a period of literary struggle and transition. The public mind tolerated, even admired, conceits, affectation, coarseness, in the service of song. Watts did much to improve the literary temper of the times; his genius, at the bidding of his piety, often soared above the taste of his contemporaries; yet, he sometimes did so unconsciously, for he himself believed that in some of his compositions, now dear to the church and admired by critics, he was sacrificing literary excellence to pious simplicity. He expected to be censured, he informs us, for a too religious observance of the inspired word, by which the verse was debased in the judgment of literary criticism.

But, powerful as his influence was upon his age, the age had power also over him, and he often succumbed to it, by the production of lyrics which the church *has* practically been willing to let die. The immediate consequence, however, in part, of the transcendent excellences of his poems, and in part of the purblind taste of the age, was, that his "Psalms and Hymns" were received in the mass, by those who accepted them at all. Multitudes sprang to greet them, vaulting over from all the hymnology that had preceded them. Their faults were sheltered by their virtues, to a degree almost

unprecedented in the history of our religious literature.
They were embraced *as a whole*, in the affections of
the church, and from that time to the present, " Watts
entire" has been the household word of many lovers of
holy song. Hymnologic taste, to this day, has been
quickened by the breath of life which the whole body
of devotional literature inhaled from the empyrean to
which Watts taught it to soar, but its pulse has beat
feverishly in the low grounds in which the pinions of
his muse were sometimes draggled.

Meanwhile, our national literature, and especially our
poetry, and still more essentially that class of poems
which are nearest of kin to psalmody, have been undergoing improvement which our hymnology must feel
— has felt. If we repel it or retreat from it, our service of song will be, so far forth, grooved into the past,
and all other poetic literature will stride in advance
of it, as that literature has done relatively to the psalmody of the kirk of Scotland. If we wisely but cordially
welcome it, and try its spirit, and test the past in part
by it, and use only that which is good, we shall expand
the range of religious song, and keep it abreast with
the noblest poetry of our language.

To mention but one fountain of the influence which
is working a change in our literature, and which has
created the taste that appreciates it — is it possible to
believe that Wordsworth has done nothing to advance
our national poetry? Has not his influence on *lyric*
writers been positive and healthful? Hymnology is
moving under an impulse which, so far as its literary
character is concerned, owes much to him. We owe
to him, indirectly, some characteristics of the poetic
forms which modern Christian life needs, in order to

express itself in the most becoming song. The impulse must be disciplinary to the public taste respecting the earlier poets. Its tendency is to prune away the excrescences of Watts's effusions, and to reduce the number of them, in our manuals of psalmody, to those which can *live* in the heart of our churches. The influence is salutary upon the reputation of Watts. He will live the longer; his truly vitalized hymns and psalms will be more permanent in the affections of the church, for their separation from those which are unworthy of him, or so inferior to later productions as to invite unfriendly criticism. Two hundred and fifty of Watts's psalms and hymns will live longer, by themselves, than any five hundred *can*. To set ourselves against this tendency to a cautious and reverent retrenchment of " Watts entire," is to oppose our hymnology to the whole current of our national poetry, and to seclude our churches from the ripest fruits of poetic taste in the future.

This tendency to the displacement of the inferior hymns of the past, by the introduction of modern hymns of superior merit, is sanctioned by the practice of the church from time immemorial. In the English church, the Psalmody of " Sternhold and Hopkins," at first an innovation, became at length the " Old Version," and contested the ground stoutly with that of " Tate and Brady," which was opprobriously termed the " New Version," but which supplanted its predecessor, and in turn has been itself largely encroached upon in the affections of the church, by the popularity of Watts's Psalms and Hymns. These, no compiler of psalmody for public worship since his day, so far as we know, has desired to discard. But, practically, Watts *is* yielding somewhat in the usage of the churches both of England and America. Compilers of hymn books who now omit very many of his once revered songs, do not create, they only express, the existing custom of the sanctuary. Many of both his psalms and his hymns, are virtually laid aside. They are not read from our pulpits; they are not sung by our choirs and congregations. They could not be thus used, as they once were, without exposing the service of song to the incredulity of our children, and the ridicule of profane minds. Who reads them? Who sings them? Who values them for any other than their historic interest? Who that is familiar with the poems of Watts, has not observed how deceptive often are their *first lines*, as an indication of the quality of the subsequent stanzas? The opening couplets of his hymns and psalms often give brilliant promises. They seem to be the preludes of faultless lyrics — outbursts of genuine song, which need only to be *sustained* to be without superiors in uninspired verse. But often they are not sustained. They are followed by stanzas which doom them in every pulpit. A specious but deceptive method of judging of the omissions of the productions of Watts from a modern Collection of Hymns, is to designate them by quotation of the first lines alone. His very questionable assertion respecting the Psalms of David, is far more truthful of his own. " There are a thousand lines in [them], which were not made for a church in our days to assume as its own." We shall illustrate this by examples in the sequel, though we would not seem to subject sacred thought, and specially inspired thought, to parody. We should follow the example of the *real life* of the churches of our time, in quietly turning aside from such lyrics, and leaving them unhonored and unsung, forgetting the things which are behind.

There are other hymns in our modern Collections which are retained only for the want of better hymns on the same themes. Every student of sacred song knows the difficulty of finding a variety of good hymns on *all* the topics of Christian experience, and of instruction from the pulpit. On some themes, our hymnology is meagre. The churches retain the hymns they have on those themes, not because they are good intrinsically, but because no others exist which are better. Every good manual of psalmody, therefore, in the present state of this branch of our literature, must contain some hymns which we could wish to see improved, or displaced by their superiors. But who *has* improved these hymns, or written richer hymns on the same subjects? We must look to future poets of the sanctuary to supply the deficiency, and when it is supplied, we must not say " the old is better." Association alone ought not to perpetuate the life of a poor hymn ; and Providence takes care that it shall not do so. For, in nothing is that binary economy which adjusts the laws of demand and supply in the life of the church, more signally illustrated than in the history of hymnology. The Christian life of any age is not long left to pine for a full expression of itself in song. The poet appears when the effusions of his muse are needed, and when the need is felt in Christian hearts. Thus St. Ephrem, Ambrose, Hilary, Clement, Gregory, sung the experiences of the ancient church, because those experiences must have an outlet in song. Thus Luther, Hans Sachs, Heerman, Gerhardt, John Frank, sung the life of the Reformation, because, as one of their successors said of himself, " the dear cross pressed many songs out of them." In like manner Watts created English hymnology, at a juncture at which it is difficult now to see how the life of English Reform could have been developed without the moral forces of his Psalms and Hymns; and Toplady, Doddridge, Wesley, Cowper, Mrs. Steele, Montgomery, and others, have improved the heritage they had received, by accretions of which the modern Christian life has expressed its need, by accepting them. It may be true, literally, as Montgomery affirms, that "our good poets have seldom been good Christians, and our good Christians have seldom been good poets;" yet we cannot but believe that the existing amount of good hymnological materials is larger than has been commonly supposed, and that it has a law of increase, dependent upon the laws of progress in the vital piety of the church. An age of poetic development is not necessarily an age of hymnological growth. Great poets are not of necessity able to write good hymns. But an age of advancement or revival in religious experience, will create poets who shall express its own individuality.

If, then, we are true to the history of the church, we shall welcome new Psalmists, who express the real life of the church in "new songs." Such songs have no 'associations' to befriend them. They may not appear under the shadow of venerable names. They may be obliged to create the taste that shall appreciate them. A new hymn, like a new doctrine of religion, or a new law in science, or a new canon of taste in literature, may be compelled to abide its time. But if it be a *true* hymn, it need not contend for its existence. It has come into being because Christian hearts need *it*— not because it needs them. They will discover its worth, and will enshrine it. Their decision may be more orthodox than that of much that passes for learned criticism. Criticism said of Wordsworth's poems, "This will never do;" but the verdict of the world is wiser. Watts's theory of psalmody was pronounced a destructive innovation; yet for that service to the church, the fourth generation of his countrymen after his decease, have celebrated the anniversary of that event, as a day of thanksgiving for his birth, and are now calling for a national monument to his memory.

The Sabbath Hymn Book illustrates, by its materials, in some measure, the views here advanced. While it retains more than two hundred and fifty of the psalms and hymns of Watts, and while the large majority of its selections are from the writings of such long-tried poets of the church as Watts, Doddridge, Toplady, Wesley, Cowper, Mrs. Steele, and Montgomery, yet in addition to the revival of many of the more ancient hymns, it comprises many contributions from living hymnologists. Of these, a considerable number have never before been published in a manual of psalmody for public worship. We believe that they will live. Some of them will take the place of more ancient productions, as being more natural, or more vivid expressions of modern religious life.

We have not space to indicate the grounds of this conviction by numerous citations. But we venture to recall a few of these modern hymns, for the sake of illustrating, by a comparison of them with those of more ancient origin, the truth of the principle for which we contend — that modern hymnology *must* be allowed, in many cases, to displace the earlier and inferior songs of the sanctuary. We confine our suggestion of hymns which we think the church should lay aside, to the productions of Watts,— the man whom, of all hymnologists, we most revere.

Is it, then, a loss to our temple-service, that we should part with Watts's version of the Fifty-third Psalm, on "Deliverance from persecution,"—

> "Are all the foes of Zion fools,
> Who thus devour her saints?"—

that we may possess in its place the following Hymn by Bonar?

> Church of the ever-living God,
>   The Father's gracious choice,
> Amid the voices of this earth
>   How feeble is thy voice!
>
> A little flock!— so calls he thee
>   Who bought thee with his blood;
> A little flock, disowned of men,
>   But owned and loved of God.
>
> Not many rich or noble called,
>   Not many great or wise;
> They whom God makes his kings and priests
>   Are poor in human eyes.
>
> But the chief Shepherd comes at length;
>   Their feeble days are o'er,
> No more a handful in the earth,
>   A little flock no more.
>
> No more a lily among thorns,
>   Weary and faint and few;
> But countless as the stars of heaven,
>   Or as the early dew.
>
> Then entering th' eternal halls,
>   In robes of victory,
> That mighty multitude shall keep
>   The joyous jubilee.

> Unfading palms they bear aloft;
>   Unfaltering songs they sing;
> Unending festival they keep,
>   In presence of the King.[1]

We think no one will have the hardihood to question that instinct of worship, which has led our churches practically to lay aside Hymn 75, Book I., of Watts, on " Love to Christ."

> " The wondering world inquires to know
>   Why I should love my Jesus so."

> " Yes, my Beloved, to my sight,
>   Shows a sweet mixture, red and white."

And we are as confident that the same instinct will lead Christian hearts to enshrine in their affections the following, by Palmer, as one of the sweetest of Hymns of Communion with Christ.

> Jesus, these eyes have never seen
>   That radiant form of thine!
> The veil of sense hangs dark between
>   Thy blessèd face and mine!
>
> I see thee not, I hear thee not,
>   Yet art thou oft with me;
> And earth hath ne'er so dear a spot,
>   As where I meet with thee.
>
> Like some bright dream that comes unsought,
>   When slumbers o'er me roll,
> Thine image ever fills my thought,
>   And charms my ravished soul.

[1] Sabbath Hymn Book, Hymn 1032.

Yet though I have not seen, and still
Must rest in faith alone;
I love thee, dearest Lord!— and will,
Unseen, but not Unknown.

When death these mortal eyes shall seal,
And still this throbbing heart,
The rending veil shall thee reveal,
All glorious as thou art![1]

Who is not willing to surrender Hymn 96, Book I., of Watts, on the doctrine of Election, —

"But few among the carnal wise,"—

and to substitute in the place of it, a hymn which, in the very grandeur of its rythm, as well as in the awe-struck feeling which it expresses, is so *sympathetic* with the doctrine, as the following hymn by Palmer? —

Lord, my weak thought in vain would climb
To search the starry vault profound;
In vain would wing her flight sublime,
To find creation's outmost bound.

But weaker yet that thought must prove
To search thy great eternal plan, —
Thy sovereign counsels, born of love
Long ages ere the world began.

When my dim reason would demand
Why that, or this, thou dost ordain,
By some vast deep I seem to stand,
Whose secrets I must ask in vain.

When doubts disturb my troubled breast,
And all is dark as night to me,
Here, as on solid rock, I rest;
That so it seemeth good to thee.

[1] Sabbath Hymn Book, Hymn 689.

> Be this my joy, that evermore
> Thou rulest all things at thy will;
> Thy sovereign wisdom I adore,
> And calmly, sweetly, trust thee still.[1]

Surely, no critic, in his fondness for ancient song, would retain Hymn 81, Book II., of Watts, on "Our sin, the cause of Christ's death,"—

> "And now the scales have left my eyes;
> Now I begin to see;
> Oh! the cursed deeds my sins have done!
> What murderous things they be!"—

if its place be needed for one so penetrative of Christian experience, as the ensuing lines, on the same subject:

> I see the crowd in Pilate's hall,
> I mark their wrathful mien;
> Their shouts of "crucify" appall,
> With blasphemy between.
>
> And of that shouting multitude
> I feel that I am one;
> And in that din of voices rude,
> I recognize my own.
>
> I see the scourges tear his back,
> I see the piercing crown,
> And of that crowd who smite and mock,
> I feel that I am one.
>
> Around yon cross, the throng I see
> Mocking the sufferer's groan;
> Yet still my voice it seems to be,
> As if I mocked alone.

[1] Sabbath Hymn Book, Hymn 237.

'T was I that shed the sacred blood;
I nailed him to the tree;
I crucified the Christ of God,
I joined the mockery!

Yet not the less that blood avails
To cleanse away my sin!
And not the less that cross prevails
To give me peace within![1]

The retention of such of the older hymns as have been here illustrated, and the rejection of the later productions of hymnology, for the sake of them, surely cannot command an enlightened defence. The adoption of "Sternhold and Hopkins" entire, to the exclusion of Dr. Watts, which to this day is a fact, in many churches of the English Establishment, would scarcely be more obsolete in policy, or more offensive. Montgomery expresses the decision of the large majority of worshippers against these obsolescent lyrics, when he says of "Sternhold and Hopkins": "To hold such a version forth, as a model of standard Psalmody for the use of Christian congregations, in the nineteenth century, surely betrays an affectation of singularity, or a deplorable defect of taste."

This comparison of the living with the dead Hymns of the Church, might be largely extended. But this is not needful. A few cases of such obvious contrast, illustrate and establish the *principle* on which the compilers of the Sabbath Hymn Book have admitted many modern hymns to this Manual.

Among the authors of the "new songs," appear the names of Conder, Bonar, Elliot, Malan, McCheyne,

[1] Sabbath Hymn Book, Hymn 747.

Duffield, Palmer, and others, well known in the literature of our times. There are some anonymous hymns, both in ancient and modern song, for whose authors we now search, as for a lost Pleiad. Some of the choice hymns of this Collection it is impossible to trace with entire certainty to their origin. Yet some of these, as well as others from living writers, we think will be accepted by the church, as expressions of genuine religious life, which should have a permanent place in our hymnology.

§ 10. *The Number of Hymns.*

The sympathy of hymnology with religious experience, suggests also the most important of the principles on which the *proportions* of a manual of song for public worship should be adjusted.

A good compilation of hymns is something more than a conglomeration of good hymns. It is a *structure*. The idea of proportion is omnipresent, and the demands of proportion are often as decisive in its framework, as in architecture. That is not *constructive* criticism of such a manual, which would judge of the exclusion, or the admission of a hymn, by its intrinsic merits alone. Its relation to the structure as a whole, should often be more conclusive than its absolute excellence or demerit. Church song, as an expression of religious life, requires that a hymn-book be vital with the life of the church *collectively*. It must possess, not only breadth of range in respect of the old and the new, but symmetry in respect of diversities of taste and culture. The pulse of its sympathy with real life must beat, not only strongly, but *evenly*.

In the first place, a modern manual of Hymnology

must contain a large number of selections. On this topic, we think that criticism has, for the most part, been singularly at fault. Yet, we are scarcely correct in pronouncing it singular. Probably every compiler of a hymn-book, within the present century, has commenced his labors with a numerical standard very far below that of his ultimate choice. The late Professor Edwards indicated, perhaps, the general feeling of those whose hymnologic culture has been directed by their individual tastes, in the conviction which he expressed, that "two or three hundred of the most exquisite songs of Zion, * * * would include all of our psalms and hymns which are of sterling value for the sanctuary." Yet so various is the religious history of different minds, and so diverse, therefore, are their responses of the heart to sacred song, that it would be a marvellous coincidence if any two persons should select, from the same resources, the *same* three hundred hymns.

The degree of this diversity is astonishing, even with the most generous allowance for differences of character. Experiments upon it are amusing. A very valuable Collection of Hymns recently published in England, numbering between eleven and twelve hundred, was submitted to fifteen clerical critics, each being requested to erase the hymns which in his judgment should be omitted. A comparison of the returns indicated a result like that of the artist's masterpiece under the criticism of the market-place. Less than *one hundred* hymns were retained by the unanimous suffrage of fifteen men. The Sabbath Hymn Book was, in a similar manner, submitted to the inspection of ten clergymen, with the request that each should select those hymns, not exceeding six hundred in number, which he should deem indispensable to a hymn-book for social conference. The result was, that of the twelve hundred and eighty-nine hymns in this Collection, the number unanimously rejected by ten critics from a book of but one-half the size of this, was only *fifty-six*.

Individual hymns, also, are the subjects of wide extremes of judgment. The quaintness of the old version of the one hundredth Psalm — "All people that on earth do dwell" — offends the modern ear of one reviewer, while another pronounces it "the gem of the book." Pope's stately hymn on the reign of the Messiah — "Rise, crowned with light; imperial Salem, rise!" — is deemed "unfit to be sung," by one hymnologist; while another is so fascinated by its "imperial" measure, that he would sacrifice to it even such a hymn as one of the choicest from Watts: "Alas, and did my Saviour bleed."

Certain hymns, yearning with the tenderness of Christian affection to the Saviour, like Hymn 418 of the Sabbath Hymn Book, —

"I close my heavy eyes,
Saviour ever near,"—

are condemned as approaching the passion of erotic songs. It is true, they may be easily parodied by profane criticism. Yet many devout worshippers hasten to learn them by heart; and more than one has affirmed them to be the richest lyrics in the language. The feminine graces of the hymns of such a writer as Bonar, are denounced by some, as "not having the true ring in them;" but many others, of less metallic tastes, give thanks for them, as "invaluable treasures."

This proverbial diversity of tastes is doubtless in

part factitious. But it is not wholly so; it is founded largely upon genuine differences of character, of mental history, and of religious wants. The human body, we are told, has such compass of temperament, that it will bear with impunity a degree of cold at which mercury freezes, and yet a degree of heat at which alcohol boils. The human soul is not less capacious in the amplitude of its religious nature. This necessitates, therefore, the expansion of a manual for public worship, very far beyond the range of the necessities of any one worshipper, or of any one class of Christian minds. That is improvident criticism which would restrict such a manual to three or four hundred, or twice four hundred " gems of the first water." A more large-hearted wisdom becomes all things to all men. It is a shallow judgment, either to approve or to condemn such a work in the spirit of a connoisseur in æsthetics. The very conditions of excellence in a body of popular psalmody, must extend its limits out of the range of a purely Attic taste. The censure of it by such a taste, may be an evidence that it has been collated with a wise eclecticism, with what Locke calls a "large, roundabout *sense*." "Hymns," says Montgomery, "ought always to be judged with a proportionate allowance by persons of different communions. And it requires no great stretch of Christian charity to do this. It is only allowing for the wind, in calculating the course of an arrow."

These views are confirmed by the actual circulation of the several collections of church songs which are used by the largest evangelical denominations of this country. They are, without exception, voluminous in the amount of their materials. The three collections which have been most extensively used in the Congregational churches during the last twenty-five years, are a proof of this. The " Church Psalmody" contains, as we count, twelve hundred and eighteen selections: " Watts and Select" twelve hundred and sixty; the "Connecticut Collection" twelve hundred and sixty-five. To these may now be added the " Plymouth Collection," which numbers fourteen hundred. " The Psalmist," extensively used by the Baptist churches of this country, comprises twelve hundred and forty-eight different pieces; and " Watts and Rippon," also employed by the Baptist denomination, numbers thirteen hundred and fourteen. Of the Presbyterian manuals, " The Church Psalmist," adopted by the New School General Assembly, contains eleven hundred and seventy-three, and the " Psalms and Hymns" of the Old School Assembly ten hundred and fifty-six. The " Methodist Hymns" number eleven hundred and forty-eight. Have not such figures some force as evidence of an existing necessity?

§ 11. *Proportion of Hymns on Prolific Themes.*

A manual of hymns for the sanctuary should *give a large preponderance to selections upon the richest subjects.* Hymnology has its favorite departments. They comprise the topics to which a healthy Christian mind turns with especial frequency and earnestness of affection. They are prolific of the richest fruits of poetry, because they are intrinsically the most fertile in suggestion of holy thought, and in the awakening of devout feeling. We can invent no criterion of proportion in respect of the themes of a manual of church psalmody, which shall be more truthful than the inquiry:

'On what themes has the spirit of devotional song actually taken upon itself form in speech, most copiously and most cordially?' If we can represent, in the proportions of such a manual, the devotional life of the church, we cannot fail to express the just perspective of truth. So shall we meet most symmetrically, the wants of Christian hearts.

Proceeding upon this principle, we find our materials clustering densely around certain focal points, while elsewhere they are comparatively sparse. For instance, hymns expressive of delight in worship are more abundant and rich than hymns upon the Scriptures. Hymns upon Affliction are more numerous, and of more precious quality, than hymns upon the Seasons. The subjective hymns, representing Christian feeling in view of God, of Christ, of sin, are vastly superior, in number and in merit, to the objective hymns upon the Ordinances, or the hymns of exhortation to the unconverted. "Ambrosial hymns," almost innumerable, are at command, on the subject of Heaven; but where shall we find one that shall approximate to some of them, in lyric or devotional worth, on the subject of Hell?

These inequalities of proportion are not invariably coincident with the differences of subjects, considered as themes of theologic belief. Doctrines which stand side by side in our creeds, by no means stand on an equal eminence in our hymn books. Thus, our resources are ample, of hymns upon most of the attributes of God severally; but we have few of superlative excellence upon the doctrine of the Trinity. We have an exuberance of supply upon the Advent, the Life, the Death, the Ascension, the Reign of Christ; but we search in vain for any redundance of choice hymns, upon either Depravity, or Regeneration, or the Decrees of God.

From such facts, we think, must be derived the principles of proportion on which a collection of hymns for public worship should be constructed. It is true, we cannot pronounce the religious life of the church perfect, either in the past, or in its present development. We must anticipate a growth of symmetry in the church of the future, which will express itself in the hymnology of coming ages. Yet, *substantially*, we must believe, the experience of the church has expressed the proportions of truth truthfully, in its adjustment to the sanctuary song. Christian hearts have sung that which a true experience of the "life that is of God" impelled them to sing. The genius of song has hovered most wistfully over those great centres of thought, with which the spirit of communion with God has the most profound affinity. Worship has a deeper insight here than mere Belief. Hymnology as it is, gives more trustworthy hints of hymnology as it should be, than we can glean from the history of creeds.

We adopt the principle, therefore, that, in a manual of church song, the larger proportion of hymns should be upon the themes, on which the experience of the church has in *fact* made "melody unto the Lord," most affluently and devoutly. We must follow the current of the actual outflowings of sacred poetry from the heart of the church. The result is, to disclose to us a beautiful coincidence between the experience of the past, and that of the present. We find that the themes on which Christian hearts *have* loved to sing, are those which still appear intrinsically most consonant with the spirit of worship. They are those which we should select *a priori*, as most genially sympathetic with holy song.

They are, for instance, such as the Being and Perfections of God, the Atoning Work, the Personal Preciousness, and the Mediatorial Reign of Christ; the Feelings of a Christian in view of sin, of God, of Christ; the Communion of Saints, the Future of the church, and the glory of Heaven. These themes, we intuitively feel to be the central topics of sacred lyric poetry. We can not merely rehearse them, we can *sing* them. They suggest themselves as the subjects of spontaneous melody. Hymns upon them are songs of the heart. " They come because they must come, and men sing them because they must sing, and the soul is borne upward by them into a height of Christian life, which animates and emboldens it for any and every special form or incident of duty."

Even of this choicest group of themes, we distinguish some which transcend the rest. The history of hymnology accords with the best forms of Christian culture, in finding the very heart of its life in the person of *Christ*. Here the rapture of holy song culminates on earth, as it does in heaven. Here every grace of religious character, and every experience of a devout life, has found freedom to express itself in hymns of worship. Where can another such body of sacred poetry be found in any language, as that which comprises the Christology of the songs of the church?

In the compilation of the Sabbath Hymn Book, the aim of the Editors has been, to devote the bulk of the volume to these standard themes of praise, and to do so, if need be, at the expense of inferior material. Of the hymns in this Collection, it will be found also, that more than one-third are upon themes in which the person of the Saviour is the preëminent object of thought.

Many of these are models of adoration of a *living* Redeemer. Protestantism does not worship a *dead* Christ. A manual of Protestant song should make much of Christ, as a risen, exalted, triumphant, reigning, blessed Lord. "The Lord is risen," was the morning salutation of the first disciples. The hymnology of the Reformation was a revival of communion with an ascended Saviour. The richest fields of that hymnology have been gleaned, to obtain for the Sabbath Hymn Book the most earnest and exultant hymns of love, of trust, of joy, in Christ as a living Friend.

In this feature of its construction, we think the book expresses the most ardent aspiration of the piety of our own times. It is a noticeable fact, that modern Christian life, after a period in which, in the Calvinistic churches at least, the worship of God as Creator, as Preserver, as Sovereign, and as Judge of men, has been largely and intensely developed in the favorite hymns of the sanctuary, is now reverting with new fervor to the conception of God *in Christ*. This conception is central in the discipline which characterizes modern Revivals. Theologic thought is drawn to it with a fresh fascination. Living hymnologists are consecrating to it their choicest effusions. And to no other subject of song, does the modern Christian heart beat in response so gratefully. The hymns of the Moravian Brethren, and of the Wesleys, on this theme, are received with an indulgence, which once would not have been accorded to them beyond the pale of the denominations to which their authors belonged.

The Editors of the Sabbath Hymn Book have recognized these facts, and have endeavored to gather into one thesaurus the most precious of these utterances of praise to Christ, of *all* times, and from *all* sources. A manual of song for the house of the Lord, *ought* thus to blend the voices of the Ages, in "the new, the old, the everlasting song of the Lamb."

§ 12. *Hymns of Worship.*

Collateral to the principle of the preponderance of the richest *themes* of worship, in a collection of sacred lyrics, is that of the *ascendency of hymns of direct address to the Godhead*. The *form* of worship, as well as its most fertile subjects, should predominate largely in such a collection. This principle also grows out of the demands of devotional culture. In fact, this class of hymns constitute the immense majority of the treasures of hymnology. Comparatively, the narrative, the didactic, the hortatory, the expostulatory, the comminatory hymns, are few in number, and inferior in merit. The gems of sacred song are almost all hymns of worship; not hymns of meditation only, not hymns of appeal to men, or of address to angelic intelligences, but of direct, living communion with God. This is as it should.be; and a manual of psalmody should correspond to this, in its proportions. Hymns of merely meditative or hortatory character should be admitted with no lavish hand. Histories in rhyme, and sermons in verse, are often the most frigid material for a hymn. They may sound mellifluent, or grand, or solemn, from the pulpit, and yet may be devoid of the lyric element, and may start not a throb of lyric emotion. Eloquence is not poetry. Poetry is not, necessarily, song. " Many of our hymns in common use," says an intelligent musician, "are so destitute of the lyric quality, that when we attempt to marry them to music, we only bring about a forced and unnatural union. A state of celibacy befits them far better." " A problem of Euclid," says another, " or an auctioneer's catalogue, is about as suitable to be sung."

A collection of lyrics for the sanctuary should be so proportioned as to invite some reform, we think, in the present usage of the pulpit respecting this class of hymns. Are they not often suggested in undue proportion, for the singing of a congregation, because they *read* well, or because they are good appendices to sermons, when a hymn of worship, unisonant with the sermon in devotional tone, would be vastly more effective for the purposes *both* of worship and of moral impression, because it would lift up the soul to a loftier plane of thought and of emotion, through direct intercourse with the Most High ? The comparative value of the two classes of hymns can be easily tested by experiment, and, we imagine, with scarcely a difference of opinion in the result.

The element of meditation and the element of worship are often finely illustrated in the same hymn. Perhaps no more felicitous example of meditative poetry exists in our collections of psalmody, than the first two stanzas of Cowper's hymn on the Atonement —" There is a fountain filled with blood." Those stanzas are inimitable in their kind. Every Christian heart melts in the utterance of them. They are a noble *preparative* to direct worship. But would the hymn ever have reached the place it now holds, in the affections of the church, if it had been *entirely* composed of soliloquy? How sweetly and yet grandly are we borne aloft, into a more ethereal realm of devotion, when we reach the third stanza, and enter into positive intercourse with Christ—"Dear dying Lamb, Thy precious blood!" Through the remainder of the hymn, we mount up on wings, as eagles.

The necessity of the precatory element to constitute a hymn of the highest order for the sanctuary, is often *felt*, when it may not be critically seen, in certain hymns which, considered as poetry only, appear to be incapable of improvement. What, for example, is more faultless than the first five stanzas of Montgomery's hymn on the Nature of Prayer—"Prayer is the soul's sincere desire"? Yet why does the *singing* of those stanzas so often "drag"? It is because they are not *worship*. They have the graces of poetry, but without the wings of song. They are purely didactic, descriptive, definitive. The living soul of prayer is not in them. They are lines *upon* prayer, not lines *of* prayer. In uttering them, ever so devoutly, one is *thinking* of prayer, not praying. What worshipper has not felt a sense of relief in the change introduced by the last stanza, in which the mind breaks away from the long dead level of description, and rises to an act of address to the Saviour—"O Thou, by whom we come to God"?

A manual of Christian song, we repeat, should be so proportioned as to *invite*, in the usage of the pulpit and of congregations, a more just ascendency than is often given to hymns of worship, over those of a meditative or a hortatory character. "Modern hymns," says a German writer, "are not lyrical, but didactic. They only preach in rhyme, and thus, they reach the head, but not the heart. If, now, the sermon preaches, and the singing preaches, and the prayer preaches, the monotony of the service will occasion weariness. But, if the sermon preaches, and the hymn sings, and the prayer prays, there will be a beautiful variety to exercise and interest all the faculties of the soul."

The Sabbath Hymn Book has been constructed with reference to this ascendency of worship over instruction, in the service of praise. A very large proportion of this manual consists of selections which are, in whole or in part, direct addresses to the Godhead. Nearly one thousand of these hymns contain some form of praise or prayer. The volume "is not meant to be a Book of Theology in rhyme, but it is called ' The Sabbath *Hymn* Book, for the service of *Song* in the house of the Lord.' " The genius of the book in this respect is expressed in the fact, that it begins and ends with the Lord's Prayer.

§ 13. *Hymns of Joy.*

"Is any merry? let him sing psalms." "My lips shall greatly rejoice when I sing unto Thee." "I will offer in his tabernacle, sacrifices of joy." "Awake up my glory; awake psaltery and harp; I will awaken the dawn." "The ransomed of the Lord shall come with songs and everlasting joy." "Make a joyful noise to him with psalms." "Sing, O Heavens; and be joyful, O Earth." Thus have inspired minds expressed the natural *association of gladness with song*. The proportions of a manual of psalmody should be such as to induce such an association in the Lord's house. The large majority of selections should be *inspiriting*.

Such *are* the richest treasures of hymnology; and these, again, express the best types of Christian life. The immortal hymns of the church are in large part the efflorescence of the invigorating graces. Love, hope, trust, courage, and therefore peace, joy, rapture, are ascendant over the sombre, or even the plaintive experiences in the noblest religious culture. So should they be ascendant in lyric devotion. So *are* they ascendant in the most precious accumulations of song.

"The worship of joy," says a living writer, "is higher than the worship of sorrow. Happiness is the spheral music, in which a God, whose name is Love, has ordained that holiness must voice itself." It is no fortuitous occurrence, then, that the songs in which Christian hearts take holiest delight, are hopeful or jubilant. Only in condescension to weakness, does the genius of praise admit any hymns expressive of disconsolate sorrow. Only in forbearance with sin, does it tolerate any wailings in spiritual darkness. So long as these are actual experiences of life, we need such standard elegies as "Oh that my load of sin were gone!" and "Oh for a closer walk with God!" and "Why is my heart so far from Thee?" etc. But we should do violence to the symmetry of truth, and should assist to *keep down* Christian experience in the low grounds of faith, if we should give to such hymns a preponderance over those of cheering and exultant aspiration. Worship in song should, as a whole, be a tonic to the worshipper. It should brace up the whole being. George Herbert, we are told, was wont to go twice a week to the Cathedral at Salisbury, twenty miles distant, and at his return he would say that the music which he heard there elevated his soul, and the place seemed to him like "heaven upon earth." Could he have experienced such exaltation, if the Cathedral service had been commonly in the strain of the "Miserere?"

A group of Christian sufferers were recently heard, beneath the ruins of a burning building, singing one of their favorite hymns of triumph, with rapid measure, in anticipation of their struggle with the flames. So, the Albigensian martyrs sung, in the prospect of their fiery translation. Such a stimulus to courage, and such a strengthener in conflict, should the prevailing *tone* of song be, in the house of the Lord. Such, therefore, should be the regnant spirit of a manual of psalmody.

The Sabbath Hymn Book contains very copious selections of this character. It abounds with hymns of adoration; hymns of delight in worship; hymns of joy in God; hymns of exulting trust in Christ; hymns of gratitude for the Advent of Christ; hymns of rejoicing in the Mediatorial Reign of Christ; hymns of communion with God and Christ; hymns of Christian triumph in victory over sin; hymns of courageous resolve in conflict; hymns of joy in affliction; hymns of general thanksgiving; hymns of national joy; hymns of hopeful aspiration after holiness; hymns of Christian assurance; hymns of delight in the church and the Ordinances; hymns of gratulation in view of the prospective enlargement of the church; hymns of jubilee, in view of the world's conversion; hymns of triumph over death; hymns of joy in the Resurrection; hymns of welcome to Christ at his second coming; hymns of exultation in anticipating Heaven. The reigning spirit of the volume is thus in unison with the state of a *redeemed* soul, which sings

> "I've found the pearl of greatest price;
> *My heart doth sing for joy;*
> And *sing I must*, for Christ is mine —
> Christ *shall* my song employ."

Such a volume is significantly characterized by the spirit of its closing hymn, on a theme which has been seldom thus sung in jubilant strains, —

> Eternity — eternity!
> O bright, O blest eternity!
> Which Jesus hath obtained for those
> Who seek in him their sure repose;
> A little while they suffer here,
> But lo! eternity is near:
> Eternity — Eternity!

> Eternity — Eternity!
> Soon shall these eyes thy wonders see;
> Oh, may I now the world despise,
> And upward raise my thankful eyes,
> And seek the joys that shall abide,
> From sin and sorrow purified:
> O bright, O blest eternity![1]

§ 14. *Comminatory Hymns.*

Hymns of commination are not favorites to a healthy Christian taste. They should not fill a large place in a collection designed for public worship. Like denunciatory preaching, they must be of rare occurrence, to

---

[1] Sabbath Hymn Book, Hymn 1290.

be effective. The Scriptures inculcate a faith which worketh by love. We have been able to discover, in the whole volume of inspired Psalms, but one passage which, correctly translated and interpreted, can be fairly regarded as a defence of hymns of comminatory exhortation to impenitent men. The imprecatory passages are not hortatory. A highly dramatic Psalm like the Fiftieth, contains the *figure* of denunciatory hortation from the mouth of *God* to the wicked; and a prophetic Psalm like the Fifty-second commences with an apostrophe to the Edomite assassin. But these are widely different, in rhetorical structure, from hymns of literal, direct appeal, in which a choir, or a congregation, echo the strain of a menacing discourse by singing, — " Sinner, art thou still secure ? " or, " Ah, guilty sinner, ruined by transgression."

It is by no means a sequence, that the becoming subject of a *sermon* should be a becoming subject of a *hymn*. That is a very natural phenomenon in the history of hymnology, in which it appears that hymns on Heaven are innumerable, and many of them of matchless excellence, while we search almost in vain for a good hymn on the world of despair; and many hymns which have been written upon this awful theme, are an abomination and a burlesque. Sacred *song* instinctively looks heavenward. It aspires, it soars, it dwells in light. We very rarely find a natural occasion for a *hymn* on Hell. A hymn upon the punitive justice of God, is not a hymn *upon* the experiences of the " second death." An earnest Christian soul is seldom in the mood of song on such a theme. When it is so, it demands a subdued, tender, tremulous strain, which shall be rather chanted, or murmured, than sung.

For instance, we can understand how a worshipper can breathe in low tones, scarcely above a whisper, such a hymn as the 1289th of the Sabbath Hymn Book, " Father — if I may call Thee so." We can imagine the quivering sensibility with which one might chant the *intimations* of woe, which seem to palpitate in some of the lines of the old Judgment Hymn, by Celano.

> The last loud trumpet's wondrous sound
> Shall wake the nations under ground:
> Where, then, my God, shall I be found, —
>
> When all shall stand before thy throne,
> When thou shalt make their sentence known,
> And all thy righteous judgment own!
>
> Thou, who for sinners felt such pain,
> Whose precious blood the Cross did stain,
> Who did for us its curse sustain, —
>
> By all that man's redemption cost,
> Let not my trembling soul be lost,
> In storms of guilty terror tossed!
>
> Give me in that dread day a place
> Among thy chosen, faithful race,
> The sons of God, and heirs of grace.
>
> Trembling before thy throne I bend;
> My God, my Father, and my Friend,
> Do not forsake me in the end![1]

But where is the congregation, or choir, that has ever sung, in *any* tone, Hymn 44, of the Second Book of Watts? We beg the reader's pardon for transcribing it.

---

[1] Sabbath Hymn Book, Hymn 1282.

With holy fear, and humble song,
  The dreadful God our souls adore;
Reverence and awe become the tongue
  That speaks the terrors of his power.

Far in the deep, where darkness dwells,
  The land of horror and despair, —
Justice has built a dismal hell,
  And laid her stores of vengeance there.

Eternal plagues and heavy chains,
  Tormenting racks and fiery coals, —
And darts to inflict immortal pains,
  Dyed in the blood of damned souls.

There Satan, the first sinner, lies,
  And roars, and bites his iron bands;
In vain the rebel strives to rise,
  Crushed with the weight of both thy hands.

There guilty ghosts of Adam's race
  Shriek out, and howl beneath thy rod;
Once they could scorn a Saviour's grace,
  But they incensed a dreadful God.

Tremble, my soul, and kiss the Son:
  Sinner, obey thy Saviour's call;
Else your damnation hastens on,
  And hell gapes wide to wait your fall.

Is this poetry? Is it a lyrical outgushing of Christian feeling? Is it, then, in any proper sense, a Christian hymn? Had any other man than Watts composed it, would it not invite the criticism of Montgomery, upon the whole class of unlyrical hymns, that they "appear to have been written by all kinds of persons, except poets"? We deny that the hymn is impressive, even. It is not a more atrocious violation of good taste, than of that chastened, awe-struck, almost heartbroken emotion with which a Christ-like mind will contemplate in *song* the existence of a world of woe. No heavenly mind can *revel* in song on such a theme. Adoration of the justice of God may, indeed, soar to ecstasy. But it will never descend from that eminence of benign emotion, to lose itself *within* the abodes of despair, and to clutch at *details* of modes and instruments of torture. Pagan Mythology could open the realm of Pluto to Orpheus only on a mission of affection. Shall the taste of Christian Theodicy, in song, be less humane?

Even of a far less terrific theme of poetry, and one never intended for the accompaniment of music, Robert Southey says: "Is there not something monstrous in taking such a subject as the 'Plague in a Great City'?[1] * * * It is like bringing racks, wheels, and pincers upon the stage, to excite pathos. No doubt but that a very pathetic tragedy might be written upon 'The Chamber of the Amputation.' * * * But actual and tangible horrors do not belong to poetry. The best picture of Apollo slaying Marsyas, or of the Martyrdom of St. Bartholomew, would be regarded as more disgusting than one of a slaughter-house, or of a dissecting-room."

Still more repulsive is that taste which dwells upon, and enumerates, and particularizes, and describes, and pictures, and seems to *handle* the machinery of eternal torment — and this in the strains of a *lyric* poem. Such a ghastly eccentricity is offensive, most of all, to that benignant and reverent spirit in which piety often an-

---

[1] The allusion is to Wilson's "City of the Plague."

ticipates the working of refined culture. Such a spirit would as soon think of singing Dante's "Inferno," or Milton's portraiture of Sin.

On the principles here suggested, the Sabbath Hymn Book gives preference to hymns of Invitation, over those of Threatening. Of hortatory and expostulatory hymns, the choice has fallen upon those which are *obviously* pervaded with an affectionate, rather than a comminatory earnestness. So far as the materials of hymnology admit, exhortations of warning and rebuke in the form of *soliloquy* are selected, in preference to others in the form of colloquial appeal. The "hymn preaches" less incongruously with the spirit of worship, if a sinner is made to address its admonitions to his own soul, by the use of the first person, than if he is assailed by it, with the second person, from the lips of another. Must not the occasion be very infrequent, on which a denunciatory hymn would be as effective as the following? —

God calling yet! — shall I not hear?
Earth's pleasures shall I still hold dear?
Shall life's swift passing years all fly,
And still my soul in slumbers lie?

God calling yet! — shall I not rise?
Can I his loving voice despise,
And basely his kind care repay?
He calls me still: can I delay?

God calling yet! — and shall he knock,
And I my heart the closer lock?
He still is waiting to receive,
And shall I dare his Spirit grieve?

God calling yet! — and shall I give
No heed, but still in bondage live?

> I wait, but he does not forsake;
> He calls me still! — my heart, awake!
>
> God calling yet! — I cannot stay;
> My heart I yield without delay:
> Vain world, farewell! from thee I part;
> The voice of God hath reached my heart![1]

Where can we find a menacing hymn of exhortation to Christians, which will be as quickening to fidelity, as the following monologue?

> My soul, it is thy God
>   Who calls thee by his grace;
> Now loose thee from each cumbering load,
>   And bend thee to the race.
>
> Make thy salvation sure;
>   All sloth and slumber shun;
> Nor dare a moment rest secure,
>   Till thou the goal hast won.
>
> Thy crown of life hold fast;
>   Thy heart with courage stay;
> Nor let one trembling glance be cast
>   Along the backward way.
>
> Thy path ascends the skies,
>   With conqu'ring footsteps bright;
> And thou shalt win and wear the prize
>   In everlasting light.[2]

§ 15. *Unity of Worship.*

Hymns of infrequent use often burden unduly a collection of songs for public worship. Fidelity to

---

[1] Sabbath Hymn Book, Hymn 556.   [2] Ibid. 535.

the best forms of religious life, requires that this class of hymns be restricted. A limit must be prescribed somewhere, to the expansion of a manual designed for *use* by assemblies of worshippers. As time augments our hymnologic resources, the work of selection becomes the more indispensable, and yet the more difficult. Is it not an evil to number the fragments of our psalmody by thousands? It is well that the *permanent* taste of the churches is frugal of its favor, and its ultimate criticism is severe upon needless accumulations. Every compiler of a hymn-book should welcome this test of his work. Only thus can the purest gold be refined from the treasures of ages.

Much may be achieved, in assistance of this purifying process, by a severe taste in the estimate of the value of hymns not often used. Here, we think, is one of the most suitable points of retrenchment. Hymns of only occasional pertinence, should yield precedence to those which are in constant demand. Even good hymns, of so specific character as to be seldom pertinent, may have no claim to a place in such a manual. The space they would occupy may be needed for hymns upon the standard themes — hymns equally good intrinsically, and better for *being* upon standard themes. We cannot wisely admit many hymns upon every distinct topic whose claim is restricted by its own range of use.

Therefore, it is a positive objection to a book of psalmody, that it contains thirty hymns upon Slavery, and forty upon Sabbath Schools, and twenty upon the Cause of Seamen, and fifty upon Foreign Missions. A collection constructed with any degree of consistency upon the principle involved in such adjustments of material, must be either overgrown in bulk, or distorted in proportions.

We speak of hymns "*upon*" topics of occasional aptness, because it is further true, that hymns *upon* such a topic are not necessarily the hymns most congenial with the devotional frame excited by that topic. Why do we choose to associate any topic of pulpit discourse with one hymn, rather than another? Clearly, in order to secure the sympathy of song with the other services of the hour. *Unity of worship* is essential to the perfect excellence of any part of worship. But what is unity of worship? On what conditions does it depend? Surely, it is not identity of thought and emotion, prolonged through the hour by repetition. Every pastor who has been studious of the proprieties of the Lord's house, must have observed that the most impressive unity, so far as it is affected by selections of psalmody, is the result of a golden mean between certain extremes of method.

On the one hand, the policy, which we have known some congregations to practise, of " singing the hymn-book through," consecutively, on successive Sabbaths, is ruinous to the coälescence of song with other elements of the service. It is open to the evils, without the advantages, of a prescribed liturgy.

On the other hand, that policy is scarcely more flexible, which demands invariable identity of theme in song and sermon. That could not have been often a natural method of association of preaching with praise, which Doddridge and Watts practised, of transmuting the synopsis of a discourse into a hymn, to be sung at its close. In view of such homiletic inspiration of psalmody, who cares to seek farther for the secret of the inequality of their productions? Orton's edition of the Works of Doddridge ascribes to him three hundred and seventy-four hymns. The editor very safely ventures the hypothesis, that possibly a *few* of these may "appear flat or obscure." In truth, not a fourth part of them can be fairly regarded now as living hymns. Even Watts could not often successfully transform homily to song. It is one of the marvels of his genius, that under the incubus of this, and certain kindred habits of composition, he could produce, in seven hundred efforts, two hundred and fifty effusions which the church will not permit to die.

Between these extremes of rigidity, there is a policy, as elastic as the air, and as genial in its working. It aims at unity of worship, not by sameness of theme, but by resemblance of spirit. It would have a sermon preceded and followed, not necessarily by a hymn on the identical subject, but by a hymn on a kindred subject, pertaining to the same group of thought, lying in the same perspective, and enkindling the same class of emotions. It would select the songs of the sanctuary, with the same *play* of adjustment to the themes of meditation, which a skilful Christian chorister practises in adjusting *tunes* to songs. The unity thus obtained is that of an indefinable affinity, which lies below the reach of procrustean art.

This latitude of adaptation between the pulpit and the choir, extends as well to the standard as to the exceptional themes of meditation. Is not a sermon on the Decrees of God, more aptly preceded by that noble hymn of Watts, "Be Thou exalted, O my God," than by the standard hymn *upon* decrees, "Behold the potter and the clay"? For the want of a better hymn *upon*

Regeneration, the pulpit has stereotyped, in the usage of the sanctuary, the formal didactic stanzas of Watts, " Not all the outward forms on earth." But this hymn contains not a solitary line of worship. It is bald, calm, prosaic preaching. Is there not a more glowing sympathy with a sermon on this doctrine, in such a hymn of *invocation*, addressed to the third Person of the Trinity, as, " Come, blessed Spirit! Source of Light"? or, " Come, gracious Spirit! heavenly Dove"? The sympathy of the liturgic with the didactic parts of the church-services, admits even of *contrast* between sermon and song. We have known a sermon upon the doctrine of Future Punishment to be followed by a hymn on Heaven, with a marvellous deepening of impression.

§ 16. *Occasional Hymns.*

This *breadth of range* in the principle of unity of worship, covers the entire area of " occasional hymns." Who does not generally prefer, for instance, at the Lord's table, to sing such hymns as, " Not all the blood of beasts," and " My faith looks up to Thee," and " Rock of Ages, cleft for me," etc., rather than hymns *upon* the sacramental feast, like that of Watts: "'T was on that dark, that doleful night," and " Jesus invites his saints "? The hymn which the " Man of sorrows" himself chanted, with his disciples, on the occasion of the Last Supper, probably was composed of the Psalms 113 and 114, — Psalms of worship, containing mysterious premonitions of the sacrifice on Calvary, but not one of the sacrament which commemorates that sacrifice. The Lord's Supper, as in itself an object of thought, and, therefore, as in itself a subject of song, is not comparable to the redemptive work which it symbolizes, — still less to the person of the Saviour, to whom the believing heart would flow forth in love. Watts wrote twenty-five odes expressly for the "Holy Ordinance." But the author himself calls attention to more than a hundred hymns in his two preceding books, which "may sometimes perhaps appear *more* suitable than any of these." Even of the twenty-five which compose his third book, more than one third are not at all *upon* the ordinance itself.

Hymns for Sabbath schools are affected by the principles we have laid down respecting unity of worship. Hymns *upon* the Sabbath school must, of necessity, be upon an inferior plane of meditation, and therefore of lyric emotion, to that of many of our standard hymns of worship, which are expressed in simple language, and which direct a child's heart to the great objects of Christian praise. Can any hymn *upon* the Sabbath school be so valuable to the spirit of worship there, as the hymn on the condescension of God:

"My God, how wonderful Thou art!
Thy majesty how bright!"[1]

or, as the hymn on communion with Christ:

"Dear Jesus, ever at my side,
How loving thou must be."?[2]

The whole subject of hymns and hymn-books for children, deserves thoughtful review. The Sabbath

---

[1] Sabbath Hymn Book, Hymn 172.   [2] Ibid., 1077.

school has become a Power of evangelical enterprise. Its healthfulness depends upon its auxiliary force, as related to the church. The spirit of worship which it cherishes should therefore be in unison with that of the church. Its songs of praise should, as far as possible, be the songs of the church. Many of its richest treasures of song *are* such. It is an evidence that the life of the church has some of its most vital roots running into and under our Sabbath School system, that hymnology has created *for* that system some of the most beautiful of modern additions to this department of our literature. The simplicity of certain of the new hymns for children, wins *all* Christian hearts. An assembly of gray-haired saints might sing them with unction. Who is not grateful for the child's hymn on Heaven, "There is a happy land"? We have seen an audience of three thousand almost lifted upon their feet, by one of these "hosannas" of the "children in the temple;" and we have recalled our Lord's words: "Yea, have ye never read, 'Out of the mouth of babes and sucklings, Thou hast *perfected* praise'?"

But, on the other hand, many of the very best hymns for children, are the standard hymns of their fathers. A Sabbath School Hymn-book, therefore, ought not to consist chiefly of hymns written exclusively *for* Sabbath schools. The large proportion of such a collection should be devoted to the very jewels of hymnologic stores. It should not be made up very largely of infantile hymns — hymns which none *but* children *can* sing. We would have children taught to sing the hymns which will *live* in their experience, when *they* are fathers and mothers, old men and women. Dr. Watts composed his "Divine Songs" that they might be " a constant *furniture* for the minds of children, that they might have something to *think* upon." Hymns which one can " think upon," are generally the most apposite songs of childhood.

It is a great error to imagine that they are unintelligible, or unattractive, to youthful minds. Even Watts, we think, was too anxious to "*sink* the language," as he says, "to the level of a child's understanding." The taste of any bright child will be sensible of the contrast, for the purposes of *worship*, between the second of Watts's "Divine Songs," — " I sing the almighty power of God," — and the twenty-second, " Against pride in clothes," —

> " Why should our garments, made to hide
> Our parents' shame, provoke our pride ? "

The first of these odes anybody can sing. The second a child very early learns to put away, as among childish things.

Walter Scott, than whom no man could more skilfully interest the young, said that it was a miserable policy to " *write down* to children." No other class of minds are so aspiring in their tastes. Those tastes can be easily vitiated by twaddling rhymes, set to frisking tunes. But they need only to be *taught* some of the solid hymns of the sanctuary, to understand them, appreciate them, love them. These once loved, are loved *forever*. The best of them, indeed, *are* youthful lyrics ; as the best of " Children's Hymns" are those which adult years love as well. *The best hymns, for anybody, are the common property of youth and age.* Immortals are always young. The charm which fascinates us all, in many a sterling old psalm of praise, is the *childlikeness* of its structure — the artlessness, the spontaneousness, the freshness, the sweetness, with which it seems to exhale great thoughts in unconscious verse. Of hymnology, as of piety in its most profound and beautiful forms, we may say, " Jesus called a little child unto him, and set him in the midst of them." That is the image enshrined in a multitude of the most precious of our church songs. Of such is the kingdom of heaven.

In confirmation of this view, a sagacious critic of "Hymns for Children," says : " After more than forty years' experience in Sunday schools, I have become entirely satisfied, that the best hymns to be committed to memory by the youngest child capable of doing so, are the solid, substantial hymns of Watts, Cowper, Newton, and such like. With some few exceptions, ... I would never store the mind of a child with *baby* hymns. The same effort required for that purpose, will suffice for fixing in the memory some of the choicest hymns in the English language, and when once committed, they will never be forgotten. .... From their very nature, infantile hymns are ephemeral. Can they not, ought they not, to be supplanted by those old familiar songs of Zion, which our fathers and mothers taught us half a century ago ?"

Most cordially we answer "Yes!" repeating "with few exceptions," and adding only, " Let us bring forth out of our treasures things *new and* old." Let the children be taught to sing chiefly hymns which the fathers sing.

> " Our lips shall tell them to our sons,
> And they again to theirs."

In this direction of the *healthy* adaptation of our temple-worship to the sensibilities of children, we look for improvement. At present they are too often a forgotten fraction of the assembly. In the dialect, rather than in the themes, of *prayer*, they often find little to win their sympathy. Still more injudiciously are they often banished from the service of praise, either by the selection of obsolete, or heavy, or prosaic, or complicated hymns, or by the " performance " of intricate tunes. In no portion of the Sabbath worship should they be more thoughtfully regarded than in this. Through the most impressible years of childhood, this, if not the only one, is the chief exercise of the sanctuary which attracts, and quickens, and *educates* them. We would adjust it to their wants, in the construction and the use of a manual of sanctuary songs.

We would do this in the two methods already hinted at. Such a manual should comprise many hymns which, either in their subjects, or in their style, or in their measure, and consequently in the tunes affixed to them, should be specially fitted to win youthful voices. Then we would have the children trained, in the Sabbath school and elsewhere, to sing, and to love *also*, and *chiefly*, the choicest models of song, as judged by adult Christian culture. The usage of the Sunday school and the usage of the church, should thus very largely lap over upon each other, and be welded together.

Of the first of these two classes of hymns, an illustration may be seen in the following group:[1]

---

[1] Selected from the Sabbath Hymn Book.

the selection. By what rule of taste or utility can a hymn-book for Sunday schools reject any considerable number of the following group?[1]

"Sweet is the work, O Lord."
"Blest morning, whose young dawning rays."
"My God, how endless is thy love!"
"Lord, Thou hast searched and seen me through."
"Jehovah God, thy gracious power."
"God is a Spirit, just and wise."
"Hark! hark! the notes of joy."
"Thou dear Redeemer, dying Lamb!"
"Come, let us join our cheerful songs."
"Shall hymns of grateful love."
"Jesus, hail! enthroned in glory."
"Jesus, exalted far on high."
"Sing of Jesus, sing forever."
"Oh could I speak the matchless worth."
"Come, gracious Spirit, heavenly Dove."
"Lord, am I precious in thy sight?"
"How sweetly flowed the Gospel-sound!"
"Alas, and did my Saviour bleed?"
"Oh for a heart to praise my God."
"Thou Prince of glory, slain for me."
"I will love Thee, all my treasure."
"My God, my portion, and my love."
"My times are in thy hand."
"My blessed Saviour, is thy love."
"And can mine eyes without a tear."
"Rock of Ages, cleft for me."
"My faith looks up to Thee."
"When blest with that transporting view."
"I lay my sins on Jesus."
"Saviour, happy would I be."
"Jesus, in whom but Thee above?"
"Dear Saviour, we are thine."
"Jesus, and shall it ever be."
"O Jesus, King most wonderful!"
"To Thee, O God! my prayer ascends."

"Almighty God! in humble prayer."
"My gracious Lord, I own thy right."
"Dear Father! to thy mercy-seat."
"How sweet, how heavenly is the sight."
"Happy the souls to Jesus joined."
"Teach me, my God and King."
"Think gently of the erring one."
"Jesus, cast a look on me."
"Oh that the Lord would guide my ways!"
"There is a safe and secret place."
"Oh happy day that fixed my choice."
"Great God, the nations of the earth."
"Wake the song of jubilee!"
"Jesus shall reign where'er the sun."
"When shall the voice of singing."
"From Greenland's icy mountains."
"Thy mighty working, mighty God."
"While with ceaseless course the sun."
"Come, let us anew our journey pursue."
"Thou must go forth alone, my soul."
"That solemn hour will come for me."
"No! no! it is not dying."
"There is a land of pure delight."
"Sweet is the scene when Christians die."
"Asleep in Jesus! blessed sleep!"
"Sister, thou wast mild and lovely."
"Oh for the death of those."
"Why should we weep for those who die."
"Far from these narrow scenes of night."
"These are the crowns that we shall wear."
"Nor eye hath seen, nor ear hath heard."
"We speak of the realms of the dead."

[1] Selected from The Sabbath Hymn Book.

"Our Father God, who art in heaven."
"Lord, in the morning Thou shalt hear."
"Awake my soul, and with the sun."
"Thou seest my feebleness."
"Glory to Thee, my God, this night."
"The pity of the Lord."
"I sing the almighty power of God."
"My God, how wonderful Thou art!"
"While shepherds watched their flocks by night."
"Hosanna! be our cheerful song."
"To Thee, my Shepherd and my Lord."
"Saviour, like a shepherd lead us."
"To praise our Shepherd's care."
"Yes, for me, for me He careth."
"One there is, above all others."
"Holy Father! hear my cry."
"How shall the young secure their hearts?"
"Holy Bible! Book Divine!"
"Give to the Lord thine heart."
"O Thou that wouldst not have."
"I love Thee, O my God."
"Jesus, the very thought of Thee."
"I love the Lord who died for me."
"My spirit on Thy care."
"Jesus, take me for thine own."
"Jesus, all atoning Lamb."
"With love the Saviour's heart o'erflowed."
"I've found the Pearl of greatest price."
"Lord of mercy and of might."
"Now is the accepted time."
"Oh! see how Jesus trusts himself."
"Pity, Lord, the child of clay."
"Glory to the Father give."
"Dear Jesus, ever at my side."
"I thank the goodness and the grace."
"O happy land! O happy land!"
"How glorious is our heavenly King!"
"See the kind Shepherd, Jesus, stands."
"There is a little lonely fold."
"There is a glorious world of light."
"Shepherd of tender youth."
"Around the throne of God in heaven."
"Remember thy Creator now."
"O gracious Lord, whose mercies rise."
"From yon delusive scene."
"When blooming youth is snatched away."
"Calm on the bosom of thy God."
"There is a happy land."
"Will that not joyful be?"
"Sun of my soul! Thou Saviour dear."
"O Thou that hearest prayer."
"All praise to Thee, eternal Lord."

These are "children's hymns;" yet many of them would be sung, *are* sung, by adult worshippers. Some of them are favorite hymns of the sanctuary. These, no hymn-book for promiscuous worship can part with.

So, on the other hand, very many of the incomparable songs of worship for a mixed assembly, would be the gems of the *best* book that can be compiled for Sabbath schools. If the reader will run his eye over the "Index of First Lines," of any good manual of psalmody, he will recognize a multitude of standard hymns, which no just principle of distinction can exclude from a copious collection for children and youth. The chief embarrassment is that of limiting

Probably not one of these hymns was composed expressly for the use of children. Yet they are all adapted perfectly to youthful capacities. A large majority of them, we think, would be indispensable to a *rich* collection for Sabbath schools.

A certain class of themes lie along the border-line between the religious and the secular domains of song. They cover some area in both. Only on the religious side of the line, have they any claim to be represented at all, in a volume designed for liturgic service. And even there, they are themes of only occasional interest. The principles we have advanced respecting occasional hymns, therefore, determine the place and proportion of such subjects in a manual of psalmody.

A representative of this class is *Civil Freedom.* As a theme of devotional feeling, this cannot demand a very large place in such a manual. It should not be excluded; but we think that a prayerful spirit will often choose to associate with it a hymn upon some more central theme of worship. Our literature contains " Odes to Liberty" in abundance, which are becoming to a week-day, and the meeting for secular reform. But, for a *Sabbath* hymn-book, a hymn on the Universality of the Atonement is a *more* thrilling protest of Christianity against slavery, than the best of such odes. A hymn of exultation in the Mediatorial Reign, or a hymn exhorting to a bold fidelity to Christ, penetrates the Christian sentiment on this subject more profoundly than the large majority of " liberty songs" can do. " Hark! the song of jubilee," breathes a Christian soul into the conflict with oppression, as no hymns can which are composed upon the model of such lyrics as "Oppression shall not always reign," and "God made all his creatures free," and "All men are equal in their birth." We feel no *spring* to the battle of reform when we sing, "O pure reformers, not in vain;" but it wakes us like a clarion in the fight, to hear Duffield's "Stand up! stand up for *Jesus!*"

The same latitude of selection should be extended to hymns for the *dedication* of a church, and for the *installation* of a pastor.

It is proverbial that poems composed by the poet laureates of Great Britain, upon the national festivals, have been generally among the least spirited of their productions. Southey groaned over the labor of creating them. Of one of them he writes, in no very "fine frenzy" of inspiration: "I have been rhyming as doggedly and as dully as if my name had been Henry James Pye. Another dogged fit will, it is to be hoped, carry me through the job; and as the ode will be very much according to rule, and entirely good for nothing, I presume it may be found unobjectionable." Wordsworth declined the honor of the laureateship, till he was assured that he might regard it as a sinecure.

So, is it not equally notorious that the majority of hymns written expressly for the services of Ordination and Dedication, are artificial, meagre, spiritless? Such occasions are sympathetic with some of the grand old hymns of the church, like the Te Deum Laudamus, or the ancient hymns of praise to the Trinity. Where can we find an "original" dedicatory hymn on our modern "Orders of Exercises" for such occasions, which is equal to Milton's version of the eighty-fourth Psalm? —

>How lovely are thy dwellings fair,
>　O Lord of hosts! how dear
>The pleasant tabernacles are,
>　Where thou dost dwell so near!
>
>My soul doth long and, fainting, sigh
>　Thy courts, O Lord, to see;
>My heart and flesh aloud do cry,
>　O living God, for thee![1]

Some of our standard hymns upon the *Church*, are among the most impressive dedicatory hymns in the language. Why must we have prosaic "originals," in place of such much-loved hymns as the following? —

>"Glorious things of Thee are spoken."
>"How honored is the sacred place."
>"I love thy kingdom, Lord."

None can be more becoming hymns of dedication than some of those expressive of *delight in worship*. Place side by side, one of the multitude of hymns which have been "made to order" for dedicatory services, and either one of the well-known versions of Psalm 122 —

>"How pleased and blest was I."
>"How did my heart rejoice to hear."
>"Oh! 't was a joyful sound to hear."

Who can hesitate in deciding upon such a comparison?

Of hymns adapted to the services of an Ordination, we know of none superior to Watts's version of Isaiah 52 : 7, "How beauteous are their feet." Yet, of other selections, we greatly prefer some of our standard

---

[1] Sabbath Hymn Book, Hymn 13.

hymns of praise, such as we have specified as suitable to dedicatory worship, to the majority of those lyrics, in a double sense "uninspired," which are constructed "expressly for the occasion" of the installation of a pastor. There is an eminent fitness to such an occasion, in a hymn of invocation to the Holy Spirit, like Hymn 447 of the Sabbath Hymn Book: "Spirit Divine! attend our prayer." A hymn upon the "Advent of Christ," may have a singular pertinence at such a time. When can we more suitably sing the stirring strain of Bowring, "Watchman, tell us of the night"?

The historical association of the appointment of the ministry, with the Ascension of our Lord, creates a rare beauty in the adaptation of hymns on that subject, and on the Mediatorial Reign of Christ, to the services of an ordination. Who has not heard the hymn of Coronation — "All hail, the power of Jesus' name!" — sung in thrilling harmony with such an occasion? With the exception of the single hymn by Watts, before referred to, we have never heard, in an installation service, another hymn which seemed to rise to the height of sympathy with the hour, and to express its grandeur so royally, as the version of the twenty-fourth Psalm by Tate and Brady, "Lift up your heads, eternal gates!"

This principle, that unity of worship is a unity of spirit, and is not necessarily founded upon identity of theme, we repeat, covers the whole range of hymns of infrequent use. Its application wisely restricts the number of those which are technically termed "occasional hymns." We anticipate the time when the public taste will so far appreciate it, as to demand even a more severe restriction of such hymns than has been adopted in the Sabbath Hymn Book.

§ 17. *Necessity of Inferior Hymns.*

An unthinking criticism condemns the expansion of a hymn-book by the admission of poor materials. Yet this is unavoidable in a manual possessing any breadth in its range of topics. The office of the editors of such a volume is, not to create, but to select and arrange. A judicious critic, who has been mindful of this fact, adds: "That any manual of sacred song should be sufficiently copious and varied to meet the demands of public service in our churches, and at the same time be free from all apparent defects, is impossible, both from the character of the material from which it must be compiled, and from the vast variety of mind, differing both in culture and custom, to which it must be adapted. Perfectly, and in all parts to meet the demands — doctrinal, devotional, associational, æsthetic, metrical, and emotional — presented in such a variety, can be expected from no compilers; and that clearly because it is impracticable in the nature of things. *The very completeness of such a work cannot fail to breed offence.* The very conditions of excellence necessitate its [liability] to defects, positive or negative." This is comprehensive and constructive criticism. The severity of æsthetic taste must not be permitted to contract the range of devotional expression in song. Our eagerness to consecrate the best part of a manual for worship to the best themes of worship, should not be suffered to exclude themes less prolific of lyric emotion. Our desire to restrict the number of hymns *upon* occasions, and other hymns of infrequent use, ought not to banish such hymns entirely. But few, on any one such occasional theme, will necessitate many, in the aggregate, upon all such. A hymn intrinsically inferior, therefore, may be *so* valuable relatively, as justly to displace a hymn which is intrinsically its superior.

These principles are so inevitable, that they will illustrate themselves to a candid review of *any* manual of song for public worship, which has been largely *used* by the churches. Such a review will disclose the fact, that certain hymns on Worship, on the Attributes of God, on the Works of God, on Providence, on the Person of Christ, on the Atonement, on the Holy Spirit, on the Bold Virtues, on Affliction, on the Church, on the World's Conversion, on Death, on Heaven, are *omitted*, which yet are superior to any that the same volume *contains*, on the Being of God, on Depravity, on Regeneration, on Justification by Faith, on the Mild Virtues, on Baptism, on the Dedication of a Church, on the Ordination of a Pastor, on Seamen, on Orphanage, on the Poor, on the Oppressed, on War, on the Seasons, on the "Second Death." The very affluence of the first of these two classes of themes, renders a choice selection of song upon them practicable; and the rejected residue will appear rich by the side of the best resources of hymnology, upon the less fertile themes embraced in the second class.

The practical question, then, is, What shall be done with an unfruitful subject of song? Theoretically, it is easy to say, 'Let us have superior hymns or none;' but practically, the problem admits of no such facile solution. Shall a hymn of only respectable merit, on Baptism, if it be the best of its class, be rejected, because it is inferior to other hymns which *are* rejected, on the Atonement, or on Heaven ? Hymns, like precious stones, must be tested relatively to the class they represent. We must not despise the most goodly of emeralds, because they are not equal to the least brilliant of rubies. That must be an extreme case, in which a weighty subject of Christian thought and emotion is wholly unnoticed in a book of psalmody.

Some such extreme cases, we think, exist. We do not know of one hymn on the subject of *Temperance*, which appears to us to rise to even the lowest level of a book of worship. Secular *odes* on temperance exist in abundance, but not religious *hymns*. We prefer therefore, until our hymnologic resources are enriched on this theme, to content ourselves with hymns which have the " unity of the Spirit" with the temperance reform. We should select from such hymns as the following :

> " I send the joys of earth away."
> " Awake my soul, stretch every nerve."
> " God is my strong salvation."
> " Sleep not, soldier of the Cross."
> " Soldiers of Christ, arise."
> " Stand up ! stand up for Jesus ! "
> " Think gently of the erring one."
> " Who, O Lord, when life is o'er."
> " So let our lips and lives express." [1]

We know of no hymns written expressly *upon* the Death of an Infant, which are not either offensive to many devout men, on account of questionable doc-

---

[1] Selected from The Sabbath Hymn Book.

trine, or repugnant to devotional taste, by reason of vague, or prosaic, or sentimental expressions. We therefore choose to turn, on such an occasion, to hymns like the following, which are delicately appropriate to the event, and yet contain no express allusion to it:

> "Father, oh, hear me now!"
> "In the dark and cloudy day."
> "Father, my spirit owns."
> "Through sorrow's night, and danger's path."[1]

Yet these are exceptional themes. On the large majority of the subjects suitable to public worship, hymnology is not destitute of materials of respectable worth. Where we find such materials extant, we must select from them, rather than to leave the class to which they belong unrepresented in a manual of praise.

One of the most emphatic illustrations of the principle here adopted may be derived from a comparison of hymns on the Bold Virtues, with those on the Mild Virtues. These two classes of hymns are signally unequal in poetic merit. Bold virtues are chivalrous themes of song. They invite heroic strains of poetry. They require a martial melody. They are more facile subjects, therefore, of lyric composition, than their opposites. The very excellences of hymns on the mild virtues border upon weaknesses. Their sedative spirit *may* subside into tameness. Their tranquil measure *may* be afflicted with languor. Their soothing melody *may* seem sluggish to the ear. Human nature is more tolerant of turbulent defects than of dulness. Therefore the gentle graces are among the most difficult themes of poetry. They require the rarest com-

---

[1] Selected from The Sabbath Hymn Book.

bination of poetic gifts, and, in fact, are not voluminously represented among the stores of hymnology. Practically, then, the inquiry concerning certain hymns of this class, touches the *existence* of these graces among our themes of liturgic song. " To be, or not to be ? that is the question."

The query, for instance, respecting such a hymn as that by Bonar, on the Inner Calm, " Calm me, my God, and keep me calm," is not, ' Cannot a more rousing ode be found upon Christian Courage, a more spirited battle-song on the good fight of Faith ?' Undoubtedly it can be. But the question is, ' Shall the ornament of a meek and quiet spirit be exscinded from the adorning of our temple service ?' This presents a plain case, on which there cannot be two opinions. Yet the principle involved in it will necessarily open a volume of church song to some inferior materials. No thoughtful criticism will object to this.

§ 18. *Omitted Hymns.*

English hymnology probably numbers, upon a low estimate, thirty thousand distinct poems. The most thankless task of a compiler of a hymn-book, is that of sitting in judgment upon questionable materials. The power of rejection is as vital as that of selection. Of the most defective hymns, none are so unworthy as not to be somebody's " favorites;" and of the most comely, few are so faultless as to pass every sentinel of criticism unchallenged. If a man can be content with none but a " perfect" hymn-book, he must construct it for himself, and *then* be content to find no second critic to confirm his judgment.

Still, an approximation to a *general* standard of excellence is practicable. We think that the main principles by which the rejection of materials from a manual of psalmody should be regulated, are suggested in the foregoing pages. Practically, they often cross each other. On one principle of taste a hymn should be approved; on another, condemned. Objections to certain hymns, therefore, are perfectly valid, and yet not conclusive. Commendations of other hymns are equally reasonable, and yet equally indecisive. The verdict often lingers in a dancing balance.

The following are the most important of the objections to materials, which, for one or *more* of the reasons here named, should be omitted from a manual of church psalmody. We notice them chiefly by recapitulation of principles already discussed or implied in other connections.

1. It is an objection to a hymn, that it is not *symmetrical in point of excellence.*

This principle is so well enforced by Montgomery, in his essay introductory to the "Christian Psalmist," that we cannot more briefly present it, than in his own words. "A hymn," he observes, "ought to be as regular in its structure as any other poem. It should have * * a beginning, middle, and end. There should be a manifest gradation in the thoughts; * * every line carrying forward the connection, and every verse adding a well-proportioned limb to a symmetrical body. The reader, * * when the strain is complete, [should] be *satisfied*, as at the close of an air in music. * * The practice of many good men, in framing hymns, has been quite the contrary. They have begun, apparently, with the only idea in their mind at the time; another, with little relationship to the former, has been forced upon them by a refractory rhyme; a third, became necessary to eke out a verse; a fourth, to begin one; and so on, till, having compiled a sufficient number of stanzas of so many lines, and lines of so many syllables, the operation has been suspended; whereas it might, with equal consistency, have been continued to any imaginable length, and the tenth or ten thousandth link might have been struck out, or changed places with any other, without the slightest infraction of the chain; the whole being a series of independent verses, collocated as they came, and the burden a cento of phrases, figures, and ideas, the common property of every writer who had none of his own. * * Such rhapsodies may be sung, * * but they leave no trace in the memory, make no impression on the heart, and fall through the mind, as sounds glide through the ear, — pleasant, it may be, in their passage, but never returning to haunt the imagination in retirement, or, in the multitude of the thoughts, to refresh the soul. Of how contrary a character * * * are those hymns which, once heard, are remembered without effort, * * are in everybody's mouth, and everybody's heart!"[1]

Is not this description clairvoyant of the process by which a very large number of hymns have been composed, which still contain some lines, possibly some stanzas, of rare merit? They are not good hymns, because they have no *sustained* excellence. Many of Dr. Watts's psalms and hymns, with their glorious proems, fall into this rank.

We have already alluded to the remarkable inequality

---

[1] Montgomery's "Christian Psalmist," Introductory Essay, p. xiv.

between the first lines or couplets of some of Watts's lyrics, and the subsequent stanzas. We would apologize for another suggestion, if the shallowness of the criticism to which hymns and hymn-books are often subjected, did not compel us to offer it. It is, that no fair judgment can be formed of the *omissions* from a manual of hymnology, by an examination of its index of first lines. That criticism which runs its eye along the columns of such an index, and censures the absence of well known, beautiful, or sublime beginnings, is sheer indolence. The truth is, respecting many of the selections in the more ancient manuals, the most that is generally known of them *is* their beginnings. The subsequent stanzas are so impotent or repulsive, that few persons read them. A preacher may be sometimes entrapped into the public reading of them by their beautiful exordiums, and a choir may sing them with stifled merriment; but the preacher soon becomes more wary, and at length the congregation do not know that such contents are within the covers of their hymn-books.

Let us test, then, this glib method of judging of omitted hymns. We turn, almost at random, to Watts's Psalms and Hymns, and read —

" My soul, the great Creator praise,
When clothed in his celestial rays."—

A noble beginning. Why should such a grand ode be rejected? But we read on, and soon we come upon —

" Tame heifers there their thirst allay,
And for the stream wild asses bray."

> "Fierce lions lead their young abroad,
> And roaring ask their meat from God."

> "There dwells the huge leviathan,
> And foams and sports in spite of man."

Shall we ask a youthful choir, or a grave congregation, to *sing* these things?

But we turn again, and our eye is charmed by the following couplet:

> "Give thanks to God, invoke his name,
> And tell the world his grace."

This is promising. Why should we discard so venerable a psalm? But shall we venture to proceed, and sing, perhaps on a midsummer's day, or at nightfall —

> "He gave the sign, and noisome flies
> Through the whole country spread,
> And frogs in croaking armies rise
> About the monarch's bed"?

Again we read a line whose lowly spirit invites us to pause:

> "Deep in the dust, before thy throne."

Could words be more becoming to the introduction of an act of contrite worship from a full, burdened heart? But how rudely is the spirit of penitent song balked, by being brought up against such a block of polemic theology as this! —

> "Adam, the sinner: at his fall
> Death, like a conqueror, seized us all;
> A thousand new-born babes are dead,
> By fatal union to their head!"

We start anew, and wander on till our eye falls upon a line, of which we say, 'Surely this is *safe*,'—

"Of justice and of grace I sing,"—

but *song* refuses to come at our bidding, when we read —

"The wretch who deals in sly deceit,
I'll not endure a night."

"I'll purge my family around,
And make the wicked flee."

Once more, we cannot avoid lingering upon the truly lyric and inspiring strain:

"Jesus, with all thy saints above,
My tongue shall bear her part,"—

but even this hosanna languishes on our tongues, when we are invoked to add—

"And sent the lion down to howl,
Where hell and horror reigns."

We do not cite these examples with irreverent design. But it is well that we should know what commodities we have, stored in our hymn-books. Shall veneration for a name prevent the repudiation of lyrics like these? Why should we retain such provocatives to the sportive curiosity of our children? But it is said that objectionable couplets and stanzas can be eliminated. This is true in many cases; not in all. Often, not always, a valuable hymn can be constructed out of the remnants, after a process of expurgation.

2. But this suggests a second principle, which must often be decisive of the omission of a hymn. It is an objection if the hymn *has no unity of character.*

A concatenation of pious lines is not a hymn. Often the result of the process of selection of five or six stanzas from the twenty which form the original, is to destroy oneness of aim. Each select couplet in itself may be poetic, lyric, devotional; but in conjunction, they all do not compose *one* strain of meditation or of worship. They are not progressive, are often refluent in thought, sometimes incoherent, even contradictory.

Often the avoidance of these evils creates another equally fatal to the usefulness of a hymn, that of excessive *length.* Unity and reasonable brevity cannot always be combined in one of these fragmentary lyrics. The originals of some of our standard hymns number twenty, thirty, even forty stanzas. From other originals, equally valuable hymns might be culled, if the conflict of unity with brevity, in a selection from them, were not an insuperable obstacle.

The iron rule, that we must have one version, or more, of every inspired psalm, works in this respect disastrously. Literally applied, the rule, as we have seen, is an impossible one. To construct a tolerable modern hymn by versions of certain psalms, we must adopt the policy of Watts and others, and *pick up* the materials of the hymn here and there, by a sort of *ricochet* movement over the area of the original. Many of our so-called versions of psalms remind one who compares them with the inspired text, of the well-known amusement of boys with slatestones on the margin of a lake. Such versions touch the originals at points only, not continuously. Yet the result of this process often is, not only the loss of the primary coherence of the psalm, but the failure to substitute in its place *any* principle of unity, in the composite fabric which is manufactured out of the fragments. This defect alone is sufficient to condemn many of the ancient versions, the whole of which cannot be sung, and the *remains* of which are fit only for respectful burial.

3. Unity may be sometimes preserved in a hymn, and yet it may *have no positive character, either of merit or demerit.*

Many of the accumulations of sacred song must pass into oblivion, for no other reason than their want of character. Are they vicious lyrics? No. Are they false in sentiment? No. Are they violations of taste? No. Are they of unmusical cadence? No. They only have no positive individuality. Would that they were 'cold or hot.'! We can give no reason for refusing them, except that we find no reason for accepting them. Some speciality must support an indifferent hymn. It must be upon a subject on which better lyrics are not extant, or it must have historic associations which we cannot part with, or some similar idiosyncrasy must outweigh the burden of its dull, heavy, lifeless rhymes. Diversity of opinion will of course exist respecting the application of this criticism to many hymns; but we are unable to discern any *striking* excellence in such as the following, from Watts:

"My God, and is thy table spread."
"Salvation is forever nigh."
"To God, the Great, the ever blest."
"Forever blessed be the Lord."

"Lord, what was man when made at first."
"The Lord is Judge; before his throne."
"Blest is the man, forever blest."

"Blest are the souls who hear and know."
"Why did the nations join to slay."
"Now Christ ascends on high."
"There is a God, all nature speaks."
"Almighty Ruler of the skies."
"As when in silence vernal showers."
"Jesus invites his saints."

"Thus the Eternal Father spake."
"To keep the lamp alive."
"Forever blessed be the Lord."
"Straight is the way, the door is straight."
"The Lord descending from above."
"Jesus is gone above the skies."

These, and a multitude like them, from other authors, are good enough negatively; they have no obtrusive defects of sentiment or form; individuals may have agreeable associations with them; but they belong to a class of lyrics which modern hymnology will inevitably encroach upon, and at last set aside. They have not merits numerous and positive enough to save them.

4. A hymn not destitute of positive worth, *may be fatally inferior to others of its class.*

Relative inferiority is in many cases so great, and so obvious, as to constitute a sufficient reason for omission. The good suffers by the overshadowing excellence of the better. It is a positive evil to place such selections in juxtaposition. For instance, is it not a waste to follow Watts's first version of the fifth Psalm, — "Lord, in the morning thou shalt hear," — with one so *much* its inferior as that by Goode, "Whene'er the morning rays appear"? Who will ever sing the second, with the first before his eyes?

On this principle, we object to very numerous versions of the same Psalm, unless, like Psalms 19, 51, 139, it be one of very rare quality, and aptness to modern use. Excepting the choicest of the Psalms, *many* versions of *one* will inevitably ensure such inequality, as to doom a part of them to respectable uselessness. Why should we burden a collection with four, six, eight versions, of which one-half can practically be of no other service than that of illustrating, by contrast, the quality of the other half? As the accretions of psalmody multiply, the sufficient reason for dropping one after another of the good, but not excellent, old hymns, must be, " the new is better."

On this principle we should exclude even the best of Watts's didactic versions of the thirty-second Psalm, and such other selections as the following:

" Lord, if thine eyes survey our faults."
" How calm and beautiful the morn."
" Thrice happy souls, who born of heaven."
" Thy mercy heard my infant prayer."
" Our spirits join to adore the Lamb."
" Not to the terrors of the Lord."
" Beyond where Cedron's water flows."
" Jesus comes, his conflict over."
" Methinks the last great day is come."
" O Lord, how many are my foes."
" Lord, I can suffer thy rebukes."
" The tempter to my soul hath said."
" My God, how many are my fears."
" O God of grace and righteousness."
" Whene'er the morning rays appear."
" Come tune, ye saints, your noblest strains."

" My trust is in my heavenly Friend."
" O Lord, our Lord, in power divine."
" Father of all, to Thee we bow."
" O Lord, the Saviour and defence."
" Return, O God of love, return."
" And let this feeble body fail."
" Lord, I commit my soul to Thee.
" Angels, roll the rock away."
" The Lord will come and not be slow."
" Lo, I behold the scattering shades."
" From every stormy wind that blows."
" Lo, He comes, with clouds descending."
" O God of mercy, hear my call."
" To God the Great, the ever blest."
" Away from every mortal care."
" O Zion, tune thy voice."
" How swift the torrent rolls."

These are by no means worthless productions. Some of them have sterling merits. But our hymnology is rich in its resources on the subjects which these hymns represent. We have, therefore, others of kindred spirit, serving the same purpose in the liturgy of song, which are superior to these, and are so numerous that these would be well-nigh useless by the side of them. The large majority of the changes which time necessitates in our public psalmody, are of this kind, — exchanges not of the bad for the good, but of the good for the better. Of the fact and the degree of improvement, of course there will be diversity of judgment. Every new compilation must speak for itself, and then accept the verdict of the general response.

5. Other things being equal, a hymn is *objectionable in proportion to the necessary restrictions upon its use.*

A hymn which can be rarely used, must be one of rare merit, or be upon a theme on which a hymn is sometimes a rare treasure, in order to entitle it to a place in a manual of psalmody. The policy of contracting the number of occasional hymns in such a manual, will exclude many selections, for no other reason than that they are not needed. Of thirty odes on Liberty, for instance, it may justly be a foregone conclusion, that but two or three should be admitted. Of four versions of a Psalm on Sickness, it may be fairly presumed that but one is necessary. Variety, exuberance, even redundance, of material may be tolerated upon a theme central to evangelical experience, like the doctrine of Christ crucified; and if any *leeway* is to be allowed for hymns of moderate worth, it should be around such a centre of Christian thought. The subject will sustain a hymn which in turn is unequal to the dignity of the subject. Multitudes of hymns *upon* occasions, and upon topics of infrequent use, may be in itself an evil. It may serve to divert attention from the standard themes and hymns which are more impressive *for* such occasional uses. It may thus cultivate an unchastened, even a vitiated taste, in the service of song.

On this principle, we would omit from a collection designed for public worship, the following hymns, among others:

"Great Lord of angels, we adore."
"Speak gently, it is better far."
"O pure reformers! not in vain."
"Oh, he whom Jesus loved has truly spoken."
"Spirit, leave thy house of clay."
"Were not the sinful Mary's tears."
"Eternal Source of every joy."
"God made all his creatures free."
"In anger, Lord, rebuke me not."
"In mercy, not in wrath, rebuke."
"Hush! my dear, lie still and slumber."
"We are living, we are dwelling."
"Who is thy neighbor?"
"Go to the pillow of disease."

These represent a large class of sacred poems, of which none are necessary, many are rarely pertinent, and some never so, to the liturgy of praise. Why should the bulk of a volume intended for *service* in the house of the Lord, be expanded by such a supplement?

6. The decisive consideration adverse to a rejected hymn often is, *some infelicity in its relation to the biblical passage of which it professes to be a version.*

Poets of the sanctuary have practised every variety of license in attaching their productions to inspired originals. At the two extremes stand paraphrases and motto hymns. Between these, we find odes of mosaic structure. They are composed of fragments of biblical thought and diction gathered here and there, with little or no regard to the *order* of inspired composition; or they are such fragments intermingled with uninspired material. These metrical nondescripts are, by courtesy, denominated "versions" of the Scriptures. But it is evident that very marked diversities must distinguish them from paraphrases, in respect of fidelity to their professed originals.

On the one hand, the biblical likeness in a metrical paraphrase may be so striking, and at the same time so spiritual, as to constitute its chief excellence. This virtue may buoy up an ode which is burdened by mediocrity of lyric merit. On the other hand, interpolated material, or inconsecutive selections, may weigh down a "version" so heavily as to sink it, if it be not sustained by singular worth in other respects. Judged as a "hymn," it may or may not be deserving; but judged as a "psalm," it may be literally good for nothing.

Here, again, that canon of psalmody which exacts rigidly the representation of every inspired psalm in a hymn-book for liturgic use, leads to deceptive results. Many of the psalms have no such representatives in any hymn-book. So-called "versions" of them are inserted for no other reason than the supposed inspiration of their parentage, when in fact portions of them are interpolated, and other portions are so abstracted from their inspired connections, that there is no Spirit left in them. Why should an inferior hymn, which, *as* a hymn, would be doomed, be retained because it professes to be a "psalm," when in fact it is not only not a paraphrase, but is not even an imitation of a psalm?

For example, Watts's version of Psalm 4, L. M., — "O God of grace and righteousness," — so far as it is "evangelized" by such lines as, "And dare reproach my Saviour's name," and "For the dear sake of Christ who died," has not a word in the original to sustain its claim as a version of the Psalm. Watts's second version of Psalm 90, C. M., — "Lord, if thine eyes survey our faults," — besides shuffling the verses of the original into an uninspired order of thought, contains, in the second stanza, absolutely interpolated material.

> "Thine anger turns our frame to dust:
> *By one offence to Thee*
> *Adam and all his sons have lost*
> *Their immortality.*"

The lines italicized have not a shadow of foundation in the original. Watts's third version of the same Psalm—"Return, O God of love, return"—is an excursus from the inspired line of thought, throughout. It comes from his pen a hymn on *Heaven*, of which not a vestige appears in the original prayer of Moses. Watts's second version of Psalm 85—"Salvation is forever nigh"—is a similar episode on the work of *Christ*, to whom not the remotest allusion occurs in the inspired text.

Now, we do not object to the principle on which these changes are founded. We believe that no other is adequate to adapt many of the Psalms to modern thought. There is good taste, and good sense, in the liberty which Watts assumed of composing a hymn as he was "persuaded the Psalmist would have done, in the time of Christianity," or as Paul would have done, "had he written a psalm-book." We admire the artless, yet reverent courage, with which this father of English hymnology so often takes a poet's liberty, by "giving to a psalm," as he says, "*another turn*." Indeed a sufficient reason for the rejection of many versions of psalms, is their mechanical fidelity to the letter of the text, like that of an exact version of Psalm 60:8— "Moab is my washpot; over Edom will I cast out my shoe."

But when a modern poet takes this license with an inspired production, the claim of *his* production is very materially modified. The foundation of that claim is shifted. That it is called a version of the Scriptures *may* be its least virtue. It may justly be required to fall back from inspired support, upon its own intrinsic merits as an uninspired ode. When the ninetieth

Psalm, for instance, is transformed into a lyric on Heaven, the question of its admission into a manual of psalmody is no longer a question respecting a version of the Psalm: it is simply, whether we have not other, and numerous, hymns on Heaven which are its superiors?

Furthermore, a version of a biblical passage may be impressive in thought, and not barbarous in diction, and yet it may fall so far below the original, as to *degrade* the original by the association. Certain paragraphs of the Scriptures are inimitable by an uninspired muse. The attempt to translate them into modern song is perilous. Some of them crowd expression to the very verge of decorous imagery. They have even been thought to overstep the boundary, in the view of Occidental taste. Hence the failure of Watts in so many of his versions from the Song of Solomon. Other Scriptures are inimitably sublime, and a *remote* approach to them, in English verse, falls flat. A single infelicitous word in such a version, may remind one of the first verse of the tenth chapter of Ecclesiastes.

For example, Watts's version of Psalm 90, S. M., is the favorite hymn of many, upon the Frailty of Life. But who can read or chant the original — " Thou carriest them away as with a flood: they are as a sleep: In the morning they are like grass which groweth up: in the morning it flourisheth and groweth up; in the evening it is cut down and withereth" — and then sing, without stammering —

> " Lord, what a feeble *piece*
> Is this, our mortal frame?
> Our life, how poor a trifle *'tis*
> That scarce deserves the name!"?

How can the spirit of worship pass from the subdued *prayer* of Moses — " So teach us to number our days, that we may apply our hearts unto wisdom " — to the colloquial *remark* of Watts —

> " *Well*, if our days must fly,
> We'll keep their end in sight." ?

Such descents as these, are like the fall of the Son of the Morning.

7. Other things being equal, a hymn is defective in proportion to *the prevalence of other than the forms of worship in its style.* Didactic, descriptive, dramatic, meditative, hortatory, and comminatory hymns, must possess superior virtues in other respects, to outweigh the evil of the preponderance of these elements in their structure. Multitude of such materials in a manual of psalmody, is in itself an evil. It invites to prosaic song, or to soliloquy, or to colloquy with men, rather than to communion with God. The personality, the presence, the friendship of the Deity, are realized to the worshipper most vividly, by services of song in which *habitually* he addresses God in the dialect of homage. That is a misuse of the church-song, which would generally subject it to the convenience of the pulpit. The aid which it renders to homiletic uses, is one of its incidents only. A very large number of lyrics, therefore, must be excluded from our hymn-books, chiefly for the sake of preserving the ascendency of the spirit of worship in their proportions. On this principle, we would check their overgrowth, by the rejection of the following hymns, among others :

"Blest are the souls who hear and know."	"Stop, poor sinner, stop and think."
"Thus the eternal Father spake."	"Sinner, hear the Saviour's call."
"Love, love on earth appears."	"Oh, blessed souls are they."
"Thus the great Lord of earth and sea."	"Happy the man to whom his God."
	"The Almighty reigns, exalted high."
"Now the Saviour standeth pleading."	"Happy soul, thy days are ended."
"Tell us, wanderer, wildly roving."	"Just o'er the grave I hung."
"Drooping souls, no longer mourn."	"Beyond the starry skies."
"Dying souls, fast bound in sin."	"Jesus comes, his conflict over."
"When the harvest is past, and the summer is gone."	"Blest is the man, forever blest."
	"The man is ever blest."
	"Happy the man whose cautious feet."

We would have a choice selection, rather than a multiplicity of such odes, purposely to restrict the inducements to the excessive use of them, and thus to facilitate the ascendency of *worship* in the temple service.

8. It is an objection to a hymn, if it is *deficient either in dignity, or in solemnity, or in sympathy, on the tragic themes of song.* No lyric virtue, which can consist with this class of defects, can atone for them.

On this principle, we would refuse the Judgment hymn, — " Oh! there will be mourning," — and Watts's hymn on the Death of a Sinner, — " My thoughts on awful subjects roll," — and the entire class of lyrics in which poetry seems to *luxuriate* in images of terror, as the machinery of operatic effect. No other hymns have so little of salutary impressiveness as these. No others are so often parodied by callous hearers whom they are designed to arouse.

9. A certain class of lyrics are objectionable, chiefly on account of *an excess of the analytic element.* Severe analysis is unnatural in song. The themes of psalmody, especially, invite free, soaring strains. One of the perils of didactic hymns is, the facility with which they subside from the buoyancy of *devotional* musing, to the prosiness of analytic thought. Some

subjects, like Regeneration, or the Decrees of God, may admit of a degree of this element; but even in such hymns, it needs to be sustained by qualities which are its direct opposites. It is a quality which never sustains *itself* in a song of praise. Other subjects positively reject it; the heart refuses to sing upon them philosophically.

A representative of a class of poems which should be rejected on this ground, is the hymn of Newton on the Sainted Dead:

> "In vain our fancy strives to paint
> The moment after death."

Song does not, naturally, even "strive" to do any such thing. It imitates the poetic silence of the Scriptures. It carols forth its visions of the *state* of departed saints, impulsively, unmethodically, most of all, unchronologically. Often it seems capricious in its hints of truths, which yet would scarcely be truths, if they were more than hints. More than these, eye hath not seen, nor ear heard.

10. A hymn must often be rejected for the *want of congruity between its sentiment and its style or metre*. The spirit of sacred song is delicate, yet imperative in its instincts. It revolts from inaptitudes of form to substance, however vivaciously they are displayed. An eccentric diction, or a fantastic measure, is as offensive in temple worship, as a funereal measure in a dance. Any violence committed by style or rythmical structure, upon the proprieties of time, place, circumstance, occasion, is resented by a healthy lyric taste, as unseemly and undevout, even though it be in elaborate artistic forms.

That is a theatrical taste, which can exhort the ungodly in such a strain of amphibrachs as —

"Oh, *turn* ye! | Oh, *turn* ye! | for *why* will | ye *die.*"
"Come *give* us | your *hand,* and | the *Saviour* | your *heart,*"

or in words in which thought is so artificially subordinated to both rythm and rhyme, as in the lines —

"*Sinner,* | *come,* | '*mid* thy | *gloom,*
All thy | *guilt* con | *fess*ing;
*Trem*bling | *now,* | *con*trite | *bow,*
Take the | *of* fered | *bless*ing."

It surely is not desirable to cultivate a taste for such rollicking lyrics as the following, in church-song:

"We're travelling home to heaven above —
 Will you go?
To sing the Saviour's dying love —
 Will you go?
Millions have reached that blest abode,
Anointed kings and priests to God,
And millions more are on the road —
 Will you go?

Oh! could I hear some sinner say:
 'I will go;
I'll start this moment, *clear the way!* —
 Let me go!
My old companions, fare you well,
I will not go with you to hell;
With Jesus Christ I mean to dwell, —
 Let me go; fare you well.'"

What is this? Is it designed for a congregation of circus-riders? Has it, either in style or measure, that congruity with its sentiment, which ought to breathe through every line of a sanctuary hymn? We have heard college glees, and convivial songs, which were less dissonant from a church-like tone.

Such are a few of the more important principles, affecting the omission of hymns from a manual designed for public worship. Diversities of opinion respecting their application are inevitable; but there can be none, we think, respecting the principles themselves. A judicious and candid application of them, must diminish very much the "disputed territory" of hymnology.

Omissions from church-psalmody, which excite the surprise of many, are often required by a *combination of several of these laws of song*. Even brilliant and forceful poems may be open to so many of the objections we have enumerated, that, with all their virtues, they must pass out of our hymn-books for public praise, and remain in collections of devotional poetry for private meditation. We have not space to illustrate this by numerous examples. Two must suffice.

We select for the first, one of the most warmly contested poems in the language, — contested as a *hymn*, yet one whose sterling poetic merits are above dispute. It has been well pronounced "that incomparable death-song, by Toplady,"—"Deathless principle, arise!" This is a lively, fervid, impulsive, bold, brilliant lyric. It merits a high place in every collection of sacred poems for private *reading*. Still, it should be omitted from a collection of hymns for public *song*.

A comprehensive reason for its omission is, that its

place can be easily supplied by better hymns for song upon the Death of a Christian. On this theme our hymnology is fertile. Again, the hymn cannot be sufficiently abbreviated to be sung, without mutilation of its vital parts. It is too long for use, even when reduced, as we commonly find it, to four double stanzas. On such a theme we are not inclined to sing a *protracted* series of vivid, stirring verses. If the lines be stimulating, rousing, we require that they be few. Yet, to abridge this hymn sufficiently, would destroy its *unity*.

Furthermore, the hymn has a rythmical structure, which is not happily adapted to the occasions on which it would be used, if used at all. These are the occasions on which the mind is most intimately conversant with death, and when, therefore, it demands the most dignified and solemn measure in the stanzas that are set to music. But the metre of this hymn is neither solemn nor dignified, as compared with the Long, Common, or even Short metres. The foot, also, which prevails in the hymn is the Trochee, and this is less elevated and subduing than the Iambus. Let any one contrast a song composed of such lines as this:

"*Swift* of | *wing* and | *fired* with | *love*,"

with a song composed of lines like the following—

" Sweet *fields* | be*yond* | the *swell* | ing *flood*."

and he will feel the superior majesty of the Iambic over the Trochaic verse.

If we could find no better hymn, we would, of course, adopt one of the Trochaic measure, for expressing, with music, the emotions of a believer in view of death. But we could not help regarding the structure of the hymn as inapposite to the imposing scenes which called it forth. "The Trochaic metre," says Aristotle, "is too tripping, and all tetrameters show it; for tetrameters are a kind of dancing rythm."[1] "The Iambus," says Dr. Campbell, "is expressive of dignity and grandeur; the Trochee, on the contrary, according to Aristotle, is frolicsome and gay."[2]

As the measure of the words, so the splendor and quick succession of the images in this hymn, are not expressively becoming to the scene of a Christian's death. In the very hour of the soul's departure, it is not natural to multiply, in such a rapid and even vehement course of song, such brilliant images as the 'native of the skies,' 'rising,' 'soaring,' 'mounting,' 'flying,' 'fearless,' the 'pearl,' 'bought,' 'wrought,' 'going to shine before the throne,' to 'deck the crown,' 'angels hovering,' 'bending,' 'waiting for the signal,' and then 'quick escorting,' the 'deathless principle,' 'bursting its shackles,' 'dropping its clay,' 'breathing,' 'singing,' 'swift of wing,' 'passing the stream,' whose 'tossing is stilled,' and 'roar hushed' by 'dying love and power;' passing through 'shade,' 'waited for by saints,' who are 'ardent,' and 'thronging the shore,' etc., etc. More *repose* is requisite for the singing of a prolonged death-song. If intensity of triumph characterize the hymn, it must be brief, like the sudden shout, 'O Death, where is thy sting? O Grave, where is thy victory?'

This unnaturalness is augmented by the fact, that

---

[1] Aristotle's Rhetoric, B. III., c. viii. § 4.
[2] Campbell's Rhetoric, B. III., c. i.

the hymn is an exhortation to one's self. A hortatory song is less apt than a supplicatory one, at the moment of departure from the world. Still further, the hymn is objectionable for the minute particularity of its reference. Scarcely can an occasional hymn be more restricted in its use than this. It is an address of "The Dying Believer to his Soul." When, and where, shall it be sung? At the couch of the departing saint? Is the Christian, in the near view of death, often disposed to hear the appropriate *music* for such an energetic, trumpet-toned exhortation? Shall it be sung in the temple? Can other than an imaginary conjunction of circumstances render it opportune there?

These queries suggest, that in fact this hymn will be used very seldom, if ever, with a musical accompaniment. It was published in the year 1776; but it has not yet been introduced into many hymn-books, and has not been often used with music, even when it has been readily accessible. The experience of the last eighty years has confirmed the judgment of Montgomery, who said of this hymn, a half century after it was written: " [It] is scarcely suitable to be sung; but it may be uttered by the 'dying Christian to his soul,' with a joy which he alone can feel, and feel only at the height, in the last moment of time, and the first of eternity."[1] It is a lyric to be *read*, at the hour, or, more properly, in the vivid imagination of the hour, when an earnest Christian rises in triumph to the skies.

The second example which we select, of hymns that violate many of the principles of a sound hymnology, is the well-known and much-disputed imitation of

---

[1] Montgomery's "Christian Psalmist," Introductory Essay, page xxvii.

Psalm Fifty-eight, by Dr. Watts, — " Judges, who rule the world by laws."

This, also, is a bold, spirited poem, whose loftiness of sentiment and diction is worthy of the stern, comminatory, imprecatory, prophetic original. We can easily imagine that, as abbreviated and altered in some collections of psalmody, and *delivered* well from the pulpit, after the enactment of a fugitive slave law, it should ring in the ears of a congregation, like the voice of an old prophet risen from the dead. Still, it is not a good liturgic hymn.

In the first place, nearly one half of it, as reduced in several modern hymn-books, is no "*version*" of the original psalm. The larger part of the first two stanzas is an interpolation. This we do not regard as a conclusive objection; but so far as the hymn is not a "version," it is to be judged upon its own merits, with no reference to the authority of inspiration; and we venture to believe that, if the interpolated lines were absent, the remainder would find no place in any manual designed for public worship, except one sacredly conservative of " Watts entire."

It is also a significant comment on the hymn, that the most vivid stanzas of the whole, and those which are most strikingly faithful to the original, are omitted from the most popular constructions, and, may we not say, are *never* sung in a public assembly. Who has ever heard, from congregation or choir, the following lines? —

> A poisoned arrow is your tongue,
> The arrow sharp, the poison strong,
>   And death attends where'er it wounds:
> You hear no counsels, cries, or tears;
> So the deaf adder stops her ears
>   Against the power of charming sounds.

> *Break out their teeth, Eternal God;*
> *Those teeth of lions dyed in blood!*
> *And crush the serpents in the dust!*
> * * * * * * *
> Or snails that perish in their slime,
> Or births that come before their time, —
> Vain births, that never see the sun."

We do not find these lines in the abbreviated forms of the hymn. Why not? They are the most pungent fragments in the whole production, and the most intensely suggestive of the original. The reason for their rejection is obvious, and we think it is unanswerable. But it excites the inquiry, whether the psalm itself has not a radical unfitness to modern liturgic use? Otherwise, why must so large and so emphatic portions of it be eliminated, and a nearly equal amount be interpolated, to adapt it to modern worship?

Be this as it may, the hymn is objectionable for its very *restricted usefulness*. Assuming the intrinsic merit of the select stanzas, how often can they be appropriately sung by an assembly of worshippers? When are they *needed?* Divest them, for the moment, of imaginary uses; bring them down to the test of the *wants* of men, women, and children congregated for the worship of the Most High; — and when, where, under what circumstances, is the hymn necessary? *It is a malediction against ungodly rulers.* How many such, have the majority of pastors in their congregations? How often is it wise to exhort them in imprecatory song? Or, assuming that the hortatory form is apostrophic, and that the hymn is an indulgence of the "righteous indignation" of worshippers against absent culprits, how often will a wise pastor deem such a strain needful to the devotions of a people?

These practical queries, which bring this poem to the test of real life, must cause the range of its liturgic usefulness, we think, to "grow beautifully less," in the judgment of sober criticism. With large assumptions in vindication of the hymn, it still must be doomed to comparative desuetude. Its use must be not only occasional, but exceptional. It belongs, upon the most favorable hypothesis, to the extreme wing of occasional hymns.

Moreover, this is not a hymn of *worship*. As abridged, it contains not a line of praise or prayer. It is didactic, descriptive, hortatory, menacing. The only communion with God expressed by the original Psalm is in the terrific imprecations, which are scarcely exceeded elsewhere in the Scriptures, and which modern song, we venture to assume, *always* omits in the use of this hymn. These omitted, the relics of the Psalm contain almost every form of hymnologic diction which is *not* devotional. True, this absence of the liturgic element is not in itself fatal to the claims of a hymn. But *with* the presence of the other elements we have indicated, it creates a strong adverse presumption. That a hymn is didactic *and* descriptive, *and* hortatory, *and* comminatory, and yet *not*, in any part of it, precative, lays upon it a very heavy burden of proof, in the assertion of its claims to a place in a manual for public worship.

We must believe that the hymn in question is one of the *eloquent poems*, in the use of which the service of the pulpit lords it over the service of song. It *reads* well — grandly. It backs up a sermon of rebuke, valiantly. It falls like a sledge-hammer, from the uplifted voice of a preacher. We can conceive of circumstances, in which its rehearsal should seem to bring inspired indignation to the relief of a speaker, like one of twelve legions of angels. But the singing of it, the worship of God with it, the blending of the voices of young men and maidens, of old men and children, in devotional recitative of such strains, with *becoming* music — is altogether another affair.

Yet, is it not an inspired psalm? Very true; and this suggests what we regard as the crowning objection to the hymn, that it is *incongruous with those occasions on which it would be used, if used at all.* The same principle which has practically excluded the imprecatory portions of the original from recent use in song, should exclude the entire hymn from our hymn-books. The *animus* of the whole poem is imprecatory. Its modern use as a liturgic song, we cannot but think, is perilous. Its inspired foundation by no means establishes its claims as a *hymn*, in *uninspired* form, for *Christian* use, in application to *ages* and *occasions* not contemplated in its divine origin. An inspired mind may utter that which one possessing no miraculous safeguard may *not*. A seer, speaking as moved by the Holy Ghost, conscious of declaring, through the medium of his own retributive instincts, the mind of God, may express those instincts, with safety to their moral equilibrium, as another man may *not*. The very consciousness of inspiration may *steady* the sensibilities of a "man after God's own heart," in the use of language, which, if applied by an uninspired worshipper to other circumstances, times, and cases, would tempt him to malign emotion. Knowledge of the doom of certain incorrigible enemies of God, may give a boldness to inspired imprecation, which would be presumptuous, if applied by any other mind, to any other instance of flagrant iniquity.

We do not say, that the appropriation by another of the imprecatory desires of an inspired mind, is not conceivably, even possibly virtuous. But we say that it is *perilous*. Our ignorance of the decrees of God renders it so. Who *knows* that the present Pope of Rome, or the despot of Madagascar, or the Chief Justice of an American court, is a doomed object of God's wrath? Anathema of wickedness is safe; but who shall venture to anathematize the wicked? This is *more* perilous in the form of an uninspired imitation of a psalm, than in the appropriation of the exact original. It is more hazardous in *song*, than in reverent perusal of the Scriptures. We believe it to be fraught with more danger in a Christian age, than in David's time, by so much as the merciful spirit of Christ is more luminous than that of Judaism. We must think that it puts in jeopardy the spirituality of worship, especially in our own day and country, in which political passions are rampant, and denunciation of rulers *needs* no stimulus.

Our churches have been influenced, consciously or unconsciously, by these considerations, in eliminating from their *use* of the hymn in question, the most appalling imprecations of the Psalm. The same principles, we repeat, require the disuse of the hymn in public song. It is a hymn to be *read* in private hours, with devout meditation upon the circumstances which called forth such utterances of the mind of Him who said, "Vengeance is mine; I will repay."

On the occasions on which this hymn would be used, if used at all, we need hymns of an entirely different character. For example: Has the supreme judiciary at the Capital, given a blow to Freedom which reverberates through the land? Has the national legislature struck down a barrier against Slavery? Have the state-courts despoiled a hundred churches of the temples where their fathers worshipped? — We would improve such a calamity by singing strains like these:

> "Dread Jehovah! God of nations!"
> "See, gracious God! before thy throne."
> "On Thee, O Lord our God, we call."
> "O Lord, our fathers oft have told."
> "Great Shepherd of thine Israel."

We would rouse a timid or inactive people with the old battle-song of Adolphus —

> "Fear not, O little flock, the foe,"—

or with the not less spirited hymn of one of our own poets —

> "Stand up! stand up for Jesus!"

We would cheer an audience of disheartened worshippers, by such psalms of worship as —

> "Our God, our help in ages past."
> "Up to the hills I lift mine eyes."
> "God is our Refuge, ever near."
> "God is our Refuge and our Strength."
> "God is the Refuge of his saints."

We would subdue the anger of an outraged community, by praising Him "which stilleth the tumult of the people," in the use of such hymns as —

> " Keep silence, all created things."
> " God moves in a mysterious way."
> " Great God! how infinite art Thou!"
> " Jehovah reigns! He dwells in light."
> " The Lord Jehovah reigns."
> " Kingdoms and thrones to God belong."
> " Wait, O my soul, thy Maker's will;
> Tumultuous passions, all be still."

We have thus considered a few of the principles of hymnology, as an outgrowth from the religious life of the church, and also some collateral principles affecting the construction of a manual of liturgic song.

Tried by the standard here set forth, any existing manual must be imperfect. None can be more sensible of this, than they who have encountered the labors of exploration; the search for originals; the accumulation of readings; the sifting of materials; the balancing of conflicting virtues; the perplexities of classification; the adopted, suspended, abandoned, resumed decisions; the testing of results by the discussions of friendly criticism; and the *affliction* of parting with such costly treasures, under the merciless economy of space — in the compilation of a hymn-book. An approximation, not to the " best conceivable," but to the " best possible," liturgy of song, is all that any reasonable editor will hope for, and all that any reasonable critic will ask for. Both have reason to welcome the diversities of candid criticism, with which every such volume must be received, but which, in the selection of any hymn-book for the temple service, *must concede much more to each other than to the book.* So hymnology grows, like everything else in the world of mind which deserves to grow.

An editor of such a manual of psalmody cannot more wisely give the result of his labors to the world, than in the spirit of the language in which Dr. Watts introduced the first edition of " The Psalms of David, imitated and applied to the Christian State and Worship": " Whensoever there shall appear any paraphrase of the Book of Psalms, that retains more of the savor of David's piety, discovers more of the style and spirit of the gospel, with a superior dignity of verse, and yet in lines as easy and flowing, and the sense as level to the lowest capacity, I shall congratulate the world, and consent to say, ' Let this attempt of mine be buried in silence.' "

CHAPTER II.

THE TEXT OF HYMNS.

The criticism on the text of church hymns is always perilous. They are associated with the most imposing scenes of the present life, or with the august realities of the future. If they become suggestive of mere verbal disputes ; if their faults be made more prominent in the popular mind than their excellences, their sanctity is impaired. It is easy to lessen the influence of these odes, because many of them abound with faults. Some of the best of them are disfigured by mixed metaphors, strained comparisons, incongruous images. They live by their own spiritual power, which triumphs over their literary defects. Indeed, their rhetorical blemishes are, in one respect, a positive gain to the influence of the poetry; for they set off, by contrast, its vital force, and attest the superiority of pure and fervid sentiment over all the graces of style. But their diction is still open to criticism. It is easy to make this criticism, and to expose many of our most precious hymns to ridicule. "Nothing is easier," said Napoleon Buonaparte, " than to find fault." There are no two books which can with more facility be made the theme of sport, than the Bible and the Hymn Book. "Wit," says Lord Kaimes, " consists chiefly in joining things by distant and fanciful relations, which surprise us because they are unexpected." The more sacred the composition, so much the more facile is it to startle men by connecting it with something secular or contemptible. This surprise is agreeable to an irreligious and vulgar mind. To such a mind, the unexpected association of solemn words with low images is one of the most fascinating, as it is the most demoralizing, species of wit. But in a free censure of some excellent hymns, there is danger of making ludicrous suggestions, and of degrading, if not spoiling, those forms of expression which are not commonly regarded as inappropriate to the worship of God. The spirit of even a just criticism often proves that the critic is unfit for his calling; that he has aspired to a sphere too lofty for him. He injures his own character, not less than his reputation, while he corrupts the minds of men who would have thought no evil, if he had not suggested it.

Still there will, there must, be discussion on the faults of hymns. Let it be conducted, then, in the spirit of decorum and of meek reverence. This discussion is most apt to arise when we are debating whether, on the one hand, we will adhere to the original form of our sacred odes, or, on the other hand, by certain changes in the stanzas, accommodate them to the real or imagined wants of the community. On this question, extravagant opinions are maintained by some advocates and by some opposers of alterations. All hymnologists unite in *practically adopting* alterations; but all do not agree in the theory that they ought to be adopted. Let us now examine, under various topics, the evils and the advantages of deviating from the original form of hymns.

§ 1. *The Relation of Changes in the Text to the Rights of Authors.*

It is affirmed by some, that an author has a perfect right to control the use that shall be made of his compositions; and that all alterations of what he has written are not merely "infringements" upon his property; they are "frauds," "trespasses," literary "theft," "robbery," "swindling," and (it has even been added) "felony." If we desire to print the hymn of an author, we must print it just as he wrote it. If we will not take his form, we have no right to take his hymn.

Now there is no question, that an author has a legal right to withhold from the community the productions of his pen; and also, if he publish them, and if he comply with certain legal conditions, he has a legal right to prevent their republication, in any form, during a limited period of time. But at the close of that period, all his legal rights expire. The benevolent law *gives* his productions, freely, to the world.

Further: there is no question that an author has a moral right to all the honor with which the merits of his work are fitted to crown him; and he may, therefore, within certain limits, claim to have his work presented to the public in that form which will be most creditable to himself.

But there are limits to this claim. The good of the community must not be sacrificed to the honor of a single individual. The whole poem may reflect a brighter glory on its author than a few detached parts of it; but those parts are all that can be sung in a church hymn, and they may be selected, even although the writer fail of securing all the praise which the omitted verses would have given him. As inapposite stanzas may be omitted, so inapposite words may be sacrificed, for more church-like phrases. If the author wrote his poem chiefly for his own fame, the omission of his inappropriate lines is a fit comment on his selfishness; if he wrote it for the general welfare, he will be willing to advance this end, even at the sacrifice of his personal reputation. When he publishes a hymn, he gives it to the coming ages; he *gives up* his control over it. If he does not mean to give it away, he should keep it to himself. We are quite free from anxiety lest the bliss of Gregory, and Ambrose, and Bernard, and Baxter should be disturbed on account of the damage to their poetic fame, from the changes in their lyrics. The lines of bishop Ken breathe the sentiment of a dying psalmist:

> "And should the well-meant song I leave behind,
> With Jesus' lovers some acceptance find,
> 'Twill heighten even the joys of heaven to know
> That, in my verse, saints sing God's praise below."

All this discussion with regard to the "rights of authorship," may be terminated by considering that a manual for church song is not designed to perpetuate the renown of men. It is designed for the worship of God; and in some respects it would, better than now, fulfil its main intent, if it contained no allusion to the majority of names connected with its hymns. A church prayer book would lower its tone of sacredness, if it should append to each separate petition the name of its original writer; and, when a church hymn book parades the names and titles of its numerous authors on the same pages with the songs, it seems almost equally adapted to the glory of God and the renown of poets. The manual for church worship must not be regarded as the original repository of sacred songs; it must not be consulted as a literary witness; it must be looked upon as a book of prayer and praise. Its materials, in their original form, are found in other places. In those places, they may contribute to the honor of their authors. But in the church manual, the fame of poets should be lost in the glory of Him whom they adore.

Men of exclusively literary tastes, and also men who affect to be the *literati* of the world, are apt to form an inaccurate and a low estimate of the very nature of a church hymn book. The book is considered as a collection of choice poems, specimens of the taste and genius of eminent composers. In this view it ought not to be, like the work of Dr. Vicessimus Knox, a volume of "Elegant *Extracts*," for an extract from a poem fails to display the symmetry of the whole. But if extracts are admitted, they must be quoted precisely as they were written. They are historical specimens. They profess to be mere reproductions. Of course, all changes of the original become falsehoods. An extract of six stanzas, which are consecutive in the hymn but not consecutive in the original, is a misrepresentation of its author. On the title-page of the book, and as a title of every song, is virtually published the announcement: "These are the beautiful or sublime words of this or that man." To deviate from these words, in such a case, falsifies the entire aim and pretension of the book. It is indeed important to have repertories or encyclopaedias of

Christian hymns in their pristine form. But when we regard a hymn book as such an encyclopaedia, or as a beautiful abridgment of such an authoritative repertory, we substitute an historical and a scholastic standard for the higher standard of piety and devotion.

§ 2. *The Relation of Changes in the Text to the Encouragement of Authorship.*

If we concede that it is right, still is it expedient, to leave an author uncertain whether the exact words of his hymn will be transmitted to posterity? Pained with the prospect of changes in his song, many an author will shrink back from giving it to the world. So far forth as a sensitive poet is deterred from authorship by the fear of these changes, they are an evil. The evil should never be encountered, except in the prospect of an overbalancing good.

But on this topic, as on the preceding, men entertain degrading views of the office of a hymn book. The poet is not dependent on the church manual for the faithful preservation of his words. They are guarded in the literary remains, in the scholastic repositories, in the archives of the university, in the historical collections. He is not injured by the fact that, superadded to all the literary and scientific channels through which his words may flow down to posterity, there are more or less exact quotations from them, in manuals for public worship. Very frequently, the changes made in his hymn are the occasion of its being more widely known in its original form, than it otherwise would have been. Its real merits would never have been discovered by the majority of worshippers, if some critic had not removed the rubbish of uncouth or fantastic words under which the solid worth of the hymn lay hidden. As amended, it became a favorite lyric; when it had become such, its original was sought out; if it had not been pruned, it would have been forgotten. A man of poetic genius ought to be stimulated, rather than discouraged, by the thought that posterity will not willingly let his verses die; and that, even if they become antiquated in their present form, they will still live in new and fresh modifications, or become the germs of other and better songs. A philosopher propounds theories in the expectation that they will be improved by the scholars of a coming age. Does this expectation repress his love of contributing to the advancement of science? Was David deterred from giving his hymns to the world, through fear that they would be modified by some future Milton or Montgomery?

There are two men who represent two classes of poets, in relation to this theme. Dr. Watts is one, and he is a representative of the larger class. These are his words, breathing forth his unselfish desire that his hymns be a "living sacrifice" to God, rising up to heaven, in any form which may be congenial with the devout aspirations of the worshipper: "If any expressions occur to the reader that savor of an opinion different from his own, yet he may observe, these are generally such as are capable of an extensive sense, and may be used with a charitable latitude. I think it is most agreeable, that what is provided for public singing, should give to sincere consciences as little disturbance as possible. However, where any unpleasing word is found, he that leads the worship may substitute a better; for, blessed be God, we are not confined to the words of any man in our public solemnities." [1]

The noble-hearted psalmist who gave this authority, even to precentors, to make extemporaneous changes in his hymns, would not have regarded it as an outrage upon his rights, if he had foreseen that Wesley and Conder and Worcester would make studied and careful changes in them.

But there is another, less numerous, class of poets, represented by James Montgomery. In the year 1819, he united with Rev. Thomas Cotterill in the publication of a hymn book, and Montgomery contributed " the benefit of his judgment in the choice and *amendment* of available compositions from various quarters." In 1824, he said : " Good Mr. Cotterill and I bestowed a great deal of labor and care on the compilation of that book: clipping, interlining, and remodelling hymns of all sorts, as we thought we could correct the sentiment or improve the expression." Speaking of his toil on a lyric of Cowper, he then remarked : " I entirely rewrote the first verse of that favorite hymn, commencing: " There is a fountain filled with blood," etc. The words are objectionable as representing a fountain being *filled*, instead of *springing up:* I think my version is unexceptionable :

> From Calvary's cross a fountain flows,
> Of water and of blood;
> More healing than Bethesda's pool,
> Or famed Siloa's flood."

---

[1] Watts's Works (Preface to his Hymns), Vol. IV. p. 149.

In the year 1835, Mr. Montgomery was officially requested, and he consented, to make an entire revision of the Moravian hymn book, containing twelve hundred hymns. "And it is hardly too much to say, that the time and thought spent in the reformation of such a mass of matter, much of it of a peculiar character, was not less than would have sufficed for the composition of a like quantity of original verse. He was often compelled either to change an obsolete or equivocal term, to soften down a too striking sentiment into a general meaning, or entirely to remodel the structure of a verse, or even of a whole hymn." He labored on these amendments, more or less frequently, through the lengthened period of twelve years. In 1849 the hymn book was published, containing a multitude, but not the whole, of his emendations.[1]

Notwithstanding this labor, continued at intervals for more than thirty years, in the modifying of sacred lyrics, Mr. Montgomery requests other men not to modify his own verses; and says, that "if good people cannot conscientiously adopt *his* diction and doctrine, it is a little questionable in them to impose upon him *theirs*." "When I am gone," he says, "my hymns will, no doubt, be altered to suit the taste of appropriators; for it is astonishing how really religious persons will sometimes feel scruples about a turn or a term."[2] What Mr. Montgomery predicted, has come to pass. There is not a hymn book, English or American, which contains twenty of his hymns, with-

---

[1] Memoirs of James Montgomery, Vol. III. p. 158; Vol. IV. pp. 69, 70; Vol. VI. pp. 266—268; Vol. VII. pp. 154—157.
[2] Memoirs, IV. p. 70.

out modifying some of them. That remarkable man, John Wesley, also requested that his poetical effusions remain unaltered. But as he made many, and some splendid, changes in the lyrics of Henry More, Watts, and others, so his own lyrics are now more deeply imbedded in the hearts of worshippers, and the original forms of them are more faithfully studied, than they would have been, if they had not, in a modified style, been ingratiated into the love of the churches. The entreaty of these and other eminent poets, that there may be no changes in their songs, reminds us of Dr. Joseph Huntington's Introduction to his "Calvinism Improved:"[1]— "The author has one request to make to all that may see or hear of this book. He asks that none would either *approve* or *censure* it, until after careful reading. And that all who may have read it with attention, and then speak freely their own opinion concerning it, as every one in that case has a good right to do, would also communicate this humble request from the author, to all such as have knowledge of it only by report." If men, because requested, are bound to withhold their condemnation of Dr. Huntington's treatise, they will soon be obligated, because they will soon be requested by some author, to purchase some particular volume of his, to circulate it gratuitously, to write reviews of it, to read it semi-annually in a standing or kneeling posture. That petition, which will more probably be granted than any other, was made by Henry Vaughan, in the preface to his Silex Scintillans, p. 7: "And if the world will be so charitable as to grant my request, I do here most humbly, earnestly, beg that none would read them [my earlier writings]."

[1] See page xxiii.

But it is asked: Should the hymns as altered, be ascribed to the poet who never indited them in that form? Is not this ascription a falsehood? We have already implied that there are evils connected with any allusion in a Hymn Book to the names of its authors, especially such authors as Barlow, Burns, Campbell, Dryden, Hogg, Thomas Moore, Pope, Walter Scott, and others who have no consecrated name in the church. Additional evils are connected with such allusions, where the stanzas appear in a new diction. If the hymn is essentially changed in style, or more especially in doctrine, and if the author's name be mentioned, there should be some announcement that the modifications are made.[1] Where the changes are not important, the notice of them would only confuse the reader. If all the alterations found in Worcester's "Watts and Select Hymns" were signified by an asterisk or dagger prefixed to the altered stanzas, the number of hymns without the asterisk or dagger would be very insignificant. But how could we, then,

---

[1] Often the Presbyterian Old School Collection makes a change in the doctrinal expression of its Psalms and Hymns, without giving sufficient notice of the change, as in the following instances:

ORIGINAL FORM.	PRESBYTERIAN O. S. FORM.
Watts's 18th *Psalm.*	
Or if my feet did e'er depart 'Twas never with a wicked heart.	Or if my feet did e'er depart Thy love reclaimed my wandering heart.
Watts's 32nd *Psalm.*	
Blest is the man to whom the Lord Imputes not his iniquities.	Before his judgment seat the Lord No more permits his crimes to rise.
Beddome.	*Hymn* 106.
When on the cross my Saviour died, A righteous God was pacified.	When on the cross my Saviour died, God's holy law he satisfied.

distinguish, whether the modifications were important or trivial?[1]

It must be observed, further, that *usage* has long ago explained the meaning of a Hymn Book when it refers an *altered* hymn to its original author. Long established custom has taught men, not to expect that the hymn will be always quoted with punctilious accuracy, not to look upon a manual for worship as a standard of weights and measures, of antique styles and historical phrases, but as a peculiar and a privileged volume, intended for nobler than antiquarian ends, and superior to the petty jealousies of authors. This being understood as the explanation of an Index to a Hymn Book, no wrong is done when a hymn is referred to a poet who did not give the present finishing touches to his lines. The reference is interpreted by custom ; it is prescriptively right. The usage began and continues on the assumption, that the sweet Psalmists of Israel, even although they were once as tenacious as Pontius Pilate of what they had written, will now suffer their hymns to rise toward heaven in the incense of devotion, and in that form which is most congenial with the devotional spirit of the worshippers.

There are so many readers who desire to know the authorship of their favorite songs, that editors who

---

[1] In Worcester's Watts there are not many changes affecting the doctrinal character of the lyrics. Where John Newton says of the Saviour: "Oh my soul, *he bore thy load,*" Dr. Worcester says: "Oh my soul, *behold the load.*" — Select Hymn, 174. Where Dr. Watts says of men: "Their hearts by nature *all* unclean," Dr. Worcester says: "Their hearts by nature *are* unclean." — B. I. H. 94. In changes like these, however, Dr. Worcester did not probably intend to modify the sentiment, but only the style.

13*

prefer to do otherwise, feel compelled to gratify the general curiosity. And then there are so many precious influences flowing from an association of these songs with names like those of Cowper and Newton, Luther and Ambrose, that editors feel bound to connect the memory of a sanctified poet with the other rich reminiscences of the hymn, even when, as individual editors, they would prefer to fasten the worshipper's mind upon the *spirit*, rather than the *origin*, of what he sings. In all this, they *mean* to be understood, and they *are* understood, as referring, not to the orthography, or punctuation, or symmetry, or completeness, or the minuter graces of the hymn, when they ascribe it to a particular writer, but rather as referring to its aim, spirit, and general phraseology. The pious Toplady, the devout Gibbons, William Bengo Collier, Josiah Conder, indeed a majority of the most accurate and exemplary compilers during the last hundred years, have openly announced that their selections from other authors have not been, in all instances, exact quotations. Here, as in a thousand other instances, common, immemorial usage interprets and justifies a well-intended deed. The conscientious Bickersteth, in the Preface to his Christian Psalmody (p. v.), thus explains the meaning of references to authors in a church hymn book: "As alterations have been made probably by every collector of hymns, the only effective way of enabling the reader to know what the hymn originally was, is to give the name of the author, by which reference may be made to it, as first written." Among the boldest advocates of the changes adopted in the Church Psalmody by Dr. Lowell Mason and Rev. David

Greene, were Professor Ebenezer Porter of Andover,[1] and Dr. Benjamin B. Wisner of Boston, both of them distinguished for their punctilious accuracy, and both of them defending alterations of hymns, on the ground that a church manual *needs* them, and has a prescriptive right to them, and cannot properly be understood as implying that all its authors wrote the lyrics in the exact form which is demanded for public worship.

§ 3. *The Immodesty of Changing the Text of Hymns.*

There are indeed not many poets who can lay claim to an equality with Addison, Gerhard, Heber and Keble. A reverent mind will hesitate long, before it will even suggest an improvement of the words of such men. There is an immodesty in allowing one jot or tittle of their writings to pass away, unless there

---

[1] It is a great error to suppose, that all the changes *adopted* in the Church Psalmody, were first *made* by its Editors. Many of them had been long *established* in England and in this country. Dr. Porter of Andover, although eminent as a judge and critic of psalmody, yet, as we think, carried his love of alterations too far. He condemned indiscriminately the erotic expressions in hymns, even such as have their parallel in the inspired word. He insisted on modifying not only such phrases as *Dear* God, but also *Dear* Lord. He once remarked, that the line "Jesus *Saviour* of my soul," was "*infinitely* better" than the endeared line of Wesley: "Jesus *Lover* of my soul." It was Dr. Porter, also, who urged more strenuously than any other man, that the Church Psalmody should have on its margins the marks for musical expression. These are a blemish to the manual, and also to Worcester's Watts. What would be thought of a Prayer Book, which appended to its supplications the following rules: "Offer this part of the prayer *mezzo piano;*" "Utter these petitions *diminuendo;*" "Now pray *affetuoso;*" "Here pray *staccato;*" or — "*swell;*" or "*fortissimo.*" A book of devotion is no more a book of elocution, than it is of antiquarian researches.

be an obvious reason for the change. But "aliquando bonus dormitat Homerus;" and even when the stanza of a great master is perfect in its pristine relations, it may be imperfect in a manual of church song. Milton wrote: "For His mercies *aye* endure;" but in our less obsolete form of his version of the one hundred and thirty-sixth Psalm we sing: "For his mercies *shall* endure." He said: "Let us *blaze* his name abroad;" an Episcopal hymn book substitutes: "Let us *sound* his name abroad." He crowds eight syllables into lines which admit only seven, and writes:

> Who by' *his* wis'dom did' create'
> The *pain'ted* heavens' so full' of state'.

The Episcopal version reduces these lines to their proper measure:

> Who' by wis'dom did' create'
> Heaven''s *expanse'* and all' its state'.

Addison, also, with all the exquisite chasteness of his imagination, wrote a stanza which it was not immodest for the English hymnologists to modify:

Original Form.	Altered Form.
	Sabbath Hymn Book, Hymn 1280.
Then see *the sorrows of my heart*	Then see *my sorrows, gracious Lord!*
Ere yet it is too late;	*Let mercy set me free,*
And add my Saviour's dying groans,	*While in the confidence of prayer*
To give those sorrows weight.	*My heart takes hold of thee.*

The exquisite Cowper, whose verses it were often profane to tamper with, has written the couplet:

> Israel's *young ones*, when of old,
> Pharaoh threatened to withhold.

This couplet appears in the 167th Select Hymn of Worcester's Watts, but there the word "*infants*" is substituted for "*young ones.*" In the 47th Select Hymn of Dr. Worcester's manual, another stanza of Cowper remains unaltered:

> Not such as hypocrites suppose,
> Who with a graceless heart
> Taste not of Thee, but *drink* a *dose*
> Prepared by Satan's art.

If now the choice minds of our most seraphic poets have sometimes let a word fall, which it is not indelicate to alter, can we regard the less admirable genius of other men as elevated above the reach of criticism? An American scholar, previously unknown to Wordsworth, suggested to him several emendations of the poet laureate's verses; and the author of the Excursion adopted, as his own, all the proposed amendments. It is not implied, in a criticism, that the critic regards himself superior to the genius in which he detects a flaw. Apelles modified his picture, at the hint of a cobbler. An artist who does not feel worthy to loosen the latchet of the shoe of Raphael, may yet discern a fault in the Transfiguration. There is no manifestation of vanity or arrogance in the editors of the Presbyterian (Old School) hymn book, adopting the following alterations of Dr. Watts's Psalms:

ORIGINAL FORM.	PRESBYTERIAN O. S. COLLECTION.
Watts's 7th Psalm. For me their malice digg'd a pit, But there themselves are cast; My God makes all their mischiefs light On their own heads at last.	Though leagued in guile, their malice spread A snare before my way; Their mischiefs on their impious head His vengeance shall repay.
Watts's 15th Psalm. While others *gripe* and *grind* the poor.	While others *scorn* and *wrong* the poor.

Original Form.	Presbyterian O. S. Collection.
Watts's 34th Psalm. To him the poor lift up their eyes, *Their faces feel the heavenly* shine.	To him the poor lift up their eyes, *With heavenly joy their faces* shine.

Watts's 35th Psalm.
 Behold the love, the generous love
    That holy David shows;
 See how his sounding bowels move
    To his afflicted foes.
	Behold the love, the generous love
	    That holy David shows;
	 Behold his kind compassion move
	    For his afflicted foes.

Watts's 37th Psalm. His *lips abhor to talk* profane.	His *soul abhors discourse* profane.
Watts's 49th Psalm. *Life is a blessing can't* be sold.	*Eternal life can ne'er* be sold.
Watts's 49th Psalm. Like thoughtless sheep the sinner dies, *Laid in the grave for worms to eat.*	Like thoughtless sheep the sinner dies, *And leaves his glories in the tomb.*

Watts's 71st Psalm.
 My tongue shall all the day proclaim
    My Saviour and my God;
 His death has brought my foes to shame,
 And drowned them in his blood.
	My tongue shall all the day proclaim
	    My Saviour and my God;
	 His death has brought my foes to shame,
	 And saved me by his blood.

Watts's 104th Psalm. *Tame heifers there* their thirst allay.	*There gentle herds* their thirst allay.

§ 4. *The Probability that a Poet's Inspiration will surpass a Critic's Amendment.*

In the glow of composition, the thoughts are more genial and healthful than in the cold business of criticism. Images throng upon the mind of the *poet*, words come of their own accord, and marshal themselves in their own places; but the *critic* looks anxiously around to find more fitting images, and he seeks after more appropriate words; and the very anxiety of his search makes his conceptions unnatural, his phrases cold and chilling. Editors are often audacious, when they venture to omit or supplement a stanza once finished by a royal poet. They would less frequently attempt their rash enterprise, if they remembered that the poet indited his words in the fervor of inspiration, and was borne onward by the impulses of a mind and heart sanctified and therefore made accurate by the true spirit of song, and, above all, by the Spirit of grace; while the *critic* comes up to his work in cold blood, and calculates, and measures, and counts syllables, and works up his faculties to find out some phrase which will *fit in*, and *fill out* a chasm made, often ruthlessly, by himself. There is no doubt that costly gems have been broken, and exquisite settings have been marred, by the hammer and file of careless menders of hymns.

Even the rhetorical structure of a lyric is often broken by a thoughtless change. Several manuals have actually destroyed Sir Robert Grant's double rhyme in the fifth stanza of his " O worship the King all glorious above ":

Original, with Double Rhyme.	Altered, without the Double Rhyme.
Oh mea'sureless *Might'!* Inef'fable Love'!	Father' Almighty', how faith'ful thy love',
While an'gels de*light'* to hymn' thee above'.	While an'gels de*light'* to hymn' thee above'.

In 1814, Dr. Worcester published his Christian Psalmody, in which he supposed that Dr. Watts's Hymn Book was "very considerably abridged, without any detriment." But many of the stanzas which he omitted, were regarded by some of his brethren as the very choicest effusions of sacred poetry. He could not satisfy the churches until he restored these stanzas in the manual now familiarly known as "Worcester's Watts and Select." Multitudes, however, have been dissatisfied with the changes yet retained in this familiar hymn book. Nor, since its publication, has there appeared a single manual for church song, which has not offended many readers by its alterations of the primitive text. Here and there a manual has pretended to admit no alterations; but every such book actually contains the most objectionable amendments. It cannot be expected that all critics will agree with regard to emendations of favorite odes. The tastes and associations of men are so diversified, that it would be well nigh a miracle for even two independent critics to coincide perfectly, with regard to the structure of the twenty thousand lines in a popular hymn-book. For ourselves, we have never studied such a book printed during the last thirty years, in which we have not found some alterations that appeared to us, for one reason or another, unadvisable. It is a fashion of recent critics, to expose the infelicitous changes in the Church Psalmody; but *any* other manual will present vulnerable points enough. Almost at random we select the following needless alterations, found either in the "Psalms and Hymns authorized and approved by the General Assembly of the Presbyterian Church," or in the manual honored by the name of the late Dr. Samuel Worcester.

Original, as in the Sabbath Hymn Book.	Alterations in the Presbyterian O. S. Collection.
Hymn 217. *In spite of all my* foes, Thou dost my table spread.	*Amid surrounding* foes Thou dost my table spread.

NEEDLESS ALTERATIONS.

Original, as in the Sabbath Hymn Book.	Alterations in the Presbyterian O. S. Collection.
Hymn 1025. How bright has his salvation shone *Through all her palaces!*	How bright has his salvation shone! *How fair his heavenly grace!*
Hymn 1025. Where his own *sheep* have been.	Where his own *flocks* have been.
Hymn 492. And make my broken *bones* rejoice.	And make my broken *heart* rejoice.
Hymn 1129. *The prisoner leaps to loose* [lose] his chains.	*The joyful prisoner bursts* his chains.
Hymn 498. Their fancied joys, how fast they flee! *Just like a dream when man awakes;* Their songs of softest harmony Are but a prelude [preface[1]] to their *plagues*.	Their fancied joys, how fast they flee, *Like dreams as fleeting and as vain;* Their songs of softest harmony Are but a prelude to their *pain*.
Hymn 121. Thy throne was fixed on high *Before the starry* sky.	Thy throne was fixed on high *Ere stars adorned the* sky.
Hymn 163. How *slowly doth his wrath arise!*	How *slow his awful wrath to rise.*
Hymn 135. Within thy circling arms I lie, *Beset* on every side.	Within thy circling arms I lie, *Enclosed* on every side.
Hymn 225. His morning smiles *bless all* the day.	His morning smiles *adorn* the day.
Hymn 254. *When through his eyes* the Godhead shone.	*The brightness of* the Godhead shone.
Hymn 1109. *Arise in thy strength*, thy redeemed to cherish! O Jesus, once *tossed* on the breast of the billow.	*Then send down thy grace*, thy redeemed to cherish. O Jesus, once *rocked* on the breast of the billow.

[1] The word *preface* is the original, but is exchanged for *prelude* in the most popular collections.

Original, as in the Sabbath Hymn Book.	Alterations in the Presbyterian O. S. Collection.
Hymn 856. Uttered' or *un*'expressed'.	*Unut'*tered or' expressed'.
Hymn 1055. While all our hearts *and all our songs* Join to admire the feast.	While all our hearts *in this our song* Join to admire the feast.

Original, as in the Sabbath Hymn Book.	Alterations in Worcester's Watts.
Hymn 756. While faith *inspires* a heavenly ray.	While faith *supplies* a heavenly ray.
Hymn 165. Oh may I *live to reach the* place.	Oh may I *reach the happy* place.
Hymn 1164. Yet *senseless mortals vainly* strive.	Yet *senselessly vain mortals* strive.
Hymn 1266. Men the dear objects of his grace, And he *the* loving God.	Men the dear objects of his grace, And he *their* loving God.
Hymn 915. Shall we go on to sin, Because *thy* grace abounds?	Shall we go on to sin, Because *free* grace abounds?
Hymn 130. The Lord our God is *full of* might.	The Lord our God is *clothed with* might.
Hymn 680. Shall quench the *spark* divine.	Shall quench the *love* divine.
Hymn 241. *And* though his *footsteps* are unknown.	*But* though his *methods* are unknown.
Hymn 241. *With reverence bow before his* seat.	*Prostrate before his awful* seat.
Hymn 286. *The wondering angels* see.	*Angels with wonder* see.
Hymn 1031. *Mourning* captive! God himself will loose thy bands.	*Drooping* captive, God himself will loose thy bands.

NEEDLESS ALTERATIONS.

Original, as in the Sabbath Hymn Book.	Alterations in Worcester's Watts.
Hymn 1061.	
Their *solemn* charge receive, In *rapture* [raptures] or *in* woe.	Their *awful* charge receive, In *happiness* or woe.
Hymn 1159	
Upward [upwards], *Lord, our spirits* raise;	*Lord, our expectations* raise.
Pardon of our sins renew;	*Former kindnesses* renew;
Teach us henceforth how to live.	*From this moment may we* live.
Bless *thy* word to young and old; Fill *us with* a Saviour's love.	Bless *the* word to young and old. *Shed abroad* a Saviour's love.

Among other alterations in Worcester's Watts, which many critics would condemn, because unnecessary, are those in Book I. 143; Book II. 107, 140; Book III. 3; Select, 9. Dr. Watts wrote B. II. 28, "His quivering lips hang feebly down, His *pulses* faint and few." Dr. Worcester writes, "His *pulse is* faint and few." The Sabbath Hymn Book has been criticised for inserting the lines in the left hand column below, and thus altering the original lines, which have been supposed to be those quoted in the right hand column. But here, as often elsewhere, the imagined alterations are the originals, and the imagined originals are the alterations.

Original, as in the Sabbath Hymn Book.	Altered Form.
Hymn 815.	
Down to the gulf of *black* despair.	Down to the gulf of *dark* despair.
Hymn 1059.	
We plead for those who plead for thee,—	We plead for those who plead for thee,—
Successful *pleaders may* they be.	Successful *may they ever* be.
Hymn 1160.	
When past — *but as* a day!	When past, *'tis but* a day.
A host of *enemies* without.	A host of *dangerous foes* without.

Original, as in the Sabbath Hymn Book.	Altered Form.
Hymn 698.	
Thou know'st *I love thee, dearest* Lord.	Thou *knowest that I love thee*, Lord.
Hymn 219.	
My steadfast heart shall *fear* no ill. *Addison.*	My steadfast heart shall *know* no ill.
Hymn 695.	
And *tremble on the brink of fate.*	And *save me ere it is too late.*
Hymn 883.	
That *leans, O Lord, on thee!*	That *trusts the Almighty hand.*
Hymn 55.	
Here afford us, Lord, a taste Of our everlasting *feast.*	Here afford us, Lord, a taste Of our everlasting *rest.*

But it is the prerogative of good judgment to use a good principle rationally. While we recognize the truth, that the original readings are commonly the best, and that ill-considered changes are apt to turn poetry into prose, or sense into nonsense, we must also remember that no lyrist has yet attained perfection, and our duty is to " cease from man whose breath is in his nostrils." The afflatus of the poet commonly wafts him onward in a graceful or a sublime movement, but now and then the gales of his fancy bear him into the dry sand. Among the sacred lyrists of the English, or of any other language, there has not arisen a greater than Isaac Watts, since the days of supernatural inspiration. But we are compelled to own, that besides other far more unworthy stanzas, he wrote the following:

> My foot is ever apt to slide,
>   My foes rejoice to *see't;*
> They raise their pleasure and their pride
>   When they supplant my feet.
>   *Psalm* 38, C. M.

> Yet, if my God prolong my breath,
> The saints may profit *by't;*
> The saints, the glory of the earth,
> The men of my delight.
>
> *Psalm* 16, C. M., *first part.*

In reading Dr. Worcester's Abridgment of Watts's Psalms and Hymns, we are surprised at the multitude of couplets and entire lyrics, so faulty "as seldom, perhaps never, to be given out in public," and therefore excluded from his Christian Psalmody. Many of these stanzas, as restored in Worcester's Watts, have never, we presume, been *sung* since their restoration; and some of them, as, for instance, Psalm 83, stanzas 4—6, have so infrequently been even *perused,* that their very existence is unknown to the great majority of worshippers using that manual.

§ 5. *Changes in the Text, as Affecting Old Associations.*

"I will make Jerusalem heaps;" "I will make Jerusalem a cup of trembling;" "I will make Jerusalem a burdensome stone;" "I create Jerusalem a rejoicing;"—such phrases are frequent, in the prophetic style. Dr. Doddridge preached a discourse on Isaiah 62: 6, 7, "Ye that make mention of the Lord, keep not silence; and give him no rest, till he establish, and *till he make Jerusalem a praise* in the earth." One of his best hymns followed that discourse:

> 2. How shall thy servants give thee rest,
> Till Zion's mouldering walls thou raise;
> Till thy own power shall stand confessed,
> *And make Jerusalem a praise.*
>
> 10. —— And Zion, *made a praise by thee,*
> To thee shall *render back the praise.*

In some recent versions, the fourth line here quoted is exchanged for another: "*And thine own church be filled with praise.*" The Sabbath Hymn Book, hymn 1122, rejected this interpolation, because it is not hallowed by common use, and is in no way an improvement upon Doddridge's own biblical quotation. Yet an advocate of the original text has quoted the line in the Sabbath Hymn Book, "*And make Jerusalem a praise*"! and has appended to it an exclamation point, as if it were a *signal* instance of "clumsy and prosaic alteration," " very objectionable innovation," and places over against it what he mistakes for Doddridge's own words: "*And thine own church be filled with praise.*" This is one among numerous examples of the love which a man acquires to verses which he has often perused, and the facility with which he sees more excellence in those verses than in any which can be substituted for them. The same writer objects to the 383d hymn in the Sabbath Hymn Book, as " in a form very different from what [he has] *been accustomed to*," and yet every word remains precisely as Mrs. Steele left it, with the exception of the first line, where instead of " Triumphant *he* ascends on high," a more appropriate beginning is chosen : " Triumphant *Christ* ascends on high."

The same Review which contains the two preceding criticisms adds the following: " All other collections [than the Sabbath Hymn Book] in which this hymn [Wesley's ' Rejoice, the Lord is King'] is found, so far as our knowledge extends, give the chorus of that hymn, repeated in every stanza, thus :

> Lift up *the* heart, lift up *the* voice,
> Rejoice *aloud, ye saints,* rejoice :

which (for some musical reason, surely, and no other) is changed by the Sabbath Hymn Book into

> Lift up *your* hearts, lift up *your* voice,
> Rejoice! *again I say*, rejoice"!

Now the truth is, that the Sabbath Hymn Book retains that chorus exactly as Wesley left it, and as it is still retained in Montgomery's Psalmist, the Revised Edition of the Methodist Hymn Book, and in other authoritative manuals. Some manuals ascribe the hymn to Dr. Rippon, and we first discovered that *changed* form of it, which our reviewer prefers, in Rippon's Selection, printed in 1813. And then, as to "*some musical reason surely, and no other*," which induced Charles Wesley to select his original reading in preference to Rippon's interpolation, — this "musical reason" is found in the fourth verse of the fourth chapter of the epistle to the Philippians: "Rejoice in the Lord always, and *again I say*, rejoice." There is music in this inspired phrase, which breathes delightfully through Wesley's biblical hymn. His expressive quotation is as much superior to the altered form "Rejoice aloud," as an inspired, quickening, cheering, and reiterated call, is better than a *loud* joy.

The three criticisms just mentioned, develop an attachment to old poetic reminiscences, which is in itself amiable, and suggestive of important rules in church song. For, very peculiarly is our worship of the Ancient of Days affected by associating it with times gone by. There are some lyrics of historical celebrity, like the first English hymn for the Old Hundredth tune: "All people that on earth do dwell," and the old Scotch version of the twenty-third Psalm: "The Lord's my shepherd, I'll not want," which in the simple homeliness of their style, transport us into the near, warm presence of our ancestors, as with tearful eye and aching heart, amid sicknesses, persecutions, and still more disheartening fears, they warbled forth these identical words. They should be in every Hymn Book. They should remain unaltered, even when a change would remove here and there a rhetorical blemish. The antiquity of their form is the prominent excellence of it. They are an exception from the general rule. They may be easily ridiculed, but in the final event, a spirit of reverence will prevail over the disposition to sneer at simple-hearted devotion.

Perhaps there are no words in the English language, that express more feelingly and more justly the importance of adhering to the original form of our sacred songs, than the following words of the late Professor B. B. Edwards. Speaking of those hymns which are "the product of earthly genius and of heavenly inspiration," "which had their origin almost in heaven," he says:[1]

"These compositions should remain unchanged, so that the ancient recollections connected with them may be preserved. It is well known, that such associations are often a principal cause of the extraordinary effects which are produced by popular music. The poetry and the music may be indifferent, but the composition was used in some great crisis of the country, in some new turn of human affairs; and

[1] Writings of Prof. B. B. Edwards, with a Memoir, Vol. I. pp. 156, 157.

tradition, and popular sympathy, and recollection impart to it astonishing power.

" In like manner, some pieces of sacred music, some standard hymns, excellent as they may be in themselves, are greatly indebted to the reminiscences that have been clustering around them for ages. They were sung in the fastnesses of the mountains, when it was unsafe to utter the louder notes; or in some almost fathomless glen, where the eucharistic wine might be mingled with the blood of the communicant. Some of them aroused the fainting spirit of the reformer, when the fate of Protestantism was depending on the turn which a half enlightened human will might take, in the caprice of a moment. Others were sung on a wintry sea by pilgrim voices. Some are hallowed by missionary reminiscences, or by all the sad, yet joyful images of the chamber of death. A thousand times have they quivered on lips, which in a moment were motionless forever. A thousand times have they been wept rather than sung, while the grave was unvailing her faithful bosom; while a mother's precious remains were descending to their last resting-place, or while they came as life from the dead to the solitary mourner, whose entire household were beneath the clods of the valley. Everywhere, in innumerable burying places, fragments of them are engraven with rude devices, teaching the rustic moralist how to die, or pointing him to the sure and certain hope. They are embalmed in the most sacred affections of the heart. They often come like unseen ministers of grace to the soul. We would not lose a line, or suffer the alteration of a word. The *slightest* change breaks the link. It is sacrilege to touch them.

They connect us with the holy dead on the other side of the ocean; they bring up the hallowed memories of Watts, and Wesley, and Cowper; they make us at home in the venerable churchyards where our forefathers' dust is garnered. We are *fellow*-citizens with the great commonwealth of the happy dead in both hemispheres. We feel new chords of relationship to the saints in glory."

The author of this eloquent protest against altering the text of hymns, and especially those hymns which are " cut in the rock forever," was advocating a general principle, and was not intending to preclude all exceptions to it; for when he was called to prepare an epitaph for his first born, "the delight of his existence," he selected the touching lines of Henry Kirke White, and adopted that alteration of them which makes them so tenderly applicable to the graves of children. He did not carve on the marble, " These ashes, *too*, this little dust,"[1] but

> These ashes *few*, this little dust,
> Our Father's care shall keep,
> Till the last angel rise and break
> The long and dreary sleep.

This incident recalls the suggestion already made, that an *altered* form often acquires more sacredness than the original. More precious associations may cluster around a *common* reading than around the first one. The same reason, then, which exists ordinarily for *avoiding* changes of the original text, becomes occasionally a reason for *retaining* them when made. Worshippers have become not only wonted to them,

---

[1] See Sabbath Hymn Book, H. 1276.

but also attached to them, and are pained, shocked, by a return to the pristine phrases which seem to them like innovations. What is old in reality, is new to them. The love of novelty in doctrine, leads one man to revive an ancient but exploded error. The prurient desire of change induces another man to adopt some antiquated ecclesiastical ceremony. The same fondness for innovation betrays another man into the use of old terms, which have been so long disused as to appear like words just coined. If we should begin to print the Bible, as it was originally written, without divisions into chapters and verses, we should gratify both the love of antiquity and the love of novelty, in scholars of a peculiar class; but we should offend the majority of plain men, who love the Bible in its modern form. If we should deviate from the arbitrary divisions made by the monk Arlott, or Bishop Langton of Canterbury, in the thirteenth century, or by the Jew Mordecai Nathan in the fifteenth, or by Robert Stephens in the sixteenth, we might improve their hallowed work; but, by substituting the accurate for the inaccurate, we should appear to be innovators, and our emendations would not be tolerated by the masses.

We often hear objections made to certain changes in a hymn, on the ground that they break up the most cherished associations, when in fact the editor of that hymn would have restored the ancient text, were it not for the fear of disturbing the sacred memories clustering around the established departure from it. We should not *alter* the original line, says the objector, because we thus divert the pious mind from the solemnity of worship to the inquiry: " Why have my favorite words been displaced?" "We should not *restore* the original," says the editor, "because we thereby distract the attention of the worshipper with criticisms upon the words, which appear to him strange, and perhaps inferior. The *reasons* for and against the accommodated style, are often nearly balanced. The balance may often be struck in favor of that style, by the fact that custom *has* sanctioned, or seems *likely* to sanction the altered form; and that a deviation from what *is*, or is destined to *become*, the common reading would give more pain than pleasure. "Go now and boast of all your stores, And tell how bright *you* shine," are words which would startle many a worshipper as a novelty; yet they are the original words of Watts. Men have become familiar with the line, "Let the dark benighted pagan," who would be startled at the *innovation* of the *original* line, "Let the Indian, let the negro." It is common to condemn changes like the following, but they are adopted in the Sabbath Hymn Book, partly for the reason that a majority of those who will ever use that manual, would be painfully disappointed if their favorite changes had not been retained.

ORIGINAL.	SABBATH HYMN BOOK.
	Hymn 132.
How terrible thy glories be!	*Great God! how high thy glories rise;*
How bright thine armies shine!	How bright thine armies shine!
Where is the power *that vies with thee,*	Where is the power *with thee that vies,*
Or truth compared to thine!	Or truth compared to thine!
	(See also Presbyterian O. S. Collection, Ps. 89.)
	Hymn 964.
Thorns of heartfelt tribulation.	*Scenes* of heartfelt tribulation.
Cowper.	

FAVORITE ALTERATIONS.

ORIGINAL.	SABBATH HYMN BOOK.
	Hymn 199.
O were I like *a feathered* dove, And innocence had wings, I'd fly, and make a long remove, etc.	Oh! were I like *some gentle* dove, *Soon would I stretch my* wings, And fly, and make a long remove, etc.
	Hymn 232.
Their *feet shall never slide to* fall.	Their *steadfast* feet *shall never* fall.
	Hymn 309.
And glory to th' eternal king Who lays his *fury* by.	And glory to th' eternal king Who lays his *anger* by.
	Hymn 431.
His loving kindness *is* so free, — "*is so* great" — "*is so* strong," — "*is so* good" —.	His loving kindness, *Oh how* free, — "*Oh how* great" — "*Oh how* strong," — "*Oh how* good" —.
	Hymn 493.
Be thou my strength and righteousness, My *Jesus* and my all.	Be thou my strength and righteousness, My *Saviour* and my all.
	Hymn 548.
But wisdom shows a *narrower* path, With here and there a traveller.	But wisdom shows a *narrow* path, With here and there a traveller.
	Hymn 548.
The fearful soul that *tries* and faints.	The fearful soul that *tires* and faints.
	Hymn 1170.
And to his heavenly kingdom *keep* This feeble soul of mine.	And to his heavenly kingdom *take* This feeble soul of mine.
	Hymn 1172.
Stoop down my thoughts that *use* to rise.	Stoop down my thoughts that *used* to rise.
	Hymn 142.
While thine eternal *thought moves* on, Thine undisturbed affairs.	While thine eternal *thoughts move* on Thine undisturbed affairs.
	Hymn 1245.
The saints above, how great their joys, *And* bright their glories be.	The saints above, how great their joys, *How* bright their glories be!
	Hymn 590.
And thou, my God, whose piercing eye *Distinct surveys each dark recess*, In these *abstracted* hours draw nigh.	O thou, *great* God! whose piercing eye *Distinctly marks each deep retreat*, In these *sequestered* hours draw nigh.

ORIGINAL.	SABBATH HYMN BOOK.
	Hymn 1157.
The eternal *states* of all the dead.	The eternal *state* of all the dead.
	Hymn 462.
Dear Lord, and shall we ever *lie* At this poor dying rate?	Dear Lord! and shall we ever *live* At this poor dying rate?
	Hymn 698.
And turn *each cursèd* idol out That dares to rival thee.	And turn *the dearest* idol out That dares to rival thee.
	Hymn 724.
Yes, and I must and will esteem All things but *lost* for Jesus' sake.	Yes; and I must and will esteem All things but *loss* for Jesus' sake.
	Hymn 629.
But ere *some* fleeting hour is past.	But ere *one* fleeting hour is past.
Watts.	*Hymn* 479.
But the *best* volume thou hast writ.	But the *blest* volume thou hast writ.
Wesley.	*Hymn* 997.
Love Divine all *loves* excelling.	Love Divine all *love* excelling.
	Hymn 124.
And on the wings of *all the* winds.	And on the wings of *mighty* winds.
	Hymn 617.
Now Satan threatens to prevail.	*Rise, Saviour! help me* to prevail.

During the last forty years, multitudes of American and English worshippers have been accustomed to the following variation of one of Doddridge's hymns; the variation making the hymn more appropriate to *public* worship.

ORIGINAL FORM.	SABBATH HYMN BOOK.
My Saviour, *I am* thine, By everlasting bands; *My* name, *my* heart, *I* would resign: *My* soul *is in* thy hands.	*Dear* Saviour! *we are* thine By everlasting bands; *Our hearts, our souls, we* would resign, *Entirely to* thy hands.
To Thee *I* still would cleave With ever-growing zeal: *Let* millions tempt *me* Christ to leave, *They never shall* prevail.	To thee *we* still would cleave With ever-growing zeal; *If* millions tempt *us* Christ to leave, *O let them ne'er* prevail!

ORIGINAL HYMN.	SABBATH HYMN BOOK.

His Spirit shall unite
  My soul to *him, my* Head;
Shall form *me to his* image bright,
  And teach *his path* to tread.
	Thy Spirit shall unite
	  Our souls to *thee, our* head;
	Shall form *in us thine* image bright,
	  And teach *thy paths* to tread.

Death may *my soul* divide
  From *this abode* of clay;
But love shall keep *me* near *his* side,
  Through all the gloomy way.
	Death may *our souls* divide
	  From *these abodes* of clay;
	But love shall keep *us* near *thy* side,
	  Through all the gloomy way.

Since Christ and we are one,
  What should remain to fear?
If he in heaven *hath* fixed his throne,
  He'll fix his members there.
	Since Christ and we are one,
	  Why should we doubt or fear?
	If he in heaven *has* fixed his throne,
	  He'll fix his members there.

That indispensable hymn of Dr. Raffles: " High in yonder realms of light," consists of forty-eight lines, as published by William Bengo Collier in 1812. As published by Dr. Raffles himself, in 1853, it consists of thirty-two lines. As it ordinarily appears, in English and American hymn books, it is variously combined and altered. The following are specimen copies:

WILLIAM BENGO COLLIER'S EDITION OF 1812.	DR. RAFFLES'S OWN EDITION OF 1853.
1	1

High in yonder realms of light,
  Far above these lower skies,
Fair and exquisitely bright,
  Heaven's unfading mansions rise:
Built of pure and massy gold,
  Strong and durable are they;
Deck'd with gems of worth untold,
  Subjected to no decay!
	High in yonder realms of light,
	  Far above these lower skies,
	Fair and exquisitely bright,
	  Heaven's unfading mansions rise;
	Glad, within these blest abodes,
	  Dwell the raptured saints above,
	Where no anxious care corrodes,
	  Happy in Emmanuel's love.

2	2

Glad within these blest abodes,
  Dwell the raptured saints above,
Where no anxious care corrodes,
  Happy in Emmanuel's love!
Once, *indeed,* like us below,
  Pilgrims in this vale of tears,
Torturing pain and heavy woe,
  Gloomy doubts, distressing fears:
	Once the big unbidden tear,
	  Stealing down the furrowed cheek,
	Told, in eloquence sincere,
	  Tales of woe they could not speak;
	But, these days of weeping o'er,
	  Passed this scene of toil and pain,
	They shall feel distress no more,
	  Never, never weep again.

WILLIAM BENGO COLLIER'S EDITION OF 1812.	DR. RAFFLES'S OWN EDITION OF 1853.
3	3

These, alas! full well they knew,
  Sad companions of their way:
Oft on them the tempest blew
  Through the long, the cheerless day!
Oft their vileness they deplor'd,
  Wills perverse and hearts untrue,
Grieved they could not love their Lord,
  Love him as they wished to do!
	'Mid the chorus of the skies,
	  'Mid the angelic lyres above,
	Hark! their songs melodious rise,
	  Songs of praise to Jesus' love!
	Happy spirits! ye are fled
	  Where no grief can entrance find;
	Lulled to rest the aching head,
	  Soothed the anguish of the mind.

4	4

Oft the big, unbidden tear,
  Stealing down the furrow'd cheek,
Told in eloquence sincere,
  Tales of woe they could not speak.
But these days of weeping o'er,
  Past this scene of toil and pain,
They shall feel distress no more,
  Never — never weep again!
	All is tranquil and serene,
	  Calm and undisturbed repose;
	There no cloud can intervene,
	  There no angry tempest blows:
	Every tear is wiped away,
	  Sighs no more shall heave the breast,
	Night is lost in endless day,
	  Sorrow in eternal rest.

5	

'Mid the chorus of the skies,
  'Mid the angelic lyres above,
Hark — their songs melodious rise,
  Songs of praise to Jesus' love!
Happy spirits! — ye are fled,
  Where no grief can entrance find,
Lull'd to rest the aching head,
  Sooth'd the anguish of the mind!
	Many worshippers would be shocked at the novelty of either of the first stanzas given above; for the following appears as the first stanza in the Church Psalmody, the Presbyterian Old School and the Dutch Reformed Church Collections; Nettleton's Village Hymns, the Sabbath Hymn Book, and many other manuals.

6	

All is tranquil and serene,
  Calm and undisturbed repose,
There no cloud can intervene,
  There no angry tempest blows!
Every tear is wiped away,
  Sighs no more shall heave the breast;
Night is lost in endless day —
  Sorrow — in eternal rest!
	High in yonder realms of light,
	  Dwell the raptured saints above;
	Far beyond our feeble sight,
	  Happy in Immanuel's love:
	Pilgrims in this vale of tears,
	  Once *they knew*, like us below,
	Gloomy doubts, distressing fears,
	  Torturing pain and heavy woe.

§ 6. *Changes in the Text, as affecting the Uniformity of Worship.*

A great evil resulting from the alteration of hymns is, that various forms are used by various congregations; and men, accustomed to sing from one manual, are confused by the new phrases which they find in another manual; and sometimes the same assembly utter, on the same notes, different words, or even different verses, and thus there is no distinction of sound, but "every-one hath a psalm," "hath a tongue," "hath an interpretation." This is an infelicity, and therefore manuals for song should adopt the original, partly because this is more apt to be the prevailing, form of the lyrics.

But *exceptions* prove the wisdom of this general rule. We must not blame the original collector of the "Psalms of David," even if we adopt a common theory, that he inserted the eighteenth Psalm in a form different from the original, as found in the twenty-second chapter of second Samuel. It has been remarked by those who believe that the Book of Samuel contains the *earliest* copy of that song, that the first notable instance of departure from the original draught of a sacred lyric, was made by the editor of the inspired Psalms. . Many persons have been "shocked," still more have been "confused," and some have been ruinously prejudiced against the revealed word, by the fact that the old songs of the temple are "altered," when cited by the apostles; and that the quotations made in the New Testament from the Old, are often so far "modified," that it is difficult, if not impossible, to recognize and identify them. We believe that, in many instances, the writers of the New Testament quoted the "changed form," simply because it had become more familiar than the original words, to the men whom the apostles immediately addressed. But the *original* form remains, and is now better known, and has become far more precious to many readers, than is the Septuagint, which the writers of the New Testament have preferred to cite. There were valid reasons for accommodating the words of the old poets and prophets to the times of the new dispensation. So there were valid reasons for giving us two different versions of the Lord's Prayer, both of them promoting an excellent end, although the "*uniformity* of worship" is not always secured by them. In like manner, there are reasons for adapting to modern tastes some of the ancient hymns, notwithstanding all the inconveniences which attend the adaptation.

It is an unwelcome fact, that these inconveniences have been incurred already, and they cannot, even by our most strenuous effort, be remedied altogether. As the manuals for song neither are, nor ever have been exactly alike, the objection that changes in the text prevent uniformity of worship, comes, in some respects, too late. We regret to say, that restorations to the original sometimes prevent this uniformity. It would be a joy to us, if all our hymn books would adopt the same version of Toplady's hallowed lyric: "Rock of Ages, cleft for me," but the ensuing columns indicate the multiplicity of changes that have hopelessly ingratiated themselves into the favor of some admirers of the hymn.

Lines Unaltered.	Lines Altered.
1	
Rock of Ages, *cleft for* me.	Rock of Ages, *shelter* me.
	Dr. Rippon and others.
Let me hide myself in thee!	
Let the water and the blood	
	From thy *wounded* side which flowed.
	Presbyterian (O.S.) Col., and others.
From thy *riven* side which flowed,	
	From thy *side a healing* flood.
	Church Psalmody, and others.

CHANGES IN TOPLADY'S HYMN.

LINES UNALTERED.	LINES ALTERED.
Be of sin *the double* cure, Cleanse me from its guilt and power.	Be of sin *and fear the* cure, Save from wrath and make me pure. *Church Psalmody.* Be of sin the *perfect* cure, Save me, Lord, and make me pure. *Presbyterian (N.S.) Col.* Cleanse *from guilt and grace ensure.* *Kempthorne.*
2 Not the labors of my hands Can fulfil thy law's demands :	
Could my zeal no *respite* know, *Could* my *tears forever* flow, *All* for *sin could not* atone :	*Should* my zeal no *languor* know, *Should* my tears forever flow, *This* for sin could not atone. *Church Psalmody, Presbyterian (N.S.) Collection, and others.* *May* my zeal no respite know, *May* my *heart with love o'*erflow. *But can this* for *sin* atone ? *Kempthorne.* *This* for sin could *ne'er* atone. *Connecticut Col.* This for sin could *not* atone. *Church Psalmody.*
Thou must save, and thou alone.	
3 *Nothing in my hand* I bring ;	*In my hand no price* I bring. *Church Psalmody, Presbyterian (N. S.) Col.*
Simply to thy cross I cling ; Naked, come to thee for dress ; Helpless, look to thee for grace ;	
Foul, I to *thy* fountain fly ;	*Vile*, I to *the* fountain fly. *Presbyterian (O.S.) Collection, and others.*
Wash me, Saviour, or I die !	
4 While I draw this fleeting breath,	
When my *eye-strings break* in death,	When my *heart*-strings *break* in death. *William Collier, 1812.* When my *eyelids sink* in death. *Kempthorne's Selection, 2d ed., 1813.* When my eyelids *close* in death. *Bickersteth's Christian Psalmody.*
When I *soar to worlds* unknown, *See thee on thy judgment* throne,—	When I soar *through tracks* unknown. *Kempthorne.* When I *rise* to worlds unknown, *And behold thee on thy* throne. *Church Psalmody, Presbyterian (N. S.) Col.*
Rock of Ages ! *cleft for* me, Let me hide myself in thee.	Rock of Ages, *shelter* me. *Dr. Rippon, and others.*

A commentary on church-song lies hidden in these columns. They develop the attachment of men to an ode, and also their conviction that something is wrong in it somewhere. It must be confessed, that several of the above-named alterations, unwise as they may have been, were still the means of ushering Toplady's hymn into common use. It was not a favorite ode until these changes were introduced into it, in 1826, by an Episcopal collection, which was imitated by the Church Psalmody, the Connecticut and several other Manuals. It must also be confessed, that *one* of the alterations (the *only* positive change adopted in the Sabbath Hymn Book) is highly important. We have heard a defence of Toplady's line : " When my *eye-strings break* in death," on the ground that, in the article of death *there is actually emitted from the eye a cracking sound,* as if the muscles and tendons were suddenly snapped and broken. But even if this were true, the songs of Zion are not anatomical treatises, and should not · divert the worshipper's mind from sacred to scientific themes. Still, there are admirers of the original text, who *will* not give up Toplady's words for any other. There are admirers of Collier and Watts, who *will* prefer the breaking of the *heart-*strings to that of the *eye-*strings ; for Dr. William Bengo Collier sings, in his 977th hymn : " When the *strings of my heart* I feel *break,*" and Dr. Watts writes : " Then will ye hear my *heart-strings break*" (altered by the Church Psalmist, Hymn 97, into : "*And while* ye hear my *heart-strings break*"). There are others who *will* choose the form adopted in the Sabbath Hymn Book : " When my *eyelids close* in death." Here, as elsewhere, entire agreement is desirable, but is absolutely unattainable. The plea for a uniform text is good, but its force is impaired by the fact, that the plea comes a century after it could serve its end. Let any man compare the 476th lyric in the Sabbath Hymn Book, with the same hymn as given first by Charles Wesley, then by Augustus Toplady; and he will be satisfied that the spell of an agreement in the same form, was broken long ago, and cannot now be restored. There are two things of which we must never complain: first, what we *can* help; second, what we *cannot*.

§ 7. *The Principle of Changes in the Text lies at the Basis of Modern English Hymnology.*

More than twenty English versions of Hebrew Psalms appeared before the time of Dr. Watts. They were written by Sir Philip Sidney, Christopher Hatton, H. Dodd, Dr. Henry King, Miles Smith, Dr. Samuel Woodford, John Milton, William Barton, Dr. Simon Ford, Sir Richard Blackmore, Dr. John Patrick, Mr. Addison, Archdeacon Daniel, Dr. Joseph Trapp, Dr. Walter Harte, Dr. Broome, George Sandys, Sir John Denham, and others. It was the aim of their versions to represent, exactly, the spirit and style of the Psalter; but every one of them frequently, though unintentionally, failed in the correctness of its translation. The Psalter, as versified by Dr. Watts, introduced a new era into English psalmody, and constitutes the basis of our modern hymnological literature. But he has designedly "altered" the Psalms of David. "I could never persuade myself," he writes, "that the best Way to raise a devout Frame, in *plain*

Christians, was to bring *a King* or *a Captain* into their Churches, and let him lead and dictate the Worship, in his own Style of royalty, or in the language of a field of Battel."[1] Accordingly, we find such notes as the following appended, frequently, to his *Imitations* of the Psalms.

Psalm 1. "In this work I have often borrowed a Line or two from the New Testament; that the excellent and inspired Composures of the Jewish Psalmist may be brightened by the clearer Discoveries of the Gospel."

Psalm 5. "Stanzas 2 and 5. Where any just occasion is given to make mention of Christ and the Holy Spirit, I refuse it not; and I am persuaded David would not have refused it, had he lived under the Gospel; nor St. Paul, had he written a Psalm Book."

Psalm 7. "In this Psalm I have not exactly followed every single Verse of the Psalmist, but have endeavored to contract the Substance of it into fewer lines, yet not without a regard to the litteral Sense and Words also, as will appear by the Comparison."

Psalm 14. "Several Verses of this Psalm are cited by the Apostle, (Romans 3: 10, etc.) to shew the universal Corruption of human Nature, wherefore I have brought more of the Apostle's Words there used into the 4th and 5th Stanzas here, and concluded this part of the Psalm agreeably to St. Paul's design."

Psalm 35. "Stanza 6. Among the Imprecations that David uses against his Adversaries, in this Psalm, I have adventured to turn

---

[1] This quotation is made from page XIII of the first edition of Watts's Psalms. It was printed in London "for J. Clark, *at the* Bible *and* Crown *in the* Poultry; R. Ford, *at the* Angel *in the* Poultry; *and* R. Cruttenden, *at the* Bible *and* Three Crowns in Cheapside. 1719." The copy of this edition now lying before us was a presentation copy of the author himself, and contains his autograph on the blank leaf: "To yᵉ Revᵈ Mʳ Stinton. — I. WATTS." From this copy the notes printed on this, and the following pages are extracted.

the Edge of them away from Personal Enemies, against the implacable Enemies of God in the World.

"Stanzas 7 and 8. Agreeably to the Spirit of the Gospel, I have here further mollified these Imprecations by a charitable distinction and Petition for their Souls, which Spirit of Evangelic Charity appears so conspicuous in the 12th, 13th, and 14th verses of the Psalm, that I could not forbear to form them into a short, distinct Hymn, enlarging on that Glorious Character of a Christian — Love to our Enemies — commanded so particularly, and so divinely exemplified by Christ himself."

Psalm 37. "This long Psalm abounds with useful Instructions and Incouragements to Piety, but the Verses are very much unconnected and independent; Therefore I have contracted and transposed them so as to reduce them to three Hymns of a moderate length, and with some connection of the sense."

Psalm 39. "I have not confined myself, here, to the Sense of the Psalmist; but have taken occasion, from the three first Verses, to write a short Hymn on the Government of the Tongue."

Psalm 40. "If David had written this Psalm in the Days of the Gospel, surely he would have given a much more express and particular account of the Sacrifice of Christ, as he hath done of his preaching, vs. 9, 10, and enlarged, as Paul does in Heb. 10 : 4, etc., where this Psalm is cited. I have done no more, therefore, in this paraphrase, than what I am persuaded the Psalmist himself would have done in the time of Christianity."

Psalm 41. "The positive Blessings of long Life, Health, Recovery, and Security in the Midst of Dangers, being so much promised in the Old Testament, and so little in the New, I have given a Turn at the end of this Hymn to discourage a too confident Expectation of these temporal things, and lead the soul to heavenly Hopes, more agreeable to the Gospel."

Psalm 55. "I have left out some whole Psalms, and several parts of others that tend to fill the Mind with overwhelming sorrows, or sharp resentment; neither of which are so well suited to the Spirit of the Gospel, and therefore the particular Complaints of David against Achitophel, here, are entirely omitted."

Psalm 67. "Having translated the Scene of this Psalm to Great Britain, I have borrow'd a devout and poetical Wish for the Happiness of my native Land, from Zech. 2:5, and offered it up in the 2d Stanza: 'I will be a Wall of Fire round about, and will be the Glory in the Midst of her."

Psalm 69. "In both the Metres of this Psalm I have apply'd it to the Sufferings of Christ, as the New Testament gives sufficient Reason by several Citations of this Psalm: From which Places I have borrowed the Particulars of his Sufferings for our Sins, his Scourging the Buyers and Sellers out of the Temple, his Crucifixion, etc. But I have omitted the dreadful Imprecations on his Enemies, except what is incerted in this last Stanza in the Way of a Prediction or Threatening."

Psalm 73. "This Psalm is a most noble Composure; the Design and Model of it is divinely beautiful, and an admirable Pattern for a Poet to copy. But it being one single Scheme of Thought, I was obliged to contract it, that it might be sung at once; though the Dignity and Beauty of the Ode suffers much by this Means."

Psalm 85. "If some Readers should suppose the English Verse here to mistake the Hebrew sense, yet perhaps these Evangelical Allusions to the Words of the Jewish Psalmist may be as agreeable and useful to the Christian worshipper."

Psalm 87. "I have explained the Second Verse at large, and transposed the last. For Singers and Players on Instruments, I have introduced Angels with Men."

Psalm 92. "Stanza 6. Rejoicing in the destruction of our personal Enemies, is not so evangelical a practice, therefore I have given the 11th verse of this Psalm another Turn."

Psalm 104. "Stanza 5. Tho' I am persuaded the Psalmist speaks here of the first Formation of the Sea and Mountains, where the Waters of the Chaos were separated from the Earth, yet the People more easily understand it of Noah's Flood, and therefore I have indulg'd such a Paraphrase as is capable of that sense."

Psalm 112. "Many of the Blessings of Wealth, and Grandeur and Temporal good Things that were the portion of a Good Man and his Children under the Old Testament, I have here abridged agreeable to the New, which foretells rather Temporal Afflictions, and Promises everlasting Rewards."

Psalm 149. "This Psalm seems to be written to encourage the Jews in their Wars against the Heathen Princes of Canaan, who were Divinely Sentenced to Destruction. But the four last Verses of it have been too much abused in later Ages to promote Sedition and Disturbance in the State, so that I choose to refer this Honour that is here given to all the Saints to the Day of Judgment, according to those expressions in the New Testament,—Mat. 19 : 28, 'Ye shall sit on twelve Thrones, Judging the Tribes,' etc.; 1 Cor. 6 : 3, 'We shall Judge Angels'; Rev. 2 : 27 and 3 : 21, 'I will give him power over the Nations; he shall rule them with a Rod of Iron,♭ etc."

It is common to speak of Dr. Watts's "Imitations" as model psalms. They are such, and they ratify the principle of occasional departures from the main text. It is a singular fact, that even although *he* is not condemned, when he exchanges the idioms of David for more prosaic idioms, his *editors* are accused of trespassing on vested rights, when they reinstate the inspired phrases in the place of Dr. Watts's acknowledged innovations. They are accused of injustice when they substitute the biblical phrase: " Within the tents of sin," for Watts's drawling line: " In *pleasurable* sin." Although many of his departures from the sacred text are needed, yet some of them are unwarrantable. What and where would be the end of the obloquy poured on a modern editor, who should interpolate into one of Watts's hymns, such stanzas as the following, which he has thrust into the old Hebrew lyric? In that magnificent eighth Psalm, which begins: " O Lord, our God, how wondrous great, Is thine exalted name," we find the sixth stanza devoted to one of our Lord's miracles:

> The waves lay spread beneath his feet;
> And fish at his command,
> Bring their large shoals to *Peter's* net,
> Bring tribute to his hand.

As the prince of English psalmists has changed not barely the words, but also the images and the ideas of the text which he versified, so have succeeding lyrists modified the style of the hymns transfused by them from the Greek, Latin, German, French, and Welch tongues. Luther's imitation of the old "Media in Vita," and his looser imitation of the "Veni Sancte Spiritus;" the versions of the hymns of Gregory, Ambrose, Bernard, Thomas von Caelano; Wesley's translations from Gerhard and other German lyrists, abound with deviations from the original text. The favorite lyric: "Guide me, O thou great Jehovah," is rather more distant from the old Welsh, than Walter Scott's lines: "That day of wrath, that dreadful day," are different from the old "Dies Irae." All the English translations of Gerhard's passion hymn: "O sacred head, now wounded," differ from the original German, as that, in its turn, is diverse from the Latin ode on which it is founded. In fact a literal translation of any, and especially an ancient, poem, must be too artificial and frigid for an English or American worshipper. As our versions of foreign lyrics are necessarily accommodated to our Anglo-Saxon tastes, so we have several favorite songs founded on antique English poems. They disagree unnecessarily, sometimes, with the stanzas from which they are derived; but even this disagreement illustrates the truth that our hymnody, as well as psalmody, has adopted the fundamental principle of departing from the original text. The hymn extracted from Milton's poem on the Morning of Christ's Nativity, is a signal example of this free accommodation. An old English poem, the manuscript of which is now in the British Museum, written we know not when, — probably, however, by some devout papist, — is itself founded on the twenty-second chapter of John's Revelation, and is the basis on which several recent hymns have been composed. We subjoin the original, and three of the "modified" copies.

A Version made by F. B. P.
To the tune of Diana.

1
Jerusalem! my happy home!
  When shall I come to thee,
When shall my sorrows have an end,
  Thy joys when shall I see?

2
O happy harbor of the saints,
  O sweet and pleasant soil;
In thee no sorrow may be found,
  No grief, no care, no toil.

3
In thee no sickness may be seen,
  No hurt, no ache, no sore;
There is no death, no ugly de'il,
  There's life for evermore.

4
No dampish mist is seen in thee,
  No cold nor darksome night;
There every soul shines as the sun,
  There God himself gives light.

5
There lust and lucre cannot dwell,
  There envy bears no sway,
There is no hunger, heat, nor cold,
  But pleasure every way.

6
Jerusalem! Jerusalem!
  God grant I once may see
Thy endless joys, and of the same
  Partaker aye to be.

7
Thy walls are made of precious stones,
  Thy bulwarks diamonds square,
Thy gates are of right orient pearl,
  Exceeding rich and rare.

8
Thy turrets and thy pinnacles
  With carbuncles do shine;
The very streets are paved with gold,
  Surpassing clear and fine.

9
Thy houses are of ivory,
  Thy windows crystal clear,
Thy tiles are made of beaten gold;
  O God, that I were there!

10
Within thy gates no thing doth come
  That is not passing clean;
No spider's web, no dirt, no dust,
  No filth may there be seen.

11
Ah, my sweet home, Jerusalem!
  Would God I were in thee,
Would God my woes were at an end,
  Thy joys that I might see.

12
Thy saints are crowned with glory great,
  They see God face to face,
They triumph still, they still rejoice,
  Most happy is their case.

13
We that are here in banishment
  Continually do moan;
We sigh and sob, we weep and wail,
  Perpetually we groan.

14
Our sweet is mixed with bitter gall,
  Our pleasure is but pain,
Our joys scarce last the looking on,
  Our sorrows still remain.

15
But there they live in such delight,
   Such pleasure, and such play,
As that to them a thousand years,
   Doth seem as yesterday.

16
Thy vineyards and thy orchards are
   Most beautiful and fair,
Full furnishéd with trees and fruits,
   Most wonderful and rare.

17
Thy gardens and thy gallant walks
   Continually are green;
There grow such sweet and pleasant flowers,
   As nowhere else are seen.

18
There's nectar and ambrosia made,
   There's musk and civet sweet;
There many a fair and dainty drug
   Are trodden under feet.

19
There cinnamon, there sugar grows,
   There nard and balm abound;
What tongue can tell, or heart conceive
   The joys that there are found?

20
Quite through the streets, with silver sound,
   The flood of life doth flow;
Upon whose banks, on every side,
   The wood of life doth grow.

21
There trees for evermore bear fruit,
   And evermore do spring;
There evermore the angels sit,
   And evermore do sing.

22
There David stands with harp in hand,
   As master of the quire;
Ten thousand times that man were blest
   That might this music hear.

23
Our lady sings Magnificat,
   With tune surpassing sweet,
And all the virgins bear their parts,
   Sitting above her feet.

24
Te Deum doth Saint Ambrose sing,
   Saint Austin doth the like;
Old Simeon and Zachary
   Have not their song to seek.

25
There Magdalene hath left her moan,
   And cheerfully doth sing,
With blessed saints, whose harmony
   In every street doth ring.

26
Jerusalem, my happy home!
   Would God I were in thee;
Would God my woes were at an end,
   Thy joys that I might see!

One Imitation of the Original Hymn.

1
Jerusalem! my happy home!
   Name ever dear to me!
When shall my labors have an end
   In joy, and peace, and thee?

2
When shall these eyes thy heaven-built walls
   And pearly gates behold?
Thy bulwarks with salvation strong
   And streets of shining gold?

3
There happier bowers than Eden's bloom,
   Nor sin nor sorrow know!
Blest seats! through rude and stormy scenes
   I onward press to you.

4
Why should I shrink at pain and woe,
   Or feel at death dismay?
I've Canaan's goodly land in view,
   And realms of endless day.

5
Apostles, martyrs, prophets there,
Around my Saviour stand,
And soon my friends in Christ below,
Will join the glorious band.

6
Jerusalem! my happy home!
My soul still pants for thee;
Then shall my labors have an end,
When I thy joys shall see.

A SECOND IMITATION OF THE ORIGINAL HYMN.

1
Jerusalem! my happy home!
Name ever dear to me!
When shall my labors have an end,
In joy and peace in thee?

2
Oh! when, thou city of my God,
Shall I thy courts ascend,
Where evermore the angels sing,[1]
Where Sabbaths have no end?

3
There happier bowers than Eden's bloom,
Nor sin nor sorrow know;
Blest seats! through rude and stormy scenes,
I onward press to you.

4
Why should I shrink at pain and woe?
Or feel at death dismay?
I've Canaan's goodly land in view,
And realms of endless day.

5
Jerusalem, my glorious home!
My soul still pants for thee;
Then shall my labors have an end,
When I thy joys shall see.

A THIRD IMITATION OF THE ORIGINAL.

1
Jerusalem, Jerusalem,
I hear those tones of love
Resounding from thy mansions fair,
And calling me above.

2
When shall mine eyes thy jasper walls
And gates of pearl behold;
Thy bulwarks with salvation strong,
And streets of shining gold?

3
Apostles, prophets, martyrs there
Shall round the Saviour stand,
With all who in his faith depart, —
One great and goodly band.

4
There all the saintly company
Who followed Christ the Lord,
Shall evermore in anthems high
His saving strength record.

5
Faint not, then, O my soul, at pain,
Nor feel at death dismay;
Let hope of Salem's heavenly peace
Thy grief and fear allay.

6
Rejoice, and with hosannas laud
Thy blest Redeemer King;
To him who reigns on Sion's hill
In strains of gladness sing.

There is no question that, in several particulars, the original of these hymns is better than either and all

---

[1] Montgomery's line was "Where congregations ne'er break up." The alteration is a nearer conformity to the original. See stanza 21. Montgomery's line is also too prosaic. See Professor Edwards's criticism on it, in his Memoir and Writings, Vol. I. p. 145.

of the abridgments and imitations; yet, for various reasons, the original cannot be introduced into our hymn books. Not only private hymns, but also the *standard* psalms of the English church, began to be altered very soon after they were printed. The first edition of the *entire* Psalter versified, and authorized to be sung in the church of England, was published in 1562, and contains in the very *first* stanza of the *first* psalm, a variation from Sternhold's original text, printed in 1549, and 1552. The edition of 1696 exhibits numerous variations from that of 1562, and the edition of 1726 adds yet more and greater amendments. The version by Tate and Brady supplanted that by Sternhold and Hopkins; but this new version never maintained a uniform text. What is true of the hymns, is also true of the tunes; they have all been varied to meet the real, or the imagined wants of various ages. Some of the amendments have been ill-advised; but the practice and the theory of the church have been in favor of *some* innovations adapted to new exigencies.

§ 8. *The principle of Deviating from another's Text, is substantially the principle of Quoting another's Words.*

When we make a quotation from a writer, we need not quote everything which that writer has affirmed. We may cite one-half, or one-eighth, or one verse, or one clause of the one hundred and nineteenth psalm, without imposing on ourselves an obligation to repeat the whole. We may quote the entire fifteen stanzas of Tate and Brady's lyric:

"Let all the land with shouts of joy," etc., or we may quote only four of them, or only four couplets, or four phrases, or four words. If the substance of the psalm be thus derived from those veteran hymnologists, the whole may, in an undiscriminating style, be ascribed to them, while it is understood that, in stricter speech, there must be some exceptions and abatements. We often pay honor to Watts, as the original versifier of the psalms and hymns ascribed to him. But he has frequently and frankly confessed his obligation to preceding writers. In the following specimens of his quotations, he has taken more liberties with his predecessors, than many of his own editors have taken with him.

Tate and Brady's Version of the 21st Psalm.	Dr. Watts's Version of the 21st Psalm.
1	1
The king, O Lord, with songs of praise Shall in thy strength rejoice, *With thy salvation* crown'd, *shall raise* *To heaven his cheerful voice.*	The king, O Lord, with songs of praise, Shall in thy strength rejoice; And blest *with thy salvation,* raise *To heaven his cheerful voice.*
5	2
Thy sure defence, through nations round, *Has spread his glorious name;* *And his successful actions crown'd* *With majesty and fame.*	*Thy sure defence thro' nations round* *Has spread his glorious name;* *And his successful actions crown'd* *With majesty and fame.*
7	3
Because *the king on God alone* *For timely aid relies;* *His mercy* still *supports* his *throne,* *And all* his *wants supplies.*	Then let *the king on God alone* *For timely aid rely;* *His mercy* shall *support the throne,* *And all* our *wants supply.*
8	4
But righteous Lord, thy *stubborn foes*[1] *Shall feel thy* heavy *hand;* *Thy vengeful arm shall find out those* *That hate thy mild command.*	*But righteous Lord,* his *stubborn foes* *Shall feel thy* dreadful *hand;* *Thy vengeful arm shall find out those* *That hate* his *mild command.*

[1] The foes of *God* in Tate and Brady's version, are the foes of King George I. in Watts.

TATE AND BRADY'S VERSION OF THE 21ST PSALM.

9
When thou against them dost engage,
　Thy just, but dreadful, doom
Shall like a glowing oven's rage,
　Their hopes and them consume.

13
Thus, Lord, thy wondrous strength disclose,
　And thus exalt thy fame;
Whilst we glad songs of praise compose
　To thy Almighty name.[1]

DR. WATTS'S VERSION OF THE 21ST PSALM.

5
When thou against them dost engage
　Thy just, but dreadful, doom;
Shall like a fiery oven's rage,
　Their hopes and them consume.

6
Thus, Lord, thy wondrous power declare,
　And thus exalt thy fame;
Whilst we glad songs of praise prepare
　For thine Almighty name.[2]

TATE AND BRADY'S VERSION OF THE 112TH PSALM.

1
That man is blest who stands in awe
Of God, and loves his sacred law;
His seed on earth shall be renowned,
And with successive honors crowned.

2
His house the seat of wealth shall be,
An inexhausted treasury;
His justice free from all decay,
Shall blessings to his heirs convey.

3
The soul that's filled with virtue's light,
Shines brightest in affliction's night;
To pity the distress'd inclin'd,
As well as just to all mankind.

4
His lib'ral favors he extends,
To some he gives, to others lends;
Yet what his charity impairs,
He saves by prudence in affairs.

DR. WATTS'S VERSON OF THE 112TH PSALM.

1
That man is blest who stands in awe
Of God, and loves his sacred law;
　His seed on earth shall be renowned;
His house, the seat of wealth, shall be
An inexhausted treasury,
　And with successive honors crown'd.

2
His liberal favors he extends,
To some he gives, to others lends;
　A generous pity fills his mind:
Yet what his charity impairs,
He saves by prudence in affairs;
　And thus he's just to all mankind.

3
His hands, while they his alms bestowed,
His glory's future harvest sow'd;
　The sweet remembrance of the just
Like a green root revives and bears
A train of blessings for his heirs,
　When dying nature sleeps in dust.

---

[1] It will be seen, at once, how far this Psalm has been altered by Dr. Watts. The Presbyterian Old School Collection has altered it still more by interpolating two stanzas.

[2] Watts's note: "I have borrowed almost all these stanzas from Mr. Tate's version, and they seem very applicable to his present Majesty King George," 1716.

QUOTATIONS BY DR. WATTS.

TATE AND BRADY'S VERSION OF THE 112TH PSALM.	DR. WATTS'S VERSION OF THE 112TH PSALM.

TATE AND BRADY'S VERSION OF THE 112TH PSALM.

5
Beset with threatening dangers round,
Unmoved shall he maintain his ground;
The sweet remembrance of the just
Shall flourish when he *sleeps in dust.*

6
Ill tidings never can surprise
His heart, that fixed on God relies;
On safety's rock he sits, and sees
The shipwreck of his enemies.

7
His hands, while they his alms bestow'd,
His glory's future harvest sow'd,
Whence he shall reap wealth, fame, renown,
A temp'ral and eternal crown.

8
The wicked shall his triumph see,
And gnash their teeth in agony:
While their unrighteous hopes decay,
And vanish with themselves away.

DR. WATTS'S VERSION OF THE 112TH PSALM.

4
Beset with threatening dangers round,
Unmoved shall he maintain his ground;
His conscience holds his courage up:
The soul that's filled with virtue's light,
Shines brightest in affliction's night:
And sees in darkness beams of hope.

5
Ill tidings never can surprise
His heart that fix'd on God relies,
Though waves and tempests roar around:
Safe on the *rock he sits, and sees*
The shipwreck of his enemies,
And all their hopes and glory drown'd.

6
The wicked shall his triumph see,
And gnash their teeth in agony,
To find their expectations crossed:
They and their envy, pride, and spite,
Sink down to everlasting night,
And all their names in darkness lost.[1]

TATE AND BRADY'S VERSION OF THE 113TH PSALM.

1
Ye saints and *servants of the Lord,*
The triumphs *of his name record;*
His sacred name forever bless,
Where'er the circling sun displays
His rising beams or setting rays,
Due praise to his great name address.

2
God through the world extends his sway;
The regions of eternal day
But shadows of his glory are.

DR. WATTS'S VERSION OF THE 113TH PSALM.

1
Ye that delight to *serve the Lord,*
The honors *of his name record,*
His sacred name forever bless:
Where'er the circling sun displays
His rising beams or setting rays,
Let lands and seas his power confess.

2
Not time, nor Nature's narrow rounds,
Can give his vast dominion bounds;
The heavens are far below his height:

---

[1] Watts's note: "Many lines of this metre, and some of the next Psalm, Proper Metre, are borrowed from Mr. Tate's version."

TATE AND BRADY'S VERSION OF THE 113TH PSALM.	DR. WATTS'S VERSION OF THE 113TH PSALM.
To him, whose majesty excels, Who made *the heaven* in which he dwells, *Let no created* power *compare.*	*Let no created* greatness dare With our eternal God *compare,* Armed with his uncreated might.
3	3
Though 'tis beneath his state *to view* In highest heaven *what angels do,* Yet he to earth vouchsafes his care; *He takes the needy from* his cell, Advancing him in courts to dwell, *Companion* to the greatest there.	He bows his glorious head *to view* *What* the bright hosts of *angels do,* And bends *his care* to mortal things; His sovereign hand exalts the poor; *He takes the needy from* the door, And makes them *company* for kings.
4	4
When childless families despair, He sends the blessing of an heir *To rescue their expiring name;* Makes her, that barren was, to bear, And joyfully her fruit to rear: O then extol *his* matchless *fame!*	*When childless families despair, He sends the blessing of an heir* *To rescue their expiring name;* The mother, with a thankful voice, Proclaims his praises and her joys; Let every age advance *his fame.*

TATE AND BRADY'S VERSION OF THE 139TH PSALM.	WATTS'S VERSION OF THE 139TH PSALM.
	First Part.
1	1
Thou, Lord, by strictest *search* hast known *My rising* up and laying down; *My* secret *thoughts are known to* thee, Known long *before* conceived by me.	*Lord, thou* hast *search'd* and seen me through; *Thine eye* commands with piercing view *My rising* and my resting hours, My heart and flesh with all their powers.
2	2
Thine eye my bed and path surveys, My public haunts and private ways; Thou *know'st* what 'tis *my lips* would vent My yet unutter'd *words'* intent.	*My thoughts, before* they are my own, *Are to* my God distinctly *known;* He knows the *words* I mean to speak, Ere from *my* opening *lips* they break.
3	3
Surrounded by *thy power, I stand;* On every side *I find thy hand.* O skill, for human reach too *high!* Too dazzling bright for mortal eye!	Within *thy* circling *power I stand;* On every side *I find thy hand:* Awake, asleep, at home, abroad, I am surrounded still with God.

QUOTATIONS BY DR. WATTS.

Tate and Brady's Version of the 139th Psalm.	Watts's Version of the 139th Psalm.
	4 Amazing knowledge, vast and great! What large extent! what lofty height! My soul, with all the powers I boast, Is in the boundless prospect lost.
4 O *could I so* perfidious be, To think of once deserting thee! *Where, Lord, could I thy* influence *shun?* *Or whither from thy* presence *run?*	6 Could I so false, so faithless prove, To quit thy service and thy love, *Where, Lord, could I thy* presence *shun,* *Or from thy* dreadful glory *run?*
5 *If up to heaven I take my flight,* *'Tis there thou dwell'st enthroned in light;* *Or* sink *to hell's* infernal plains, *'Tis there* almighty *vengeance reigns.*	7 *If up to heaven I take my flight,* *'Tis there thou dwell'st enthroned in light;* *Or* dive *to hell,* — *there vengeance reigns,* And Satan groans beneath thy chains.
6 *If I the morning's* wings could gain, And *fly beyond the western* main, *Thy swifter hand would first arrive,* *And there arrest thy fugitive.*	8 *If,* mounted on a *morning* ray, *I fly beyond the western* sea, *Thy swifter hand would first arrive,* *And there arrest thy fugitive.*
7 *Or should I try to shun thy sight,* *Beneath the* sable *wings of night,* *One glance* from *thee, one piercing ray,* *Would kindle darkness into day.*	9 *Or should I try to shun thy sight,* *Beneath the* spreading *veil of night,* *One glance* of *thine, one piercing ray,* *Would kindle darkness into day.*
8 *The veil of night is no disguise,* *No screen from thy all-searching eyes:* *Through midnight shades* thou find'st the way, As in the *blazing noon* of day.	11 *The veil of night is no disguise;* *No screen from thy all-searching eyes:* Thy hand can seize thy foes as soon *Through midnight shades,* as blazing noon.
	Second Part.
10 I'll praise thee *from whose hands I came,* *A work of such a curious frame:* The *wonders* thou *in me* hast shown, My soul with grateful joy must own.	1 'Twas *from thy hand,* my God, *I came,* *A work of such a curious frame:* In me thy fearful *wonders* shine, And each proclaims thy skill divine.

Tate and Brady's Version of the 139th Psalm.	Watts's Version of the 139th Psalm.
11 *Thine eyes my* substance *did survey,* While *yet* a lifeless mass it *lay,* In secret how exactly wrought, Ere from its dark enclosure brought. **12** Thou didst the shapeless embryo see, Its parts were registered by thee : *Thou saw'st the daily growth they took,* *Formed by the model of thy book.*	**2** *Thine eyes did* all *my* limbs *survey,* Which *yet* in dark confusion *lay;* *Thou saw'st the daily growth they took,* *Formed by the model of thy book.*
13 Let me acknowledge, too, O God, That *since* this maze of *life I* trod, *Thy thoughts of love to me surmount* *The power of numbers to recount.*	**6** Lord, *since* in my advancing age I've acted on *life's* busy stage, *Thy thoughts of love to me surmount* *The power of numbers to recount.*
14 Far sooner *could I* reckon o'er The *sands* upon *the ocean's shore :* Each morn revising what I've done, I find th' account but new begun.	**7** *I could* survey *the ocean* o'er, And count each *sand* that makes *the shore,* Before my swiftest thoughts could trace The numerous wonders of thy grace.
	Third Part. **2** Does not my soul detest and *hate* The sons of malice and deceit ? Those that oppose thy laws and thee, I count them enemies to me.
17 Who practise enmity to thee, Shall utmost *hatred* have from me ; Such men I utterly detest, As if they were my foes profest.	
18 Search, try, O God, my thoughts and heart, *If mischief lurks* in any part ; Correct me *where I go astray,* And guide *me in thy perfect way.*	**4** Doth secret *mischief lurk* within ? Do I indulge some unknown sin ? O turn my feet, whene'er *I stray,* And lead *me in thy perfect way.*[1]

---

[1] Watts's note: "In this noble Psalm I have not refused the aid of my predecessors, chiefly Mr. Tate. In some places where I have borrowed, I hope I have improved the verse; and in others, my own design constrained me to leave out the words of a more poetic sound, such as 'infernal plains,' 'morning's wings,' 'western main,' 'sable wings of night,' 'shapeless embryo,' 'maze of life,' etc. : yet I have endeavored to maintain the spirit of the Psalmist in plainer language."

QUOTATIONS BY DR. WATTS.

BISHOP PATRICK'S VERSION OF THE 6TH PSALM.

1
Lord, *I can suffer thy rebukes,*
 When thou with kindness dost chastise;
But *thy fierce wrath I cannot bear;*
 O let not this against me rise.

2
Pity my languishing estate;
 And those perplexities *I feel,*
While crushéd by *thy heavy hand;*
 O let thy gentler touches heal.

4
See how I pass my weary days
 In sighs and groans; and when 'tis night,
I drown *my bed* and self in *tears:*
 My grief consumes and dims my sight.

DR. WATTS'S VERSION OF THE 6TH PSALM.

1
Lord, *I can suffer thy rebukes,*
 When thou with kindness dost chastise;
But *thy fierce wrath I cannot bear;*
 O let it *not against me rise!*

2
Pity my languishing estate,
 And ease the sorrows that *I feel;*
The wounds *thy heavy hand* hath made,
 O let thy gentler touches heal!

3
See how I pass my weary days
 In sighs and groans; and when 'tis night,
My bed is watered with my *tears;*
 My grief consumes and dims my sight.[1]

BISHOP PATRICK'S VERSION OF THE 63D PSALM.

1
Early, O Lord, *my fainting soul*
 Thy mercy doth implore;
No traveller in desert lands
 Can thirst *for water more.*

2
I long to appear as I was wont,
 Within thy holy *place;*
Thy power and glory to behold,
 And to obtain *thy grace.*

3
For *life* itself, *without thy love,*
 No relish doth *afford;*
No other *joys* can equal this,
 To serve and praise *the Lord.*

4
I'll therefore make *my* prayers *to* him,
 And praise him *whilst I live;*
This, like the choicest *dainties,* will
 Both *food* and *pleasure give.*

DR. WATTS'S VERSION OF THE 63D PSALM.

2
My thirsty fainting soul
 Thy mercy doth implore;
Not travellers in desert lands
 Can pant *for water more.*

3
Within thy churches, Lord,
 I long to find my place,
Thy power and glory to behold,
 And feel *thy* quickening *grace.*

4
For *life without thy love*
 No relish can *afford;*
No joy can be compar'd to *this,*
 To serve and please *the Lord.*

5
To thee *I'll* lift my hands,
 And praise thee *while I live;*
Not the rich *dainties* of a feast
 Such *food* or *pleasure give.*

---

[1] Watts's note: "Part of the three first stanzas I have borrowed from Dr. Patrick, being pleased with the agreeable turn he gives to David's sense."

Bishop Patrick's Version of the 63d Psalm.	Dr. Watts's Version of the 63d Psalm.
5	6
When others sleep, my *wakeful* thoughts Present thee *to* my *mind;* And in the *night I think how* good My God has been and *kind.*	In *wakeful* hours at *night* I call my God *to mind;* *I think how* wise thy counsels are, And all thy dealings *kind.*
6	7
Since thou alone *hast been my help,* *To thee* alone I *fly;* And on *thy watchful* Providence, With *cheerfulness rely.*	*Since thou hast been my help,* *To thee* my spirit *flies,* And on *thy watchful* Providence My *cheerful* hope *relies.*[1]

Sir John Denham's Psalms.	Dr. Watts's Psalms.
Psalm 23. 1.	
My shepherd is the living Lord.	My shepherd is the living Lord.
Psalm 80. 1.	
Great Shepherd of thy Israel! Who Joseph like a flock dost guide, Between the cherubims dost dwell.	Great Shepherd of thine Israel, Who didst between the cherubs dwell.
Psalm 89. 1.	
From age to age I will record The truth and mercy of the Lord. His faithfulness as firmly stands, As heaven established by His hands.	Forever shall my song record The truth and mercy of the Lord; Mercy and truth forever stand, Like heaven, established by His hand.
Psalm 94. 1.	
O God, to whom revenge belongs.	O God, to whom revenge belongs.
Psalm 95. 1.	
Come let us sing Jehovah's praise, And in His name rejoice; To our salvation's Rock we'll raise, In sacred hymns, our voice.	Sing to the Lord Jehovah's name, And in His strength rejoice; When his salvation is our theme, Exalted be our voice.
Psalm 100. 1.	
Ye nations of the earth, rejoice.	Ye nations round the earth, rejoice.

[1] Watts's note: "After I had finished the Common Metre of this Psalm, I observed several pious turns of thought in Dr. Patrick's version, which I have copied in this Metre, though with some difficulty because of the shorter lines."

DENHAM.	WATTS.
Psalm 104. 1.	
My soul, thy great Creator praise, When clothed in His celestial rays, He in full majesty appears, And like a robe His glory wears.	My soul, thy great Creator praise, When cloth'd in His celestial rays, He in full majesty appears, And, like a robe, his glory wears.
Psalm 104. 2.	
The skies are for His curtains spread, Th' unfathomed deep He makes his bed, The clouds are His triumphant car, The winds His fleeing coursers are.	The heavens are for his curtains spread, Th' unfathom'd deep he makes his bed; Clouds are His chariot, when He flies On wingéd storms across the skies.
Psalm 104. 3.	
Angels whom His own breath inspires, His ministers, are flaming fires: The earth's foundations by His hand Are poised, and shall forever stand.	Angels, whom His own breath inspires, His ministers, are flaming fires. The world's foundations by His hand Are poised, and shall forever stand.
Psalm 104. 13.	
God from His cloudy cistern pours On the parch'd earth inriching showers.	God, from His cloudy cistern, pours On the parch'd earth enriching show'rs.
Psalm 104. 35.	
But I shall to my Lord and King Eternal Hallelujahs sing.	I to my God, my heavenly King, Immortal Hallelujahs sing.
Psalm 105. 1.	
Give thanks to God, invoke His name.	Give thanks to God, invoke His name.
Psalm 124. 1.	
Had not the Lord maintained our side.	Had not the Lord maintained our side.
Psalm 142. 3.	
My soul was overwhelmed with woe, But thou my paths didst know.	My soul was overwhelm'd with woes, My heart began to break.

It is evident, that some of the psalms here quoted cannot properly be ascribed to the sole authorship of Dr. Watts, as they are by Dr. Worcester and others. If they be attributed to any versifiers, they should be referred in a general way to Watts *and* Tate and Brady, or Dr. Patrick or Sir John Denham, from whom the characteristic features of them were borrowed. It is further evident that these altered forms of the psalms must have "confused" the minds of worshippers in 1719, as much as other quotations have "created disturbance and confusion" in the nineteenth century. The old forms of these psalms were inwrought into the fond associations of thousands. The "new version" of Tate and Brady was an authorized part of the English church service. The dissenting poet of Southampton "dislocated" the favorite stanzas of men, "inverted" the order of long-cherished phrases, impaired the "uniformity" of worship, etc. These were real evils. Were they not counterbalanced by superior advantages? It is also evident, that the charge of "plagiarism," wrongly made against recent poets who have borrowed lines from their predecessors, may, with equal propriety, and, we prefer to say, with equal impropriety, be made against the very prince of our sacred lyrists. From the days of Homer down to those of Shakspeare, from Shakspeare to Longfellow, men have blended with their own verses the phrases, the metaphors, the prevailing air and tone of other poems. The principle on which these and similar poets have incorporated the words of preceding writers with their own words, is the very principle on which the lyrists of the sanctuary have constructed hymns embodying entire stanzas from their predecessors.[1] They have

---

[1] When we begin to insist on entire originality in a hymn, we know not where we can end. Pope writes:

> He from thick films shall purge the visual ray,
> And on the sightless eye-balls pour the day.

There is a striking similarity to these lines in one of the most noted

borrowed sometimes more, sometimes less, from lyrics in which they discovered elements too precious to be lost; but whether more or less, they esteemed the borrowed words as substantially a quotation, and equally justifiable with every other quotation. In all our more popular hymn books, there are what may be termed *composite lyrics,* which are made up of extracts from other songs, and which fuse into *one* hymn the better portions of two or three. In the Presbyterian (Old School) Collection, the 14th, 21st, 33d, 66th, 75th, and 124th Psalms; the 129th, 139th, 169th, 174th, 381st, 559th, 601st hymns, are either "*composite lyrics,*" or else contain new interpolated lines or stanzas; so in the Presbyterian (New School) collection, are psalm 21; hymns 6, 137, 205, 350, 533, 553, 624, 661, and others; likewise in the Connecticut Collection, are the 152d, 220th, 393d, 373d, 699th, and other hymns; also in Mr. Beecher's Plymouth Collection, are the 75th, 215th, 264th, 273rd, 545th, 688th, 813th, 1113th, 1158th, 1256th, 1291st, 1317th, 1318th, and other hymns.

§ 9. *Difficulty of Ascertaining the Original Text of some Hymns.*

" If four persons have used four different selections [of lyrics], it will be found on comparison that many a verse has four different readings, while perhaps the hymns of Doddridge. He was no plagiarist, and still wrote:

> He comes from thickest films of vice
> To clear the mental ray,
> And on the eye-balls of the blind
> To pour celestial day.

original differs from them all; in coming, therefore, to the use of one book, three of them, at least, must find a different reading from that with which they are familiar. In some popular hymns, the various readings are so numerous that identity is almost lost, and the original cannot now be ascertained."[1]

This fact suggests the reason why it has become so common to condemn certain phrases as *departures* from the original, when in fact they are *returns* to it. The author's own words have been stigmatized as innovations, even in a lyric so celebrated as:

> Lo! on a narrow neck of land,
> 'Twixt two unbounded seas I stand;
> *Secure*, insensible! etc.

> O God, my inmost soul convert,
> And deeply on my *thoughtful* heart
> Eternal things impress, etc.[2]

The Village Hymns of Dr. Nettleton, the manual commonly known as Worcester's Watts, the Presbyterian (N. S.) Collection, the Reformed Dutch Hymn Book, and more than one Episcopal Selection, substitute for the second and fifth of the preceding lines: "*Yet how* insensible," "And deeply on my *thoughtless* heart." These latter readings have been even cited, as illustrating the great superiority of the author's own words to the interpolations of critics. But in the first editions of Wesley's lyrics we find the words "*secure*," "*thoughtful*."

---

[1] Preface to the fifty-third edition of the English Baptist Selection of Hymns, p. vi.
[2] See Sabbath Hymn Book, Hymn 495.

Even a hymn so noted and so new as Montgomery's "Forever with the Lord" (Sabbath Hymn Book, 1237), is seldom published correctly. Often it is made to contain the following words:

> My father's house on high,
> Home of my soul, how near
> At times to faith's *far-seeing* eye
> Thy golden gates appear.

Frequently the word *discerning* is substituted for *far-seeing*. In the dislike of such a prosaic term, some have exchanged it for *aspiring*, thus imitating Doddridge, who sings of an "aspiring eye." But others who commend this phrase in Doddridge, condemn it as infelicitous when it appears in Montgomery, and insist that the original *discerning* is more poetic. But the truth is, that not one of these three words was chosen by Montgomery. His term was, — and it is superior to either of the other three, *foreseeing*. It so appears in the earlier and better editions of his works.

The Missionary Hymn of Heber is generally printed with the following inaccuracies:

> "*Shall* we whose souls are lighted," etc.
> "*Shall* we to *man* benighted," etc.
> "Till *earth's* remotest nation," etc.

The editors of the Sabbath Hymn Book originally printed these lines as they were written by their author:

> "*Can* we whose souls are lighted," etc.
> "*Can* we to *men* benighted," etc.
> "Till *each* remotest nation," etc.

By the importunity of a friend, who remonstrated against violating the sacred associations of the word *shall* in the first two of the above cited lines, the editors were induced to restore the common, which is, however, what certain critics are pleased to call a "*garbled*" reading. But it has been necessary to consult numerous editions of Heber's writings, before his own chosen words could be indisputably ascertained. Dr. Raffles of Liverpool possesses the identical manuscript which Bishop Heber sent to the press, and we have now lying before us an exact copy of that manuscript, corresponding precisely with the first printed impressions of the Missionary Hymn, and with the version in the Sabbath Hymn Book (H. 1132) except in the use of "*can*" for "*shall.*"[1]

[1] In a letter from Dr. Raffles to Dr. Lowell Mason, he gives the following information with regard to the origin of the Missionary Hymn:

"Heber, then Rector of Hodnet, married the daughter of Dean Shipley, Rector or Vicar of Wrexham, in North Wales. On a certain Saturday, he came to the house of his father-in-law, who resided at the rectory or vicarage, to remain over Sunday, and preach, in the morning, the first sermon ever preached in that church for the Church Missionary Society. As they sat conversing after dinner in the evening, the Dean said to Heber, 'Now, as you are a poet, suppose you write a hymn for the service to-morrow morning.' Immediately he took pen, ink and paper, and wrote that hymn, which, had he written nothing else, would have immortalized him. He read it to the Dean, and said, 'Will that do?' 'Aye,' he replied, 'and we will have it printed and distributed in the pews, that the people may sing it after the sermon.' 'But,' said Heber, 'to what tune will it go? — Oh,' he added, 'it will go to "'Twas when the seas were roaring."'' And so he wrote in the corner, at the top of the page, ''Twas when the seas were roaring.' What that tune is, I do not know, but it may easily be ascertained. The hymn was printed accordingly, and from the file of the printer I obtained the manuscripts.

I" have seen another version of the story of the hymn, which states that it was on Whitsunday, 1819, and that it was for a sermon in aid of the Society for 'the Propagation of the Gospel in Foreign Parts.' I

• Now if in four such favorite compositions from authors so recent and eminent as Charles Wesley, James Montgomery, and Bishop Heber, the common readings have been inaccurate for so many years, how much more difficult must it be to ascertain the exact form in which older and less familiar hymns, from less conspicuous authors, originally appeared? The difficulty is greater than can be rewarded by the *practical* (we do not say the *historical* and *antiquarian*) results of the

cannot vouch for the correctness of either. "I tell the tale as 'twas told to me.'"

"The only correction in [Heber's] MS. occurs in the seventh line of the second stanza, where he had originally written: "The savage in his blindness," which he altered to: "The heathen in his blindness."

Below the stanzas is written in pencil: "A Hymn to be sung in Wrexham Church, after the sermon, during the collection."

While occupied with this literary reminiscence, we are tempted to publish the notes of the tune to which the Missionary Hymn was first sung; but which has been now supplanted in common use by the tune of Dr. Lowell Mason. The original notes are:

search. Still further, in numerous instances it is not barely arduous, it is impossible to determine which is the primitive of many conflicting versions; and in these instances, the charge of departing from the primitive style is made in blank uncertainty whether the charge be true or false. Here, the author is unknown; there, the original copy is unknown. Even in an author so near us and so noted as Doddridge, we are not always sure that we have his own words. The honest Job Orton, who first edited Doddridge's hymns, says in his first Preface to them, p. x.: " There may perhaps be some improprieties [in these hymns] owing to my not being able to read the author's manuscript in particular places, and being obliged, without a poetic genius, to supply those deficiencies, whereby the beauty of the stanza may be greatly defaced, though the sense is preserved." With some persons, if a hymn deviates from Worcester's Watts, the deviation is thought to be a departure from the original; but a careful scrutiny has disclosed the fact that in only nine hundred and twenty-five of even the more common lyrics in that manual, there are fourteen hundred and fourteen alterations, besides a large number of omissions. There is a multitude of readers who rely implicitly on the text of the Presbyterian (Old School) Collection, and regard every instance of departure from this text as a violation of the rights of authorship; yet in seven hundred and forty of the more common lyrics in that Collection, there are thirteen hundred and twenty-seven variations, exclusive of the frequent omissions. In the preface or advertisement of that manual it is stated: " The psalms have been left without alteration; the Committee believing that it would be extremely difficult to furnish a more acceptable version than that of Watts. The hymns, as may be seen, have undergone great and essential modifications," p. 3. But in the three hundred and forty-five versions of psalms contained in the Collection, there are six hundred and ninety-seven alterations. Indeed there are not one hundred and ten of these psalms unaltered. In seven hundred and seventy-four of the most noted hymns in the Presbyterian (New School) Collection, there are thirteen hundred and thirty-six variations of the original text. In eight hundred and ten familiar hymns of the Connecticut Hymn Book (two hundred and fifty at least of which are hallowed by long use), there are eleven hundred and twenty-six changes. In five hundred and fifty well-known hymns of Mr. Beecher's Plymouth Collection, there are nine hundred and seven changes. In many English manuals for song, the departures from the original text are still more numerous. We believe that there has not been published, either in England or America, during the last thirty years, a single hymn book in which there are not more changes of the text than there are hymns. Among the less noted lyrics, the diversity is greater than among the more noted; and amid all this diversity the labor of determining the author's primitive reading is often great, and not seldom utterly fruitless. If editors have blundered in altering the text, critics have blundered far more in conjecturing what was the first draught. On this theme, as well as others, we are apt to be positive in proportion to our ignorance.

There has been a singular and a prolonged misunderstanding with regard to both the text and the authorship of a noted hymn, which appears in the following, among other versions:

Hymn as Ascribed to Toplady.	Hymn Represented as Altered.

Blow ye the trumpet, blow,
  The gladly solemn sound ;
 Let all the nations know,
  To earth's remotest bound :
 The year of jubilee is come,
 Return, ye ransom'd sinners, home !
	Blow ye the trumpet, blow
	  The gladly-solemn sound ;
	 Let all the nations know,
	  To earth's remotest bound :
	 The year of jubilee is come ;
	 Return, ye ransom'd sinners, home.

Exalt the Lamb of God,
  The *sin*-atoning Lamb ;
 Redemption *by* his blood,
  Through all the world proclaim :
 The year of jubilee is come ;
 Return, ye ransom'd sinners, home.
	Jesus, our great High Priest,
	  Hath full atonement made :
	 Ye weary spirits, rest ;
	  Ye *mournful* souls, be glad :
	 The year of jubilee is come ;
	 Return, ye ransom'd sinners, home.

Ye who have sold for nought,
  The heritage above,
 Come take it back unbought,
  The gift of Jesus' love :
 The year of jubilee is come ;
 Return, ye ransom'd sinners, home.
	Extol the Lamb of God, —
	  The *all*-atoning Lamb ;
	 Redemption *in* his blood
	  Throughout the world proclaim :
	 The year of jubilee is come ;
	 Return, ye ransom'd sinners, home.

Ye slaves of sin and hell,
  Your liberty receive ;
 And safe in Jesus dwell,
  And blest in Jesus live :
 The year of jubilee is come ;
 Return, ye ransom'd sinners, home.
	Ye slaves of sin and hell,
	  Your liberty receive ;
	 And safe in Jesus dwell,
	  And blest in Jesus live :
	 The year of jubilee is come ;
	 Return, ye ransom'd sinners, home.

The gospel trumpet hear,
  The news of *pard'ning* grace ;
 Ye happy souls, draw near,
  Behold your Saviour's face :
 The year of jubilee is come,
 Return, ye ransom'd sinners, home.
	Ye who have sold for naught
	  Your heritage above,
	 Shall have it back unbought,
	  The gift of Jesus' love :
	 The year of jubilee is come ;
	 Return, ye ransom'd sinners, home.

Jesus, our great high priest,
  Has full atonement made ;
 Ye weary spirits, rest ;
  Ye *mourning* souls, be glad :
 The year of jubilee is come,
 Return, ye ransom'd sinners, home.
	The gospel trumpet hear, —
	  The news of *heavenly* grace ;
	 And, saved from earth, appear
	  Before your Saviour's face :
	 The year of jubilee is come ;
	 Return, ye ransom'd sinners, home.

This hymn is ascribed to Toplady in Worcester's Watts, in the Methodist Protestant, the Presbyterian (Old School), the Connecticut, the Dutch Reformed Church, the Plymouth, and, indeed, in nearly all the

Collections that adopt the hymn as it is given in the left hand column above. Many admirers of Toplady seem to reason thus: "*he* was a more gifted lyrist than his successors; *therefore* his version is superior: the original is always better than the altered form; his is the original; therefore it is the preferable one." But the fact is, that Toplady did not publish this hymn until 1776, and the hymn is found as early as 1755, in a little tract entitled "Hymns for New Year's Day," containing only seven odes, and all of them by Charles Wesley. Toplady *altered* the hymn somewhat, and published it *as modified*. Some of his admirers, then, must reason thus: " Toplady was superior to Wesley; therefore his version of this hymn is to be preferred to Wesley's: the original is always superior to the altered form; therefore Wesley's *first* draught must be preferred to Toplady's *second*." The Sabbath Hymn Book has rejected nearly all of the alterations made by Toplady, and has omitted (as several other manuals have done) the fourth and fifth of Wesley's stanzas. But an advocate for the original readings has condemned the Sabbath Hymn Book, because it has "omitted" these twelve of the original thirty-six lines, and has "altered" the hymn; and then the reviewer adds: two of the stanzas are "*most unpoetically transposed. By a curious coincidence the genius of Toplady is again the victim.*" It is indeed curious. But the transpositions are all on the other side. The Sabbath Hymn Book rejects the transpositions made by the "genius of Toplady"; it holds fast the greater part of the words given up by that genius, and excludes the greater part of his interpolations, which may now be called superior, because original![1] This is one of a hundred instances in which we believe that a verse is admirable, when we imagine it to have come from a favorite lyrist, but if that same good come out of Nazareth, it is a root out of a dry ground.

§ 10. *Changes in the Text, as affecting its Biblical and Evangelical Character.*

"We must have versifications of all the Psalms, because our hymn books must be modelled after the Bible." This is a common plea. It is an extravagant expression of a great truth. Our hymn books *must* be conformed to the standard of the inspired word. A *sacred* song becomes, often, the more poetical by becoming more biblical. The word of God has in and around itself a *poetic* association. When a hymn is transformed from its mere human to a divine idiom, it is restored to its proper original. If there come forth an aroma from the very name of Watts, there comes a still more fragrant incense from the name of David. If there be a kind of poetry in the mere fact that a phrase has been sanctioned by Reginald

---

[1] When the preceding paragraph was originally written, we supposed that *all* of the changes commonly made in Wesley's hymn were the work of Mr. Toplady. But on a recent inspection of Toplady's "Psalms and Hymns for Public and Private Worship," First Edition, 1776, we find that he transposed the stanzas, and altered about a dozen of the words. One of his alterations is not copied into the popular version of the hymn. He writes: "*Through all the lands* proclaim," for the original, "*Throughout the world* proclaim." On the other hand, he retains Wesley's words in the following, commonly altered, lines: "*Extol* the Lamb of God," "*Shall have* it back unbought," "Redemption *by* his blood," " Ye *mournful* souls, be glad."

Heber and Henry Kirke White; yet more, that it has been sanctified by Isaiah or Jeremiah. A profound emotion is often excited, by the sudden out-breaking of an inspired thought or phrase from the human song. The Bible, too, is our standard of sentiment, as well as style, and it is often an advantage to see that our poetry is the exact expression of revealed science. "Show thy *reconciling* face," is not only more poetical, but more instructive and biblical than "Show thy *reconciled* face,"[1] as, in the scriptures, God is repeatedly affirmed to "reconcile" men to himself; never, to be "reconciled" to men.

In such changes as the following, the biblical language is more nearly retained, by altering the phrases of the hymn:

Original Form.	Sabbath Hymn Book.
	Hymn 170.
What's man, say *I*, Lord, that Thou *lov'st* To *keep* him in thy mind?	Lord, *what is man, that thou shouldst deign* To *bear* him in thy mind?
	Hymn 219.
Thy friendly *crook* shall give me aid.	Thy friendly *rod* shall give me aid.
	Hymn 253.
The *med'cine* of my broken heart.	The *healing* of my broken heart.
	Hymn 312.
Till Christ, with his reviving light, *Over* our souls arise.	Till Christ, with his reviving light, *Upon* our souls arise.
	Hymn 461.
Nor in thy righteous anger swear, T' *exclude* me from thy people's rest.	Nor in thy righteous anger swear *I shall not see* thy people's rest.
	Hymn 600.
Mark and revenge iniquity.	*Be strict to mark* iniquity.

[1] Sabbath Hymn Book, Hymn 55. See also Presbyterian (O. S.) Collection.

Original Form.	Sabbath Hymn Book.
	Hymn 1038.
A *fane unbuilt* by hands.	*A house not made* by hands.
Being of beings! may our praise Thy courts with grateful *fragrance* fill.	*Lord God of hosts!* oh! may our praise Thy courts with grateful *incense* fill.
Sweet cherubs learn Immanuel's name.	*Bright seraphs* learn Immanuel's name.
The *antidote* of death.	The *conqueror* of death.
Fanned by some *angel's purple* wing.	Fanned by some *guardian angel's* wing.
"The Lord has risen indeed : *Then hell* has lost its prey."	The Lord is risen indeed : *The grave* has lost its prey.
	Hymn 474.
Jesus, our Lord, *arise!* Scatter our enemies And *make them* fall.	Jesus, our Lord, *descend;* From all our foes defend : Nor let us fall.
	Hymn 1210.
Up to the Lord our *flesh* shall fly.	Up to the Lord our *souls* shall fly.
	Hymn 316.
That were a *present* far too small.	That were an *offering* far too small.
	Hymn 855.
The *Patron* of mankind appears.	The *Guardian* of mankind appears.
	Hymn 952.
Come, *at the shrine of God* fervently kneel.	Come *to the mercy-seat,* fervently kneel.
	Hymn 1193.
Where is, O Grave! thy victory now? And where, insidious Death, thy sting?	O Grave, where is thy victory now? And where, O Death, where is thy sting?
	Hymn 388.
Say "Live forever, *wondrous* king : Born to redeem and strong to save! *Then ask the monster, where's his sting,* And *where's* thy victory, boasting grave?	Say, "Live forever, *glorious* King, Born to redeem, and strong to save; *Where now, O Death, where is thy sting?* And *where's* thy victory, boasting grave?
Nor leave thy *sacred* seat.	Nor leave thy *mercy* seat.
	Hymn 873.
And, *midst th' embraces of his God.*	And, *in the Father's bosom blest.*

EVANGELICAL STYLE OF HYMNS. 209

ORIGINAL FORM.	SABBATH HYMN BOOK.
Thy sacramental cup I'll take.	*Salvation's sacred* cup I'll take.
Oh *bid us turn, Almighty Lord!*	Oh *turn us, turn us, mighty* Lord!
	Hymn 363.
Erect your heads, eternal gates.	*Lift up* your heads, eternal gates.

There are many hymns which, if they do not become more biblical in language, yet become more biblical, or at least more evangelical in sentiment and spirit, by slight modifications of their style. Sometimes they contain phrases of classical but pagan origin; sometimes, of the fashionable secular poetry; sometimes, of economical prose; which may well be exchanged for phrases more intimately associated with the Gospel.

ORIGINAL FORM.	ALTERED FORM.
He rears his *red right* arm on high, And *ruin bares* the sword.	He rears his *mighty* arm on high, *They fall before* his sword.
The *muse* stands trembling while she sings.	*My soul* stands trembling while she sings.
Chained to his throne a volume lies.	*Before* his throne a volume lies.
Go, return, immortal Saviour!	*Reäscend,* immortal Saviour!
He bids his *blasts* the fields deform; Then, when his thunders cease, He *sits like an angel 'mid* the storm, And *smiles* the winds to peace.	He bids his *gales* the fields deform; Then, when his thunders cease, He *paints his rainbow on* the storm, And *lulls* the winds to peace.
The king of terrors, then, would be A welcome messenger to me, *That bids* me come away: Unclogged by earth or earthly things, I'd mount *upon his sable wings* To everlasting day.	The king of terrors, then, would be A welcome messenger to me, *To bid* me come away: Unclogged by earth or earthly things, I'd mount, *I'd fly with eager* wings, To everlasting day.

It is indeed a biblical truth that there are evil spirits, and that incorrigible men will be consigned

18*

to "everlasting fire, prepared for the devil and his angels." But the Bible does not inform us of the unrenewed soul, that "*devils plunge it* down to hell." This line of Dr. Watts produces an impression more exactly biblical, and better adapted to the spirit of sacred harmony, if it be modified, at least as much as in the Sabbath Hymn Book, H. 1172:

> Up to the courts where angels dwell,
>   It [the soul] mounts triumphant there,
> Or *plunges guilty* down to hell,
>   In infinite despair.

Hymnologists have differed among themselves with regard to the propriety of the line: "When God the mighty Maker died."[1] The Connecticut Hymn Book has written it: "When Christ, the Lord of glory died." The Church Psalmody has: "When Christ th' almighty Saviour died." Others have: "When Christ, the mighty Saviour died," or "When the almighty Saviour died," or "When Christ, the mighty Maker died." The line is thus changed, because it is said to be unscriptural, as well as revolting, to speak of the death of God. Others contend that the idea is scriptural, and they refer to the passage (of which there are various readings, however): "Feed the church of *God*, which *he* hath purchased with *his own* blood;" Acts 20:28. But the contested line of Watts has become endeared to so many Christians, and is so carefully inwrought into the inmost texture of his celebrated Hymn (the ninth of his second

---

[1] An old German hymn contains the couplet:

> O welcher noth
> Gott selbst ist todt.

book), that it is probably safer to retain it, even although it is repugnant to the tastes of a large, and certainly an honored, minority of those who use it. A similar reason exists for retaining the lines, "Beheld our rising God," and "The rising God forsakes the tomb," in the Sabbath Hymn Book, Hymns 59, 358. Still there can be no doubt, that the ordinary style of the Bible is to represent *Christ*, rather than *God*, as dying; just as it represents God, and not the son of Mary, as eternal. The usual style of the Bible then is more exactly represented by the lines:

> "Oh, the sweet wonders of that cross
> Where *my Redeemer* loved and died;"
> (*Hymn* 348.)

than by the original lines of Watts:

> "Oh, the sweet wonders of that cross,
> Where *God the Saviour* loved and died."

One of Dr. Watts's deeply affecting hymns begins thus: "Here at thy cross, my *dying* God." The Presbyterian (Old School) Collection modifies the line: "Here at thy cross, *incarnate* God." The Sabbath Hymn Book substitutes the words, "my *gracious* Lord." In the fourth stanza of the hymn, Watts wrote:

> Hosanna to my *dying* God,
> And my *best honors* to his name.

The Presbyterian (Old School) Collection expunges *dying* and supplies its place by "Saviour." The Sabbath Hymn Book has:

> Hosanna to my *Saviour* God,
> And *loudest praises* to his name.

Whatever of doubt may linger in any mind with regard to the wisdom of these changes, there can be none with regard to the impropriety of such stanzas as those of Watts, Book I. 13:

> " This infant is the mighty God,
> Come to be suckled and adored."

Dr. Worcester omitted this couplet from his Christian Psalmody, but felt compelled to insert it in his Worcester's Watts.

We are accustomed to the biblical phrases: Christ will *draw* all men unto him, the Father *draws* his children to him; but we are not so much wonted to the phrase, that God *forces* us to become his friends. Therefore, it is more agreeable to the inspired idiom to celebrate the love " That sweetly *drew* us in," than the love " That sweetly *forced* us in;" see Sabbath Hymn Book, Hymn 1055.

§ 11. *Alterations in the Text, as affecting its Dignity.*

" Lift up thy feet, and march in haste." This is the call sent up to Jehovah in the seventy-fourth of Dr. Watts's Psalms. It is made more harmonious to an occidental ear, by an alteration in the Church Psalmist:[1] " Oh, come to our relief in haste." It is defended by some as an imitation of the old Hebrew Psalm 74:3. But this may be translated: " Lift thy steps to the perpetual ruins." Besides, if our English version were the only accurate one: " Lift up

---

[1] Presbyterian (New School) Hymn Book, Ps. 74.

thy feet unto the perpetual desolations," it would not justify the paraphrase of Watts. There are inspired words, which ought not to be repeated except with literal exactness. This version of Watts is one example; there are many far more faulty instances, proving that in the heat of the first composition, an author sometimes neglects, if he does not despise, that elevated manner, which, even when dependent on the *minutiæ* of rhetoric, is singularly conducive to the great ends of worship. A change so insignificant as that of the familiar, for the solemn style, will often elevate a domestic song into a sacred hymn, a stirring lyric into a solemn prayer. "To what a stubborn frame, *Hath* sin reduced our mind," is a more dignified couplet than the original "*Has* sin," etc. A mother, retiring from her household for her twilight devotion, may well sing, "I love to steal awhile away, From *little ones* and care;" but when she prepares these lines for the sanctuary, she may exalt them by saying, "From *every cumbering* care." Dr. Watts, in view of death, addresses his Saviour thus: "Scarce shall I feel death's cold embrace, If Christ be in my arms." The Presbyterian (N. S.) Hymn Book has made the line less indecorous by changing it thus: "While in the Saviour's arms." Many a hymn composed for the seclusion of private thought, has admitted commonplaces which need to be transformed into more select idioms, when that same hymn is transferred from the closet to the temple. The persecuted Madame Guyon wrote in a familiar way:

> "*My Love*, how full of sweet content
> *I pass my years of banishment!*"

but in the assembly of worshippers at the house of God, it is more appropriate to sing:

> " *O Lord*, how full of sweet content
> Our years of pilgrimage are spent!"[1]

A favorite hymn of Watts[2] begins with the stanza:

> He dies, the *Heavenly Lover* dies!
> *The tidings strike a doleful sound*
> On my poor heart-strings: deep he lies
> *In the cold caverns of the ground.*

But there is a greater majesty, as well as a delicate and biblical propriety, in the stanza as thus transformed by John Wesley:

> He dies! the *Friend of sinners* dies;
> *Lo! Salem's daughters weep around:*
> A solemn darkness vails the skies;
> *A sudden trembling shakes the ground.*

So in the following instances, there is either a familiarity or an uncouthness which may fitly give place to a more elevated style:

Original Form.	Sabbath Hymn Book.
	Hymn 433.
When *he*, dear Lord, will bring me home.	When *my* dear Lord will bring me home.
	Hymn 435.
I yield to thy dear *conquering* arms.	*Incarnate God!* now to thine arms.
	Hymn 1252.
Sweet Jesus! every smile of thine.	*My Saviour!* every smile of thine.

[1] Sabbath Hymn Book, Hymn 140.   [2] Ibid., Hymn 358.

DIGNITY OF HYMNS. 215

ORIGINAL FORM.	SABBATH HYMN BOOK.
	Hymn 440.
O dear almighty Lord.	*O thou* almighty Lord.
	Hymn 441.
Jesus! my Shepherd, *Husband,* Friend.	Jesus, my Shepherd, *Guardian,* Friend.
	Hymn 442.
Shepherd, Brother, *Husband,* Friend.	Shepherd, Brother, *Lord and* Friend.
	Hymn 703.
Oh, that I could forever sit *With Mary, at the Master's* feet. (Wesley.)	Oh that I could forever sit *In transport, at my Saviour's* feet.
	Hymn 788.
Oh that I could forever dwell *With Mary, at my Saviour's* feet. (Dr. Reed.)	Oh that I could forever dwell *Delighted at the* Saviour's feet.
	Hymn 886.
While his [God's] *left hand my* head sustains.	While he *my sinking head* sustains.
	Hymn 952.
Here speaks the Comforter, *in God's name,* saying.	Here speaks the Comforter, *tenderly* saying.
	Hymn 312.
And breaks the *cursed* chain.	And breaks *th' accursed* chain.
	Hymn 1267.
By power oppressed, and mocked by pride,— *O God!* is this the crucified?	By power oppressed, and mocked by pride,— *The Nazarene,* the crucified.
Things of precious Christ he took, Gave us hearts and eyes to look.	*Filled our minds with grief and fear, Brought the precious Saviour near.*
	Hymn 1007.
Meet it is that we should own, What thy grace has done for us: Saved we are by grace alone; And we joy to have it thus.	*Joyful are we now to own, Rapture thrills us, as we trace All the deeds thy love has done, All the riches of thy grace.*
	Hymn 13.
My soul doth long, and *almost die,* Thy courts, O Lord, to see.	My soul doth long, and *fainting sigh,* Thy courts, O Lord, to see.
	Hymn 1135.
He shall be damned, who wont believe.	*And they condemned who disbelieve.*
	Hymn 1237.
Uphold thou me, and I shall stand, *Fight,* and I shall prevail.	Uphold thou me, and I shall stand, *Help,* and I shall prevail.

Original Form.	Sabbath Hymn Book.
Such peace as reason never planned, As *worldlings* never knew.	Such peace as reason never planned, Nor *sinners* ever knew.
	Hymn 635.
I want a principle within Of jealous, godly fear; *A sensibility to* sin, A pain to feel it near.	*Oh for* a principle within, Of jealous, godly fear; *Oh for a tender dread of* sin, A pain to feel it near.
	Hymn 708.
I want that grace *that* springs from thee. (Cowper.)	*Oh for* that grace *which* springs from thee.
	Hymn 1034.
And when his saints complain, It sha'nt be said, etc.	*Nor* when his saints complain, *Shall it* be said, etc.
	Hymn 461.
From now my weary soul release.	*O Lord*, my weary soul release.
	Hymn 592.
Oft *abused Thee to* thy face.	Oft *have sinned before* thy face.

§ 12. *Changes in the Text, as affecting its Vivacity.*

"There is no other name than thine," "O speak of Jesus," "I lay my sins on Jesus," "O gift of gifts, O Grace of Faith," "'Tis not that I did choose thee," "Oh where is he that trod the sea," "Come, let us sing the song of songs," "I've found the pearl of greatest price," "There is laid up for me a crown," "Thou must go forth alone, my soul," "That solemn hour will come for me," "Gently, my Saviour, let me down," "No, no, it is not dying," "I love thee, O my God," "Jesus, the very thought of thee," "Thy mighty working, mighty God," "Oft in sorrow, oft in woe," "Stand up, stand up for Jesus," "Oh where are kings and empires now,"[1] — as we listen to the

---

[1] Sabbath Hymn Book, 302, 434, 746, 240, 297, 339, 439, 753, 1173, 1174, 1183, 1177, 681, 687, 1154, 896, 902, 1038.

ring of the true metal in lyrics like these, we long for the day when men will be allured to the sanctuary by the liveliness of the song, and the heartiness with which the whole assembly offer it to the Lord. We are confident that often the vivacity of hymns has been impaired by so altering them, as to secure some other excellence. In aiming at one perfection, critics have, here and there, sacrificed a different and a higher one. The allegation is not true, however, that the changes in our psalmody have always been intended to improve its musical adaptation, at the expense of its poetic liveliness. Certainly this has not been the design of such changes as : " *Swift* on the wings of time it flies," for " On *all* the wings of time it flies;" "*Wide* let the earth resound the deeds;" for ",Let the wide earth resound the deeds;" " *Come let us* bow before his feet," for " *Now we may* bow before his feet." Instead of deadening our psalmody, wise alterations will enliven it. Many hymns, — frequently those of Doddridge, — gain a new animation by so slight a change as that of a masculine or feminine for a neuter pronoun; a singular for a plural noun; the present for the past tense, thus:

ORIGINAL FORM.	SABBATH HYMN BOOK.
	Hymn 736.
Still would my spirit rest on thee, *Its* Saviour and *its* God.	Still would my spirit rest on thee, *My* Saviour and *my* God.
	Hymn 736.
Till love dissolves my inmost soul, At *its* Redeemer's feet.	Till love dissolves my inmost soul, At *my* Redeemer's feet.
	Hymn 736.
And tell the boldest *foes* without That Jesus reigns within.	And tell the boldest *foe* without That Jesus reigns within.
	Hymn 961.
God of my life through all *its* days	God of my life through all *my* days.

ORIGINAL FORM.	SABBATH HYMN BOOK.
	Hymn 961.
When death o'er nature shall prevail,	When death o'er nature shall prevail,
And all *its* powers of language fail.	And all *my* powers of language fail.
	Hymn 356.
In wild dismay |*Fell* to the ground	In wild dismay |*Fall* to the ground
The guard around|And *sunk* away.	The guard around|And *sink* away.

It is an interesting fact, that the same excellences which augment the solemnity of worship, may also favor its vivacity. While they prevent giddiness they promote liveliness. The *prayer* is more animating than the *history;* the personal appeal, than the instructive comment. Dr. Watts wrote the inimitable poem, " *Keep silence all created things,*" in twelve stanzas, not designed at first for public worship, but now adapted to the sanctuary by omitting a third or half of its verses. As thus accommodated we often find the animated prayer: " My God, I *would not long* to see, My fate with curious eyes." But in the original, we have the more biographical and less precative announcement: " My God, I *never longed* to see," etc.

The following Hymn of Doddridge becomes the more inspiring, when it is felt to be our own *present* utterance in relation to *present* scenes; our united expression of what *is*, rather than an individual and historical narrative of what *was*.

THE PRIVATE POEM.	THE GENERAL HYMN.[1]
My Helper God! I bless *his* name:	*Our* Helper God! *we* bless *thy* name,
The same *his* power, *his* grace the same.	The same *thy* power, *thy* grace the same;

[1] See Sabbath Hymn Book, Hymn 1151. The same is found in the Presbyterian (N. S.) Collection, and with different modifications in "Hymns for the Church of Christ," compiled by Drs. Hedge and Huntington.

THE PRIVATE POEM.	THE GENERAL HYMN.
The tokens of *his friendly* care, Open, and crown, and close the year.	The tokens of *thy loving* care Open and crown and close the year.
I 'midst ten thousand *dangers* stand, Supported by *his* guardian hand; And see, when *I* survey my ways, Ten thousand monuments of praise.	*Amid* ten thousand *snares we* stand, Supported by *thy* guardian hand; And see, when *we* survey *our* ways, Ten thousand monuments of praise.
Thus far *his* arm hath led *me* on; Thus far *I* make *his* mercy known; And while *I* tread this desert land, New mercies shall new songs demand.	Thus far *thine* arm hath led *us* on; Thus far *we* make *thy* mercy known: And while *we* tread this desert land, New mercies shall new songs demand.
My grateful *soul*, on Jordan's shore, Shall raise one sacred pillar more; Then bear in *his* bright courts above, Inscriptions of immortal love.	*Our* grateful *souls* on Jordan's shore, Shall raise one sacred pillar more; Then bear in *thy* bright courts above, Inscriptions of immortal love.

Sometimes the vivacity of a hymn is increased, by changing its measure from the long to the common. The common metre is more permanently enlivening, than any other. Hence it is the prevailing measure of the old English ballad. By repeating several times continuously a stanza in the long metre (having four lines, each of them divided into eight syllables, four feet), and then immediately repeating a stanza of the common metre (having four lines, of which the first and third have four feet, eight syllables, and the second and fourth have only three feet, six syllables), we cannot fail to notice the superior ease, elasticity, liveliness of the more varied measure. Let the experiment be tried on the simple letters of the alphabet, arranged in Iambic feet, and by frequent repetition of them, especially with music, we soon become wearied with the long-drawn monotony of the one measure, and are suddenly relieved by the quicker, more flexile movement of the other. We are aware that the sentiment of some hymns requires the majestic and uniform rhythm of the old hundredth psalm. "Not to the mount that burned with flame," "Lord, my weak thought in vain would climb," "Thee we adore, eternal Lord," are the first lines of hymns too majestic for the measure of the English ballad. But the sentiment of many other hymns is more congenially expressed in that ballad form. For instance, the eighteenth psalm of Tate and Brady, contains forty-four stanzas in long metre, of which four are ordinarily extracted for a modern hymn. The following are the four stanzas, and in a parallel column are the same in the more quickening measure:[1]

Original Form.	Altered Form.

No change of *times* shall ever shock
  My *firm* affection, Lord, to thee;
For thou hast always been my rock,
  A *fortress and* defense to me.
	No change of time shall ever shock
	  My trust, O Lord, in thee;
	For thou hast always been my Rock,
	  A sure defense to me.

Thou *my* deliverer art, *my* God;
  My trust is in thy *mighty* power;
Thou art my shield from foes
    abroad,
  At home, my safeguard and my tower.
	Thou *my* deliv'rer art, O God;
	  My trust is in thy power;
	Thou art *my* shield from foes
	    abroad,
	  My safeguard, and *my* tower.

To thee *I will* address my prayer,
  To whom all praise *we justly* owe;
So shall *I*, by thy watchful care,
  Be *guarded* from *my treach'rous* foe.
	To thee *will I* address my prayer,
	  To whom all praise *I* owe;
	So shall *I*, by thy watchful care,
	  Be saved *from* every foe.

Who then deserves to be adored
  But God, on whom my hopes depend;
Or who, except the mighty Lord,
  Can with resistless power defend?
	Then let Jehovah be adored,
	  On whom *my* hopes depend;
	For who, except the mighty Lord,
	  His people can defend?

[1] The altered form is found in the Sabbath Hymn Book, Hymn 669. Substantially the same alterations are in the Psalmist, the popular Hymn Book of the Baptists, also in the Church Psalmody, and other collections. For similar changes of metre in the Connecticut Collection, see Psalm 93, second version; also Hymn 319.

A favorite hymn in six stanzas by William Bengo Collier has been reduced to four stanzas, and also pruned of its superfluous words, and in becoming more concise, has taken a movement more rapid, and more appropriate to the stirring sentiment of the lines:

ORIGINAL FORM.	CHURCH PSALMODY.
	Hymn 263.
Return, O wanderer, return!	Return, O wanderer, *now* return!
He *heard* thy *deep repentant* sigh;	He *hears* thy *humble* sigh;
He *saw* thy softened spirit mourn,	He *sees* thy softened spirit mourn,
When no *intruding ear was* nigh.	When no *one else is* nigh.
Return, O wanderer, return,	Return, O wanderer, *now* return,
And wipe *away* the falling tear;	And wipe the falling tear!
'*T is God who says*, no longer mourn;	*Thy Father calls* — no longer mourn;
'*T is mercy's voice* invites thee near.	'*T is love* invites thee near.[1]

In like manner, a hymn of Swain, "*Firmly* I stand on Zion's mount," "The lofty hills and *stately* towers," "The vaulted Heavens shall *melt away*," was reduced by the editors of the Connecticut Collection from the common to the short metre by simply omitting the words "firmly" and "stately," and changing *melt away* into "*fall.*" Is not the change vivifying? Compare Sabbath Hymn Book, Hymn 681, with Church Psalmody, Hymn 429.

The old English ballad metre not only gives to some hymns more vivacity than they would have in the stately march of four uniform feet, but it also sometimes makes their style less flaunting, and more

---

[1] The adverb "*now*" is inserted in the first line of each stanza because the word "wanderer" is in fact ordinarily *sung* with only two syllables, and has a drawling sound when *sung* with three. The Psalmist, edited by Rev. Dr. Baron Stowe, and by Rev. S. F. Smith, avoids this trisyllabic utterance of "wanderer," so tedious in song, by substituting the words: "Return, *my wandering soul*, return."

appropriate to the worship of God. The majestic hymn of Mrs. Barbauld, "When as returns this solemn day,"[1] if used as a poem to be *read*, should not be reduced to the common metre; but when it is sung in the solemn assembly, there is a greater chasteness, a more modest reverence, more sober earnestness in the lines : " Shall clouds of incense rise ; " " The costly sacrifice ; " " Thine offerings well may spare ; " than in the original lines : " Shall *curling* clouds of incense rise ; " " The costly *pomp of* sacrifice ; " " Thy *golden* offerings well may spare."

" Praise to the Spirit *Paraclete ;* " " Above the *ruinable* skies ; " " Sweet *lenitive* of grief and care ; " " In all the *plenitude* of grace ; " " Be universal honors paid, *Coëqual* honors done ; " " Their *name* of earthly gods is vain ; " " An *instantaneous* night ; " " Thou dwellest in *self-existent* light ; " " With *serious industry* and fear ; " " Ye *dangerous inmates,* hence depart ; " " Tell me, *Radiancy* divine ; " " *Unmeasurably* high ; " " *T'* *invigorate* my faint desires ; " " Ye *specious* baits of sense ; " " With *diligence* may I pursue ; " — all verses like the above, containing long, Greek, Latin, abstract, or prosaic words, tend to benumb a lyric, and may sometimes be made more vivid by modifications like the following :

Original Form.	Sabbath Hymn Book.
	Hymn 234.
Great God ! I would not ask to see What *my futurity* shall be.	Great God ! I would not ask to see What in my *coming life* shall be.
	Hymn 360.
Jesus *dissipates* its gloom.	Jesus *scatters all* its gloom.

Sabbath Hymn Book, Hymn 41.

Original Form.	Sabbath Hymn Book.
	Hymn 425.
Dark and cheerless is the morn Unaccompanied by thee.	Dark and cheerless is the morn, *If thy light is hid from me.*
	Hymn 531.
Oh, sweetly *influence* every breast.	Oh, sweetly *reign in* every breast.
	Hymn 802.
Should I, to gain the world's applause, Or to escape its harmless frown, Refuse to *countenance* thy cause.	Should I, to gain the world's applause, Or to escape its harmless frown, Refuse to *love and plead* thy cause.
The captive surety now is freed.	Now *is the mighty captive* freed.
Thine *obvious* glory shine.	Thy *power and* glory shine.

§ 13. *Alterations in the Text, as affecting its Solemnity.*

Among the mysteries of music is its suggestive and its exciting power. A certain combination of sounds, even when no words accompany them, will carry the mind captive into a train of warlike sentiments, and stir it up to martial exploits; while a different combination will awaken festive emotions, and quicken both the soul and the body for a joyous dance. It is needless to say, that such musical combinations are improper for the temple song. It is equally needless to say, that they are often introduced into the sanctuary. "The truth is," — we quote without fully endorsing the words of a scientific musician, — "most of the music at present heard in our churches *essentially* differs from no *other* music; sacred and secular music are nearly identical, so far as style is concerned. Our psalm and hymn tunes are constructed on the form of the German popular part-songs. The old English glee has also served as a model. German convivial songs, soldiers' songs, students' songs, are actually found bodily transferred to our books of church psalmody, and are sung in our churches as sacred music. "*Bekranzt mit Laub den lieben vollen Becher*," — " Wreathe with green the flowing goblet"—(a German convivial song), is now enthusiastically rendered to sacred words. And, on the other hand, many American psalm tunes are of so essentially uproarious a character, that they might equally well be transferred to German *Kneipen*, and as admirably serve the purpose of these gatherings — so far as the music goes."

Now in order to resist the fashion of introducing into the sanctuary the "tripping triplet measure" of the music for the ball-room, and the stately march of the music for the army, we must have hymns which will prompt to the selection of strictly ecclesiastical tunes, and which will also control the expression of doubtful melodies. The words which are sung often interpret the musical sounds which accompany them, and they also lead to the choice of appropriate airs; yet as our choirs occasionally sing tunes borrowed from the opera, so there are Hymn Books containing lyrics written for the political, and the festive gathering. The tunes are modified somewhat, and so are the hymns. But there are lyrics primarily designed for the sanctuary, and still devoid of that solemn expression characteristic of the true church-song. These should be either rejected or amended. It is not so well to sing out the order: "Shun the world's *bewitching* snares," as to qualify it in imitation of the mandate: " If sinners *entice* thee, consent thou not." In a political ode we sing cheerily of "*leathern* hearts," but we regret that a Book of Sanctuary Songs has not put some other material into the place of *leather*.

One of the most effective methods of promoting

solemnity in the temple song, is to make it a direct address to Jehovah. The inspired Psalms would be less solemn than they now are, if all of them were written in the same style as the 1st, 2d, 11th, 23d, 24th, 29th, 47th, 50th, 53d, 81st, 87th, 91st, 95th, 96th, 98th, 100th, 103d, 105th, 107th, 110th, 111th, 112th, 113th, 114th, 117th, 122d, 127th, 128th, 129th, 133d, 134th, 136th, 146th, 147th, 148th, 149th, 150th. But in many modern hymn books, a large number of the inspired Psalms which *do* contain express appeals to God, are so altered that they come to resemble the above-named Psalms which do *not* contain such appeals. We cannot vouch for the accuracy of the statement, but we have seen the statement made by a professional musician, that in the Episcopal Prayer Book only sixty-three in a hundred lyrics are "*purely* devotional," in the Church Psalmist only fifty-three in a hundred, while in the inspired Psalms there are ninety-two in a hundred; in the Episcopal Prayer Book fifteen in a hundred are "*instructive and* devotional," in the Church Psalmist there are twenty-three in a hundred, and in the Biblical Psalms only eight in a hundred; that in the Episcopal Prayer Book twelve in a hundred are "purely *instructive*," in the Church Psalmist there are seventeen in a hundred, but in the inspired Psalms only two in a hundred. Such a disproportion would not exist, if the poet who versified the inspired Psalms, had not changed their spirit and style by omitting their direct appeals to God. Compare the appended columns:

David's Psalm v. Verse 12.	Episcopal Prayer Book. Psalm 5. Stanza 12.
"For *thou* Lord wilt bless the righteous; With favor wilt *thou* compass him, as with a shield."	To righteous men, the righteous Lord *His* blessing will extend, And with *his* favor all *his* saints As with a shield defend.

We presume that if a modern hymnologist should restore to this stanza of Tate and Brady the original second person, he would be accused of trespassing on the rights of that venerable company. The Sabbath Hymn Book has been censured, because in a stanza (H. 474) intended mainly for direct prayer and praise to Jehovah, the article " To *the* great One in three " has been changed into the pronoun " To *thee*, great One in Three." If this change of one letter be for the worse, it cannot be *much* for the worse; but if it be for the better, it *must* be much for the better. It transforms an indirect, into an immediate and palpable act of homage. We bring the Most High nearer to us, when we sing verses of petition, confession, or praise *to* Him, than when we are left to sing verses of meditation *about* Him, or about persons and things inferior to Him; and a hymnologist heightens the solemnity of our temple service when he elevates a poem *for* worship into a psalm *of* worship. An admirable lyric of Mrs. Steele begins in many Collections with the third stanza of the original, which may be easily translated from a distant history of Christian experience to a present solemn expression of homage to the Deity.

Mrs. Steele.	Sabbath Hymn Book.
	Hymn 9.
3. Oft in the temples of *his* grace *His* saints behold *his* smiling face, And oft have seen *his* glories shine, etc.	1. Oft in the temples of *thy* grace, *Thy* saints behold *thy* smiling face, And oft have seen *thy* glories shine, etc.

There is one class of discourses and odes, in which a want of dignity is the most fatal of all faults. Those compositions which introduce Jehovah as making an address, need to be guarded with the most sacred care against the slightest departure from the majestic diction. They are the most critical and difficult of all compositions. In various printed sermons, we find the Deity speaking in low, uncouth, ungrammatical, or otherwise indecorous phraseology. In various hymns, also, the words ascribed to him are far beneath the imposing solemnity which is demanded.

It is a grave question, whether a hymn containing a *lengthened* address from Jehovah, a *prolonged* " quotation" from his real or imagined remarks, ought ever to be sung by a public assembly. There are objections against even that solemn hymn of Watts, B. III. 1: "'Twas on that dark and doleful night;" but these objections arise from the historical, narrative, rubrical style of some of the stanzas, not from their indecorum. But where is the propriety of singing such words (and there are many having the same general character), as those ascribed to the " victorious God," by Watts in his Book III. 21, — words which Dr. Worcester wisely omitted from his Christian Psalmody, but felt a necessity of inserting in " Worcester's Watts and Select:"

> " But while I bled, and groaned and dy'd,
> I ruined Satan's throne ;
> High on my cross I hung and spy'd
> The monster tumbling down."

" I beheld Satan as lightning fall from heaven." These are solemn and sublime words. But the attempt to stretch them out, or press them down into a rhythm and metre just right for a certain tune, has led a devout man to " alter " the words and damage the sentiment. Is the critic an innovator, if he restore the Biblical simplicity to these lines? Does he trespass on the property of the uninspired poet, by bringing back the stanza to the model of the original author? Such a stanza, so far from its lofty model, is not only an offence against a delicate taste, but also against the spirit of reverence.

The solemnity of a Hymn Book is affected by its method of expressing the terrific realities of our faith. *There are certain facts in the clear view of which men do not sing.* Jacob did not burst forth into a strain of music, as soon as he saw the many colored coat of Joseph, nor David when he first heard of Absalom's tortures in death. There are vivid conceptions of mere woe, at which every mouth must be stopped. There are methods of depicting everlasting punishment which are not congenial with the spirit of church-song, and do not leave a solemn impression when they are accompanied with church music. They might horrify the soul, if they were set off by the instruments and voices of an opera, but they "petrify the feeling" when associated with the simple tunes of the sanctuary, — tunes not at all adapted to such overwhelming realities. The Presbyterian (Old School) Hymn Book substitutes the "*justice*" of God, or some other phrase, for the original words which represent Jehovah as taking "*revenge*" on men. It even substitutes the "*followers*" of Christ for his "*favorites*," the idea of *favoritism* being neither dignified nor solemn enough for a sanctuary song. Dr. Worcester was so particular in avoiding the seemingly harsh expressions of some hymns, that he substituted for them words of a directly opposite signification. He even went so far as to exchange "*kill*" for "*give*" in the following stanza of Watts:

> "Great was the day, the *joy* was great,
> When the divine disciples met;
> What gifts, what miracles he gave!
> And power to *kill* and power to save."[1]

We are, therefore, not at all surprised that Dr. Worcester omitted from his Christian Psalmody the 45th Hymn of Dr. Watts's First Book, and the 44th and 52d hymns of his Second Book; nor that he enclosed them within brackets in his "Watts and Select." But we are amazed that, as he mollified the temper of so many hymns, he did not also allay the severity of those lines which portray eternal punishment in colors too fearful to elicit song. Those lines ought to have been made either more biblical or more tender. There is a need for terrible denunciations of wrath; but on earth music is silent and adores when they come. There is, too, a distinction between the terrible and the solemn. In the former we are engrossed with the mere appeal to fear. In the latter we are appeased with the element of tenderness and love. This element ought to chasten our hymns on everlasting woe. A model ode, because a melting and subduing one on this theme, — the most critical theme over which the spirit of song can hover, is the following:

> 1. Father! — if I may call thee so, —
>   I tremble with my one desire;
>   Lift up this heavy load of woe,
>   Nor let me in my sins expire!

---

[1] Book II. Hymn 144. With an entirely different meaning Montgomery prays for "*killing*," and for "quickening grace." Dr. Worcester changes even this phrase into "quickening and confirming grace." Select Hymn, 406.

2. I tremble, lest the wrath divine,
   Which bruises now my sinful soul,
Should bruise and break this soul of mine,
   Long as eternal ages roll.

3. Thy wrath I fear, thy wrath alone,
   This endless exile, Lord, from thee!
Oh, save! oh, give me to thy Son,
   Who trembled, wept, and bled for me![1]

But this is a modification of stanzas from an author to whom Dr. Watts is said to have confessed his own inferiority. Is not the tone of these lines far more solemn and majestic, than the tone of the following, which are still not the most sharply pointed of Dr. Watts's comminatory lines.

WATTS, B. II. *Hymn* 52.	ALTERED IN PRESBYTERIAN (NEW SCHOOL) HYMN BOOK.

3
Awake and mourn, ye heirs of hell,
  Let stubborn sinners fear;
You must be driven from earth, and dwell
A long *for ever* there.
	Awake and mourn, ye heirs of *woe!*
	  Let stubborn sinners fear;
	Why will ye sink to flames below,
	  And *dwell* forever there.

4
See how the pit gapes wide for you,
  And flashes in your face;
And thou, my soul, look *downwards* too,
  And sing recov'ring grace.
	See how the pit gapes wide for you,
	  And flashes in your face;
	And thou, my soul, look *downward* too,
	  And sing recov'ring grace.

§ 14. *Changes in the Text, as affecting its Neatness.*

While the words chosen in the fervor of original composition, are apt to be more vivid than those which

---

[1] Sabbath Hymn Book, Hymn 1289.

the critic substitutes for them; yet, on the other hand, the liveliness of a hymn is often gained at the expense of its neatness. There are graces of style, there are delicate niceties of structure, which are overlooked in the onward march of the first composition. They may be supplied in the critical review. Often the neatness of a hymn may be promoted by even a *literal* change in its phraseology. Why need the most punctilious opponent of alterations in the text, forbid our singing: " And bends his footsteps *downward* too," " Our soaring spirits *upward* rise," " *Upward*, Lord, our spirits raise," instead of " *upwards* " and " *downwards*," as in the original? What harm to the rights of authorship will come from our singing: " Wonder and *joy* shall tune my heart," instead of the original, " *joys*." It is certainly neater to say:

"In thee I shall conquer by flood and by field,
Jehovah my anchor, Jehovah my shield;"—SAB. H. B. 1006;

than to mingle the incongruous metaphors :

"In thee I shall conquer by flood and by field,
My cable, my anchor, my breast-plate, my shield."

Sometimes the want of chasteness in the style of a hymn, calls away the attention from its religious aim; and the mind is repelled, by disagreeable associations, into a train of thought uncongenial with worship. The following instances will suggest others of a still more objectionable character.

ORIGINAL FORM.	SABBATH HYMN BOOK. *Hymn* 274.
And on the *eye-balls of the blind* To pour celestial day.	And, on the *eyes long closed in night*, To pour celestial day.

ORIGINAL FORM.	SABBATH HYMN BOOK.
	Hymn 424.
His heart is made of tenderness, His *bowels* melt with love.	His heart is made of tenderness,— It *melts with pitying love.*
Oh, let thy *bowels* answer me.	Oh, let thy *mercy* answer me.
	Hymn 547.
My *bowels yearn* o'er dying men.	My *spirit yearns* o'er dying men.
	Hymn 318.
And *dances his glad heart for joy.*	And *bounds his gladdened heart with joy.*
	Hymn 359.
A moment *give a loose to* grief: Let grateful sorrows rise; And wash the *bloody* stains away With torrents from your eyes.	A moment *now indulge your* grief: Let grateful sorrows rise; And wash the *crimson* stains away, With torrents from your eyes.
	Hymn 516.
Then will the angels *clap their wings* And bear the news above.	Then will the angels *swiftly fly To* bear the news above.
	Hymn 566.
I lay my soul beneath thy love: Beneath *the droppings of thy* blood, *Jesus, nor shall it e'er* remove.	I lay my soul beneath thy love: *Oh, cleanse me with atoning* blood, *Nor let me from thy feet* remove.
	Hymn 705.
My God, my God! on thee I call; Thee only would I know; *One drop of blood on me let fall,* And wash me white as snow.	My God, my God! to thee I cry; Thee only would I know: *Thy purifying blood apply,* And wash me white as snow.
H. K. *White's Hymn on the Resurrection.*	Hymn 1276 (see, also, Conn. Hymn Book, H. 393).
And the long-silent *dust shall burst* With shouts of endless praise.	And the long-silent *voice awake,* With shouts of endless praise.
	Hymn 1210.
Why should we tremble to convey Their bodies to the tomb? There the dear flesh of Jesus lay, And *left a long perfume.*	Why should we tremble to convey Their bodies to the tomb? There the dear flesh of Jesus lay, *There hopes* unfading bloom.
	Hymn 286.
And *there's no* weeping *there.*	And *weeping is not* there.
	Hymn 725.
To *snatch* me from eternal death.	To *save* me from eternal death.

ORIGINAL FORM.	SABBATH HYMN BOOK.
	Hymn 780.
And thy rebellious *worm* is still.	And thy rebellious *child* is still.
	Hymn 1180.
Behold the *gaping* tomb.	Behold the *opening* tomb.
	Hymn 882.
In the dear bosom of his love.	*Safe in the* bosom of his love.
Those wandering cisterns [clouds] *in the sky,*	Hymn 1150.
Borne by the winds around,	*Thy showers the thirsty furrows fill;*
With wat'ry treasures well supply	And ranks of corn appear;
The furrows of the ground.	Thy ways abound with blessings still —
The thirsty ridges drink their fill,	Thy goodness crowns the year.
And ranks of corn appear;	
Thy ways abound with blessings still,	
Thy goodness crowns the year.	
	Hymn 518. (2 Cor. 6 : 2.)
Come, ye sinners, poor and wretched,	Come, ye sinners, poor and wretched,
Weak and wounded, sick and sore.	*This is your accepted hour:*
	Hymn 1002.
May purge our souls from *sense and sin.*	May *purify* our souls from sin.
	Hymn 524.
Compelled by bleeding love,	*Drawn by his* bleeding love,
Ye wandering sheep, draw near;	Ye wand'ring sheep, draw near;
Christ calls you from above,	Christ calls you from above;
His charming accents hear.	*The Shepherd's voice now* hear.
Let whosoever will now come,	Let whosoever will now come;
In *mercy's breast* there still is room.	In *Jesus' arms* there still is room.
	Hymn 585.
And though his arm be strong to smite,	*His arm, though it* be strong to smite,
'Tis also strong to save.	*Is* also strong to save.
	Hymn 676.
Wait thou his time; *so shall this* night	Wait thou his time; *the darkest* night
Soon end in *joyous* day.	Shall end in *brightest* day.

It is often objected that we make a hymn feeble by making it neat. The attempt to prune it of its rank growth, results in destroying its masculine vigor. But a song may be energetic, and yet chaste in its diction.

20*

Indeed, an immodest or extravagant air is often fatal to the manly robustness of a sacred lyric. The strength of it is impaired, when it contains any word which dissipates the thoughts of the singer by awakening a suspicion of excess or wildness in the poet. There is a degree of soberness which is the hiding of the Christian lyrist's power. The line of Mrs. Steele, "*Tremendous* judgments from thy hand," is not so forcible as the altered line, "*Dark frowning* judgments from thy hand" (Sabbath Hymn Book, H. 1118). It is very true that some of the alterations made for the beauty of a hymn may interfere with its energy. Some of them may mitigate the force of a *single line*, by toning down its boisterous spirit, while the power of the entire hymn is heightened, by giving a more considerate meaning to its violent words. Some of the changes in the Presbyterian Old School Collection are tamer than they need be; still they augment the general impressiveness of the lyrics which contain them; thus

Original Form.	Presbyterian O. S. Hymn Book.
Watts, 6th Psalm.	
In anger, Lord, *rebuke me not*, Withdraw the dreadful storm, Nor let *thy fury grow so hot* Against a feeble worm.	In anger, Lord, *do not chastise*, Withdraw the dreadful storm, Nor let *thine awful wrath* arise Against a feeble worm.
Watts, 9th Psalm, also 99th.	
And make his *vengeance* known.	And make his *justice* known.
Watts, 11th Hymn.	
On impious wretches he *shall* rain *Tempests of brimstone, fire and death.*	On impious wretches he *will* rain, *Sulphureous flames of wasting* death.

§ 15. *Changes in the Text, as Affecting its Vigor.*

The great evil in the alteration of hymns, consists in its lessening their energy. It is better that they be forceful and rough, than "coldly correct and critically dull." Nothing but a taste well cultivated, can determine when to leave an extravagant phrase in its pristine wildness, and when to chasten it. But we err, if we suppose that all the changes in a hymn are designed to augment its refinement and delicacy. Some of them are intended to invigorate its more languid phrases. When we are singing of *God*, we form a weaker conception of his omniscience, if we say, with Watts, that he "*often*" looks down upon our dust, than if we say, as in the Sabbath Hymn Book, H. 1274,

> God, my Redeemer, lives,
>   And *ever* from the skies
> Looks down and watches all my dust,
>   Till he shall bid it rise.

Injudicious criticisms are often made on an alteration of lyrical phrases, because it suggests no one *prominent* reason in its favor. But in fact there may be several different reasons combined in its behalf; as in the following instances, where vigor is one of the attributes gained in the change:

Original Form.	Sabbath Hymn Book.
	Hymn 824.
The joy and *labor* of their tongue.	The joy and *triumph* of their tongue.
	Hymn 1056.
O mem'ry! leave no other name [than Christ's]. So deeply graven there.	O mem'ry! leave no other name But his *recorded* there.
	Hymn 1279.
Our *cautioned* souls prepare.	Our *anxious* souls prepare.
	Hymn 704.
Jesus! in that *important* hour.	Jesus! in that *momentous* hour.

ORIGINAL FORM.	SABBATH HYMN BOOK.
	Hymn 325.
To Jesus, our *superior* King.	To Jesus, our *eternal* King.
	Hymn 310.
Atoned for *sins* which we had done.	Atoned for *crimes* which we had done.
	Hymn 308.
And hence our hopes arise.	*Hence all* our hopes arise.
	Hymn 118.
Creatures *as numerous as they be.*	Creatures *that borrow life from thee.*
	Hymn 723.
I urge no merits of my own, For I, alas! am all that's vile.	I urge no merits of my own, *No worth to claim thy gracious smile.*
	Hymn 558.
Come, *humble* sinner.	Come, *trembling* sinner.
	Hymn 380.
His the *fight,* the arduous toil.	His the *battle, his the* toil.
	Hymn 366.
Grant that we, too, may go.	*Oh, grant that we may go.*
	Hymn 1236.
No cloud those blissful regions know, *Forever* bright and fair.	No cloud those blissful regions know— *Realms ever* bright and fair.
	Hymn 1234.
No chilling winds *or* poisonous breath, Can reach that healthful shore.	No chilling winds, *no* poisonous breath, Can reach that healthful shore.
	Hymn 159.
Let *the whole earth* his power confess; Let *the whole earth* adore his grace; *The Gentile with the Jew shall join* In work and worship so divine.	Let *every land* his power confess; Let *all the earth* adore his grace; *My heart and tongue with rapture* join, In work and worship so divine.
	Hymn 703.
Stronger his love than death *and* hell, *Its riches are unspeakable;* The first-born sons of light *Desire in vain* its depths to see; They cannot reach the mystery, *And* length, *and* breadth, *and* height.	Stronger his love than death *or* hell: *No mortal can its riches tell, Nor* first-born sons of light: *In vain they long* its depths to see; They cannot reach the mystery— *The* length, *the* breadth, *the* height.

§ 16. *Alterations in the Text, as Affecting its Poetical and Lyrical Character.*

> Then seek the Lord betimes, and choose
> The ways of heavenly truth;
> The earth affords no lovelier sight
> *Than a religious youth.*

This fourth line suggests a wholesome thought, but is not a *lyrical* ending of a hymn. Yet the excellent Dr. Thomas Gibbons has admitted it as the close of a church lyric. The final verse of a hymn should often condense into itself the whole spirit of the preceding verses; and, like the rudder of a ship, control all that goes before it.

> "His love hath animating power."

This is a didactic peroration of an affecting ode by Doddridge. It is a judicious verse, but is not poetry. The hymn will close with a line more in sympathy with all that precedes it, if it be modified in one of the following methods:

> "His work my hoary head shall bless,
> When youthful vigor is no more,
> And my last hour of life confess
> *His dying love's constraining power.*"
> *(Connecticut, and Plymouth, Collections)*; or,

> "*His saving love, his glorious power.*"
> *(Church Psalmody)*; or

> "*His dying love, his saving power.*"
> *(Sabbath Hymn Book, Hymn 832.)*

> Let the sweet hope that thou art mine,
>   My life and death attend;
> Thy presence through my journey shine,
>   And crown my journey's end.
>   (*Sabbath Hymn Book, Hymn* 926.)

This is the closing line of a hymn by Mrs. Steele. It is like the final tone of an anthem. It appears in all our choicest hymn books. But it is not the line with which her exquisite hymn closed at first. *Her* concluding words were less crowning:

> "*And bless its happy end.*"

A lyric is that kind of poetry which prompts us to *sing*. We are not incited to utter in musical cadence, phrases merely instructive; turns of economical or philosophical discourse. It is more in harmony with the very nature of a lyric to exclaim: " In the cold prison of the tomb, The *great* Redeemer lay," than " The *dead* Redeemer lay" (we need not hear that he was deceased, if he was entombed); to sing: "*When in want, or when in wealth,*" than "*Whether then in want or wealth;*" to cry out: " Nor could *the bowers of* Eden give," than " Nor could *untainted* Eden give." All feeble, stale, hackneyed phrases, like Watts's " Yet I would not be much concerned," " Nor milk nor honey taste so well," may be exchanged for lines better adapted to awaken the spirit of song. The following are specimens of numerous alterations made in one standard Hymn Book, on purely lyrical grounds:

Original Form.	Presbyterian O. S. Collection.
Watts, 105*th Psalm.*	
A *little, feeble* band.	A *small and feeble* band.
Watts, 105*th Psalm.*	
Each some Egyptian spoils *had got.*	*Rich with* Egyptian spoils *they fled.*

ORIGINAL FORM.	PRESBYTERIAN O. S. COLLECTION.
Watts, 107th *Psalm.*	
'Twas the right path to Canaan's ground.	And brought their tribes to Canaan's ground.
Watts, 107th *Psalm.*	
Who trade in floating ships.	Who tempt the dangerous way.
Watts, 112th *Psalm.*	
While envious sinners *fret* in vain.	While envious sinners *rage* in vain.
Watts, 113th *Psalm.*	
And *makes them company for* kings.	And *seats them on the thrones of* kings.
Watts, 132d *Psalm.*	
Not Aaron in his costly dress, *Made an appearance* so divine.	Not Aaron in his costly dress, *Appears so glorious,* so divine.
Watts, 132d *Psalm.*	
But we have no such lengths to go, Nor wander far abroad; Where'er thy saints assemble now, There is a house for God.	*We trace no more those devious ways,* Nor wander far abroad; *Where'er thy people meet for praise,* There is a house for God.
Watts, 144th *Psalm.*	
Happy the country where the *sheep, Cattle, and corn,* have large increase, Where men securely work or *sleep,* etc.	Happy *the land in culture drest, Whose flocks* and corn have large increase, Where men securely work or *rest,* etc.
Watts, 135th *Psalm.*	
Their gods have tongues that *cannot talk,* etc.	Their gods have tongues that *speechless prove,* etc.

Dr. Watts, in more than one hymn, speaks of " wild world;" more vivid than " wide world," to which Dr. Worcester changes it, Bk. ii. 73 and 138. Dr. Watts writes : " We shout with *joyful* tongues ;" more animating than " *cheerful* tongues," as written by Dr. Worcester, Bk. ii. 42. " And unbelief *the* spear," is the line of Watts; made less lively by Worcester : " And unbelief *a* spear," Bk. ii. 95. Cowper writes: " And if her faith was firm and *strong,* Had *strong* misgivings too ;" which, feeble at best, is still feebler in Worcester's Watts : " Had *some* misgivings too." (Select Hymn, 76.) Dr. Watts writes : " As potter's earthen *work* is broke;" Worcester does not *mend* this line by saying: "As potter's earthen *ware* is broke," Ps. ii. The following alteration is not disrespectful to the Olney Hymns:

John Newton's original.	Connecticut and Plymouth Collections.
He himself has *bid thee pray*,	He himself *invites thee near* —
Therefore will not say thee nay.	*Bids thee ask him* — *waits to hear.*

The spirit of song often disdains the trammels of a precise philosophy. It flies aloft, and leaves the rules of logic in the low ground of unimpassioned thought. The naked statement of a truth is sometimes poetical; but at other times the truth must be intimated in metaphors, or veiled in some attractive drapery. When the rationalists of the last age gained possession of the German pulpit, they found that the poet had written in their hymn book, concerning the midnight hour: " Now *all* the world is locked in sleep." But this is not philosophical. The earth is round; therefore the rationalists merged the poet's hyperbole into the more undeniable theorem : " Now *half* the world is locked in sleep." The Presbyterian (Old School) Collection of hymns has stumbled at the simple line of Watts, concerning *that* sound which " Bid the new-made *heavens* go round." This line is not true. It falsifies the Copernican system. The " *heavens* " do not go round. Hence that Collection has reduced the poetry of the line to accurate astronomy, thus : " That bid the new-made *world* go round."

On the same principle, the Hymn of Watts: " Once more, my soul, the rising day," is changed from an expression of lively praise, " To Him that *rolls* the skies," into the more philosophical dictum: " To Him that *rules* the skies." In another instance, however, a scientific line is metamorphosed by the same Presbyterian Collection into the freer poetical form; the poet wrote: " How *most exact* is nature's frame;" the critic has preferred to write: " How *fair and beauteous* nature's frame." The 65th Psalm of Watts affirms that sailors are especially affrighted

" When tempests rage, and billows roar,
 At dreadful distance from the shore."

It has been objected, that the further off from the shore the sailors are in a tempest, so much the safer are they. But, however this may be in prose, it is not so in poetry. A favorite hymn asserts: " Fire ascending seeks the sun." This is not the fact in *midnight* prose; but shall we therefore qualify the poetic assertion?

If a hymn leaves a decidedly erroneous impression, and is adapted to deprave the moral sentiment by its false doctrine, it should be either omitted or amended. Truth is more essential than poetry. An injurious influence is worse than a prosaic expression. If, however, the hymn does not inculcate an unsound doctrine by its unscientific style; if it merely employ a less technical, or more indirect, or ambiguous phrase, than is demanded by a precise theology, the uses of the hymn require that the old form be retained for the explanation of a didactic hour, rather than that the flow of song be checked by a rigid analytic emendation. We query whether the Presbyterian Old School Manual (Hymn 549,) has at all heightened the moral excellence of Mrs. Steele's stanza, by translating the affectionate words:

> " 'T is thine, *Almighty Saviour*, thine,
> To form the heart anew,"

into the more accurate language: " 'T is thine, *Eternal Spirit*, thine," etc. On the other hand, the Connecticut Hymn Book, Hymn 86, has made a more healthful impression by describing the divine goodness as "*unceasing*," than was made by Doddridge, who represents it as "*redundant.*"

While all poetry shrinks from the cold argumentative methods of science, lyrical poetry urges a peculiar demand for the lively, impassioned, stirring diction. In the present state of hymnology, we cannot look for a strict adherence to the rules; still, the rules are admirable which are thus laid down in the Preface to the Church Psalmody (p. vi.):

"Sentences and clauses should contain, as far as is practicable without occasioning a stiff and tedious uniformity, *complete sense in themselves*. A succession of clauses bound together by weak connectives, exhausts the performer, by allowing no opportunity for pausing; while, by multiplying unmeaning words, and keeping the mind too long on the same course, it also wearies the hearer. It contributes greatly to the spirit and force of the hymn, as well as to the ease of the performer, to throw off rapidly, in a concise form, one thought after another, each complete in itself, and with each beginning a new rhetorical clause.

The structure of each stanza should be such that the *mind shall perceive the meaning immediately.* All hypothetical clauses, placed at the beginning, or other clauses containing positions or arguments having reference to some conclusion which is to follow, are to be avoided. They contain no meaning in themselves, and bring nothing before the mind expressive or productive of feeling, till the performer reaches the important words at the close of perhaps the second or fourth line. The only method of wading through such lines, set to music, is for the performer to suspend all thought and feeling, and struggle hard and patiently, till he shall come to the light. The first word should, if possible, express something in itself, and every word should add to it. But, from a spirited clause at the beginning, the mind may derive an impulse which shall carry it through a heavy one that may follow. Clauses, however, which follow the main one, to qualify it, connected by a relative, are always heavy and injurious."

In all our hymn books we can discover many violations of this rule. Prof. B. B. Edwards has cited the following violation in a manual, which is remarkably free from this species of fault.[1]

"The 15th Psalm, 2d part of the Church Psalmody, furnishes a specimen of the complex [structure of hymns]. In the second stanza begins a protasis, and the fifth stanza contains the apodosis. Thus the second stanza introduces the condition:

> The man who walks in pious ways,
>   And works with righteous hands;
> Who trusts his Maker's promises,
>   And follows his commands;——

The third and fourth stanzas continue in the same style, and the last two lines of the fifth introduce the consequence:

> His [whose] hands disdain a golden bribe,
>   And never wrong the poor:—
> *This man shall dwell with God on earth,*
>   *And find his heaven secure.*"

One of the most radical emendations of a church song is that made by Logan on a hymn of Doddridge,

---

[1] Writings of Prof. B. B. Edwards, with a Memoir, pp. 143, 144.

and subsequently modified by an English hymnologist.[1] The main superiority of the amended over the original hymn, is the quicker and more direct expression of its thought, the avoidance of the far-separated protasis and apodosis, and also of the apparently *conditional* homage.

ORIGINAL FORM.	AMENDED FORM.
O God of Jacob, by whose hand Thine Israel still is fed, Who thro' this weary pilgrimage Hast all our fathers led.	O God of Bethel! by whose hand Thy people still are fed; Who through this weary pilgrimage Hast all our fathers led; —
To thee our humble vows we raise, To thee address our prayer, And in thy kind and faithful breast Deposit all our care.	Our vows, our prayers, we now present Before thy throne of grace; God of our fathers! be the God Of their succeeding race.
If thou, thro' each perplexing path, Wilt be our constant guide; If thou wilt daily bread supply, And raiment wilt provide;	Through each perplexing path of life Our wandering footsteps guide; Give us, each day, our daily bread, And raiment fit provide.
If thou wilt spread thy shield around, Till these our wand'rings cease, And at our Father's lov'd abode, Our souls arrive in peace:	Oh, spread thy covering wings around, Till all our wanderings cease, And at our Father's loved abode, Our souls arrive in peace.
To Thee, as to our Cov'nant God, We'll our whole selves resign: And count that not one *tenth* alone, But all we have is thine.	Such blessings from thy gracious hand Our humble prayers implore; And thou shalt be our chosen God, Our portion evermore.

§ 17. *The Adaptation of a Hymn to the State of Mind in Public Worship.*

We are living, we are dwelling,
In a grand and awful time,
In an age on ages telling,
To be living is sublime.

---

[1] Logan's modified emendation is found in the Sabbath Hymn Book II. 216, and in nearly all the recent manuals.

> Hark! the waking up of nations,
>   Gog and Magog to the fray.
> Hark! what soundeth? is creation
>   Groaning for its latter day?
>
> Will ye play, then, will ye dally,
>   With your music and your wine?
> Up! it is Jehovah's rally!
>   God's own arm hath need of thine.
> Hark! the onset! will ye fold your
>   Faith-clad arms in lazy lock?
> Up, O up, thou drowsy soldier;
>   Worlds are charging to the shock.
>
> Worlds are charging — heaven beholding;
>   Thou hast but an hour to fight;
> Now the blazoned cross unfolding,
>   On — right onward, for the right.
> Oh! let all the soul within you
>   For the truth's sake go abroad!
> Strike! let every nerve and sinew
>   Tell on ages — tell for God!

This lyric, found in one of our church hymn books, is an excellent illustration of certain principles, easily misunderstood. A song may be vivid, vigorous, highly poetical, and still not church-like in its tone. The statements already made in the 12th, 15th, and 16th sections, may be misapprehended as favoring that kind of giddiness which we often find in an Independence ode, but which we never ought to find in a sanctuary hymn. As men of exclusively literary tastes are prone to sigh for the standard old text, so men of exclusively poetical aspirations are prompted to cry for verses that are soul-stirring, that "sound like a trumpet." The flowers of rhetoric cannot grow too luxuriantly and rankly for these children of the imagination. They insist upon retaining all such lines as " Now resplendent shine his [Christ's] *nail-prints*," " A *bottle* for my tears," " My prayers are now a *chattering* noise," " And *fling* his wrath abroad," " Then will the angels *clap* their wings," " And *claps* his wings of fire," " Behold what *cursed* snares," " *Dress thee in arms*, most mighty Lord," " How terrible is *God in arms*," " Wind, hail, and *flashing* fire," " And pours the *rattling* hail." Such lines are good because they are rousing, it is said. Many of them may be sung with an accompaniment of drum and fife.

But a just and refined taste is needed for distinguishing between the appropriate brilliancy or strength of a church song, and that of a martial or even a temperance ode. A delicate Christian sentiment in regard to hymns, is like common sense in regard to the affairs of daily life; it knows how, where, and when, to make an exception to a rule. Vivid images, glowing metaphors, breathing words, do give immortality to a song of praise. Critics, however, mistake the nature of a hymn book, when they treat it as a bouquet of bright flowers, or a coronet of glistening jewels. That is not always the best church song, which sparkles most with rhetorical gems. There are spangled hymns, which will never excite devotional feeling. The state of a congregation during the worship of God, is peculiar. The rich and the poor, the learned and the ignorant, the strong-minded and the superannuated, are uniting in a solemn address to Jehovah. When the conceptions of the song are too brilliant, when its rhetoric is too gorgeous, when its allusions are too brisk and lively, there are untutored minds which *cannot* comprehend them, and there are cultivated minds which *will* sympathize with the unlettered, and demand a simpler mode of speech. *Alleviating* the line of Watts, who says that God "*pushed*" the wheels of the universe "into motion first," Dr. Worcester wrote "*put* them into motion first," Bk. ii. 13. Many young men will prefer "pushing" to "putting;" not so with the old, however. Frequently a hymn is a prayer; and it is a rule for the structure of prayers, that they exclude all those recondite figures, dazzling comparisons, flashing metaphors, which, while grateful to certain minds of poetic excitability, are offensive to more sober and staid natures, and are not congenial with the lowly spirit of a suppliant at the throne of grace. All individualities of expression, all idiosyncracies in which few worshippers will feel a sympathetic interest, and from which the majority will turn away with disgust or mere indifference, are infelicitous parts of a church song. A simile may be shining, but it may not be exactly chaste; and a hymn prefers pure beauty to bedizening ornament. In his one hundred and forty-eighth Psalm, Dr. Watts has written :

> Ye creeping ants and worms,
> His various wisdom show;
> And flies, in all your shining forms,
> Praise him that drest you so.

All such lines may be called *lively*, but they are too *buzzing* for a hymn of worship. It were better to retain Mrs. Steele's long word: "Their bright *inimitable* dyes," than to introduce Dr. Worcester's more *picturesque* alteration: "The smallest worms, the meanest flies," Select H. 1. It is true, that sometimes Dr. Worcester has added to the intensity of the original verses by such changes as: "Can make this *world* (for *load*) of guilt remove," Bk. ii. 41; but more frequently he has relieved the intense phrases, as: "Nor let thy fury *grow* (for "*burn*") so hot," Ps. 6; "Herself a *frighted* (for "*frightful*") ghost," Bk. ii. 2; "Rebelled *against* (for "*and lost*") their God," Bk. ii. 78; "Impatient (for "*insatiate*") panting for thy blood," Select, 16; "And scatters slaughtered *millions round*" (for "*heaps around*") Select, 114. Often, if he does not chasten a rank phrase, he marks the entire hymn for omission, as: "*lumps* of lifeless clay," "*heaps* of meaner bones," "My wrath has struck the rebels dead, My *fury stamped them down*," Bk. i. 24 and 28. The Connecticut Hymn Book contains many lenient alterations; as: "*Before the moth we sink to dust*," for "*A moth may crush us in the dust.*" Hy. 61; "And put the *hosts* of hell to flight," for "*troops* of hell," Ps. 68; "Of *dust and worms* thy power can frame," for "Of *meanest things* thy power can frame," Ps. 8; see, also, Hymns 84, 380, and others. The terms *wretch, wretched*, are so often used in an extravagant and ironical way, that they may, here and there, be exchanged for more biblical terms; as in Sabbath Hymn Book, 595, 73.

The Presbyterian (Old School) Collection abounds with instances of the less expressive phrases, inserted in the place of the more expressive originals. Some, but not all, of these changes are wisely made; as in the following instances:

Original Form.	Presbyterian (O. S.) Form.
Watts's 3d Psalm.	
And all my *swelling* sins appear	And all my *growing* sins appear
Too *big* to be forgiven.	Too *great* to be forgiven.
Watts's 6th Psalm.	
And hears *when dust and ashes* speak.	And hears his *mourning children* speak.
Watts's 10th Psalm.	
And *still thy saints devour.*	And *slight thy righteous cause.*
Watts's 18th Psalm.	
In all the wars *that devils* wage.	In all the wars *the proud can* wage.
Watts's 26th Psalm.	
With hands well washed in innocence.	*Arrayed in robes of* innocence.
Watts's 35th Psalm.	
See how his sounding bowels move.	*Behold his kind compassion* move.
Watts's 41st Psalm.	
Shall find the Lord has *bowels* too.	Shall find the Lord has *mercy* too.
Watts's 53d Psalm.	
Where his own *carcass* lies;	Where his own *body* lies;
For God's *revenging* arm	For God's *avenging* arm
Scatters the bones of them that rise	*Shall crush the hand that dares to* rise
To do his children harm.	To do his children harm.
Watts's 55th Psalm.	
With inward *pain* my heart-strings *bound.*	*What* inward *pains* my heart-strings *wound.*
Watts's 69th Psalm.	
He saved me from the dreadful deep,	He saved me from the dreadful deep,
Nor let my soul be drowned.	*Where fears beset me round.*
Watts's 74th Psalm.	
Where once thy churches prayed and sang,	Where once thy churches prayed and sang,
Thy foes profanely *roar.*	Thy foes profanely *rage.*
Watts's 91st Psalm.	
Shall keep thee from the fowler's snare,	Shall keep thee from the fowler's snare,
Satan the fowler who betrays.	*From Satan's wiles, who still* betrays.
Watts's 74th Psalm.	
Thy [God's] children in their *nest.*	Thy [God's] children in their *rest.*

ORIGINAL FORM.	PRESBYTERIAN (O. S.) FORM.
Watts's 105*th Psalm.*	
And frogs in *croaking* armies rise.	And frogs in *baleful* armies rise.
Watts's 112*th Psalm.*	
While envious sinners *fret* in vain.	While envious sinners *rage* in vain.
Watts's 139*th Psalm.*	
Or *dive* to hell, there justice reigns.	Or *plunge* to hell, there justice reigns.
Watts's 121*st Psalm.*	
Whose never-ceasing *brawlings* cease.	Where never-ceasing *quarrels* cease.
Watts's 129*th Psalm.*	
The Lord *grew angry* on his throne.	The Lord *in anger* on his throne.
Watts's 145*th Psalm.*	
The Lord supports our *tottering* days.	The Lord supports our *sinking* days.
Watts.	*Hymn* 413.
Labor, and *tug*, and strive.	Labor, and *toil*, and strive.
Doddridge.	
My God, what *silken* cords are thine.	My God, what *gentle* cords are thine.

§ 18. *Changes in the Text, as affecting the Fundamental Qualities of the Style.*

Perspicuity is one essential excellence of a lyric. " I will sing with the spirit, and I will sing with the understanding also." " In the church, I had rather speak five words with my understanding, that by my voice I might teach others also, than ten thousand words in an unknown tongue." The worshipper should not be driven to ask: " What does my prayer signify? Has my language of praise any meaning at all?" The words which he sings should be so perspicuous, that he cannot fail to see through them at once. The perfection of a Christian lyric consists in the fitness of every line to awaken, immediately and simultaneously, the devout feelings of a congregation. That is an imperfect hymn which diverts the worshipper's attention from the inner spirit of the stanzas, to the obscurity of their diction. Not seldom has a man been either baffled or troubled in ascertaining the exact significance of the following lines, as left by their authors:

Original Form.	Sabbath Hymn Book.
	Hymn 144.
Till *a wise care of piety* *Fit us to die*, and dwell with thee.	Till *by thy grace, we all may be Prepared to die*, and dwell with thee.
	Hymn 147.
God reigns on high, but *not* confines.	God reigns on high, but *ne'er* confines.
	Hymn 594.
My crimes are great, but *not* surpass.	My crimes are great, but *ne'er* surpass.
	Hymn 160.
The *small respects that* we can pay.	The *best obedience* we can pay.
	Hymn 184.
And awfully adore.	*In awe and love* adore.
	Hymn 701.
The sense of *our* expiring love, Into my soul convey.	The sense of *thine* expiring love, Into my soul convey.
	Hymn 1006.
Jehovah, *Tsidkēnu*, my death-song shall be.	Jehovah, *my Saviour*, my death-song shall be.
	Hymn 1192.
Sweet is the scene when virtue dies.	*How blest the righteous when he* dies.
	Hymn 1192.
Its duty done, as sinks the day, Light from its load the spirit flies.	*Life's labor done*, as sinks the day, Light from its load the spirit flies.

The following amendment, while it makes the stanza more luminous, makes it also more devotional:

Doddridge's Original.	Presbyterian New School Hymn Book, Hymn 606.
When death shall *interrupt these* songs, And seal in silence mortal tongues, Our *Helper — God*, in whom we trust, *In better worlds our souls shall boast.*	When death shall *close our earthly* songs, And seal in silence mortal tongues, Our *helper, God*, in whom we trust, *Shall keep our souls, and guard our dust.*

There are many congregations who do not comprehend the line of Henry Kirke White, " Though not thus buried or *inane*," and who utter in blank amazement such words as " Praise the mount, — I'm fixed upon it," or " Praise the mount, Oh, fix me on it," " Death of death, and hell's destruction," etc. Therefore, in the majority of recent hymn books, such phrases are modified, if not into the more poetical, at least into the more intelligible. See the 1276th, 648th, 1221st, 1222d hymns of the Sabbath Hymn Book.

Precision is another fundamental quality of style which is often promoted by a slight modification of a hymn. When Watts, in his study at Newington, was inditing verses in regard to public worship, he wrote: " Peace to this sacred house, For *there* my friends and kindred dwell;" " *There* God my Saviour reigns;" " He sits for grace and judgment *there*;" but when these verses are sung *in* the " sacred house," it is more definite and vivid to exchange the distant adverb, *there*, for the present adverb, *here*. So it is more precise and more grateful to speak of " Jesus, the name that *calms* our fears," than with Wesley to speak of the name that "*charms*" our fears. It is more exact, and more endearing to say,

>Jesus, and didst thou leave the sky,
>To bear our sins and woes,

than with Mrs. Steele to say that he left the sky, "*For miseries* and woes." It is more definite, and more devotional to sing:

>" *Let every moment*, as it flies,
>Increase thy praise, improve our joys; — H. 385;

than with Watts to sing:

"*Each following minute*, as it flies,
Increase thy praise, improve our joys."

When Charles Wesley, in Hymn 409, is contrasting the believer with the Master, he says: "*False* and full of sin *I am; Thou art full of truth and grace.*" A very common reading of this line is: "*Vile* and full of truth and grace." The Sabbath Hymn Book (Hymn 409) has departed from this common reading, and returned to the first draught, which is more precise; yet an advocate for the "original text" has censured the Sabbath Hymn Book for here deviating from, when it has gone back to, Wesley's own words.

Instances of phrases made more exact and accurate by slight alterations, are:

ORIGINAL FORM.	SABBATH HYMN BOOK.
	Hymn 944.
And those that choose thy upright path, Shall in *those paths* go on.	And those *who* choose thy upright path, Shall in *that path* go on.
	Hymn 1229.
Our journey is a thorny maze, But we *march* upward still, Forget these troubles of the ways, And *reach at* Zion's Hill.	Our journey is a thorny maze, But we *press* upward still, Forget these troubles of the ways, And *march to* Zion's hill.
	Hymn 780.
Then, my Redeemer, then I find The *follies* of my doubts and fears.	Then, my Redeemer, then I find The *folly* of my doubts and fears.
	Hymn 768.
I know, with healing in his wings, The Sun of righteousness shall rise.	*And soon*, with healing in his wings, The Sun of righteousness shall rise.
	Hymn 582.
Jesus demands this heart of mine, Demands my *wish*, my joy, my care.	Jesus demands this heart of mine, Demands my *love*, my joy, my care.
	Hymn 500.
Till *terribly* I saw.	Till I *with terror* saw.
	Hymn 432.
All *my capacious* powers can wish.	All *that my loftiest* powers can wish.

Original Form.	Sabbath Hymn Book.
	Hymn 643.
How vain a toy is glittering wealth, If once compared *with* thee.	How vain a toy is glittering wealth, If once compared *to* thee.
	Hymn 1000.
There shed thy choicest *loves* abroad.	There shed thy choicest *love* abroad.
	Hymn 607.
The burden which I feel, Thou *canst alone* remove.	The burden which I feel, Thou *only canst* remove.
	Hymn 144.
Or dust was fashioned *to a* man.	Or dust was fashioned *into* man.
	Hymn 36.
We are his *works*, and not our own.	We are his *work*, and not our own.
	Hymn 1252.
Haste, my Beloved, *fetch* my soul, Up to thy blest abode.	Haste, my Beloved, *raise* my soul Up to thy blest abode.

Propriety is another fundamental excellence of style, which will not be disdained by a good hymn, and which may be often increased by slight changes of words. In such phrases of Watts as "Wisdom *and* power belongs," "Thy power and love *has* made," "Wisdom, power, and love, *shines* in their dying Lord," "Each of us *cry* with thankful *tongues*," "And each fulfil *their* part," "Thou doth chastise," "Thou boasted," there is no more tendency to excite a devotional spirit, than there is in those phrases modified according to the more approved standard of the language. Will any modern hymn book insert unaltered the lines:

> "Thy power and glory *works* within,
> And *breaks* the chains of reigning sin,
> *Doth* our imperious lusts subdue,
> And *forms* our wretched hearts anew."—*Watts*, B. II., 133.

The mind is rather diverted from religious contemplation by any such verbal impropriety as, " The *orders* [for *order*] of thy house," " Or do the *sin* [for *ill*] I would not do," " And *hearken what* [for hearken *to* what] his children say," " *Indulged* [for *allowed*] my doubts to rise," " *Avow* [for *accept*] our temples for his own," " Come, Holy Ghost, descend *from high*," " From men of prudence and of *wit*" (Old English), " With the same blessings grace *bestows* [for *endows*] the gentiles," etc.

An *unusual* word or construction may sometimes be needed for the poetical dignity of a hymn;[1] but where not required, may well be exchanged for a phrase more accordant with the general custom. In Newton's celebrated song, " Safely through another week," he prays to the Redeemer: "*Shine* away my sin and shame." Bonar adopts the same language. This unusual phrase is sometimes very expressive; but in Newton's hymn, it has been commonly changed into "*Take* away my sin and shame." The line of Mrs. Barbauld, " Ten thousand *differing* lips shall join," has been modified into the more customary form, " Ten thousand *thousand* lips," etc. The favorite phrases of Watts, concerning Him that " built us," " built our bones," are usually changed to " formed," or " made" us and our bones.

Original Lines.	Sabbath Hymn Book.
	Hymn 265.
Fly, my tongue, such guilty silence.	*Break*, my tongue, such guilty silence.
	Hymn 484.
I love the *volumes* of thy word.	I love the *volume* of thy word.
	Hymn 555.
Let *old* ingratitude provoke, etc.	Let *past* ingratitude provoke.

---

[1] A *cant* word in a lyric is an offence; as in the line: " This may distress the *worldling's* mind."

Original Lines.	Sabbath Hymn Book.
	Hymn 587.
And all *my carriage* mild.	My *words and actions* mild.
	Hymn 1202.
Tremblers beside the grave.	*Trembling* beside the grave.

On the other hand, the original phrases are oftener more conformed to general usage than are the alterations. Baptist Noel's verse, " While yet *in anguish he* surveyed," is better than the change in the Presbyterian N. S. Hymn Book (Hymn 507): " While yet *his anguished soul* surveyed."

§ 19. *Alterations in the Text, as affecting the Service of Song.*

It is a general rule, that a church lyric should retain its marked character from the beginning to the close of it; that it should not commence with a jubilant and end with a pathetic strain; that its first stanzas, if gentle and tender, should not be followed by stanzas bold, rugged, exultant. When a hymn thus diversified is to be merely *read*, the free voice can overcome all the difficulties attending the heterogeneous composition. Indeed, the change from "grave to gay, from lively to severe," may impart a new freshness and energy to the hymn. But when it is to be sung in an ordinary standard tune, the same notes are to be used for both the melting and the rapturous words; and, therefore, cheering sentiments will be uttered with plaintive tones, or mournful thoughts will find vent in exhilarating strains. There are various methods in which this evil may be remedied in some degree; still it commonly remains an evil.

It is also a general rule, that the musical accent be the same with the syllabic, and that the correspondent lines of a stanza contain the like succession and kind of poetic feet. When the lyric is to be merely recited, the unfettered voice can hide the faults arising from the want of uniformity in the feet of one line, and the want of symmetry in the successive stanzas of a couplet, or the alternate stanzas of a quatrain. Sometimes, indeed, the irregular accentuation, breaking up the monotony of a poem, may give relief to the ear and add vivacity to the lines. There are no inflexible marks of notation to which the reader is bound, and he may so manage the cesural pause as to refresh and enliven the stanzas which otherwise might have a *humdrum* air. In music, however, there is a fixed system of notation, and the musical bars will not bend this way and that, for a wrong accent of the composer. The musical accentuation is a strong emphasis, and when a decided stress is placed on the wrong syllable, the idea is not given forth with its becoming power; occasionally it is hidden under the gross impropriety of utterance. A preacher would divert the mind of his auditors to a very unedifying topic, if in reading Doddridge's hymn " Gird on thy conquering sword," he should conform to the rhythm of the stanza:

> " Fair truth' and smil'ing love',
> And in'jured right'eous*ness*',
> In thy' *reti'nue* move,
> And seek' from thee' redress'.

In some tunes a man is compelled to utter the following lines with a style of emphasis, which would expose him to ridicule if it were heard in a recitation: "God *of'* my strength', how long' shall I';" "The praises' *of'* my God' shall still' My heart' and tongue' employ';" "An an'gel *of'* the Lord' came down';" "Sing *to'* the Lord' with cheer'ful voice'."

The faults of a hymn are often made the more conspicuous by this want of conformity between the accents of the verse, and the accents of the music. Thus two old Psalms of the Church of England have been often sung with this inaccurate emphasis:

"And as' thou art' of all' men judge',
O Lord', so judge' thou me'
Accord'ing *to'* my right'eousness',
And mine' integ'ri-*ty'*.
For this' our tru'est in'terest is',
Glad hymns' of praise' to sing';
And *with'* loud songs' to bless' his name',
A most' delight'ful *thing'*."

In the more recent, as well as in the more ancient English hymns, the accents of the verse often fail to correspond with those by which the music is measured. This is an *imperfection;* often, indeed, a necessary one, one to which we must submit, — but for all that, except in some peculiar cases, it remains an *imperfection.*

We often hear of va'n*ity'*, glor*y'*, captiv'*ity'*, humil'*ity'*. wor'ship*per'*, ter'ri*ble'*, insen'si*ble'*, etc., in our tunes, although not in our speech. Nor is this a matter of mere sound. Sometimes the meaning of a stanza is marred by the dissonance between the accents with which the verse is read, and those by which the music is measured. Even Addison's most perspicuous version of the twenty-third Psalm, may be sung in such a manner as to proclaim the following sentiments: "The Lord' my past'ure *shall'* prepare':" He *shall* do it; there is an imperative force upon him; "And feed' me *with'* a Shep'herd's care';" as if *with* were to be carefully distinguished from *by*, which expresses a more distant relation; "His pre'sence *shall'* my wants' supply';" there must be no attempt to evade this mandate; "And guard' me *with'* a watch'-ful eye';" *with* it as if He might be suspected of guarding *without* such an instrument. The transparency of Addison's hymn would leave even this emphasis intelligible, but would not make it felicitous or impressive.

English lyrists have been far more inattentive than were the old Latin and Greek poets, to the due correspondence between the accents required by music, and those required by the sense of the verse, or by the laws of pronunciation. Indeed, some of the most admirable hymnists have occasionally intermingled the Trochee with the Iambus, so that their verses cannot be even *read* harmoniously without giving a wrong accent to some one syllable. In the recitation of Cowper's touching lyric, "Far from the world, O Lord, I flee," we have often heard sad blunders:

"There *if'* thy Spi'rit touch' the soul',
And grace' her mean' abode',
Oh *with'* what peace' and joy' and love',
She *com'munes* with' her God'."

Dr. Nettleton,[1] who did not hesitate to introduce

[1] In his preface to these hymns he says, pp. v. vi.: "In all cases, excepting the hymns of established reputation, wherever abridgment or

many accentual changes into his Village Hymns, has modified the final line thus: "She *there' com'munes with God'*." Unless we adopt this modification, we must read the word com'-mune, with an accent which will of itself attract the attention from the sentiment of the line to a question of orthoepy. Dr. Nettleton's alteration ought to be adopted in any *ordinary* hymn; but so many precious associations cluster around this stanza as it was first written, that perhaps it were wiser to leave the line as Cowper left it.

This introduces the question: How far may the structure of a stanza be modified, so as to obtain a symmetry between the successive lines of a couplet, or the alternate lines of a quatrain. We have no hesitation in answering, that such modifications have been carried to an extreme. Musical difficulties have been too much magnified, and the facility of overlooking faults of accent has been underrated. Changes have been introduced into established hymns with some gain to the sound, but with much loss to the sense; or else with some gain to both the sound and the sense, but not enough to justify the disturbance of old associations.

But a man need not become insane, merely because he has found out one truth. Although too many sacrifices have been made to the symmetrical accentuation of our songs, we still believe that this excellence, so marked in the lyrics of Greece and Rome, may conduce to the spirituality of our worship. Our hymns were written with the design that they be uttered in

---

alterations were deemed conducive to the design of this volume, they have been made without hesitation." His changes in hymns of established repute, may have been made *with hesitation*, but they were made, nevertheless.

measured cadence. If not written according to the laws of musical delivery, they may here and there be made more significant, more emphatic, more solemn, by giving the prominent position to the syllable expressing the prominent idea. "And *swift* fulfil his word," is a more sensible phrase than "Swift *to* fulfil his word." Watts put the accent right in "Not *all'* the dainties of a feast." Dr. Worcester added no force to the line by changing the accent, "Not *the'* rich dainties of a feast." The order of the words is often inverted, not *merely* for the music, but also for the sentiment, not always to avoid a ridiculous *error* in elocution, but sometimes to make the words more expressive of their meaning. The following are specimens by no means more decisive than many others of accentual changes, aiding rather than impairing the significance and the decorum of the hymn.

ORIGINAL.	SABBATH HYMN BOOK.
	Hymn 13.
Who on'ly on' thee dost' rely', And in' thee on'ly rest'.	*Who* doth' on thee' alone' rely, In thee' alone' doth rest'.
	Hymn 203.
From whence' my bless'ings flow.'	*Whence all'* my bless'ings flow'.
	Hymn 723.
O deign' to *list'en* to' my voice'.	Oh deign' to *hear'* my mourn'ful voice'.
	Hymn 1067.
With full' consent' thine *I'* would be'.	With full' consent' I *thine'* would be'.
	Hymn 1099.
Like us' thou *hast'* a mour'ner been'.	Like us' a *mour'ner thou'* hast been'.
	Hymn 230.
How blest' *they are'* and on'ly they', Who in' his truth' confide'.	How blest' are *they'*, and on'ly they', Who in' his truth' confide'.

Original.	Sabbath Hymn Book.
	Hymn 866.
Still I' am noth'ing with'out love'.	Still *am'* I noth'ing with'out love'.
	Hymn 1171.
If I' must die', Oh! let' me die', Trusting' in Jes'us' blood'.	If I' must die', Oh! let' me die', *With hope'* in Jes'us blood'.
	Hymn 1194.
The pains', the groans', the dy'ing strife' Fright our' approach'ing souls' away', Still *we'* shrink back' again' to life'.	The pains', the groans', the dy'ing strife', Fright our' approach'ing souls' away', We *still'* shrink back' again' to life'.
	Hymn 1201.
Cease *then'* fond na'ture, cease' thy tears'.	Then *cease'*, fond na'ture, cease' thy tears'.
	Hymn 1268.
Bless'ing and' fore'ver blest',	*Ev'er bles'sing*, ev'er blest'.
	Hymn 362.
The world', sin, death', and hell' o'er-threw'.	Who sin', and death', and hell','o'er-threw'.

The impression has been extensively made, that the accentual changes of hymns are found only, or chiefly, in the Church Psalmody of Dr. Lowell Mason and Rev. David Greene. But they are found with still greater frequency, in many English Manuals, and are numerous in all the Hymn Books published in this country. The following is a specimen of changes for the sake of accent found in the Presbyterian [Old School] Collection.

Original Form.	Altered Form.
Watts's 4th Psalm.	*Presbyterian Old School Collection.*
Counting' the min'utes as' they pass.	And count' the min'utes as' they pass'.
Watts's 18th Psalm.	*Presbyterian Old School Collection.*
Then *did'* his grace' appear' divine'.	And *proved'* his sav'ing grace' divine'.

Original Form.	Altered Form.
Watts's 18*th Psalm.* Sweet *is'* the peace' my Fa'ther gives'.	*Presbyterian Old School Collection.* *While heav'enly peace'* my Fa'ther gives'.
Watts's 25*th Psalm.* Till *the'* dark eve'ning rise'.	*Presbyterian Old School Collection.* Till eve'ning shades' arise'.
Watts's 29*th Psalm.* *Over'* the o'cean *and'* the land'.	*Presbyterian Old School Collection.* Through ev'ery o'cean, ev'ry land'.
Watts's 32*d Psalm.* Through *his'* whole life' appears' and shines'.	*Presbyterian Old School Collection.* Through *all'* his life' appears' and shines'.
Watts's 34*th Psalm.* They *in'* his praise' employ' their breath'.	*Presbyterian Old School Collection.* His praise' employs' their tune'ful breath'.
Watts's 50*th Psalm.* Call *up'on me'* when trou'ble's ne'ar.	*Presbyterian Old School Collection.* *Invok'e* my *na'me* when tro'uble's ne'ar.
John Newton. Now when' the eve'ning sha'de prevails.'	*Ibid., Hymn* 400. But now', when eve'ning shade' prevails'.

Watts's 4*th Psalm.*
Know that' the Lord' divides' his saints,'
  From all' the tribes' of men' beside' ;
He hears' *the cry' of pen'itents'*.
	Presbyterian Old School Collection.
	Know that' the Lord' divides' his saints,'
	  From all' the tri'bes of men' besi'de ;
	He hears' and pit'ies their' complaints'.

Watts's 31*st Psalm.* How *won'drous is'* thy grace', And trust' thy *pro'mises'*.	*Presbyterian Old School Collection.* How *sweet'* thy *smil'ing face'*, And trust' thy *prom'ised grace'*.
Watts's 31*st Psalm.* Among' mine en'emies' my name' *Was a' mere pro'verb* grown'.	*Presbyterian Old School Collection.* Among' mine en'emies' my name', *A pro'verb vile' was* grown'.
Watts's 84*th Psalm.* Blest are' the saints' who sit' on high,' Around' thy throne' *of maj'esty'*.	*Presbyterian Old School Collection.* Blest are' the saints' who sit' on high,' Around' thy throne' *above' the sky.*

What has been said with regard to the *kind* of feet in consecutive verses, applies also to the *number* of feet. This number must be uniform in the correspondent lines. An occasional excrescence of a verse may promote the vivacity of a poem which is to be simply recited; but if it is to be sung to an established measure, with regularly recurring accents, the words must be fitted to this measure.

ORIGINAL COUPLETS.	REGULAR COUPLETS.
Nor ever may we parted be, *Till I become one spir-it with thee.*	*May I be one, O Lord, with thee,* *And never parted may we be.*
The trees of life immortal stand, In *flour-ish-ing* rows at thy right hand.	The trees of life immortal stand, In *beauteous* rows at thy right hand. *Watts, Book II., Hymn* 15.

Formerly the word *prayer* was pronounced in two syllables. At present, it is uttered in one; and the word *pray-er*, in two syllables, would suggest the *person who prays*. In the hymns of Watts we find the following lines:

ORIGINAL.	WORCESTER'S WATTS.
	Book I., Hymn 1.
Those are the *pray-ers* of the saints.	These are the *prayers* of *all* the saints.
	Book II., Hymn 123.
And *pray'er* bears a quick return.	And *prayers'* produce a quick return.
	Book II., Hymn 156.
For *pray'er* and devotion are But melancholy breath.	For prayer' and *grave* devotion are But melancholy breath.

The word *heaven* is sometimes pronounced in two syllables, but more properly in one; therefore the original lines, "Our *heav'en* is' begun'," "And bowed' the *heav'ens* high'," are changed into "Our *heaven'* is *here'* begun'," "And bowed' the *heavens' most* high'." In a common metre line admitting only six syllables, Henry Kirke White has written: "In the distant peal it dies;"

but the line is generally altered into, "In distant peals it dies."

There is an exquisite hymn of Phœbe Carey, which has appeared in at least four different forms, and which must be either excluded from the songs of the sanctuary, or must be divested of its original rythmic inequalities.

ORIGINAL FORM.	SABBATH HYMN BOOK.

One sweetly solemn thought
  Comes to me o'er and o'er, —
I am nearer home to-day,
  Than I have ever been before ; —
	One sweetly solemn thought
	  Comes to me o'er and o'er,
	Nearer my parting hour am I,
	  Than e'er I was before.

Nearer my Father's house
  Where the many mansions be ;
Nearer the great white throne,
  Nearer the jasper sea ; —
	Nearer my Father's house,
	  Where many mansions be ;
	Nearer the throne where Jesus reigns;
	  Nearer the crystal sea ;

Nearer the bound of life,
  Where we lay our burdens down ;
Nearer leaving the cross,
  Nearer gaining the crown.
	Nearer my going home,
	  Laying my burden down,
	Leaving my cross of heavy grief,
	  Wearing my starry crown ;

But lying darkly between,
  Winding down through the night,
Is the dim and unknown stream
  That leads at last to the light.
	Nearer that hidden stream,
	  Winding through shades of night,
	Rolling its cold, dark waves between
	  Me and the world of light.

Closer and closer my steps
  Come to the dark abysm ;
Closer death to my lips
  Presses the awful chrysm.
	Jesus ! to thee I cling ;
	  Strengthen my arm of faith ;
	Stay near me while my way-worn feet
	  Press through the stream of death.

Father, perfect my trust ;
  Strengthen the might of my faith ;
Let me feel as I would when I stand
  On the rock of the shore of death,—	

Feel as I would when my feet
  Are slipping o'er the brink ;
For it may be I'm nearer home,—
  Nearer now than I think.	

The principles laid down with regard to symmetry of accent and of poetic feet, are also applicable to the character of the sounds in a lyric. Many a hymn, when silently *read*, will admit such lengthened words as enfeeble it when it is *sung*. The line, "*Praise him in evangelic* strains," cannot be uttered in music with as much vivacity as the substituted line, "*Sing to his name in lofty* strains" (Sabbath Hymn Book, Hymn 1285); nor can the words, "How *honorable* is the place," appear so quickening as the words, "How *honored is the sacred* place" (*Ib.*, 1028). In song, the lingering of the voice on the line, "The world's *allurements, Satan's* snares," is heavier than the delay upon "The world's *alluring, fatal* snares" (*Ib.*, 984). We feel the tediousness of *singing* the words of Conder:

"*For there the great Propitiatory
Abolished all* my guilt."

But we can readily sing the substituted line, which equally agrees with the principal aim of the hymn:

"*My soul is melted at the story
Of him who bore* my guilt." — *Sab. H. B., Hymn* 367.

"For good is the Lord, *inexpressibly* good," may well be exchanged for "Good is the Lord, *ever gracious and* good," because the polysyllable is not only too drawling and sibilant, but also too much in the style of fashionable boarding-schools.

The Connecticut Hymn Book substitutes "*afflicted*," for "*dispeopled;*" "In times of *danger and* distress," for "*general* distress;" "*ordainest*," for "*determinest;*" "*enduring*," for "*substantial;*" "*deep, repentant*," for "*penitent;*" " And *soon he brings* them low,". for " And *he reduced* them low;" "*At once eternal* night," for "*An instantaneous* night;" "O, *for the day,*" instead of " O, *happy period;* "—and so in numerous instances.

The long, open vowels, and the liquid consonants, are also preferable, in song, to the short vowels and the mute consonants. Dr. Worcester inserts, " At Emanuel's birth," in the place of " At Jesus' birth." "*Omnipotence* with wisdom shines," is often exchanged for "*Almighty power* with wisdom shines." The line of Wardlaw, " Loads every *minute* as it flies," is altered into " Loads every *moment,*" etc. For the same reason, the line of Worcester's-Watts, " Oh, for a sight, a *pleasant* sight," should be restored to the original, " Oh, for a sight, a *pleasing* sight;" and the verse in the Connecticut Hymn Book, " And let thy *excellence* be known," should be restored to Doddridge's original, " And let thy *various charms* be known."[1]

There are some lyrics which require rough and even harsh words. A sterling hymn should nor be sacrificed because here and there it has admitted a jagged syllable. Still, the general rule demands mellifluous cadences for our sacred songs. In despite of the grating syllables found so often in the lyrics of Watts, it is evident that he strove after " the concord of sweet sounds," and did not mean to be understood literally, when he sung:

"How jarring and how low
Are *all* the notes we raise."

In some of his most exquisite hymns, he resorts to the quaint aphæresis, for the sake of euphony:

[1] Sabbath Hymn Book, H. 256, 1235, 1024.

ORIGINAL.	WORCESTER'S WATTS.
	Book II., Hymn 36.
Now may our joyful tongues Our Maker's *honors* sing; Jesus, the Priest, receives our songs, And bears 'em to the King.	Now may our joyful tongues Our Maker's *honor* sing; Jesus, the Priest, receives our songs, And bears *them* to the King.
	Book II., Hymn 41.
Vanish as though I saw *'em* not.	Vanish as though I saw *them* not.
	Book II., Hymn 77.
Thy Jesus nailed *'em* to the cross, And sung the triumph when he rose.	Thy Jesus nailed *them* to the cross, And sung the triumph when he rose.
	Book II., Hymn 23.
And stand and bow amongst *'em* there.	And stand and bow amongst *them* there.

While the following changes promote the symphony of the hymns, they also conduce to their impressiveness:

ORIGINAL.	SABBATH HYMN BOOK.
	Hymn 5.
Whilst thou o'erlook'st the guilty stain, And *washest out* the crimson dye.	*For grace shall cleanse* the guilty stain, And *wash away* the crimson dye.
	Hymn 693.
Tabor's glorious *steep* I climb.	Tabor's glorious *mount* I climb.
	Hymn 783.
That wished for period soon will come.	*Ere long that happy day* will come.
	Hymn 890.
Shall melt away, and *drop*, and die.	Shall melt away, and *droop*, and die.
	Hymn 1035.
And joyful from the *mountains'* tops.	And joyful from the *mountain* tops.
	Hymn 1047.
And seals the *blessings* sure.	And seals the *blessing* sure.
	Hymn 536.
"Listen, sinner;" "Hasten, sinner."	"Hear, O sinner;" "Haste, O sinner."
	Hymn 889.
Where *thy' great cap'tain Sa'viour's gone'*.	Where *Je'sus thy' great Cap'tain's gone.*

Our hymns often contain abrupt transitions which confuse the singer. Therefore such lines as, " But what to those who find ? ah! this, Nor tongue, nor pen can show," " And endless praise. Amen," " Oh! for a seraph's wing of fire ? No, — on the mightier wings of prayer," — may well be smoothed down, as in the Sabbath Hymn Book, Hymns 687, 1170, 978.

We are aware of the objections urged against all alterations of hymns for the mere service of song. But we must be also aware, that the very idea of a metrical version of David's Psalms, is the idea of changing their structure for the sake of the tunes. The title-page of a renowned manual for song is: " A New Version of the Psalms of David, *fitted to the tunes used in churches.* By N. Brady, D. D., late Chaplain in Ordinary, and N. Tate, Esq., late Poet Laureate to the King of England." Dr. Watts did not intend even to *imitate* the internal structure of the inspired Psalms; but he transformed them, in order to adapt them to certain tunes. He appends the following notes to various Psalms:

Psalm 50. Pause 2. "If the former Heroic Metre do not fit the old Proper Tune of the fiftieth Psalm, for want of Double Rhymes at the end of every stanza, I have here altered the form of it much, in order to fit it exactly to the old Proper Tune; adding a Chorus, or (as some call it) the Burden of the Song, betwixt every Four Lines. I hope it will not be displeasing to the more Musical Part of my Readers, to be entertained with such a Variety."

Psalm 104. "This Psalm may be sung to the Tune of the old 112th or 127th Psalm, by adding these two lines to every stanza, viz.:

> Great is the Lord ; what tongue can frame
> An equal honor to his name ?

Otherwise it must be sung as the 100th Psalm."

Psalm 139. "The Epiphonema, or the Burden of the Song, that I have inserted three times in the first Part, was not introduced by any means to add Beauty to the Poem, but merely to reduce it to convenient lengths for Singing, which has too often confined the Ode and debased it."

Psalm 148. "This Psalm may be sung to the Tune of the old 112th or 127th Psalm, if these two lines be added to every stanza, viz.:

> Each of his works his name displays,
> But they can ne'er fulfil the praise.

Otherwise it must be sung to the usual Tunes of the Long Metre."

§ 20. *Changes in the Text, as resulting from Changes in the Application of a Hymn.*

"You may alter the *phraseology*, but you must not alter the *meaning* of a song." This is often asserted. But the words and the idea of many a hymn are changed, in consequence of a change in its application from one *place* to another. Thus "*British* lands" become "*Christian* lands;" the "*British islands*" become "*Gentile nations*" or "*these western climes;*" simple "*Britain*" becomes *Zion;*" "*this northern isle*" becomes "*these western shores.*" Where can there be a more decided abandonment of an idea, than in the following change of the old national song of England?

Dr. Watts's Version, B. II. 111.	The American Version.
Long may the *King, our Sovereign* [George I.] *live*, To rule us by his word ; And all the honors *he* [Geo. I.] can give Be offered to the Lord.	*Still* may the *King of Grace descend*, To rule us by his [Jehovah's] word ; And all the honors *we* can give, Be offered to the Lord.

The following are specimens of nearly fifty such alterations.

DR. WATTS.	DR. WORCESTER.
	Psalm 60.
Great Britain shakes beneath thy stroke, O heal the *island* thou hast broke.	*Our nation trembles at* thy stroke, *Oh* heal the *people* thou hast broke.
	Psalm 67.
Shine, *mighty God, on Britain* shine. *While British* tongues exalt his praise, And *British hearts* rejoice.	Shine *on our land, Jehovah,* shine. *Let ev'ry tongue* exalt his praise, And *ev'ry heart* rejoice.
	Psalm 96.
In Britain is Jehovah known.	*Among us* is Jehovah known.
	Psalm 100. *2d Part.*
The *British* isles shall send their voice.	The *northern* isles shall send their voice.
	Psalm 104.
What noble fruit the vines produce! The olive yields a *shining* juice; Our hearts are cheered with gen'rous wine, With inward joy our faces shine.	What noble fruit the vines produce! The olive yields *an useful* juice; Our hearts are cheered with gen'rous wine, With inward joy our faces shine.
	Psalm 104.
O bless his name, ye *Britons* fed With nature's chief supporter, bread.	O bless his name, ye *people* fed With nature's chief supporter, bread.
	Psalm 115.
O Britain, trust the Lord: thy *foes in vain.* And *Britain* bless the *Lord that* built the skies.	*In God we trust; our impious* foes in vain. And *Zion* bless the *God who* built the skies.
	Psalm 135.
O Britain, know thy living God.	*Ye saints, adore the* living God.
	Psalm 145.
Let *Britain round her shores* proclaim.	Let *ev'ry realm with joy* proclaim.
DR. KIPPIS.	*Select* 433.
Oh, still may God in *Britain* reign.	Here still may God in *mercy* reign.

The seventy-fifth psalm of David, being formally applied by Watts "to the Glorious Revolution by King William, or the Happy Accession of King George to the throne," declares that

" Britain was doomed to be a slave,"

and that William or George received his crown from the divine hand,

" And sware to rule by wholesome laws;"

but the second and third stanzas of that ode were essentially altered by Joel Barlow, in his edition of Watts's Psalms for the churches in Connecticut; and Barlow's alteration has been adopted by succeeding hymnologists. The one hundred and forty-seventh psalm of David is entitled by Dr. Watts, " A Song for Great Britain;" and after the opening appeal

" O Britain, praise thy mighty God,"

the psalm is made to assign the reason why that prospered island should send up notes of thanksgiving to Jehovah:

" He feeds thy sons with finest wheat,
And adds his blessing to their meat."

" To all the isle his laws are shown,
His gospel through the nation known;
He hath not thus revealed his word
To every land: Praise ye the Lord."

The presence of these distinctively British songs in Watts's Biblical Psalms, and the fact that he had not hesitated to alter the inspired odes, both in phrase and in *idea*, both in form and in *spirit*, was sufficient to justify the action of the General Association of Connecticut, at their meeting in June, 1784, when "it was thought expedient that a number of the Psalms in Doctor Watts's version, which are locally appropriated, should be altered and applied to the state of the Christian Church in general, and not to any particular country; and, finding some attempts had been made to alter and apply those Psalms to America, or particular parts of America, tending to destroy that uniformity in the use of Psalmody so desirable in religious assemblies, they appointed the Rev. Messrs. Timothy Pitkin, John Smalley, and Theodore Hinsdale, a Committee to confer with, and apply to Mr. Joel Barlow, of Hartford, to make the proposed alterations."

Occasionally, the application of a hymn is changed in regard to *time*. John Newton wrote a "Divine Song" for Saturday evening; but men who have loved his ode have desired to utter it on the Sabbath. Accordingly, it has been sung by thousands at Sabbath-morning Prayer-meetings, and at the opening of the more stately morning service in the temple; but with words differing somewhat from those of its pious author.

Newton's Form.	Common Form.
Safely through another week, etc.	Safely though another week, etc.
On the approaching Sabbath day.	*Waiting in his courts to-day.*
When the morn shall bid us rise.	*Here we're* [we] *come thy name to praise.*
When we in thy house appear.	*While* we in thy house appear.
There afford us, Lord, a taste.	*Here* afford us, Lord, a taste.

Sometimes, also, the application of a hymn is changed in regard to the *occasion* of its use. Addison celebrated his rescue from shipwreck by a touching poem of ten stanzas, which he never dreamed of hearing sung in the temple of God. But long after his decease, pious men adapted it to a public occasion, and inserted *general*, in the room of his more *personal*, phrases :

Addison's Hymn.	Altered Form.
How are thy servants blest, O Lord, etc.	How are thy servants blessed, O Lord, etc.
Through burning climes *I passed* unhurt,	Through burning climes *they pass* unhurt,
And *breathed* in tainted air.	And *breathe* in tainted air.
For though in dreadful whirls we hung.	*When by the dreadful tempest borne.*
The storm *was* laid, the winds *retired*, Obedient to thy will;	The storm *is* laid, the winds *retire*, Obedient to thy will;
The sea, that *roared* at thy command,	The sea, that *roars* at thy command,
At thy command *was* still.	At thy command *is* still.

In many hymns, the pronoun " I " need not be exchanged for " we," as the singular number is used *representatively* for the plural. The Rev. and Hon. Baptist Noel exchanges the singular for the plural, where he should have adhered to the old form; as in the line, " No more, O God, *we* boast no more." Occasionally, however, the pronoun " I " is so used in a lyric as to give it a special fitness to the hour of secret devotion; and, by substituting the plural for the singular, the general for the individual, the vivid present for the historical past, we make an individual, private song attractive to the band of worshippers. Such modifications of Addison's poem have given it the currency which it has enjoyed during the last thirty years.

An impressive Hymn of Mrs. Barbauld, "How blest the sacred tie that binds," is often sung at the Marriage Festival, and is termed the "Wedding Hymn." When so used, its original form is retained, for it was at first written to celebrate the "pious friendship" of *two* persons :

> "Together *both* they seek the place,
> Where God reveals his awful face."

But when the hymn is used to describe the mutual love of *all* Christians, its form is changed, and in our manuals for public song we read,

> "Together *oft* they seek the place," etc.

So the "Thanksgiving Hymn" of Mrs. Barbauld was not originally adapted to the service of the sanctuary, but has become deeply seated in the heart of many congregations, by a few changes like the following:

Mrs. Barbauld's Hymn.	Sabbath Hymn Book, H. 1142.
Praise to God, immortal praise, etc.	Praise to God, immortal praise, etc.
For the *vine's exalted juice,* For the *generous olive's* use.	For the *joy which harvests bring,* *Grateful praises now we sing.*
Clouds that drop *their fattening* dews; Suns that *temperate warmth* diffuse;	Clouds that drop *refreshing* dews; Suns that *genial heat* diffuse;
These, *my* God, to thee we owe.	These, *great* God, to thee we owe.
And for these *my soul* shall raise Grateful vows, etc.	And for these *our souls* shall raise Grateful vows, etc.

One of our best hymns for the dedication of a sanctuary, begins with the line: "*When in these courts we seek thy face;*"[1] but the original hymn of Montgom-

---

[1] Sabbath Hymn Book, Hymn 1071.

ery begins: "*This stone to thee in faith we lay.*" Montgomery's second stanza commences: "*Here, when thy people seek thy face.*" His hymn was written for "Laying the foundation stone of a place of worship." It must therefore be accommodated, when used for a Dedication hymn.

On the same principle, the hymns of Dr. Doddridge are often modified. "Being composed to be sung after the author had been preaching *on the text prefixed to them*, it was his *design* that they should *bring* over again the *leading thoughts in the sermon*, and naturally express and warmly enforce those devout sentiments which he hoped were *then* rising in the minds of his hearers, and help to fix them on the memory and heart."[1] It is difficult to over-estimate the effect which must have been produced by these pertinent hymns, when they had all the advantage of extemporaneous effusions. A sermon had been preached on the words: "My son, be of good cheer; thy sins be forgiven thee." Then the hymn prepared for that sermon broke forth in a prayer:

> "My Saviour, let me hear thy voice
> Pronounce *these words* of peace."

But when no discourse has been preached on "*these words*," the hymn, as adapted to general worship, may supplicate for "*the word*" of peace.[2]

There are some odes, written for a particular denomination of Christians, and containing phrases like "mother church," "dear holy church," "our goodly

---

[1] Dr. Orton's Preface to Doddridge's Hymns. Original edition.
[2] Sabbath Hymn Book, Hymn 609.

church," which have become rather technical with that denomination, but which are not familiar to the mass of worshippers in other sects. It may divert many an humble suppliant from his song of prayer, if he be requested to sing, with Sir Robert Grant: "*Hear our solemn litany*," when he might, with equal propriety, and with more of a home-like feeling, utter the petition:

> Turn on us a favoring eye,
> Hear, oh hear, our solemn cry.[1]

§ 21. *The indispensable Necessity of some alterations in some hymns.*

There are critics who will tear down the defaced front of a mansion, leave the halls and chambers unprotected from wind, storm, vagrants, and robbers, and boast all the while that they have not altered the house; but if any architect put up a wall of freestone in place of the dilapidated brick, *he* makes a change! But in fact, he leaves the house more like the original, than it was left by the critics who tore much down and built nothing up. To take away the first or the last stanza of a hymn, is like knocking out the buttress of a structure which must depend either upon it or upon some new support. The new support is more substantially like the old one, than the absolute vacancy is. The 238th hymn of the Sabbath Hymn Book contains only four stanzas of Watts's original eight. These four are unaltered. But the spirit, logical order, and force of the hymn are more affected by

[1] Ibid., Hymn 740.

these bare omissions, than the 201st hymn is affected by its mere alterations. Many lyrics which are said to be curtailed but "unchanged," would be far more similar to their primitive form, if, while abridged, they were *also* made self-consistent and self-poised. When one of its lines, or even words is *exchanged* for another, the hymn is said to be "mutilated"! But if a couplet is *lopped off* altogether, and nothing put in its place, then the lyric is not "mutilated"! There is a precious hymn of Dr. Watts, containing *five* stanzas, from which Mr. Toplady has cut off *three*, but this abscission is not condemned as injurious — still he has altered the words of the second stanza, and *here* he is said to have maimed the original! He sings:

1

When I survey the wondrous cross,
  On which the Prince of Glory died,
My richest gain I count but loss,
  And pour contempt on all my pride.

2

Forbid, O Lord, that I should boast,
  Save in the *cross* of Christ my God.
I have, and wish to have, no trust,
  But in his righteousness and blood.

This is *the whole* of Mr. Toplady's 334th hymn. Now, in fact, he has marred the ode by his excisions of stanzas, far more than by his changes of single terms. In strict speech, the word *mutilate*, refers to a cutting off of verses, rather than a verbal change in them; and those hymn books which profess to quote the stanzas as the author left them, often contain the very sorest mutilations. They pretend to make no changes of words, but they leave out words, metaphors, ideas, the more important ideas, from the very hymn which they represent as at first so exquisitely finished that it will not endure the alteration of a particle. They scorn to prune a line, therefore they cut off a stanza. They disdain to change one offensive phrase, therefore they omit the entire hymn. They are like a florist who shrinks from straightening one crooked twig, and therefore cuts up root and branch of the whole plant.

In citing a passage from our present version of the Bible, if we substitute a phrase or two of Wickliffe's translation, for some of the words authorized by King James, we may indeed impair the force of the passage, but often we may impair it far more by entirely dropping a few clauses, while exactly retaining the other words of King James. "For I am persuaded that neither death nor life shall be able to separate me from the love of God," is a more fearfully "mutilated" quotation than: "For I am certain that neither death nor life, neither angels, neither principalities nor powers, nor things present nor things to come, neither height, neither deepness, nor any other creature, shall be able to separate us from the charity of God that is in Christ Jesus our Lord." The *most highly finished* lyric has its beginning, middle, and end; its members are organized into one living system; each stanza is a complement to the preceding or the succeeding; all the stanzas modify, or introduce, or emphasize, or exalt each other. We break the chain, whatever link we strike. The once symmetrical composition we make disjointed and disproportioned, by leaving out a single couplet. The least beautiful line was a robe for all the others; if we take it away, they are left ragged or naked. We disturb the unity of the thoughts, we mar the brilliancy of the images, if we break up the relation in which they have stood to each other. We often disturb this relation by leaving out the couplet which once came between and cemented the parts. Not infrequently does it require a far more critical sagacity to ascertain what stanza should be omitted, than how a line can be advantageously altered. In compiling a hymn book, there is often more anxiety in determining what to leave out, than what to put in. There is the long one hundred and twenty-first psalm, " Up to the hills I lift mine eyes," a lyric which Dr. William E. Channing pronounced the grandest of all Dr. Watts's psalms, and one which nothing but an unpardonable audacity will tempt an editor to abridge. All its seven stanzas in long metre must be retained unaltered. But that exquisite ninety-second psalm of Watts: " Sweet is the work, my God, my king," containing the same number of verses in the same metre, and also that hymn which was the special favorite of President Edwards: " Ere the blue heavens are stretched abroad," containing only six stanzas in long metre, are usually and may be wisely curtailed. Good taste and good sense, rather than a fixed, arbitrary rule, must govern the hymnologist, here as elsewhere.

Notwithstanding all the evils resulting from the alteration of hymns by abridging them, the abridgment must, now and then, be made. In their original shape, our sacred songs consist often of ten, fifteen, twenty, or even fifty stanzas. All of these will not, cannot be sung at one time. Some of them must be left out, either by the editor, the minister, or the choir. It is better that they be omitted by the editor, leisurely, considerately, conscientiously, than that they be omitted by the clergyman or the singers, on a sudden, and without care or thought. Often the extemporaneous request that singers pass by several stanzas, leads them to sing nonsense, or something more fatal. When Dr. Lowell Mason was conducting the music in one of our city churches, the preacher read the entire hymn: " When thou, my righteous Judge, shalt come," and then requested that the singing of the second stanza be omitted. This omission left the following course of thought:

1
When thou, my righteous Judge, shalt come
To take thy ransomed people home,
Shall I among them stand?
Shall such a worthless worm as I,
Who sometimes am afraid to die,
Be found at thy right hand?

3
O Lord, prevent it by thy grace.

The Connecticut Collection has deliberately omitted the second stanza, and has adjusted the third to the first by the change: "*Blest Saviour, grant* it by thy grace."

But even when there is a connection preserved between the stanzas from which two or three have been extemporaneously stricken out, the fact that the preacher has omitted them, diverts the mind of worshippers to the query: *Why* did he omit them? or, Why did he omit *these* rather than *those?* or, Why were the omitted stanzas ever written? still more, Why were they ever republished?

In his Christian Psalmody, Dr. Worcester dispensed altogether with the fifteenth hymn of Watts's second book: "Let me but hear my Saviour say." He went too far; for the first three stanzas of the hymn, with slight modifications, are excellent. Afterwards, conceding to the popular demand for "Watts *entire*," the same editor felt compelled to insert, in his Worcester's Watts, all the five stanzas of the hymn unaltered. But will not every careful minister request his hearers to omit, and will he not, by that very request, tempt them to read, and will they derive any *sober* lesson from perusing, the monstrous fifth stanza: "So Samson, when his hair was lost," etc., etc.?

Other things being equal, the Hymn Book most congenial with the soul of public worship, and with all the demands of the Lord's day and the Lord's house, is that which contains the choicest variety of hymns fitted in their sentiment, their style, their length, to be sung just as they are printed, without any parade of verses to be read but not sung, and without any abrupt or jagged transitions which rouse the suspicion, that a critic's hammer has struck away some golden links. Even if it should be necessary, it would be a necessary evil, to request an audience to unite in the Lord's Prayer, omitting the supplications for daily bread and the forgiveness of sins. The best hymn is a prayer.

It is sometimes objected, that the entire hymn should be printed, even although a part only can be sung, because the worshipper ought to have a clear view of the ode in its original symmetry. But this objection overlooks the fact, that the ode is not sung for a literary exercise, but in the very act of communing with God.

The mind of the *worshipper* should not be occupied with an analysis, or with a scholar's admiration, of the hymn, but with an expression of its devout thoughts. Why should not the entire Litany of the Romish Church be printed in the Episcopal Prayer Book, in order to reveal the symmetry of the original address to Jehovah? — "But if the ode be one of the Psalms of David, shall we dare to curtail it? Shall not the complete work of inspiration be presented to the reader"? "We *must* have Watts entire, because we thus obtain David entire." — Now what does Dr. Watts himself confess? In a note to his 150th Psalm he writes, and he might have appended a similar remark to some other of his versions: "The greatest part of this Psalm suits not my chief design. I have therefore imitated only the two first verses, and the last, in a short Doxology or Song of Praise." The truth is, that in Watts we obtain *some parts* of *not all* the inspired odes; and if we demand a fac-simile of all the parts, we must abandon Watts's Imitation for Rouse's Version; and even then we shall not secure a copy of the Psalms complete.

§ 22. *Changes in the Text, as affecting its Consistency with itself.*

When an infant is baptized, is he offered to God by the whole family, — by the parents and by all their other children? This is a new theory of Infant Baptism. We find it implied, however, in one hymn-book which professes to insert its hymns unaltered. The genesis of the strange theory is the following. Dr. William Bengo Collier wrote three " *Family* Hymns for *Private*

Baptism," the first he entitles "Introductory;" the second, "Before the Administration;" the third, "After the Administration, *for the family.*" This third hymn contains six stanzas, and is, of course, too long for a baptismal ode. Therefore the second and third stanzas, are generally omitted. But the first stanza offers a prayer for the "*waiting family,*" the second for the "father," the third for the "mother," the fourth for the children of the father and the mother. When, therefore, the second and third stanzas are left out, and the remaining stanzas are not changed in accommodation to the first, the words which Dr. Collier applied to the parents, are transferred to the entire household, and we are left to pray for "the babe whom *they* [*i. e.*, the waiting family] devote to God.

Collier's Hymn.	The Abridged Hymn.
1	1
United prayers ascend to thee, Eternal Parent of mankind; Smile on this waiting family, Thy face they seek, and let them find.	United prayers ascend to Thee, Eternal Parent of mankind: Smile on this waiting family; Thy *blessing let Thy servants* find.
2 *The father of the household bless, The priest, the patriarch, let him move, That all his family may trace, In him thy law, in lines of love.* 3 *Regard the mother's anxious tears, Her heart's desire, her earnest prayers, And while her infant charge she rears, Crown with success her pious cares.*	[The second stanza, praying for the *father* is here omitted; the third stanza. praying for the *mother*, is also omitted; therefore, the next stanza has grammatical reference to the *waiting family*, who offer to God their babe.]
4 Let the dear pledges of their love, Like tender plants around them grow,	2 Let the dear pledges of their love Like tender plants around them grow;

COLLIER'S HYMN.	THE ABRIDGED HYMN.
Thy present grace, and joys above, Upon their little ones bestow.	Thy present grace, and joys above, Upon their little ones bestow.
5	3
Receive at their believing hand, The *babe whom* they devote as thine, Obedient to their Lord's command— And seal with power the rite divine.	Receive, at their believing hand, The *charge which* they devote as Thine, Obedient to their Lord's command, And seal, with power, the rite divine.
6	4
To every member of their house, Thy grace impart, thy love extend ; Grant every good that time allows, With heavenly joys that never end.	To every member of their house Thy grace impart, Thy love extend ; Grant every good that time allows, With heavenly joys that never end.

Did the Gentiles go through the wilderness, pilgrims and strangers on the earth ? So we are informed in a popular hymn book :[1]

* * * * * * * *

Gentiles the ancient promise read,
And find his truth endure.

Like pilgrims through the countries round,
Securely *they* removed. .

The trouble is, that the fourth and fifth stanzas of the psalm are omitted, the sixth is made to follow the third immediately ; and, therefore, the words which were meant for the Jews, are grammatically applied to the Gentiles.

These are two of the many examples proving, that if lyrics are modified by leaving words out, they must be still further modified by dovetailing together the words which are left in. That must be a remarkable

---

[1] Presbyterian New School Collection, Psalm 105.

hymn, and often a remarkably poor one, which will allow some of its component parts to be stricken out, and its remaining parts to come into a new connection, without any new connective words. Often, if a song be compact and symmetrical, its stanzas will be so inwoven with each other, that they cannot be transposed at pleasure, and its particles of transition will need to be new modelled in order to make the sixth stanza happily follow the third. A perfect hymn is an organism not a mere collection of words.

> *And* oh! whate'er of earthly bliss
> Thy sovereign hand denies.

Can we begin a lyric with this couplet? It commences the *eighth* stanza of a sanctuary song by Mrs. Steele. Our choicest hymn books omit the first seven of her song, and are therefore compelled to modify the eighth, when it becomes the first, by the address:

> *Father!* whate'er of earthly bliss
> Thy sovereign *hand* denies;[1]

The author of a favorite lyric never intended to *introduce* it by the words:

> Majestic sweetness sits enthroned
> Upon *his awful* brow.

His? Whose? This couplet introduces the *third* stanza of the original hymn. But when it stands in

---

[1] Nearly all our manuals of song contain the hymn thus modified, and nearly all substitute the word *will*, in the second line, for the word *hand*, which is the original. See the Presbyterian (O. S. and N. S.), the Dutch Reformed Church, and the Connecticut Collections.

the *first* stanza, it must be made more definite : " Upon the *Saviour's* brow," or, " *On my Redeemer's* brow."

The hundredth psalm of Watts, that to which the Old Hundredth tune was so wonderfully adapted, begins :

1 Sing to the Lord with joyful voice ;
Let every land his name adore ;
The British isles shall send the noise
Across the ocean to the shore.

2 *Nations attend, before his throne,*
With solemn fear, with sacred joy ;
Know that the Lord is God alone,
He can create, and he destroy.

Does the second of these stanzas, unmodified, conform to the laws for the introduction of a hymn ? Yet in almost all our American Collections, the second stanza becomes the first, and there retains the magnificent alteration made by John Wesley :

Before Jehovah's awful throne,
Ye nations, bow with sacred joy.

When a convert first approaches the table of his Lord, he begins his solemn hymn with the words :

" *While to thy table I* repair,
And seal the sacred contract there,
Witness, O Lord! my solemn vow ;
Angels and men attest it too."

But these lines were designed by their author, President Davies, to be the *fifth* stanza of a *common* sacramental hymn, and were therefore written in the ensuing form, which is not peculiarly appropriate for the *first* stanza of an *initiatory* communion hymn.

> "*Be thou the witness of my* vow,
> Angels and men attest it too,
> That to thy board I now repair,
> And seal the sacred contract there."

The *middle* stanza, which Davies wrote for an *ordinary* sacramental ode, is:

> Thine would I live, thine would I die,
> Be thine through all eternity;
> The vow is past beyond repeal,
> Now will I set the solemn seal.

But these lines are now sung by the convert, as the *concluding* lines of his *first* sacramental ode. Therefore, they are transposed so as to rise in the form of a climax, and to make the final words expressive of a full, spiritual surrender to God:

> The vow is past beyond repeal,
> Now will I set the solemn seal;
> Thine would I live, thine would I die,
> Be thine through all eternity.[1]

We have rarely seen in a church manual the entire hymn of Cowper, "There is a fountain filled with blood," printed as it was originally written (see Sabbath Hymn Book, Hymn 300). The Presbyterian [Old School and New School], the Reformed Dutch, the Connecticut, and the Plymouth Collections, introduce

---

[1] See three different arrangements of President Davies' ode in Sabbath Hymn Book, H. 1067, 1068, and Presbyterian (O. S.) Collection, H. 272.

various verbal changes. Besides the positive alterations, these hymn books omit the two final stanzas of the hymn. The positive alterations are often condemned; the mere omission is justified. And yet the mere omission is itself an important change. Cowper wrote the hymn so that it should end in sounding " no other name but" the Redeemer's. When, however, his two closing stanzas are omitted, the hymn is left to end with a " poor lisping, stammering tongue," " silent in the grave." In an English Hymn Book, printed in 1827, which closes with Cowper's fifth stanza, instead of his seventh, the evil of the omission is lessened by a transposition of couplets in the fifth stanza, and by thus making the abridged hymn end with a climax like that of the original. See Sabbath Hymn Book, Hymn 301. The following are the three stanzas closing the hymn in its three forms:

ORIGINAL TERMINATION.
'T is strung and tuned for endless years,
And formed by power divine,
To sound in God the Father's ears,
No other name but thine.

FIRST FORM OF THE MODIFIED TERMINATION.	SECOND FORM OF THE MODIFIED TERMINATION.
Then in a nobler, sweeter song, I'll sing thy power to save, When this poor, lisping, stammering tongue Lies silent in the grave.	And when this feeble, stammering tongue Lies silent in the grave, Then in a nobler, sweeter song, I'll sing thy power to save.

We are well aware that, in the present state of our literature, an entire self-consistency in a hymn cannot always be attained. Some of our most admirable songs for the temple are, in certain respects, incongruous with themselves. But we may innocently approximate to the desired congruity, by occasional variations of the original text; as when, for instance, the singular pronoun "I" needlessly alternates with the plural "we;" the *past* tense of a verb, with the *present;* the *solemn* style, with the *familiar,* etc. A celebrated hymn of Watts begins thus:

> Nor eye *hath* seen, nor ear *has* heard,
> Nor sense nor reason *know.*

One of our own spirited lyrists has written of the church, that she is unshaken while *rocked* to and fro:

> Though earthquake shocks are *rocking* her,
> And tempests are abroad —
>
> *Unshaken* as eternal hills,
> *Immovable* she stands.

It will certainly do no harm, either to the church or to this ode, if the shocks, instead of "rocking" this "unshaken" house, should merely "threaten" it, as in Sabbath Hymn Book, H. 1038.

§ 23. *Changes in a Hymn as affecting its Availability.*

"Shall *Simon* bear the cross alone?" A lyric beginning in this way would seldom be read from the pulpit. Therefore we find a better name than Simon's in the first line: "Must *Jesus* bear the cross alone?" — The Sheffield poet has written, "Faith, hope, and charity, — *these three;*" but where is the minister willing to commence a song of praise with this arithmetical announcement? —"*Eighteen* centuries have fled," says Josiah Conder; but Mr. Beecher would not probably have inserted this hymn, unless he had given up the notation, thus: "*Many* centuries have fled."

> "*Strange as it is, yet this may be,*
> *For creature-love* is frail;
> But thy Creator's love to thee,
> O Zion, cannot fail."

This stanza will not properly introduce a temple-song. Then a favorite ode of Mrs. Steele, on Isaiah 49:14—16, will remain unsung, unless its first available stanza be modified in some such manner as:

> "*Forgetful can a mother be?*
> *Yes: human love* is frail;
> But thy *Redeemer's* love to thee,
> O Zion! cannot fail."
> *Sabbath Hymn Book, Hymn* 420.

"The lofty tune let Michael raise," "Sat simply chatting in a rustic row," "Bids the rash gazer wipe the eye," "A box where sweets compacted lie," "His heralds are despatched abroad," "Pale-faced death will quickly come," "'T is palsy, dropsy, fever," "New Ebenezers to his praise," "My spirit labors up thine hill," "Christ to the young man said, Yet one thing more," "Thus much, and this is all we know," — these lines, unmodified, make the hymns containing them unavailable for church song; yet these very hymns, *with these stanzas modified*, are admitted into Mr. Beecher's Plymouth Collection.

Toplady, while in severe illness, wrote a sweet hymn

of fifteen stanzas, and sent it to the Countess of Huntington. It commences with the well-known lines:

> When languor and disease invade
> This trembling house of clay,
> 'T is sweet to look beyond *our cage*,
> And long to fly away.

The hymn closes with another allusion to *the cage*:

> Oh may the unction of these truths
> Forever with me stay,
> 'Till from *her sinful cage* dismissed,
> My spirit flies away.

For public worship, this mellifluous hymn must be abridged. It ordinarily closes with Toplady's fourteenth stanza:

> If such the sweetness of the stream,
> What must the fountain be,
> Where saints and angels draw their bliss,
> *Immediately* from thee!

But Toplady never intended to conclude his hymn with the polysyllabic "immediately." In order to give to the abridgment a more appropriate conclusion, the slow-moving adverb is exchanged for a more obvious address to Jehovah: "*Direct, O Lord*, from thee." If this hymn remain entirely unaltered, it will seldom be let loose from its cage.

That eminently Biblical, as well as popular hymn, "Had I the tongues of Greeks and Jews,"— shall we sing it? But it is like fifty other excellent hymns, containing one line unfit to be sung. For that one line, shall we drop the hymn from our Manual? Will not the volume be maimed and mutilated without it? May we not more wisely expurgate two words from the obnoxious line?

Original Form.	Sabbath Hymn Book.
Should I distribute all my store, To feed the *bowels of* the poor.	Should I distribute all my store, To feed the *hungry, clothe* the poor.

There is a solid hymn of Doddridge, " Lord of the Sabbath, hear our vows;" but this hymn, in the original form, has made confusion among hymnologists. Dr. Worcester's Watts has given one modification of it; the Presbyterian [Old School] Collection, another; the Church Psalmody has given a different version, altogether superior to the two preceding. The Sabbath Hymn Book has inserted this (Hymn 1254); and also Doddridge's original (Hymn 1253). But probably the abridged and amended form, although *perused* less, will be *sung* more, frequently than the lengthened form, as it was left by Doddridge himself.

We have no right to demand that *every* alteration made in the text of hymns, should increase their poetic excellence. Their religious use exceeds in value their merely rhetorical perfection. Some odes *will not* be sung in the sanctuary, unless they first undergo a modification. It were a signal blessing, if this modification could *always* augment their brilliancy as poems. But, alas! they must now and then suffer an abatement of their rhetorical splendor, in order to secure their acceptance with the majority of worshippers. Thus they are better *hymns*, while they are poorer *odes*. The question is: Shall we allow a poem to be useful in the *church*, at the expense of its popularity in the *school?* Shall we permit its religious utility to prevail over its artistic finish? Shall the Gothic cathedral be shorn of some rich ornaments, in order to adapt it, as an auditorium, to Protestant worship? The famed ode of Hillhouse, too dazzling, perhaps, for a sanctuary lyric, will be sung, as abridged in the Sabbath Hymn Book (H. 614), with more interest, and with far more frequency, than if its prolonged train of sentiment had been admitted entire.

§ 24. *Concluding Remarks.*

There are various other topics, requiring too large a space for our present notice, and intimating reasons *for* some changes, and *against* others.

The relation of a phrase to the ode which contains it, often suggests an argument for modifying that phrase, although in itself it may be superior to the words put in its place. Unexceptionable as it may be in any *other* ode, it may still help to make this ode monotonous, or gaudy, or stiff, or hard. When the entire hymn is in danger of too much *ring*, it is better to say: "Loud *sound* the harps around the throne," than "Loud *ring* the harps." The common reading of the sixth line in Watts's brilliant lyric: "What equal honors shall we bring," is, "The Prince of *Peace*, who groaned and died." Perhaps this reading should be retained, *because* it is so common; it was sanctioned by Toplady in 1776. It is not, however, the original. Watts wrote: "The prince of *Life*." Both designations are biblical. The reason for the well-nigh universal change of one Scriptural title for another is, that the hymn is already full of contrasts; it has the fault of many old English poems which *tire* their readers by strained, quick-returning antitheses; it sometimes becomes prosaic in the accuracy of its antagonisms, as: " *Wisdom* belongs to Jesus, too, Though he was charged with *madness* there;" and hence the mind is relieved by the absence of a striking opposition in the phrases of the sixth line : " The prince of *life* who groaned and *died*," — although, in almost any other hymn, this line would be preferable to the words now substituted for it.

The symmetry not only of a single ode, but also of an entire Collection, may require for one Manual such changes as are not demanded for another. Pope writes, " See lilies spring and sudden *verdure* rise;" but in one of Addison's exquisite hymns he admits the term, " *sudden* greens." This phrase has developed the verdancy of many readers. It has been changed by some hymnologists into " *sudden green*," by others into " *lively* green," and by others still into " lively *greens*." It is better to let the phrase bloom as Addison planted it. But there is no need of having it more than once in one Manual. Such a phrase, however, when it blossoms in a hymn of Addison, will certainly be transplanted into other odes. But when it is borrowed by inferior lyrists, may we not transform it into some new flower? Must we reiterate :

> " The effusions of his love shall share,
> And *sudden greens* and herbage wear."
> *Dr. Rippon's Hymn.*

> " With *sudden greens* and fruits arrayed,
> A blooming paradise."— *Dr. Gibbons's Hymn.*

Why are certain stanzas omitted or altered in the Sabbath Hymn Book? For a good reason; the same stanzas *are substantially* repeated elsewhere in that Manual. Why are those stanzas unaltered in the Church Psalmody? For a good reason; they are *not* substantially repeated elsewhere in that Manual. In order to determine the propriety or the impropriety of various omissions and new adjustments of verses, a critic must form a clear and comprehensive view of the entire Collection; of its aim, its plan, its mutual internal fitnesses, the relation of part to part, and of the various portions to the symmetrical whole. A maniac can slash upon a grove, but it can be well pruned by none other than a circumspect arborist.

It would often require a long time to enumerate all the reasons which combine to favor a single change of an original hymn; but here a convenient test for our criticisms may be furnished by this question: — If the author of the hymn had written it in its present modified form, should we have imagined that it would be improved by changing it into he form which he actually did select for it? If improved as a *poem*, would it be improved as a *hymn?* Perhaps we may not be able to specify the one prominent reason for the following changes; but would any one think of altering the stanzas of the right hand column, supposing them to be the author's own draught, into the stanzas of the left hand column, supposing these to be innovations upon the author?

Original Form.	Altered Form.
Our sins, alas! how strong they be, And, like a *vi'lent sea*, They break our duty, Lord, to thee, And *hurry us away*.	Our sins, alas! how strong they *are!* And like a *raging flood*, They break our duty, Lord, to thee, And *force us from our God*.

TEST OF PROPER ALTERATIONS. 297

ORIGINAL FORM.	ALTERED FORM.
For she *has* treasures greater far Than east *or* west unfold, And her *reward is more secure* Than *is the gain of gold.*	For she *hath* treasures greater far, Than east *and* west unfold, And her *rewards more precious are* Than *all their stores of gold.*
Come, almighty to deliver, Let us all thy grace receive; *Suddenly* return, and never Never more thy temples leave!	Come, almighty to deliver, Let us all thy grace receive; *Hasten thy* return, and never Never more thy temples leave!
Thee we would be always blessing, *Serve thee as thy hosts above,* *Pray and praise thee* without ceasing, *Glory in thy perfect love.*	*Dwell in us, with thy rich* blessing, *Dwell in us with all thy love;* *We will praise thee* without ceasing, *Serve thee as thy hosts above.*
If human kindness meets return, And owns the grateful tie; If *tender feelings in* us burn, *Because* a friend is nigh.	If human kindness meets return, And owns the grateful tie; If *tender thoughts within* us burn, *To feel* a friend is nigh.

The preceding discussion leads us to the following inference: that no short, indiscriminate, unbending rule can be laid down with regard to alterations of hymns; that every change must be judged by itself, and by its relation to the contents of the manual which allows it; that the main excellence of a lyric is neither its newness nor its oldness, but its inherent or relative fitness to express religious emotion; that we are not to sacrifice the best reading to our love of novelty nor to our love of antiquity, but are to sacrifice all our fondnesses for the novel or the ancient, to that reading which is the best in itself and on the whole; that a reading may be the best in itself, and yet not the best in all its relations; that long continued usage, popular prejudices, accidental associations, and general symmetry, may warrant a preference for a phrase which, in its own individual character, is unworthy of such a preference; that alterations always have been, always will be, and always must be, admitted into the sacred odes of different communities and different ages; but that the original text should be retained, unless there be imperative reasons for abandoning it.

CHAPTER III.

THE DIGNITY AND THE METHODS OF WORSHIP IN SONG.

§ 1. *Existing Feeling and Usage respecting the Service of Praise.*

THERE is at present, in the American churches, a widely prevalent, and rapidly growing dissatisfaction with the manner in which the praises of God are sung in his sanctuaries. It is felt that the legitimate and main object contemplated by them fails of being realized in any suitable degree, and that probably, in multitudes of instances, they do not convey to the Supreme Being any act of the heart, and therefore are not worship. Many a man who carefully interrogates his own experience will confess, that while the voice of public prayer readily engages his attention and carries with it his devout desires, it is not so with the act of praise; that he very seldom finds his affections rising upon its notes toward Heaven, — very seldom can say at its close that he has worshipped God. The song has been wafted near him as a vehicle for conveying upward the sweet odor of a spiritual service, but the offering has been withheld, and the song ascends as empty of divine honors as sounding brass or a tinkling cymbal.

The heartlessness which he discovers in himself, he very naturally suspects in others; and it is melancholy to observe, how few are the instances in which there is positive and satisfactory evidence that it does not exist. There is but little manifestation of interest in the service, either by voice, attitude, expression of countenance, or even by so much as a fixed attention. In saying this, we must except the case of those whose attention is gained by the interest which they feel in a musical performance. These give their attention, but they do not necessarily worship. Their minds are absorbed by the pleasure of sweet sounds, but not in any contemplation of the Being addressed by means of them. They do not make melody in their heart to the Lord.

There are many things in the appearance of our religious assemblies, which indicate that by general consent a less degree of sacredness is attached to the act of praise than to any other service of the hour. There is a degree of listlessness and inattention, which, if it were exhibited during the sermon, would be considered indecorous, if during the prayer, irreverent. The attitude of the audience, seated in easy, careless posture, their eyes often wandering in idle vacancy or inquisitive curiosity, indicates a very wide difference in their estimation between praise and prayer as claiming their reverent and devout attention. If one enters the sanctuary while prayer is offering, he pauses at once, and waits until the prayer is concluded. But if one enters during the singing, he may pace the whole length of the aisle, if need be, without an apparent suspicion that he interrupts any one's devotions. The singing is the time for the multifarious performances of the sexton. If strangers are to be seated, if notices are to be carried to the pulpit, if the blinds are to be adjusted, if ventilation is required, the singing of the hymn is supposed to furnish an intermission to the more important and sacred parts of divine service, during which these operations may, with impunity, be going on. It may be that even the minister's thoughts are wandering. He is finding the next hymn, and deciding which of the stanzas it will be best to omit; or, pencil in hand he is correcting his manuscript; or he is surveying his audience, to ascertain what portion of the uncertain and irregular attendants upon his preaching have honored him with their presence to-day. If there happen to be two ministers in the pulpit, the singing furnishes a convenient time to deliberate upon an equitable division between them of the several parts of the service. What a change does this show from the habits of our pilgrim fathers, whose reverence for the songs of the Lord's house was so great that it extended to the musical notes in which the psalms were sung! They uncovered their heads, as they would in prayer, whenever they heard one of the tunes sung, though not a word of the psalm was uttered.

This indifference to the religious import of the service being general, both in the pews and in the pulpit, it is not to be expected that the singing-gallery should form an exception. Very often the choir is composed largely of irreligious persons; or if not, they are usually young, and in the exertion of religious influence in the church to which they belong, they are rather followers than leaders. We have no right to look to them for any higher degree of religious edification from the act of praise, than is demanded by the general voice of the church. If the choir have reason to believe that it is not edification but entertainment, that is desired, it would be strange enough if they should not endeavor to furnish entertainment. As things now are, our choirs perfectly understand that their singing is not regarded as in any emphatic sense a religious act, but rather as a skilful performance, whose chief end is either musical gratification, a relieving variety in the order of worship, or at best, an enlivening influence preparative for what is to follow. It is true, that a plea may be instituted in favor of furnishing musical delight in the sanctuary, on the ground of its attractiveness to those who have no delight in prayer and preaching. But this plea is not a sufficient warrant for making pleasure-seeking or pleasure-furnishing a chief end in any service of the house of God. If, however, the church admit the plea, or if they do not strenuously resist it, they may be sure that the choir will meet its demands if it is possible. They will obtain every variety of music, sacred and secular, which the tune-venders can supply. They will indulge without stint the insatiable hankering after what is new and popular. They will have tunes made of songs, ballads, glees, minuets, martial airs; tunes drawn from German, French, and Italian operas; strains resembling as nearly as possible those which give delight in the drawing-room, at the banquet, on the parade-ground, in the popular concert-room, or even at the play-house. When an old and standard tune is sung, in which harmonies that are richly ecclesiastical adorn a plain, animated, stately melody, it will be with a feeling of condescension to those who cannot keep pace with the progress of the age, and will always require an apology to the musically enlightened.

In all this the choir are less to be blamed than we imagine. They do but meet the demand which is made upon them by the congregation. The fault lies mainly with the churches, which seem, until quite recently, to have dismissed all care for the honor of God in psalmody, and to have felt no responsibility about a service which it was their duty to guard with a wakeful and holy jealousy. Churches that would have quickly detected irreverence or lightness in prayer, or a pervading savor of secularity in the sermon, have shown a surprising insensibility to the domination which worldliness has usurped over the service of public praise. "If there is any department of practical duty," says the *Christian Examiner*, "in which the churches 'are carnal and walk as men,' it is here." Is it too much to say, of the great majority of our churches, that the spirit of piety has long since ceased to preside over their public songs, and that it is to be feared that these songs do neither express the devotions of the churches, nor promote their edification? The power of a psalmody purely religious in aim, in character, in association, and in the whole manner of its performance, is not experienced. Its wonderfully quickening influence upon the faith, hope, love, and zeal of the churches, such as it has been known to exert in some of the most interesting of its historic periods, is not now felt. There are hundreds of churches in our land, whose psalmody can hardly be called either an act of devotion or a means of grace. Its glory has departed; and with it, alas! much of that fervid glow of piety, and genial warmth of Christian affection, which have so often descended as heavenly gifts through the cloud of ascending praise.

Within a few years past, and especially since the recent religious revival, attention has been awakened more than ever before, to the evils which we have attempted to describe; and it has become a question deeply engaging the thoughts of many of the ministers and churches of the land, — How MAY OUR PSALMODY BE RESTORED TO ITS PROPER POSITION AND INFLUENCE IN THE SERVICES OF THE SANCTUARY?

In attempting to answer this inquiry, so far as we may be able, it is proposed, first, to offer a few thoughts upon *the importance of praise as an essential part of instituted worship*; and, then, to inquire *what manner of performing this service is most consonant with the ends which it contemplates.*

§ 2 *The Importance of Praise, as seen in its Nature.*

An act of praise is, by its nature, an exercise of elevated and direct worship. It is common for us to speak of the ordinary services of the sanctuary, as services of worship. Strictly speaking, however, the only services of worship are prayer and praise. We worship when we confess our sins and supplicate the divine favor, and we worship, when in devout contemplation of the adorable attributes and beneficent works of Jehovah, we thank and praise him. But in listening to divine instruction, or in preaching the word, there is not necessarily any act of worship. The dignity, sacredness, and solemnity of that act by which mortals approach the infinite Jehovah in the language of direct, personal address, belong to prayer and praise alone. However at fault our public praises may be, however they may fail of the high ends which they professedly contemplate, they still hold as conspicuous a place among the services of the house of God as prayer. Professedly, one half of our worship is praise. By general and almost universal consent, praise is so important a part of divine worship, that it is allowed to stand side by side with prayer, even though the manner of its performance is such, that often man seems to be praised, rather than God; human art and skill, rather than divine goodness and grace. And it accords with reason that God should be worshipped as much by praise as by prayer; that our minds should be as much occupied with the divine character and works, as with the thought of our own sins and wants. To worship God, is to pay him the honors which are his due. We worship him in confession and supplication, by the honor which is thereby paid to his forgiving and saving grace. But were it not for sin, and for the innumerable wants which sin occasions, our worship would not take this form. The worship of holy beings in heaven is chiefly praise. It concerns itself not with the wants of the creature, but with the perfections of the Creator. We do not say that affectionate, believing prayer, may not be as pure and acceptable an act of worship from the saints on earth, as praise. But it is less elevated, and less direct. Prayer is often a step toward praise; as when David says, "Bring my soul out of prison, that I may praise thy name." Such prayer relies on the grace whose exercise will furnish an occasion for praise; and thereby, indirectly, though truly, honors that grace. Indeed, we cannot deny that the faith which expects the grace which it supplicates, but has not received, pays peculiar honor to the hearer of prayer, through the confidence which it reposes in him. He is pleased with such faith. But must he not be still more pleased with those thankful ascriptions which refer the existence of that faith ultimately to him? "The praise of God," says an old English divine, "is the choicest sacrifice and worship under a dispensation of redeeming grace; this is the prime and eternal part of worship under the gospel."

§ 3. *The Dignity of Praise seen in the Divine Appointments respecting it.*

We see still further the importance of praise, when we notice the conspicuous part which God has caused it to form in the worship of both the Hebrew and the Christian church.

And let it be first observed, that the nation which he chooses to be peculiarly his own, and to illustrate to the world his will, as well in regard to the manner of his worship, as to other things, is an intensely musical nation. Poetry, song, and instruments of music, were the Hebrews' delight. No doubt their songs had cheered their hours of toil in Egypt, and mitigated their wearisome bondage.

He who "giveth songs in the night" had furnished them this solace in the long years of their oppression. For no sooner do they stand upon the shores of the Red Sea, a free nation, and safe from the fury of their pursuers, than they are ready, with timbrel in hand, for the performance of the triumphal ode, elaborate, and highly artistic in its structure, which Moses indites for them. In the haste of their flight from the land of their task-masters, they forget not to take with them their instruments of musical recreation and delight. The idolatrous service with which the people soon after worshipped the golden calf, was rendered by the aid of song. "The noise of them that sing, do I hear," said

Moses, as he came down from the mount. They celebrated their victories with music. David returns from the slaughter of the Philistine, to meet the welcome of singers and players from all the cities of Israel. The army of Jehoshaphat returns from its victory over the allied forces of Ammon, Moab, and Mount Seir, with psalteries, and harps, and trumpets. The social life of the Hebrews bore witness to their love of music. " The harp and the viol, the tabret and pipe, were in their feasts." The bringing of the ark from the house of Obed-Edom to Jerusalem, was an occasion of a very imposing musical performance. And on more ordinary occasions than this, the journeys of the people toward Jerusalem, in companies, from the towns and villages of the land, were enlivened by song. The collection of psalms commencing with the 120th, and ending with the 134th, were probably used on these occasions. " Ye shall have a song," says the prophet Isaiah, " as in the night when a holy solemnity is kept; and gladness of heart, as when one goeth with a pipe to come unto the mountain of the Lord." Evidently David had taken part in those musical processions, and his delight in them is shown by the pathetic allusion which he makes to them, during his temporary exile from the holy city. " When I remember these things, I pour out my soul in me; for I had gone with the multitude; I went with them to the house of God, with the voice of joy and praise." A greater than David was once found in one of those travelling companies, on its way to Jerusalem from Nazareth. He was then but twelve years of age; but he was a Jew, and doubtless partook of the characteristic tastes of the nation to which he belonged. Did not he also, like David, mingle his "voice of joy and praise," with the voices of his parents, his "kinsfolk and acquaintance"? We know the pleasure with which, in after-life, he listened to the hosannas of other Jewish children in the temple, and we always expect the children of a musical people to be singers. Perhaps there is no more striking illustration of the love of music in the Jewish people, than their taking their harps with them to Babylon, when they went there as captives. Exiled from their homes, and from their native hills and valleys, cut off from the joy of their great annual festivals in the city and temple of their pride, reduced to a humiliating subjection under an idolatrous power, they seemed to have looked upon their harps and songs as the only delight which remained to them. And when their captors call upon them for one of the songs of Zion, we discover that this national characteristic of the Hebrews is fully understood in Babylon.

He who knows the heart which he has created, saw fit very largely to use this national love of song in the religious training of the Hebrew people. In a great variety of ways he employed it as one of the most powerful means of raising their warmest thoughts, their best and highest impulses toward himself.

The national existence of this long-oppressed people was commenced in one of the most sublime outbursts of song which the earth has ever heard. The chosen captains of Pharaoh, his horses, his chariots, and his mighty host, were drowned in the Red Sea. They sunk to the bottom as a stone, and the depths covered them. On the eastern shore stood two and a half millions of liberated bondmen, still agitated by the conflict between hope and fear, while waves of joy were breaking in upon their hearts, like the returning billows upon which they gazed. How shall this day of wonders be made to teach this emancipated and exulting people its appropriate lesson? How shall these swelling and rapturous emotions upon this birth-day of a nation's freedom, which naturally would minister to pride and self-glorying, be turned into the channel of praise to God? Immediately, doubtless on that very morning, a song is furnished for the occasion from the lips of their inspired leader, picturing in most graphic expression the scene which had just been witnessed, and ascribing its glorious result, in almost every phrase, to Almighty power and goodness.

The heavenly pæan is caught from him, and reëchoed from more than a million of voices, till the air, now filled with morning light, is flooded with their song. "I will sing unto the Lord, for he hath triumphed gloriously; the horse and his rider hath he thrown into the sea." The vivid description proceeds, only pausing at the close of each stanza for another million of voices, led by Miriam, to pour in the sublime antiphonal refrain, "Sing ye to the Lord, for he hath triumphed gloriously; the horse and his rider hath he thrown into the sea."

Many things conspire to put it beyond question that this remarkable song, the most ancient now in existence, was dictated by the Spirit of inspiration, — its intrinsic grandeur and simplicity, the importance of the occasion, the desirableness that this first great national exercise of worship should embody a model form of praise, and, more than all, the reference which is made to it in the Apocalypse, as constituting a part of the song of final victory sung by martyrs in heaven, standing upon the sea of glass mingled with fire, — " And *they* sing the song of Moses, the servant of God, and the song of the Lamb."

Passing to the time when the Jews were established in their own land, and the elaborate system of Levitical worship was fully developed, we find under David and Solomon four thousand Levites praising the Lord with instruments of music, and two hundred and eighty-eight cunning men, well instructed in the songs of the Lord, praising with the voice. This expensive and magnificent musical establishment existed by special divine appointment. "For so was the commandment of the Lord by his prophets." Out of thirty-eight thousand Levites, four thousand were selected "to stand every morning to thank and praise the Lord; and likewise at even."

Not only did God select a musical nation to be his peculiar people, but he selected for its most celebrated king, a man who, while he was the greatest monarch and warrior of the nation, was at the same time its most gifted poet, and its sweetest psalmist.

He who furnished, for the use of public praise, a collection of sacred lyrics unrivalled in his own nation and in every other, who left an example to the world of enthusiastic, unfaltering, and almost heavenly praise, who from youth to old age, from a stripling to the time of gray hairs, with psaltery and harp and voice showed forth the loving-kindness of God every morning, and his faithfulness every night, — was he whom "the Lord commanded to be captain over his people," when he "sought him a man after his own heart."

The ancient ritual, when it had fully served the purpose intended by it, was destined to disappear.

Many things belonging to it utterly vanished away. But not so the temple songs. Our Saviour, when he sang with his disciples the passover hymn, not only conferred the highest honor upon the service of praise, as practised by the Jews, but, by connecting it as he did with the impressive ordinance which he was then establishing, most clearly indicated his will that, to the end of time, those who meet to remember him in the sacramental supper should remember him also in the hymn of praise and thanksgiving. If the collection of psalms commencing with the 113th, and ending with the 118th, was sung at the institution of the supper, as is commonly supposed, it certainly was not inappropriate to the occasion; for it contains the warmest sentiments of grateful recollection, holy joy, and cheerful consecration.

But the effusions of ancient inspiration, lofty and devout as they were, and in many respects unequalled, as they always will be, could not be expected to meet fully the wants of a new and vastly superior economy. Accordingly, we find provision made at a very early day for a new psalmody in the Christian Church. Among the supernatural gifts enumerated by Paul as bestowed upon the Corinthian church, the psalm is the first which he mentions. We cannot doubt that Paul himself possessed the gift, and that he refers to his exercise of it, when he says, " I will sing with the Spirit, and I will sing with the understanding also." We have historical evidence that the Christians, at about the close of the first century, were in the habit of meeting " to sing hymns to Christ as God." Such hymns must, of course, have originated in the Christian Church; and "it may not be improbable," says

Olshausen, " that the first Christian hymns, such as, according to Pliny, were sung by the Christians in their meetings, owed their origin to those persons who were endowed with that form of the gift of tongues called ψαλμὸν ἔχειν."

The gift of psalms to the early church, sets a new and broad seal of divine approbation upon that part of the worship of God which consists of praise. In addition to this, we find the duty of a proper attention to psalmody urged upon the churches in at least four of the apostolic epistles. These apostolic precepts carry with them, of course, the weight of inspired authority. They call the attention of Christians everywhere to a duty which is made binding by the force of express and reiterated injunction.

§ 4. *The Manner of Praise, as indicated by the Nature of the Service.*

Having considered thus far the importance of Praise as an essential part of instituted worship, we are prepared to inquire, as was proposed, what manner of performing this service is most consonant with the ends which it contemplates? *Should the praise of God be conducted exclusively by selected choirs, or should it be principally congregational, including always the help and lead of a choir selected from the congregation?*

In advocating, as we propose to do, the latter method, our first argument will be drawn from several considerations suggested by the nature of the service; and first, *the general principle that utterance in worship is a help to devotion.*

It needs no argument to prove that the devout

interest felt by each individual in an act of worship is greatly assisted by his taking the words of devotion upon his own lips. To speak what we feel is natural. We do this in our closets; not because it is necessary that God should hear our words, nor because we wish others to hear us when we pray in secret; but because speech is, both by necessity and by habit, our ordinary medium of communication with other minds. Strong emotions also *demand* utterance. They often lay hold of the organs of speech, and press them into service, almost before the will has had time to issue its orders. A pang of grief, or a thrill of joy, flies to the lips, and is spoken, without the help of a deliberate volition. The strong emotions which we feel toward God, tend spontaneously toward language, and quickly frame for themselves a form of utterance. The desire which· is fraught with intensity, moves the lips, as Hannah's were moved, even when articulation is purposely avoided. The joy which is too full to be adequately expressed, does not therefore remain silent, but *declares* itself to be "unspeakable, and full of glory." A praying soul is not usually satisfied that its intercourse with Heaven should be merely an unspoken and spiritual communion. It muses, the fire burns, and then the tongue speaks. "I cried unto the Lord with my voice," said the psalmist; "with my voice unto the Lord did I make my supplication." "Deliver me from blood guiltiness, O God; . . . and my tongue shall sing aloud of thy righteousness." "Open thou my lips, and my mouth shall show forth thy praise."

Secondly, this general principle, that utterance in worship is a help to devotion, *has a still stronger application when our worship is public.* The natural tendency of devout feeling toward language, which shows itself even in our closets, is strengthened by the presence of a worshipping assembly. We are social beings; and freedom of vocal utterance, is one of the prime demands of our social natures. The chief object of public worship is *united worship.* We join our fellow Christians, that we may worship *with them.* We instinctively seek the society of our kind. We do this the more, as we discover how similar to our own are the mental experiences of others. When we go to the sanctuary, we comply not less with the demands of these social impulses, than with the dictates of religion. It is a pleasure to us to go to the house of God in company with those whose wants, griefs, hopes, joys, aspirations, are like ours, that we may unite with them in expressing these emotions. We do not meet to be auditors and spectators of the devotions of a delegated few, appointed and set apart to worship for us, but to mingle, in sympathetic exercise, and harmonious, blended utterance, those devout affections which characterize in common the great Christian brotherhood; to gather together in one the thanksgivings, the aspirations, the praises, of scores and hundreds that are one in Christ Jesus, and that are "agreed as touching" the sentiments which they speak; to add flame to flame, from the private altars of individual hearts, until the fire of devotion from the great altar of the sanctuary, fanned on every side by the general breath of praise, mounts upward "like mingling flames in sacrifice."

Thirdly, *the service of praise in the sanctuary,* MEETS *the principle of which we have spoken, both in its individual and in its social application.* It admits a general vocal participation. The hymn to be used on a given occasion is in every one's hands. The tune may also be. Simple laws in relation to time, make it possible for hundreds and thousands of voices to give to each word and syllable a simultaneous utterance. Other laws regulating the pitch of sound, not only secure unison, or harmony of intonation, but conduct these hundreds or thousands of voices through those pleasing modulations of tone, which add the delights of music to the advantages of simultaneous expression.

Upon the very face of such a service as this, is written the obvious intention that every voice should take part in it. Its whole structure, provided the musical notation be not too intricate, shows it to be an express and beautiful provision for a general want. Its existence for thousands of years is to be traced not merely to the letter of divine precept, but to the instinctive demands of the devout mind, claiming for itself the privilege of uniting with heart and voice in at least *some* portion of the public worship of God. In this view, congregational singing is to be regarded as a Christian privilege. It is to be encouraged, as affording to every one an opportunity of expressing for himself, and in concert with others, the devout exercises of his own heart. Such is the nature of song, that it carries with it an invitation to all, who can do so without disturbing the devotions of others, to bring their thanks, and pay their vows audibly, by means of it. There are a few who do this in every worshipping assembly. Why not all? Why should any be deprived of the enjoyment, and of the personal edification which they would experience by using the faculties which God has given them in publishing his praise?

It will not be denied that it is one advantage of the

use of written forms of prayer, that it permits each individual to accompany the minister "with a pure heart and humble voice." This advantage is thought, however, by most Christian denominations, to be outweighed by the far superior advantages of extemporaneous prayer. But, since extemporaneous prayer renders the vocal participation of the assembly impracticable, there is the more need that the singing should be congregational, so that there may be some exercise in which every one may feel that he has a part to perform.

§ 5. *The Manner of Praise, as indicated by the Common Effect of Choir-singing.*

If the provision which is made for a general participation in the song be disregarded, and only a few engage in it with the voice, then we not only lose the pleasure and the benefit of this intensely social exercise, but we shall experience such evils as might be expected from violating the evident design of public song as indicated by its nature. The natural tendency of devout feeling toward language being checked, the feeling itself will be in a measure repressed. All personal interest in the service will be very liable to be dismissed. There will be a feeling, on the part of some, that the choir, and those who sustain it, are exercising an unjust monopoly over the praises of the sanctuary, are standing between them and the adorable object of their worship, and depriving them of a privilege of which God does not deprive them. A far greater number, however, will surrender themselves to the attractions of music, and become a mere auditory. There is always a tendency, when a service is conducted in our hearing, in which we do not audibly engage, to fall into the passive attitude of listeners. Let the special and exclusive function of using the voice in a given service, be devolved on a selected few, and, spontaneously, we become their audience. This tendency *may* be felt even in public prayer; and it may sometimes require an effort so far to resist it as to heartily unite in the petitions which are offered in our hearing. In song, this tendency is much stronger, and much harder to resist, than it is in prayer. It is so strong as to create a *probability*, to say the least, that those who do not sing, are rather listeners than worshippers. Music is an absorbing thing. There is no art whose power is so widely felt and acknowledged. From the cradle of the world's history, its potent appeal has elicited a response from almost the universal heart of mankind. It is one of the most frequent and fruitful sources of public and social entertainment. Would we be soothed or exhilarated — we court its aid, yield to its power, and passively wait to feel ourselves wafted upon its gentle wings, or stirred by its inspiring call. In either case, we are expecting the power of art to bring us its ministry of pleasure, by which, without any activity of our own, we are to be wrought upon as the mere objects and recipients of an influence. Into this passive and pleasure-loving attitude we are accustomed to compose ourselves whenever music of an attractive sort is within our hearing. At the fireside, at the social gathering, in the concert-room, it is our habit to listen to music merely for enjoyment. This is our acknowledged end. And with the American people there is almost nothing to counteract the influence of this habit. The discontinuance, long ago, of the custom, which was universal with our fathers, of congregational singing, and with it singing in family worship, has left us almost no opportunities of singing for strictly and exclusively devotional ends. The consequence of this is, that the singing in the house of God finds us under the power of the inveterate habit of regarding what is sung as only a production of cultivated art, and listening to it as such. Instead of being a worshipping assembly, we are an audience, and almost as much so in the singing as in the sermon. This habit is greatly fostered by the choir, at least by many choirs, whose evident purpose it is, if we may judge from the nature of their selections, and the style of their performances, to gratify the musical fancies which they know to exist. Whether they succeed in this or not, the result is the same upon the religious state of the congregation, whose devotions are no more assisted by their disappointment, than they would be by their gratification.

Let now the words of the song be put into the mouth of every worshipper, let the inspiring notes of melody be taken upon every one's lips, and how quickly is the whole mental attitude of this congregation transformed! From being a passive, receiving, criticizing, or coldly indifferent audience, it rises to the posture of lively, elevated, enthusiastic devotion. He who before was supinely waiting to be either entertained or impressed, is now in active communion with the Father of his spirit. In this general sacrifice of the assembled multitude, he feels that he too has something to offer as well as they, and he is personally engaged in presenting his own oblation. Instead of regarding with an idly curious speculation the manner in which others worship, his faculties of both body and soul are now enlisted in the work of praise. Mind, and heart, and voice, are called into action. Thus engaged, there is not only nothing to hinder the actings of a genuine spirit of devotion, but everything to favor and assist such a spirit. A hearty participation in the song by every voice, removes the liability to be seeking for mere musical gratification; while the fact that all are singing, and none are merely listening, removes from those who have leading voices the temptation to sing to the ear of men rather than to the praise of God.

It may be questioned, whether congregational singing is not the only method of praise which can be reasonably expected to be largely devotional; whether it is not the only effectual corrective that can be administered to the habit of singing, and listening to song, in the house of God, with the same ends in view which prevail in the concert-room; whether there is not a certainty, not to say a necessity, that a congregation of worshippers will always become a congregation of auditors, whenever praise is sung by a selected company only; whether a choir, stationed in the organ-loft, and having the sole charge of the singing, is ever regarded as an integral part of the assembly, in full sympathy with it in the utterance of devotion, and not rather as an orchestral group of performers, whose musical exhibitions may properly be subjected to the coldly calculating estimate which mere performers commonly expect. If this be so, then there can be but little question, what mode of praise should be chiefly encouraged by those who would see the *devotions* of the churches expressed in their public songs.

§ 6. *Choir-singing appropriately Jewish.*

Under the old economy, it was not the privilege of all the people, but only of selected classes, to take part in the established temple service. The worship was representative in its character, including many a wall of partition, by which the people generally were debarred the privilege of a personal participation. They were kept at a distance from the object of their worship, that his dread might fall upon them, and that they might fear to sin against Him. Priests only might enter the tabernacle or the temple. Only the high-priest could enter the most holy place, and he only once a year, and then not without blood. The sacrifices of the people must be offered for them, and not by them. They must provide victims to be offered for their sins; but they might not approach the altar, or enter the court where the priests offered them. They might be present when the songs of Zion were sung, and at the conclusion of them utter some brief response; as, on the occasion when the ark was brought to Zion and set in the midst of the tent that David had pitched for it, a psalm, filling a large part of the 16th chapter of 1 Chronicles, was sung by Asaph and his brethren, who were Levites, at the end of which all the people said "Amen," and praised the Lord. Some have inferred, from such responses as this, that all the people had at least some small part in the psalmody of the temple. But there appears no reason for supposing that these responses were sung. The probability is, that they were merely spoken. At the conclusion of the prayer of Solomon, at the dedication, we read that the people worshipped and praised the Lord, saying, " For he is good; for his mercy endureth forever." But the occasion, and especially the attitude of the people, who "bowed themselves, with their faces to the ground, upon the pavement," makes it very improbable that their response was sung. The same may be said of the answer of the people, saying "Amen! Amen!" when Ezra opened the book to read in their presence "and blessed the Lord." To suppose that there was singing on the occasion of Nehemiah's rebuking the usurers by whom the people were oppressed, and to whom their lands and houses were mortgaged, would be quite absurd. But we read that "all the congregation said Amen, and praised the Lord."

There seems no reason to question, that the psalmody of the established temple service was conducted by the Levites alone, and that it was as rigidly confined to them as was the offering of the sacrifices to the priests. They were expressly appointed to this duty; all the Scripture injunctions in reference to it are addressed to them; and whenever mention is made of the persons by whom the singing was performed on any given occasion, we are invariably told it was by the Levites. When it is said that "David and *all Israel* played before God with all their might, and with singing, and with harps, and with psalteries, and with timbrels, and with cymbals, and with trumpets," at the removal of the ark, we are probably to understand that it was only in the playing of instruments that "all Israel" took a part, while the singing was exclusively by Levites. This, it is true, was not a temple service proper; but the occasion was one of great solemnity, and would doubtless require an exact and scrupulous adherence to the methods of the temple ritual. Lightfoot calls attention to the distinction which we have made, and says, that if any man of worth or piety, not a Levite, but in near affinity with the priesthood, were skilful in musical devotions, and should offer his services, wishing to join the temple chorus, "they refused him not, but let him put in with his instrument among the instruments; but among the voices he might not join, for that belonged only to the Levites."

"*In the tabernacle and the temple*," says Horne, "the Levites (both men and women) were the lawful musicians; but *on other occasions*, the Jews were at liberty to use any musical instruments, with the exception of the silver trumpets, which were to be sounded only by the priests."

Choir-singing belonged appropriately to the Jewish system of religion, and was a legitimate result of the principle pervading the system, by which the mass of the people were to be sedulously excluded from all near approach to Jehovah in acts of worship. The "bounds" which were set at the base of Mount Sinai to keep both people and priests from attempting to ascend its sides when Jehovah should come down upon it, illustrate this principle. Everywhere the sword of divine displeasure was seen flaming forth, in more or less menacing aspect, to remind them that their sins were a wall of separation between them and Him. He could be approached by the nation only through the ministry of a selected priesthood, sanctified for this express purpose. They were to appear in the temple as the representatives of the nation. Their worship at the altar of sacrifice, at the altar of incense, and in song, was official and vicarious. They worshipped *for* the people, who, as individuals, had not the privilege of so near an approach to God as to come to the inner courts of his house, and who probably could not, even upon their great national festivals, when assembled at Jerusalem by thousands, join in those lofty temple songs, commemorative of national prosperity and renown, by which every heart was touched, and which doubtless every tongue was well qualified to sing.

§ 7. *The Manner of Praise, as indicated by the Nature of the Christian Dispensation.*

An economy widely different from the Jewish has supervened. There is now a better covenant, and the bringing in of a better hope. At the offering of the great sacrifice, of which all others were typical, the veil was rent, and the way into the holiest of all was made manifest. The priests in the temple and at the altar, the Levites beyond the altar, and the Jews in the surrounding court, might all, without exception, " draw nigh unto God." The middle wall of partition also was broken down, so that the occupants of the great outer court might enter, and Jew and Gentile " both have access by one Spirit unto the Father." Boldness of personal access to God by Jesus Christ, with a true heart in full assurance of faith, is the distinguishing gospel privilege. Between the individual believer and the mercy-seat in the heavens, nothing intervenes but the ministry of the " merciful and faithful High Priest" who is now " in the presence of God for us."

The ministry of priest and Levite, while it was representative in its character, was also typical of the rank and privilege that should be enjoyed under the gospel by the whole body of believers. The believer is himself a priest. He has a dignity both sacerdotal and "royal." He may approach the King of kings. He may come even into his presence-chamber. The incense of prayer, and the sacrifice of praise, he may offer without human intervention.

As he acknowledges no ministry standing officially between him and the throne of grace in prayer, so he can acknowledge no representative class interposed between him and God in the offering of praise. Under the gospel, the worship of God by substitutes, either in prayer or praise, is of no efficacy. Exclusive choir-singing has at least the appearance of an attempt to worship by substitutes; and is, so far, an offence against the letter and the whole spirit of the New Testament. And in whatever light it may be viewed, it is as contrary to the genius of the New Testament as congregational singing would have been to the ritualism of the Old. Accordingly, we find that the precepts of the New Testament, in relation to psalmody, are as general in their phraseology, and in their application, as in relation to any other subject of duty. In the epistles to the Corinthians, to the Ephesians, to the Colossians, to the Hebrews, and in the epistle of James, psalmody is made the subject of preceptive remark. And in all these epistles it is urged upon the attention of Christians, as such, and not upon any particular class of Christians. To the Ephesian church, Paul writes: "Be filled with the Spirit; speaking to yourselves in psalms, and hymns, and spiritual songs, singing, and making melody in your heart to the Lord, giving thanks always for all things, unto God and the Father, in the name of our Lord Jesus Christ." To the Colossians, he writes: "Let the word of Christ dwell in you richly in all wisdom; teaching and admonishing one another in psalms and hymns and spiritual songs, singing with grace in your hearts, to the Lord." To all the Hebrew Christians, whether they belonged originally to the tribe of Levi, or to any other tribe, whether their ancestors belonged to the old choir establishment of the temple, or to the common classes of the people, the exhortation is addressed: " Let us offer the sacrifice of praise to God continually, that is, the fruit of our lips, giving thanks to his name. But to do good, and to communicate, forget not: for with such sacrifices God is well pleased." To the "twelve tribes scattered abroad," the apostle James says: " Is any among you afflicted? let him pray. Is any merry? let him sing psalms." How widely different is the whole tone of these exhortations from what we find under the Levitical economy: " And David spake to the chief of the Levites, to appoint their brethren to be the singers."

As we read the apostolic precepts, and mark the connection in which they are found, how very unnatural is the supposition, that they were intended, not for the whole body of the churches thus addressed, but only for a few individuals, or a select class. They occur in such a context as at once to refute any such supposition. Does the duty of being filled with the Spirit, of giving thanks always to God, of receiving the word of Christ richly into the heart, of teaching and admonishing, of kindness and liberality, belong only to choirs — then the duty of praising God in psalmody may be incumbent only upon them. The range of obligation is as wide in one case as in the other. If divine precept is an acknowledged basis of obligation, and if the epistles of the New Testament are received as a part of the great repository of divine instruction, then who can deny that it is the duty of professing Christians generally, to participate in the singing of psalms and hymns and spiritual songs in their public assemblies, so far as they have the ability to do so? If any one, having the ability to sing, or to acquire the art of singing, tries to excuse himself, and to justify exclusive choir-singing in the public worship of God, does he not do this in the face of apostolic precept? And might he not almost attempt to absolve the great body of the church from the duty to "pray without ceasing," and affirm that this duty may be sufficiently performed by a praying few in each congregation acting as representatives of the whole? The New Testament being our guide, the duty of praise can no more be performed by proxy than the duty of prayer. Both can be performed in this way under a levitical system, or under a papal system; but official religion, and substituted worship, are neither Protestant nor Christian. Revelation is progressive; and it has pleased God to show unto us, in these latter times, a more excellent way than that which he permitted to obtain three thousand years ago. Happy would it be for that portion of Christendom which professes to see the light of this progressive revelation, and to walk in it, if it would no longer adhere to that feature of the ancient ritual and of a twilight economy, which, eighteen hundred years ago, decayed and waxed old, and, for a time at least, vanished away. To the law and to the testimony! As in the time of King Josiah, the discovery of the long lost book of the law, by the high-priest Hilkiah, led to deep repentance and reformation, so may the New Testament show us our sins in relation to psalmody; and may its inspired teachings upon this subject, which seem to have been overlooked by us for a century and a half, become a light to our feet, while we endeavor to retrace our steps.

We are aware that it may be said, in reply to the remarks just made, that no one pretends that we can worship by substitutes, or that praise by a choir is accepted for the congregation any further than the congregation unite *in spirit* with the choir. And it may be asked, Why is it not enough to unite in spirit with the singing, as well as to unite in spirit with the prayer? This inquiry is to be answered by referring to what has been already said upon the *nature* of the service of praise, as *admitting* a general participation with the voice. It allows this, not only without injury to the best effect of the service, but with such immense advantage, that the concurrence of a large number of voices becomes its very life and soul. This cannot be said at all of extemporaneous prayer, for "God is not the author of confusion, but of peace;" and it would be true only to a very limited extent, of written prayer. The rule, " Let all things be done unto edifying," is a safe guide.

§ 8. *Singing Habits of the Early Christians.*

Those who lived so near the time of the Apostles as the Christians of the first three centuries, may be supposed to have rightly understood the precepts of the New Testament, and to have imbibed, almost from the lips and lives of those devoted men, the distinctive spirit of the gospel. And, what is still more than to be chronologically near them, they were near them in sympathy. The type of their piety was very similar to that of the Apostles. It took its shape in the apostolic mould. The rays of divine instruction, therefore, as they passed from the inspired sources into these congenial minds, encountered no refracting medium of hostile prejudice or dead indifference.

What, now, was the spirit of the gospel, as it existed in the experience of believers in the apostolic age? It was preëminently a glad and joyous spirit. They had received by faith a gospel, which brought them glad tidings of great joy, and their daily walk was in the fear of the Lord and in the comforts of the Holy Ghost. A natural, and, with them, the *habitual*, expression of this joy was praise. No sooner was the Lord parted from his disciples and carried up to heaven, than they returned to Jerusalem with great joy, and " were continually in the temple, *praising* and blessing God." Praise was a part of the daily expression of that pentecostal gladness with which thousands of new converts at Jerusalem received the first great outpouring of the Spirit. " And they did eat their meat with gladness and singleness of heart, praising God." At midnight, in the inner prison at Philippi, two prisoners, with their feet fast in the stocks, were overheard praying, and singing *praises* to God. The peace which passeth all understanding kept their hearts, and one who never sleeps, and who had promised never to forsake them, was near. Both they and their companions in the faith were often in tribulation; but as the sufferings of Christ abounded in them, so their consolation also abounded by Christ. They knew how to be abased, and how to abound; how to be full, and how to be hungry; and in whatsoever state they were, therewith to be content. Whether they were in favor with all the people, or were led forth to prison and to death, they went out with joy, and were led forth with peace. They knew not what a day would bring forth; but they were careful for nothing, casting all their care on him who cared for them.

Blessed be God! the joy which prison-walls, and chains, and midnight darkness could not extinguish, was not confined to the apostolic age. The history of Christianity, down to the time of Constantine, presents the great body of believers as being pervaded, to an extent never since realized, with the spirit of religious joy expressed by praise. The living spring of gladness which had been opened in their hearts, poured itself forth in exuberant, never-failing streams of sacred melody. It sent these streams winding and purling along all the paths of life, making them, like the garden of the Lord, a perpetual delight. In their social gatherings, in their homes, and in their daily private walks, the early Christians lived and moved in an atmosphere of praise. Generally, no season of household worship was without it. The reading of the Scriptures, prayer, and sacred song, besides opening and closing the active labors of the day, accompanied their ordinary meals. Through a portion, at least, of the period which we are now contemplating, the notes of tuneful worship might have been heard ascending from their happy dwellings four times in a day. And there were those who, like the psalmist, rose at midnight to give thanks; a custom which is said to have originated in those persecuting days in which Christian assemblies were compelled to seek the cover of night for safety. "Songs dedicated to the praise of God," says Jamieson, "formed their pastime in private, and their favorite recreations at their family and friendly meetings." When the family group dispersed from the loved household altar, each to his daily occupation, their songs still cheered them in their toils. Jerome, writing from the rural retirement which he had sought as a "peaceful port" after a stormy life, says: "Here, rustic though we are, we are all Christians. Psalms alone break the pervading stillness. The ploughman is singing hallelujahs while he turns his furrow. The reaper solaces his toil with hymns. The vineyard-dresser, as he prunes his vines, chants something from the strains of David. These are our songs, and such the notes with which our love is vocal." He might have added, that hymns were the solace of the mourner; for the Christians of that day did not cease their singing in their funeral processions, or around the graves of their deceased friends. And as they did not sorrow for those that were asleep, as others that had no hope, these funeral anthems were always joyous, never sad. Pains were taken to have their children sing; not merely or mainly that they might acquire a pleasing art, but that by means of it the great theme of Redemption, which was ever the burden of their songs, might find an early welcome in their hearts. Melodious speech, from hour to hour, concerning Jesus and salvation by him, dropped like the rain, and distilled like the dew, upon the tender buds of thought and feeling in the household, until they became trees of righteousness, the planting of the Lord.

To suppose that this passionate love of song was completely suppressed in their public assemblies, and that, singing as they were all their lives, in their homes, and at their toils, they could stifle this breath of praise when met together expressly for the public and united worship of their Redeemer, would be contrary to reason. To have sat in silence while a deputed fraction of their number, a handful of singers, were uttering sentiments which were burning for expression in every bosom, must have seemed to them an occasion for the stones immediately to cry out. The choir would no sooner have struck the psalm, than it would have broken from every lip in the congregation. Its opening upon them, by a few leading voices, would have been like cutting away the sluice in a dam. The only protection against the gush of a general inundation of praise, would have been to exclude singing altogether from their worship.

Agreeing with this most natural supposition in regard to the mode of public praise in the primitive church, is the ample testimony of several of the early Fathers. "It was the ancient custom, and it still is with us," said Chrysostom, about the close of the fourth century, " for all to come together and unitedly join in the singing. The young and old, rich and poor, male and female, bond and free, all join in one song. . . . All worldly distinctions here cease, and the whole congregation form one general chorus." The contemporaneous testimony of Augustine, and of Hilary, a little earlier, is to the same effect. A Father in the church, writing in the third century, informs us that "men, women, youths of both sexes, and even children, joined in the psalmody of the churches." And in describing the effect of their singing, he compares their loud and harmonious voices to the sound of waves beating against the seashore. "Their celebration of the Lord's Supper," says

Coleman, "besides being begun and concluded with some solemn form of praise and thanksgiving, in which the whole body of the communicants joined, was with the singing of psalms *during the distribution.*" Another writer remarks, that "the early Christians spent whole days and nights almost, in psalmody." And he adds, that from the apostolic age, for several centuries, the whole body of the church united in the singing.

This being the universal custom, it was very natural that the Book of Psalms should be regarded, not as a book to be read through, like the law and the prophets, but as a collection of songs to be sung. As such, they were uniformly regarded. They probably were never read in public, and the only use made of them was to sing them. When we consider what a favorite portion of the Bible the Psalms have always been, and how much oftener they are now read, probably, than any other portion, — "a little Bible in themselves," as Luther called them, — we cannot wonder that, in a community where they were never used but to be sung, they should be sung frequently, and sung by all, and that in the use of them, "young men and maidens, old men and children, should praise the name of the Lord."

§ 9. *The Mode of Song adopted by the Reformers.*

The Reformation consisted in a rejection of the false doctrines and corrupt usages of the Romish church, and a return to the Bible as the only sufficient rule of religious faith and practice. The reformers received the Bible as their guide in regard to psalmody, as well as in regard to other things. Congregational singing, as introduced and practised by them, is referred to here, not merely as furnishing a successful historical example of this mode of praise, but chiefly as showing how the teachings of the Bible upon this subject were understood by men whose reverence for it was so profound.

Exclusive choir-singing was one of the abuses which crept into the Romish church, in connection with its gradually declining piety, in the centuries succeeding the third. The change from the primitive method was gradual. It commenced in the fourth century, at which time the choir was not expected to monopolize the singing, but only to lead it. This, however, gave them the opportunity of introducing a style of music, not only unfit for the church on account of its theatrical associations, but unfit for the use of the congregation on account of its intricacy. The introduction of tunes too difficult for any but trained singers to execute, was the first step towards debarring the people from their ancient privilege of praise. They might still unite in some simple chorus or response, but this was rather by privilege than by right. Even this privilege was at length denied them, and they were taught that the singing of God's praise was too sacred a duty for the lips of the laity, and belonged to the clergy alone. And the clergy, to make their monopoly of the singing still more exclusive, sang only in Latin. By the sixth or seventh century the voices of the people were effectually silenced, and for nearly a thousand years God was no longer praised as at the first. But this long night of darkness and silence slowly rolled away, and the light of returning day in Germany was ushered in with song. Its approach had been heralded by song, a century before this, in Bohemia, in the time of John Huss and

Jerome; and even in the fourteenth century, while "the Morning Star of the Reformation" was still visible, praise broke the silence of the waning watches in England. As in the mornings of the long days in summer, a few woodland notes may be heard here and there in the groves in advance of the general chorus which hails the day, so there were voices before Luther, both in England and on the continent, which anticipated the melodies of his time. But when the empire of the night was fairly broken, and this great chorister of the Reformation arose, he awoke the whole forest into harmony.

One of the first efforts of Luther in fulfilment of the great mission of his life, was to publish a psalm-book. Both hymns and tunes were composed mainly by himself. About sixty hymns were written by him, at a time when the history of fifteen centuries could not furnish more than two hundred hymns that had been used in Christian congregations. In this great undertaking he had a twofold object: first, to restore to the people their ancient and long-lost New Testament right to the use of psalms in public worship in their own tongue; and secondly, by the graces of verse, and the charms of melody, to lodge the word of God effectually in their memory. He took care to embody in his verse the great foundation truths of the Bible, that, being sung over and over by the people, they might never be forgotten. This object he announced in a letter to Spalatin, written in 1524, in which he says: "It is my purpose after the example of the ancient Fathers of the church, to make psalms or spiritual songs for the common people, that the word of God may dwell among them in psalms, if not otherwise. We are looking around everywhere for poets. I entreat you to help us. I would that new and courtly words might be avoided, and that the language be all suited to the capacity of the people, as simple as possible." So successful was Luther in this endeavor, that priestly influence might in vain have attempted to check the progress of the Reformation by destroying the Bible. Its doctrines were the soul of his songs, and the songs were embalmed in the people's memory.

In providing these simple psalms for the common people, Luther had his mind also upon the children. " I desire," he says, " that the young who ought to be educated in music as well as in other good arts, may have something to take the place of worldly and amorous songs, and so learn something useful, and practise something virtuous. I would gladly see all the arts, and especially music, employed in the service of Him who hath created them and given them to man. Alas! all the world is too negligent and forgetful to educate and teach the poor youth." " In the schools founded on the plan of Luther and Melancthon, nearly one fourth part of the school hours were devoted to music."

As a result of such efforts as these, psalms became the ballads of the people. They were sung everywhere. The singing habits of the early days of Christianity were fairly revived. " The hymns spread among all classes of people, and were sung not only in the churches and schools, but also in the houses and in the workshops, in the streets and in the market-places, in the barns and in the fields." Wherever the principles of the Reformation were received, whether in Germany, France, or Britain, psalm-singing was an almost universal practice. This was the blossom which the root of the new doctrines invariably produced. So contagious was this practice, and so wonderful the power of Luther's psalms in propagating his doctrines, that his enemies were obliged to adopt the same practice in self-defence. "The Papists, finding that the people would sing them, and were almost running wild with delight in so doing, published hymn-books of their own, in which, with slight alterations, they incorporated almost all of the Reformer's pieces." The hymns found their way even into the French court; but they contained seeds of truth which it was not for the interest of the Romish church to have planted, and about the middle of the sixteenth century all Papists were prohibited from singing them. From that time, the name "psalmodist," or "psalm-singer," was applied to the Protestants, in derision. It became synonymous with Reformer, Huguenot, Calvinist, Heretic.

"Next to theology," said Luther, "it is to music that I give the highest place and the greatest honor." He had reason to say this, for it was music next to theology, and sometimes more than theology, that gave success to his cause. "In the city of Hanover, the Reformation was introduced, not by preachers, nor by religious tracts, but by the hymns of Luther, which the people sung with delight." A Protestant contemporary of Luther says: "I doubt not that the one little hymn 'Now rejoice, dear Christians, all' (the first one that Luther published), has brought many hundred Christians to the faith.... The noble, sweet language of that one little song has won their hearts, so that they could not resist the truth; and, in my opinion, the spiritual songs have contributed not a little to the spread of the gospel."

The views of Luther and the English Reformers, in regard to congregational singing, were a little different from those of Calvin and Knox. The latter would have no other singing than that of the congregation. The former made provision for a choir service besides. Luther's accomplished skill in music, and his enthusiastic love of it, may account in part for the difference, the songs for the people being of necessity extremely simple. But all the reformers, German, Swiss, English, and Scotch, were equally zealous that the people should consider praise as appropriately and peculiarly *their part* in the services of the sanctuary. With great effort did they achieve for the people this "freedom to worship God." And now, the advocates of exclusive choir-singing in America are surrendering again, to Popery, the very territory which was acquired in the battles of the Reformation. They willingly relinquish to the Man of Sin a stronghold captured by the sturdy valor of such men as Luther and Calvin and John Knox, and are content that the praise of God should be sung in Protestant churches in the popish manner.

§ 10. *Congregational Psalmody in its Moral and Religious Influence.*

The *refining* influence of sacred music is everywhere acknowledged. "The young should be constantly exercised in this art," said Luther, "for it refines and improves men." It is well known that the Prussian schools are always opened and closed with religious exercises, of which the singing of hymns forms a part. Teachers in those schools, say that they regard the singing as the most efficient means of bringing a scholar under a perfect discipline by moral influence; and that, in the case of vicious youth, the reading of the Bible and the singing of religious hymns are among the most efficient instruments employed for softening the hardened heart, and bringing the stubborn will to docility. "There is in music," says Melvill, "a *humanizing* power. The poor, taught to sing, are likely to be less wild, less prone to disorder, and therefore more accessible to the ministrations of religion. I thoroughly believe that in improving the tastes of a people, you are doing much for their moral advancement. I like to see our cottagers encouraged to train the rose and the honeysuckle round their doors, and our weavers, as is often the fact, dividing their attention between their looms and carnations; for the man who can take care of a flower, and who is all alive to its beauty, is far less likely than another, who has no delight in such recreations, to give himself up to gross lusts and habits."

Of the *refreshing* and *sustaining* influence of sacred music, no better illustration can be given than is found in the experience of Luther. It is said of him, that so soon as he heard good music his temptations and his gloom flew away. So he said: "The devil specially hates good music, because thereby men are made joyful; for he loveth nothing better than to make men unbelieving and cowardly by means of melancholy and gloominess." "Music is the best soother of a troubled man whereby his heart is again quickened, refreshed, and made contented. It gives a quiet and joyful mind. My affection overflows and gushes out toward it, so often has it refreshed me and relieved me from great sorrows." "One day when some fine music was performing," says D'Aubigné, "he exclaimed, in transport:

'If our Lord God has shed forth such wondrous gifts on this earth, which is no better than a dark nook, what may we not expect in that eternal life in which we shall be perfected!'" It is related of him, that, in times of discouragement, he was wont to arouse himself from desponding thoughts by saying to his friends: " Come, let us sing the forty-sixth psalm, ' God is our refuge and strength,' or the one hundred and thirtieth psalm, ' Let Israel hope in the Lord.'" In this method he was accustomed to chide himself for his depression, and to say, as the Psalmist did, " Why art thou cast down, O my soul, and why art thou disquieted within me?"

We can but remember, in this connection, the singing of the Saviour with his disciples, just before he entered the garden of suffering. The power of darkness was about to exercise the fulness of its rage against him. He stood, as it were, in full view of his agony. It was hardly a time, we should suppose, for singing; and if singing were indulged, we should expect only strains of sorrow. But let us listen to the anthem which he sings: " The Lord is my strength and song, and is become my salvation. The voice of rejoicing and salvation is in the tabernacles of the righteous. Oh, praise the Lord all ye nations: praise him all ye people. For his merciful kindness is great toward us: and the truth of the Lord endureth forever."

And this cheerful language is not merely spoken, it is sung. Was it inappropriate? Were these reflections upon the goodness of God, uttered in the gladdening strains of music, unsuitable at such a time? Were they not the best possible preparation for the scene of sorrow which was then at the door? Did they not help to arm the Saviour's soul for the fiery conflict on which he was about to enter? Were they not the casting anew his anchor of hope and trust within the vail, the renewed planting of his foot of confidence on the everlasting rock? The sentiment of confidence in God is what we need to cherish, when descending the valley of suffering, if ever. Then, if ever, we need that the loins of our faith should be girded with it. Then, if ever, we need to hide ourselves in the secret place of his pavilion, to feel that the eternal God is our refuge, and that underneath are the everlasting arms. And how, at such times, can we better put in exercise this holy confidence, than by praising Him in those cheerful songs which enliven the soul, while they direct aright its meditations?

We are in danger, in the time of trouble, of coming to God with nothing but supplication. We forget his goodness and mercy, and omit to thank and praise him. And in our prayers, our minds are so much occupied with the thought of our distresses, that we speak to him of almost nothing else. We nourish our disquietudes by brooding over them, even at the throne of grace, until our prayer betrays our secret anxiety and discontent. It is true that God is a Father who pities his children, and permits, yea, invites them to pour out their heart before him. When they cry to him out of the depths for help, he hears them. But to make what we suffer the only topic of our communion with him, in the hope of thereby obtaining relief, is both unphilosophical and unscriptural. "Be careful for nothing," is the inspired direction, "but in everything, by prayer and supplication *with thanksgiving*, let your requests be made known unto God." If, in seasons of darkness, praise and thanksgiving were more largely mingled with our prayers, we should more honor God, and we should obtain his promised help. " Offer unto God thanksgiving," says the Psalmist Asaph, "and (thus) pay thy vows unto the Most High; *then* call upon me in the day of trouble : *I will deliver thee*, and thou shalt glorify me." More praise would lead to a better spirit in prayer; to more faith, and less complaint; and this would make our prayers more effectual. If the captive Jews had continued singing the Lord's songs in the "strange land" to which they were led, instead of yielding to immoderate grief, they would sooner have had a heart to pray for deliverance. We need to learn how to cast our burden on the Lord, by trusting in him. We need to encourage our faith by remembering his former benefits, how we sought him in time past, and he heard us, and delivered us from all our fears; how this poor man cried unto the Lord, and the Lord heard him, and saved him out of all his troubles. We are never at liberty, because of trouble, to hang our harps upon the willows, and cease praising God. We are never in so great adversity, that we may be excused from remembering and acknowledging the years of the right hand of the Most High. We sinfully defraud our great Benefactor of his due, when we cherish such a spirit as disqualifies us for praise. For, whatever be our sorrows, it is always true that "God's merciful kindness is great toward us, and the truth of the Lord endureth forever."

We have already seen the value of psalmody as a working power in the hands of the reformers. It was used in a similar way, with effect, by Felix Neff, in his labors among the high Alps in the south-east of France, and by Eliot, in his labors among the native tribes of New England. With these men it was an instrument for propagating their faith. But, distinct from this, it exerts a *quickening influence upon the religious affections*, of which no body of Christians should be willingly deprived. This is preëminently true of *congregational* psalmody. It is this form of singing that has always elicited the strongest expressions in regard to its power over Christian hearts. " Nothing," says Chrysostom, " so lifteth up, and as it were wingeth the soul, so freeth it from earth, and looseth it from the chains of the body, so leadeth it unto wisdom and a contempt of all earthly things" as this.

Augustine, in his Confessions, speaks with great warmth of the power of the music over him on the occasion of his baptism. He says: " Oh! how freely was I made to weep by these hymns and spiritual songs; transported by the voices of the congregation sweetly singing. The melody of their voices filled my ear, and divine truth was poured into my heart. Then burned the sacred flame of devotion in my soul, and gushing tears flowed from my eyes, as well they might.".

" When many voices join heartily in praise," says Melvill, " it is hardly possible to remain indifferent. Every one feels this. In a congregation where few attempt to sing, how difficult it is to magnify the Lord! But who can resist the rush of many voices.? whose bosom does not swell, as old and young, rich and poor, mingle their tones of adoration and thankfulness?

" You may tell me there is not necessarily any religion in all this emotion. I know that; and I would not have you mistake emotion for religion. But we are creatures so constituted as to be acted on through our senses and feelings; and, whilst emotion is not religion, it will often be a great step towards it. The man who has imbibed, so to speak, the spirit of prayer and of praise from the surrounding assembly, is far more likely to give an attentive ear to the preached word, and to receive from it a lasting impression, than another, whose natural coldness has been increased by that of the mass in which he found himself placed. In teaching, therefore, a people to sing with the voice "the songs of Zion," we cannot but believe that, God helping, much is done toward teaching them to sing with the understanding and the heart. A faculty is developed, which God designed for his glory, but which has, comparatively, been allowed to remain almost useless. Yes, a faculty which God designed for his glory; and if so designed, it cannot lie idle without injury, nor be rightly exercised without advantage. And I seem to learn from our text (Matt. 26:30), that it is not enough that we praise God with speech. Christ and his apostles 'sang an hymn.' Nay, there is music in heaven. Why, then, should music ever be out of place, with those whose affections are above?"

"In England and in Scotland," says John Angel James, "at least among non-conformists, the people would think themselves almost as much defrauded, if they were denied the *service of song* in the sanctuary, as they would do, if denied the sermon. What, for real sublimity and acceptableness to God, is the finest music performed by hired solos or the most effective choir, compared with the swell of hundreds of human voices, pouring forth in one grand diapason the raptures or the sorrows of hundreds of regenerated hearts?"

Rev. Dr. Raffles, of Liverpool, in a letter to one of

the editors of the Sabbath Hymn Book, says: "How is it that in your country people do not sing in the house of God; but leave it to the choir to sing for them, and are thus content to perform the most exhilarating and delightful portion of public worship by proxy? I confess I have often been astonished at this, and have deplored that loss of high spiritual enjoyment which our transatlantic brethren are willing, by reason of such a practice, to suffer. How beautiful, and true as well as beautiful, the jubilant exclamation of our own great hymnologist, Watts:

> 'Lord, how delightful 't is to see
> A *whole* assembly worship thee;
> ˉAt once they sing, at once they pray;
> They hear of heaven and learn the way.
> I have been there and still would go,
> 'T is like a little heaven below."

"But one half of that 'little heaven below' is lost to those who leave all the singing to the choir, and instead of themselves taking each his part in the offering of praise, merely listen to those who are appointed (and perhaps paid) to do it for them. For my part, I wonder, when some of the glorious hymns contained in your book are sung by the functionaries in the orchestra or singing-seats, how the people in the pews can hold their peace! I fear that if I were one of them, I should disturb and astonish the congregation, for I am sure I could not keep silence."

We need not add anything upon this topic, except to say, that wherever, even in our own country, congregational singing has prevailed, and the proper means have been used to give it success, testimony similar to what has just been cited, is not wanting. Among unprejudiced and devout Christians, we believe the feeling is general, that it is the singing of the congregation, above all other, that reaches the heart. It is felt that, however pleasing to the ear choir-singing may be, it is in its religious influence unsatisfactory and meagre. There is no desire to return to it. Substantially the same sentiment exists in many churches where choir-singing still prevails. It shows itself in the expressions which we often hear in regard to the singing at meetings for prayer and conference, where all sing who can. Those who make these expressions may not pretend that such singing deserves to be compared, musically, with the performances of the choir, but they say it seems devotional, and is helpful to religious feeling.

Quite beyond these natural results of psalmody, considered as a means of grace, is its prevailing power with God; its efficacy in securing a divine blessing. *God answers praise as well as prayer.* Both were answered in the case of Paul and Silas, in their own immediate and miraculous deliverance from prison, and in the conversion of the jailer and all his house. On another occasion, after the offering of prayer and praise by the apostles, " the place was shaken where they were assembled together, and they were all filled with the Holy Ghost."

But the most remarkable answer to praise was given at the dedication of the temple. On that occasion, Jehovah, by the cloudy symbol in which he was wont to appear, visibly entered the house which had been built for him, and took possession of it as his habitation. The priests, arrested by the insupportable splendor of the glory which they beheld, or perhaps by " the thick darkness" of the cloud which veiled it, could not proceed with their ministrations. And as at Sinai, God spake to the people " out of the midst of the cloud, of the fire and of the thick darkness," so now he seemed to say, by this august symbolic entrance into his earthly temple, " This is my rest forever: here will I dwell; for I have desired it." We should have expected this wonderful divine manifestation, if at all, at the moment when the ark, brought by priests into the oracle, was deposited under the wings of the cherubim, no more to be moved while the temple should stand. But, instead of this, it occurred afterward, during the ascent of a song of praise and thanksgiving. " And it came to pass, when the priests were come out of the holy place, . . . as the trumpeters and singers were as one, to make one sound to be heard in praising and thanking the Lord; and when they lifted up their voice with the trumpets and cymbals and instruments of music, and praised the Lord, saying, For he is good; for his mercy endureth forever: that *then* the house was filled with a cloud, even the house of the Lord; so that the priests could not stand to minister by reason of the cloud: for the glory of the Lord had filled the house of God."

This answer to praise was as direct and wonderful as any answer ever obtained by prayer. While they were yet speaking, the answer came, in most signal fulfilment of that Scripture, the import of which is, that whoso offereth praise *shall have occasion* to praise. God will surely fulfil his promises. They who acknowledge his goodness, and sing his praise, and in everything give thanks, obtain his approbation. They shall have new causes for gratitude, new themes for praise; new songs shall he put into their mouth.

Doubtless one reason for the favor with which God regarded the song of praise at the dedication, was the *unanimity* with which it was offered. " The trumpeters and singers *were as one*, to make *one sound* to be heard in praising and thanking the Lord." God is pleased with the worship which comes from united hearts. The Saviour gives special encouragement to those requests in prayer in which his disciples are agreed, and he answered their prayer in a most wonderful manner on the day of Pentecost, because they sought him with one accord. In the same manner the answer was obtained when the cloud filled the temple. And there is something in an act of praise, in which many unite, that is eminently suited to obtain answers from God. Let the hymn to be sung embody those great and simple truths of religion which are the corner-stones of faith, let its expressions in regard to them be those which every believer adopts as his own, and the fervid utterance of those sentiments by a large number of voices in concert, will be not only a delightful illustration of Christian unanimity, so far as it already exists, but it must tend powerfully to promote it. The harmonies of music contribute to this effect. And when a whole congregation, old and young, lift up their voices with strength to magnify the Lord and to exalt his name together, they employ a most hopeful instrumentality for promoting a general concurrence of devout feeling. We will not call this concert of voices anything more than an instrumentality; but it is one upon which we may hope that God will look with favor, and use in making his people "as one." And then they may expect his larger gifts. Such an exercise is favorable to *intensity* of feeling also, as well as to unanimity. There is something in the tide of song which may be set in motion by a large assembly, which helps the soul upward in those kindling aspirations toward God, and those emotions of holy delight in him, which, while they show the influence of the Spirit already enjoyed, invite his still nearer approach. God will fill the mouth that is opened wide to him. The number of voices and instruments employed at the dedication, must have been very large. It is not impossible that the whole four thousand, whose business it was to play and sing in the temple, were in active service upon that occasion. Yet all hearts were as one to make one sound to be heard in praising and thanking the Lord. Was it strange that God should regard such a sacrifice as this, and give demonstration of his approval? He is the same yesterday, and to-day, and forever. His veracity is still pledged to crown the offering of praise with fresh occasions for praise. With this promise before us, and with the illustration of its fulfilment which we have been contemplating, why should we hesitate to attach as much importance to praise as the heavenly-minded McCheyne did? "My dear flock," said he, " I am deeply persuaded that there will be no full, soul-filling, heart-ravishing, heart-satisfying outpouring of the Spirit of God, till there be more praise and thanking the Lord. Learn, dearly beloved, to praise God heartily; to sing with all your heart and soul in the family, and in the congregation; then am I persuaded that God will give his Holy Spirit to fill this house, to fill every heart in the spiritual temple."

§ 11. *Elevated Religious Feeling usually seeks Expression in Song.*

It is a remark of Spurgeon, that "congregational singing and united prayer always accompany a revival." In the revivals mentioned in the Old Testament, under the reigns of Hezekiah and Josiah, the hearts of the people overflowed with praise. The early history of Christianity, from the day of pentecost onward, is the history of one long continued revival. The Reformation was a revival; and both these periods illustrate the remark just quoted. The history of New England shows that religion and psalmody have prospered and declined together.

Cotton Mather, who was a champion in the cause of musical reform, said, in the year 1721 : " It is remarkable that, when the kingdom of God has been making any new appearance, a mighty zeal for the singing of psalms has attended it and assisted it." Edwards, in an account given by him of the revival in Northampton, in 1734-36, says : " It has been observable that there has been scarcely any part of divine worship, wherein good men amongst us have had grace so drawn forth, and their hearts so lifted up in the ways of God, as in singing his praises." In his " Thoughts on the Revival of 1740," he makes a similar remark. " I believe it to have been one fruit," he says, " of the extraordinary degrees of the sweet and joyful influence of the Spirit of God, that there has appeared such a disposition to abound in this divine exercise [of singing praises] ; not only in appointed solemn meetings, but when Christians occasionally meet together at each other's houses." A similar disposition to sing has attended all the great revivals which the American churches have enjoyed. It was a marked feature of the recent awakening, whose happy influence, we may believe, is still felt in directing the thoughts of the churches, more than ever before, to the practice of singing by the congregation.

It is common for *Christians in the last hours of life* to call for singing, and to engage in it. The dying grace which God gives them, lifts them into the region of praise, and the way into the dark valley seems to them "steps up to heaven." The prevailing character of their devout exercises is about to change forever, and the change often commences upon their dying-bed. They cease praying, and begin to praise. Among the last words of Toplady were these: "The consolations of God are so abundant, that he leaves me nothing to pray for. My prayers are all converted into praise." It is related in the memoir of the missionary Stoddard, that, in the early part of his last sickness, he called chiefly for hymns of prayer, such as "Jesus, lover of my soul," "Father, whate'er of earthly bliss," "When languor and disease invade." But, as he drew nearer heaven, he desired hymns of a very different character, and for such psalms as the 103rd and 146th. The end of his journey was crowned with praise. A part of the 146th psalm, commencing "I'll praise my Maker with my breath," together with the hymn, "Rise my soul, and stretch thy wings," and "The dying Christian to his soul," were selected by Payson, a few days before his death, and were sung in his chamber by members of his choir. The prophet Isaiah announced that when the ransomed of the Lord should return and come to Zion, it would be with songs. How often is this prophecy fulfilled in the approach of believers to their heavenly home. Their faces become radiant with anticipated joy, and their tongues are unloosed in strains prelusive, at least, to the everlasting song, if indeed they are not its actual beginning. Martyrs in the flames have sung until they breathed their last. Eusebius speaks of having been a witness to scenes like this. During the persecutions by Simon de Montfort, in the early part of the thirteenth century, it is related that one hundred and forty Albigensian Christians were singing psalms while they precipitated themselves into the flames, which had been lighted for their destruction. They have been called the first Protestant martyrs. Magaret Wilson, condemned to suffer for her faith, and fastened to a stake in Solway Frith to await the advancing tide, "prayed and sang verses of psalms till the waves choked her voice." How noble does the faculty of speech appear, when it thus publishes, to the glory of divine grace, the triumph of the soul over bodily suffering and the fear of death, and sings it away to everlasting bliss! God has clothed our tongue with song, that he may receive from us not merely such reflected praise as arises from his inanimate works, and from the speechless tribes of the animal creation, but such uttered hallelujahs as are heard in heaven. He is honored when his works praise him, but more when his saints bless him; when they abundantly *utter* the memory of his great goodness, and sing of his righteousness.

The use of speech in song would appear to be the noblest employment in which the angelic choirs are ever engaged. The most ecstatic emotions, the most momentous themes, the most extraordinary and pregnant occasions in the development of the "eternal thoughts" of God, have called forth in heaven the rapturous response of song. When the foundations of the earth were settled, and its corner-stone was laid, the praise of the Builder was not lost in the silence of a ravished contemplation, but the morning stars sang together, and all the sons of God shouted for joy. When the brightness of the Father's glory took on him our nature, and salvation was born in Bethlehem, a multitude of the heavenly host brought their songs from heaven to earth, and sung them in the ear of shepherds. The visions of Jehovah's glory, by Isaiah and John, centuries apart, were substantially the same. They both beheld him receiving the most profound and adoring ascriptions from the exalted beings near the throne, who, with amazing powers, rest not day and night, crying one to another, "Holy, holy, holy, Lord God Almighty, which was, and is, and is to come." But a still more impressive scene was witnessed by John, when he heard a new song in heaven, addressed to him that sitteth upon the throne, and to the Lamb. All the choirs of heaven took part in it. Not a voice was silent. Every bosom swelled with emotion, and every tongue was laden with its utterance. Their number was ten thousand times ten thousand, and thousands of thousands. But even then, the chorus was not full. The circling wave of song continued to expand, until "every creature which was in heaven, and on earth, and under the earth, and in the sea," had joined in it. The four living creatures were but precentors in an anthem whose responses flowed in from the remotest borders of creation. The angels that excel in strength, the hosts of the Lord, his ministers that do his pleasure, wherever in the universe, on errands of love and duty, they might have been, reëchoed the strains which their cherubic leaders had commenced. Holy beings of every rank, were as one in this triumphant ascription. Myriads of hearts were in unison, myriads of voices were in harmony. Not a jarring note, not a discordant feeling, not an indifferent mind, not one passive, curious, listening angel, dropping into silence to be delighted by the inexpressible grandeur of such a symphony; but all hearts kindling with holy rapture, " increasing with the praise," and wishing, doubtless, for " a thousand tongues " with which to utter it. What a picture is this of the sublime oneness in feeling and act which, we believe, will characterize the worshippers of Jehovah and the Lamb, when at last the whole family in heaven and earth are met, when our Father's house is filled, and a multitude which no man can number will unite, saying, " Salvation to our God which sitteth upon the throne, and unto the Lamb!"

What soul ransomed by the blood of Christ, would not enjoy, even here, if it be possible, an earnest of what he hopes to enjoy hereafter in the great assembly of the saints? And if it is always inspiring to Christian hearts to use, as we may do, the very language of the "new song," why should we not desire to conform, as nearly as we can, to the method of uttering it which was heard in heaven? Can we doubt that such will be our desire and our *practice*, if we ever reach that happy world? Can we doubt that it would be our *present* practice, without a dissenting or an indifferent voice, if our love were now perfect? Would not the language of such love be this: " If I am surpassed by any in the honors which I pay to my Redeemer, it shall be by those whose powers are above my own. No faculty which he has given me for his glory shall lie dormant. This *body* has been presented to him a living sacrifice.

> ' Shame would cover me, ungrateful,
> Should *my tongue* refuse its praise.'

He has cleansed me of my leprosy, and though but one of all the cleansed should return to give him glory, I will be that one. I may have a 'feeble, stammering tongue,' but he who 'out of the mouth of babes and sucklings' can perfect praise, shall have praise from me"?

How delightful would be the scene, if in all our earthly temples the Sabbath-songs of praise were to flow from such sentiments as these, and flow from every consecrated tongue! How delightful, if, commencing with those who walk most closely with God, as the hosannas of heaven commence with those nearest the throne, they could be swelled by the according voices and the sympathizing hearts of all, without exception, who love our Lord Jesus Christ in sincerity! This would be doing what they expect to do, and what, perhaps, at the close of every prayer they offer, they ask for the privilege of doing, when their love and joy shall be forever perfect. It would be a preparation for the anticipated joy. It would remind them most impressively of their oneness in Christ, and in the hope of being with him where he is. It would cause their hearts to flow together in the sweet union of Christian fellowship, and they would seem to one another like partners in a pilgrimage, whose way they could beguile, and whose toils they could enliven, as did the Jewish companies on their journeys to Jerusalem, "with the voice of joy and praise." The valley of Baca, as they pass through it, would become to them a fountain of delight. They would go from strength to strength, and they would come to Zion with songs and everlasting joy upon their heads.

§ 12. *Practical Remarks on Congregational Singing.*

A few thoughts of a practical nature respecting the introduction and proper management of congregational singing, may appropriately follow the considerations already presented.

And, first, *let the pulpit become a leader in the movement in favor of this mode of praise.* A subject affecting, so vitally as this does, a large part of the devotions of the sanctuary, surely deserves the attention of the ministry.

Twice in the history of the American churches, have the pulpits of the land called loudly and earnestly for improvement in psalmody. The period of greatest musical degeneracy ever known in our country was reached at about the year 1720. At that time, there was so little knowledge of music, that few congregations could sing more than three or four tunes; and these were sung so badly, that, to those who possessed any degree of musical culture, the singing was intolerable. The best and ablest ministers in the colonies, including such men as the Mathers, Edwards, Stoddard, Symmes of Bradford, Wise, Walter, Thatcher, Dwight of Woodstock, and Prince of the old South Church in Boston, devoted their energies to the cause of musical reform. They wrote sermons with reference to it. They exchanged pulpits with one another, that the sermons which each one had prepared might be preached to different congregations. Associations of ministers met to hear essays upon the subject, to discuss the topics embraced by them, and to endorse, with numerous signatures, their publication. The recommendatory preface to Mr. Walter's singing-book, published in 1721, and calling upon all, especially the young, " to accomplish themselves with skill to sing the songs of the Lord," was signed by fourteen names of leading men, mostly ministers, and among them two who had filled the office of President of Harvard College, and three others who had been elected to that office.

These efforts toward reform were stoutly resisted. The churches were thrown into a tempest of excitement, which continued to rage, with more or less violence, for ten years. Singing by note, or "regular singing," as it was called, was considered popish. " The old way was good enough." The singing of two or three tunes at the same time by different portions of the congregation, either ignorantly or intentionally, or, what was no uncommon thing, the singing of some one tune, professedly, in almost as many different ways as there were voices, according to each one's caprice, or fancy for embellishment, so that, to use the description of Mr. Walter, it sounded "like five hundred different tunes roared out at the same time," did not offend the blunted musical sensibilities of the age. But the reform was accomplished, the tempest subsided, and the prayer, " O Lord, send now prosperity," was answered.

A second period of great musical degeneracy was occasioned, not, as before, by a total neglect of musical culture, but by the introduction of the coarse, noisy tunes of Billings. These tunes brought with them the doom of congregational singing, and a general perversion of musical taste. They continued in use about thirty years; just long enough for a singing generation to pass away, and a generation wholly unaccustomed to congregational song to come into its place; just long enough to break the thread of this mode of praise, and abolish a custom which otherwise would have descended by gradual transmission to us.

To drive, as with a whip of small cords, these ruthless invaders from the sanctuary, and to correct the mischief which they had wrought in corrupting the taste of the people, was an object worthy of the efforts which were put forth in this reform. These efforts commenced at about the beginning of the present century. They originated with ministers of the gospel. Foremost among them were Rev. Drs. Prince and Worcester, of Salem; Rev. Dr. Pierce, of Brookline; Prof. John Hubbard, of Dartmouth College; and Rev. Dr. Dana, of Newburyport. The latter, in a sermon preached at Boxford, in 1803, said: " Our country has been for years overflowing with productions, not destitute of sprightliness perhaps, but composed on no plan, conformed to no principles, and communicating no distinct or abiding impression, — fugitive, unsubstantial things, which fill the ear and starve the mind." Dr. Worcester said, in an address delivered at Concord, N. H., " The influence of psalmody in respect to religion is vastly important. Genuine psalmody tends to promote genuine religion; spurious psalmody tends to promote spurious religion. . . . How different in all respects from what it ought to be, is a great part of the music in our churches! It is low, it is trivial, it is unmeaning; or, if it has any meaning at all, it is adapted to sentiments and emotions altogether different from those of pure and elevated devotion. . . . It is a mere rhapsody of sounds, without subject, without skill, without sentiment, and without sense."

That the reäction of the public sentiment against this music should be violent, was not strange. Nor was it strange that this reäction should lead to tunes as stiff and dull as their predecessors had been frivolous and unmeaning. As a consequence of this, the religious benefit which the churches derived from the change was rather negative than positive. A style of music which tended to dissipate all serious thought was excluded, it is true, but it was followed by such slow, uninteresting tunes as Winchester, Mear, Barby, Abridge, and St. Martin's, which could not confer upon the churches the positive religious advantages which lie within the power of animated as well as dignified psalmody. Nor in the use of such tunes could there be much hope of success in an attempt to restore congregational singing. It has been left for the present generation, to complete the reform which was so worthily and resolutely inaugurated fifty years ago. To whom can we look for its accomplishment, if not to ministers of the gospel? Choirs will not move in it; and congregations are apt to be timid about new measures, the introduction of which would involve division of sentiment, and perhaps strife. But let ministers find in the precepts of the New Testament upon the subject of praise, a duty and a privilege for all Christians; let them consider how much this privilege has been worth to the church in its most flourishing periods — what a help to devotion, what a means of grace, what a source of spiritual enjoyment it might now be, — and they may address an appeal to the consciences and hearts of those who love the Redeemer's kingdom, which, with the blessing of God, will not be in vain. And both ministers and churches will be surprised to discover how greatly the services of the sanctuary are enriched by the change,. and how much it will contribute to the religious benefit of men. Both the reformatory movements of which we have spoken, began in the right quarter, and were conducted boldly, zealously, conscientiously, and, no doubt, prayerfully. They were successful; that is, they attained the results which they sought. Are there none in the pulpits of the present day on whom the mantle of Edwards, and the Mathers, and Prince may fall in so good a cause as this? Are there none who will take up and carry forward the work of Worcester and his co-laborers, toward the restoration of a mode of psalmody which nourished the faith of our fathers, and which is legitimately ours by inheritance?

Secondly, *Churches should interest themselves in the musical education of children.* If to worship God in song is a Christian duty, it is equally so to become qualified for this service. The Westminster Assembly, in 1644, pronounced the singing of psalms to be a duty in which all Christians should engage, both in the congregation and in the family. "And that *the whole congregation may join herein*," said they, " every one that can read is to have a psalm-book; and all others, not disabled by age or otherwise, are to be exhorted *to learn to read*."

We should hardly feel warranted in exhorting adults of all ages to learn to *sing*. Few persons, probably, who have come to mature years without any practical knowledge of music, could become proficients in the art of song without great painstaking; and we would not urge any one to take part in the songs of the Lord's house who cannot do so without disturbing the devotions of his candid and charitable fellow-worshippers. But the labor of teaching *children* to sing is eminently a practicable labor. In early childhood the ear is quick, the vocal organs are flexible, and there is usually such a disposition to exercise them in imitating musical sounds, and such a facility in doing this, that the labor of both teacher and scholar is rather a pleasure than a task. It may be, and always is undertaken, by those who have had experience in teaching, with perfect confidence of success. Dr. Thomas Hastings, of New York, remarks, that early cultivation in this art, when rightly directed, is *uniformly* successful. "The measure of success," he adds, "is not always equal; but in those districts of country, both here and in Europe, where juvenile instruction prevails, the imaginary distinction between natural and unnatural voices is never thought of. All make progress, and receive impressions lasting as life." In Prussia it is the prevailing belief that all who have the power of speech may learn to sing. It is well known that Luther would give no encouragement to schoolmasters who could not sing; nor would he have less than an hour a day devoted to singing in the schools under his direction.

We cannot expect complete success in congregational singing in our American sanctuaries, until they are filled with a generation taught to sing from childhood. The work of Billings and his associates, in its influence upon the psalmody of the land, was like leveling ancient forests. The injury cannot be repaired in a day. We must encourage a new growth, and wait for time to mature it. Common schools must be its nurseries, and vocal music have an allotted place with other branches of daily instruction. But the first seeds of song are to be sown at the parental fireside. In musical families, the ear even of infancy is under such educational influences, that often the way is prepared for skill in song long before the lessons of the schoolroom are received; and no congregation that is composed of families in which singing by old and young is a part of daily household worship, need be without good congregational singing on the Sabbath.

The duty of parents toward their children, in respect to this branch of their education, is a *Christian* duty. The chief end to be held in view is not the possession of an accomplishment, which, in the language of Luther, " maketh fine and expert people," but the use which God may make of this accomplishment in perfecting his praise; and in this view a high degree of skill in song is not to be despised, but is rather to be sought the more diligently, because it is to be consecrated to the uses of religion. But skill in this art is usually the result of early training. No one, therefore, who would bring to the sanctuary the best offering which he can command, rather than an inferior one, will undervalue the importance of early instruction.

But it is not merely with reference to a future advantage, that we would sow these seeds of song in childhood. We shall begin almost immediately to reap the fruit of our labor. After a very little instruction, children may join in the psalmody of the churches. And this they should be encouraged to do. They should be reminded of the tender interest with which the Saviour regarded children when he was on earth, and of the words of special approbation which he spoke when his attention was directed to their youthful hosannas. They should be taught that, as the Jewish children came near his person and received his blessing, so they may come near him in spirit with their songs. They should be taught that he is offered as a Saviour and protector to them as well as to others, and that they have every reason to love and praise him. Before they have learned to say, in the language of fashionable apology, " I have no voice," or " I have no ear;" before they have begun to be affected either with fear or vanity by knowing that their voices are heard ; before pride whispers that it is beneath their dignity to engage in a service in which *anybody* may join, — they should be taught to open their mouth and utter cheerfully, heartily, and devoutly, the praises of their divine Redeemer. They will thus be forming, at the right time of life, a habit which will, probably, never forsake them ; and which, we may hope, will get the start of that foolish pride which, lurking often under a garb of modesty, closes the lips of many who are well able to sing.

The children who take part in the singing will be found to be greatly interested in it. The house of God will present a new attraction to them. The hour of worship, which they now too often only endure, they will then enjoy. They will anticipate it with pleasure, because it has a service *for them;* one that is always in itself pleasing to them, and doubly so when it occurs on the Sabbath, in the sanctuary, in company with their parents and elders. Parents also will feel a new interest in the singing, when they hear the voices of their children mingling with their own. They will feel the power of a new motive for being qualified to sing, that they may be a help and a guide to their children; and for their children's sakes they will take pains to sing with promptness, with accuracy, with distinctness, with animation, with full voice, with all those qualities, in short, which make good congregational praise; at the same time, the interest felt by children in taking part with "grown people" in so important a service, and in so public a manner, will greatly increase the facility with which they naturally learn to sing. They will be found to follow with sweet docility and surprising correctness in the track of other voices, even when the tune is new to them. Trusting mainly to their ear, which becomes very rapidly educated, and confiding implicitly in the voices on which they lean, they will not feel that a tune must be perfectly known to them before they can attempt to sing it; and hence, after a little practice, they will render very important aid in the introduction of new tunes. Besides this, there is something peculiarly pleasant in the sound of children's voices mingling in a general chorus. If the children retain the unaffected, artless ways which belong to childhood, and have not been made prematurely bold by being exhibited to admiring audiences, their singing cannot fail to please, and even their errors will be cheerfully overlooked. Not feeling concerned about their musical reputation, and not apprehending any one's displeasure in view of their occasional mistakes, their voices will disclose whatever natural sweetness and flexibility they possess, and their manner of singing will be with freedom and vivacity.

This participation by the children in the service of song, will be to them the most valuable of all the services of the sanctuary. Pulpit instruction rarely engages the attention of young children. They gain a better knowledge of religious truth from the language and acts of direct worship, and especially from psalmody, than they can do from set discourses. Metre, rhyme, song, the concurrence of many voices, the felicity and sententiousness of poetic expression combine to strike the ear and command the attention. Then, in the best hymns, we find the language, not of formal didactic statement, but of tender sensibility, and often of gushing emotion. Such language is usually simple, easily understood, forcible. Being the language of the heart, it goes to the heart. Breathing with emotion, it carries conviction of its practicalness. Accordingly we find that, of all the pious lessons of early childhood, the best remembered in after-years are those which were embodied in compact simple verse. Let these lessons be received every Sabbath through the five or six hymns which are used in public worship — let the graces of verse be coupled with the delights of song upon the children's lips, and an amount of divine truth will be lodged in their minds whose value, both present and future, will be incalculable. " Let me make the ballads of the nation," said the great English moralist, "and I care not who makes their laws." Let the choicest Christian lyrics be made as familiar to the young as ballads, and all the munitions of law could not so surely protect their welfare.

Not only will they become familiar with divine truth, but they will be likely to receive a right impression of the nature of the Christian religion. There is much in the psalmody of the Christian church that is fitted to throw an appropriate aspect of cheerfulness over the whole field of religious truth and duty. The songs of the Lord's house are cheerful songs. The young, educated under their influence, and assisting in their utterance, will not be likely to grow up with a dread of religion as something gloomy and repulsive, producing sadness of countenance, austerity of manners, and servility of spirit. They will have learned from the hymns of worship which have been so often on their tongues, that the spirit which the gospel requires is such a spirit of love, confidence, gratitude, reverence, dependence, submission toward God, and joy in him, as is in the highest degree filial, and therefore both delightful and ennobling to those who imbibe and cherish it.

Thirdly, it is desirable that, in introducing congregational singing, the services of good and well-disposed choirs should be retained. There is an impression, quite general, that the advocates of this mode of praise would have it introduced in the old Genevan, Scotch, and English Puritan form, and would have every choir disbanded. But the experience of the New England churches in the first hundred years of their history is sufficient to warn us of the danger of constant musical degeneracy in congregational psalmody, without such assistance as may be afforded by choirs. It is true that music as an art is much more highly cultivated now than it was then, and we may to some extent rely upon this fact for the success of our present efforts; but with this increased culture there is also a fastidiousness of taste which it will require an effort to conciliate, and which, though it deserves rebuke, it is better that we should endeavor to conciliate than needlessly to offend. We may remind the lovers of fine music that singing in the house of God is not meant for entertainment, and that when we are professedly engaged in an act of worship the love of sensuous delight in song should be held in subordination. But, while we do this, we are still permitted to derive from music, as an art, all the assistance to devotion which it can bring. In the singing of the congregation, music is invoked to assist the devotions of *the greatest number*; and as we cannot expect the people generally to become accomplished vocalists, we must adopt for their use an easy and simple style of tune. Having done this, there is no reason why we should not endeavor to sing the tune well. To sing it poorly when, with suitable provision and painstaking, it might be sung well, would be like bringing the lame for sacrifice. It would not be presenting to God our best offerings.

But, in order that the congregation may bring its *best* offering in song, there can be no question that it needs the help and lead of a choir. A company of well-trained singers, having, what good singers usually have, such a love of music as keeps them in habits of constant vocal practice, and makes that practice a pleasure, have it in their power to impart invaluable assistance to the congregation. They are able to sing with confidence. They are masters of the music which they perform. Their bold, firm, spirited tones assure the timid of support, and encourage all who can sing, even moderately well, to put forth their voices heartily. They may direct the movement of the tunes, securing promptness and precision of utterance, and preventing those dilatory habits of singing, to which congregations are always liable. Their help in tunes that are not very familiar, and in learning new tunes, by which the stock of musical material in use by the congregation may be gradually enlarged, is of great importance.

A good choir will also wish to be furnished with a library of anthems, motets, and such more highly elaborated compositions as belong appropriately to professed singers. The use every Sabbath of a selection of the best music of this character which can be found, while it will keep alive the interest of the choir, will exert, insensibly, a musically educating influence upon the congregation. That practised singers should desire, at least a part of the time, to use a style of composition raised to the level of their capacity, is not unreasonable. And though the love of musical exhibition would doubtless require to be carefully watched, just as an eloquent preacher may often have occasion to guard himself against a tendency toward oratorical display, yet if the choir really possess devout feeling, and desire to express it in song, they may do it without being confined to strains appropriate to a simple psalmody for the people. And the people also, if they will, may find a help to their own devotion in such singing; although it must be confessed that *direct worship* by the congregation, through an anthem by the choir, is not ordinarily easy.

We do not assert that choirs are indispensable to the success of congregational singing. A choir may be composed of such material as to be rather a hinderance than a help. It might be such in character that no bond of religious sympathy could exist between it and the congregation; or it might regard the singing of the congregation with dislike, and endeavor to thwart it, either by its manner of singing, or by selecting unsuitable tunes. But if a congregation is so fortunate as to enjoy the services of a choir of good singers, who sing not for display, but for worship, and who are willing to assist the humblest worshippers in the sanctuary, and even children, in making their praises vocal, it should by all means, and most thankfully, avail itself of such assistance. And such a choir have a noble service to perform; a generous and self-denying service; a reasonable one, to be sure, and one which we have a right to expect from them if they profess godliness, but one in which they may manifest a spirit of genuine consecration, holy and acceptable to God. They deny themselves, in great measure, the delights of such music as their cultivated tastes could appreciate, and their practised skill produce, that they may assist those who need assistance in bringing to God their humbler offering. If they are animated by right motives in doing this, they are giving many a cup of cold water to Christ's little ones, for which they will in nowise lose their reward.

Fourthly, let the congregation, male and female, so far as it is convenient for them, sing upon the treble or leading melody of the tune. It is not true, as many seem to suppose, that any musical proprieties are violated by doing this. In the music of the greatest masters, in the choruses of Handel, in the symphonies of Beethoven, and in all the higher orchestral music, the melody is frequently found moving in octaves. This is especially the case when it is the object of the composer to produce an impression of sublimity. An example of this kind is found in the Hallelujah chorus of the *Messiah* in connection with the words, " For the Lord God omnipotent reigneth." Dr. Crotch, in his remarks upon different styles of music, the sublime, the beautiful, and the ornamental, says : " A passage performed by many voices or instruments in unison or octaves, produces sublimity."

Unisonous singing is, then, peculiarly *appropriate* to songs of worship. It befits the grandeur of the themes which form their basis, and the solemnity of the act in which we take it upon us to speak unto the Lord. If any songs should be characterized by grandeur, they should be the songs of the sanctuary. Beauty and grace of performance should yield, in the house of God, to strength and dignity. Hundreds of voices, addressing the Supreme Being in solemn, elevated praise, may well afford to dismiss the thought of that carefully adjusted balance of the parts, which, though it be essential to good choir singing, is a feeble excellence compared with a magnificent unison. Hogarth relates that when Haydn heard a psalm sung in unison by four thousand children in St. Paul's Cathedral, he was moved to tears, and declared that that simple and natural air had given him the greatest pleasure he had ever derived from music. The same incident, probably, is referred to by Mr. Havergal, although in his account of it, instead of four thousand voices, he mentions six thousand, and the support of a sufficient instrumentation ; and he adds, that the tune which was sung was the Old Hundredth Psalm Tune.

But we are to discriminate between the singing which is strictly in unison, and that which is by unisons and octaves united. Effective as a strict unison of trebles, by thousands or even hundreds of voices must always be, there is great significancy in the accession to it of the bold, muscular tones of men's voices. A peculiar impression of stateliness arises from the junction of a manly tenor with an already well-sustained treble. Its effect is like that of the majestic double-diapason stop in the larger church organs. While the enlivening effect of the treble-octave is retained, its comparative shrillness is attempered by its union with the tenor; and the result is, that gravity and dignity of tone which are so much to be desired in sacred song, and which are more happily secured in this way than they could be in any other.

Another reason for singing in this way is that it makes congregational singing *practicable*. To demand of a congregation the whole four parts of a tune in proper balance, is a very different thing from asking of them only one part, and that a pleasing and easily-remembered melody. There are few congregations in which there are not singers enough to sustain, ably and vigorously, *one part* of a tune. Let this part be a treble that is adapted to a moderate compass of voice, let all sing upon it whose pitch of voice allows them to do it easily, and if there be a general disposition to sing, there is no reason why respectable congregational song should not be at once realized in the great majority of our churches. There will be, in this case, a far greater number of voices upon the treble than are ever heard upon that part in ordinary choir singing. The treble will thus have its appropriate preëminence among the parts. It will stand forth so distinctly from them, and so conspicuously above them, as to be readily followed by those unpractised singers whose voices would otherwise be drifted hither and thither upon the staff, by the shifting preponderance of treble, tenor, and bass.

Strength of utterance, also, as well as distinctness of treble, will mark this mode of performance. The concentration upon one part of the great majority of the voices which unite in song, produces an impression of strength which could not be produced by the same voices distributed. The effect is like that of an accumulation of military forces upon a single point in a line of battle. It was a frequent art in the war-policy of Napoleon, to dispose his troops in the form of a wedge, and with it pierce and turn the enemy's centre. If he could break that, the battle was his. There is something in the singing of a large assembly upon one part, led by a resolute choir, which reminds one of a wedge-shaped attack. The charge is made upon the treble, which is emphatically the centre of the tune. If that is carried, all is carried. And in an attempt of this kind, there can be scarcely any doubt of success. Ordinarily, a confidence of success will show itself at once in every one's tone and manner. The effect of this will be to encourage a large class of persons to sing, who are usually silent lest they should be heard. There are singers in every congregation whose voices are good, and whose ear is correct and quick, but who, because they cannot sing by note, will not venture upon the simplest melody unless they can lean upon other and stronger voices for support. Give them this support, and they will sensibly augment the volume of the general chorus. A congregation may contain scores of such persons, and even hundreds, if we include children, and yet among them all there may be very few who can sing the simplest tune correctly without help. A choir of twenty or thirty singers concentrating their vocal energies mainly upon the treble, and singing with clear, distinct articulation, with bold, commanding tone, and with firm, steady, unvarying movement, may set before the congregation such a plain and inviting path of song, and may inspire with such confidence all who have the ability to sing, that the result will be a successful and even admirable illustration of the people's chorus. A hundred little rivulets, no one of which could find its way to the sea alone, may join the river that passes near them, and be wafted safely to the ocean; but the stream that conveys them owes much of its grandeur to these little tributaries.

In the production of this great melodic chorus, a strong lead of men's voices upon the treble is indispensable. The value of men's voices for dignity and impressiveness of tone has already been alluded to; but their chief value, in the chorus of which we speak, is their strength. In the singing of a congregation, vocal power is the chief element of success. Weakness is failure. Weakness of *treble* is failure, though the other parts were well sustained. There is but little danger of our exaggerating the importance of producing a large body of tone upon a treble. We do not mean by this to commend such feats of strong lungs, as would give to half a dozen stentorian voices a noisy and pretentious isolation from all the rest of the assembly. Such vociferation should neither be encouraged nor tolerated. But that power, the effect of which we feel in the singing of a multitude, in which voices of every degree of strength and color of expression lose their individuality in the river of song which they help to swell, can hardly be too great. Let it be poured forth until it fill the house. Let the vocal current roll its ample volume with a momentum that shall seem to float the voices of which it is composed. Let the whole atmosphere of the place seem to have started into vibration, and to be charged with song to its utmost capacity. Let this mighty vocal unison be supported, as such singing always should be, by the ponderous bass, and the pealing modulations of the noblest of all musical instruments. Let the peerless organ open all its mines of sonorous wealth, and load the air with its golden harmonies.

Another reason for singing in unisons and octaves is, that this mode of song admits of different harmonies by organ and choir, in connection with any given melody. The advantage of the introduction of these varied harmonies would be twofold. First, it would furnish a needed variety of musical performance in any congregation whose members prefer to confine their singing to a small number of tunes; and secondly, it would open the way for all needed improvements in harmony. The period of the Reformation furnishes a historical example in point. The earliest use of the people's chorus at that period was entirely unisonous. No other mode of song was contemplated by the Reformers. The tunes in use were nothing but simple melodies. Old and young, male and female, sang these melodies without a thought of bass, tenor, or alto. But at length the lovers of music desired to press into the service of sacred song a more liberal contribution from the resources of musical science. In 1563, competent composers began to harmonize the simple melodies of the time, not with any purpose of interfering with the prevailing mode of praise, — for the people were still expected to sing as stoutly as they pleased upon the part which had always belonged to them, — but with the desire of enriching this plain song of the people by the addition of choir parts for trained voices. The melodies in common use were not only simple, but few in number. It was not strange, that practised singers should desire a richer and more copious musical vocabulary in which to express their public praises. And what method of attaining this was so practicable, and at the same time so satisfactory, as the introduction of harmony? Each of the few melodies which the people sung could be harmonized in many different ways; and so long as the melody itself remained untouched, it would be a matter of comparative indifference to the people what the choir sung; and the choir might gratify their love of vanity by diversifying their harmonies at pleasure. And this they did. Composers were ambitious of exercising their skill in varying the harmonies of a given melody. The Rev. Mr. Havergal has collected twenty-eight different methods in which the Old Hundredth Psalm Tune has, at different times, been composed into parts. In the loom of song constructed in this way, skilful choirs wove across the plain warp of the people's melodies the richest woof of many-colored harmonies, and the result was a texture with which all were satisfied. Those who desired musical gratification, found it, and at the same time the people enjoyed the privilege of participating in the song. It may not be necessary, now, to resort to such a plan of song as this; but the plan is one upon which good choir-singing, and successful congregational singing, might both be realized without requiring of the people the knowledge of many tunes.

The other advantage mentioned is the opening of the way for needed improvements in harmony. If the voices of the people are distributed upon the several parts, scarcely can a note in the bass of a familiar tune change its place, but the peace of the congregation that sings it is put in jeopardy. There is a large class of persons with whom "alteration" is a sacrilegious offence. The perfection of psalm-singing consists, in their view, in singing as we always have sung. One could hardly whisper the possibility of improving the harmony of the Old Hundredth, without being accused, by such persons, of irreverence for sacred things, and a wanton disregard of old and hallowed associations. And yet no one, of only moderate musical culture, can notice the too frequent recurrence of the tonal harmony in this tune, especially in connection with the initial and terminal notes of each strain, without perceiving its monotonous effect, and wishing that a tune, so venerable with age, and of such intrinsic worth, were honored with such harmonies as it deserves, and with such as would have been written for it by the best masters two hundred years ago. If it were the custom of the congregations to sing chiefly upon the treble part, the needed changes, both in this and in other tunes might be introduced. One of the doors now closed against progress would be thrown open, and we should witness improvement in the methods of sacred harmony, as in other branches of science.

Fifthly, let the singing be regarded as an act of worship, and let all the details of the service be such as to favor the expression of devout feeling.

If the singing is regarded as an act of worship, we shall not be likely to speak of it as *music*. We commonly and very properly associate with the word music, the thought of artistic exhibition and sensuous enjoyment. An American traveller in Germany, a few years since, asked, in what church he could find the best music. The answer was, " There is no music here, except once or twice a year, on the occasion of some great festival."—" But, do not the people sing in church ? "—" O, yes; they sing hymns, but there is no music." If we were to observe as clear a distinction as this remark indicates between psalm-singing and musical entertainment, a great barrier to the success of congregational singing would be removed.

If the singing is regarded as an act of worship, the congregation will wish to *stand* when they sing. Standing is one of the appropriate attitudes of reverence, and is therefore one that is fit to be taken in a devotional exercise. It is also the best position for a free and vigorous use of the vocal organs. The body is erect, the chest is easily expanded, and by the very act of rising and standing upon one's feet, something is done toward overcoming that spirit of indolence which closes the lips of many who might sing, or makes their singing spiritless and dull. In the singing of a congregation there is almost always a tendency toward a heavy and tedious drawling of the notes.

To sit in singing is to encourage this tendency. Pew-seats are one of the acknowledged homes of languor and drowsiness. We could not recommend congregational singing in any place, where the love of ease would be so far indulged as to hold the people in their seats while they sing. It is both painful and humiliating to observe the evidences which every Sabbath furnishes of the physical debility of the present generation. Our Pilgrim Fathers sometimes sang thirty common metre verses at one singing, and they stood through the whole, beside standing through their very long prayers. The singing of a single psalm often occupied half an hour, and the prayers were still longer than that.

If the singing is regarded as an act of worship, the congregation will stand *in the attitude of worship* facing the pulpit. To turn around, so as to face an organ and choir opposite the pulpit, is no help to devotion but a hinderance to it. No one will maintain that he worships better for turning around, or that he has any better reason for such a change of position than a desire to see the choir and the organ, and that part of the congregation which he cannot see while facing the pulpit. Just in proportion to his curiosity about seeing these objects, will be their diverting influence upon him. They can be no help to his devotion.

If the organ and the choir, or precentor, were in front of the congregation, and near the pulpit, the principal alleged reason for turning around would be obviated, and the confusion which is caused by this unbecoming and awkward movement would be avoided. And there are very decided incidental advantages to be secured by placing the organ in this position. The ground floor of the house is the place from which to exhibit to the best advantage the power of the instrument. Its nearness to the congregation makes it easy for all who sing to follow it. And, then, its location on the same level with the pews, and in full view from every part of the house, would make it obvious at once, that the organ is intended for the people, and is played for their benefit, and not merely to help an isolated choir in a remote organ-loft. And this would do much toward inclining the people to sing.

If the singing is regarded as an act of worship, the congregation will take pains to *become familiar* with the hymns and tunes which they are to use. The less one is embarrassed by the effort to sing *correctly* in respect to tune, time, and the delivery of the words, the easier will it be to sing devoutly. For this reason, and for other reasons, such as the duty to bring to God our best services, and the duty to sing so as to help rather than hinder the devotions of others, there should be frequent meetings for practice. We never expect good choir-singing where there are not diligent rehearsals. Why should we expect more from congregations than we do from choirs? It ought not to be supposed, that the end which we have in view is of so easy attainment that it can be gained without effort. All analogy teaches, that the most valuable results in any field of endeavor are to be secured only by persevering and laborious pursuit; and we should be degrading the object at which we aim, to imagine that it lies within the reach of indolence and indifference. Every congregation should in some way secure for itself the benefit of a weekly practice. If there be times or places in which this cannot be done, something approaching to it might be attempted, with advantage, on the evening of the stated weekly prayer-meeting of a church. Often the singing at such a meeting may be in the use of the same hymns and tunes, or a part of the same, which are to be used on the coming Sabbath. The two or three tunes with which the people are least acquainted, may thus be made familiar. An increased attendance upon the prayer-meeting might be an incidental and not inconsiderable advantage of this plan.

The practice of *using a given hymn always with the same tune* diminishes the labor of learning new tunes, and greatly assists the effort of retaining both hymn and tune in the memory. The association which is thereby formed in the mind, between lines of poetry and the musical strains in which we pronounce them, so that one suggests the other, is the secret of this advantage. In Germany, in any given locality, every hymn has its tune, from which it is rarely, if ever, separated. Upon a Sabbath morning, the hymns for the day are indicated by figures posted on a tablet near the pulpit, where all can see them. As soon as the hymns are found, it is known what tunes are to be sung. Indeed, the tunes are not known by proper names, such as Dalston, Amsterdam, but by the first few words of the hymn, as " How pleased and blest," " Rise my soul." By this intimate connection between the hymn and its tune, both are far more permanently lodged in the memory, than if the hymn were sung now in one tune, and now in another, and never, perhaps, in any tune twice. The only way in which such a practice can be made common, where it does not already exist, is by the use of a book in which hymns and tunes have been brought into appropriate alliance by competent editorial labor. The hymn and its tune should stand upon one page. The singer has then but one book to hold, and his eye easily passes to and fro between words and notes. If suitable tunes are provided, and fit connections formed between tunes and hymns, the desired association of words with notes will soon be established.

The use of such a book affords great encouragement to individuals and families to learn to sing. All the private labor which they expend in becoming familiar with the book, is so much direct preparation for the psalmody of public worship. The tune, in which a family at household worship on Sabbath morning sings the words " Welcome sweet day of rest," is the tune which will be sung to those words in the sanctuary, if the congregation should use that hymn.

If the singing is regarded as an act of worship, the congregation *will not perplex itself with the refinements of technical musical expression.* It will dismiss all thought of that kind of expression, which is obtained by mechanical methods to be learned from a table of musical signs. It will not deny, that we should sing with appropriateness, and with discernment of the distinctive emotional character of each hymn and each stanza. But what that manner of singing is which is appropriate in each instance, it will allow an intelligent and cordial sympathy with the sentiments which are sung to prescribe. Let a congregation be required to sing, now soft, now loud, now fast, now slowly, now crescendo, now diminuendo, now with tones short and sharp, and now with prolonged and gliding notes, and always with such deference for punctuation that a comma would bring an entire assembly to a sudden, startling pause, and the attempt to do this, beside being in itself a pretentious failure, would defeat every religious end which psalmody contemplates. Some would be perplexed, and would abandon the singing altogether; some would feel that they were doing exploits, and all who do sing would be tasking themselves to produce the appropriate lights and shades of musical expression. Those careful modulations of the voice, by which, if they are used moderately and with concealed art, a skilful choir may impress an audience, are not needed in the people's chorus, in which there is no audience, and they would be of very doubtful advantage if they could be used. Even if we consider this chorus in the light of its impressiveness, it is chiefly its grandeur that makes it impressive, and the effect which it derives from this source would be rather weakened than assisted by the addition of the finer graces of art. Dr. Lowell Mason has well said, in illustration of this thought, that the grandeur of the ocean does not depend upon the purity of its waters, nor the grandeur of a mountain upon the richness of its soil.

Ordinarily, a hymn should be sung in steady, unvarying movement, from beginning to end. If there should be anything in what is sung to lead a congregation spontaneously, without premeditated purpose, and almost unconsciously to itself, to accelerate or slacken its time in a particular part of the hymn, there is, perhaps, no objection to its obeying such an impulse. But the change which is made should be very slight, and never such as to attract attention. The labor after expression, by means of a fluctuating movement, is one of the poorest attempts which choirs ever make. For a congregation to make this attempt would be to invite confusion at once. Not only should it be the aim of a congregation to sing a hymn in exact and uniform time throughout, but it should take the greatest pains to realize this aim. A steady time, as steady as the motion of the planets, is not only demanded by the laws of music, but it is necessary to the comfort and confidence of those who sing.

The current of song should be *continuous*, also, as well as uniform in its progress. It should not be interrupted by pauses. In reading, the pauses arrest the voice, and enjoin upon it a momentary silence. But the nature of *tonal* utterance forbids such interruption. Tonal utterance requires *prolongation* of sound. When this necessary condition of song is wanting, as it must be, if every pause which the sense of the hymn admits is allowed to suspend the voice, melody is destroyed, and singing becomes declamation. Even that momentary cessation of tone which is necessary in taking breath, constitutes an imperfection in singing, and the art of concealing the act of breathing, so as to break as little as possible the flow of a melody, is always cultivated by the best vocalists. A good organist never lifts his hands from the keys till his playing is done. The successive progressions which come under his skilful finger, are wrought into a compact framework of harmony, in which no chord is separated from the adjacent chords by any perceptible interval of time. So, in singing, our endeavor should be to give every note its full length, and to let the voice be constantly heard; otherwise the song, which should be continuous, and, as nearly as possible, unbroken in its flow, is disfigured with unseemly gaps, such as appear in the singing of one who is short-breathed. And with many a person, much of the usual pleasure of singing is prevented by the fear that at some unguarded moment, when he is not watching for commas, his slender voice will be left alone, like a solitary suspension-wire, bridging a chasm of silence.

There cannot be, in singing, such an observance of pauses as there is in reading, without giving an *undue importance* to the pauses, so as to thrust them upon every one's attention. A sudden stop, a "flash of silence," in the midst of a full and animated chorus, surprises an audience. Its effect is too much like those abrupt and startling transitions which are to be expected in dramatic exhibition. And the notice which is thereby taken of an ordinary mark of punctuation is so extravagant, and so far beyond what the sense of the hymn can demand, that, in the judgment of good taste, it is better to make no attempt to observe pauses by any absolute suspension of the voice.

The habit of lingering at the end of the lines is a very common fault in singing. Much of the life of the song is thereby lost, both by the encouragement which is given to a dilatory habit, and by the loss of the sense of that regularly recurring musical pulse, or beat, which should be always in the mind.

Musical expression, even in choir-singing, is often *extravagant*, and at variance with the simplicity which is becoming in worship. There is a labored and painfully dramatic style of performance, which savors more of art than of devotion, and which appeals to fancy more than to religious sentiment. Those singers whose thoughts are more upon the tune than upon the hymn, are usually lavish of expression. They crave the entertainment which is afforded by high musical coloring. The singing of a plain tune several times through, is monotonous to them, and their "expression" is an effort after relief and variety. Hence its exaggeration. But with those whose chief interest centres upon the hymn, and who are fed by its embodied sentiment, instead of merely reciting its phraseology as a needed metrical form upon which to display their musical ornaments, the case is very different. Their taste demands, and their devotion is most assisted by, such simple yet earnest and elevated tonal utterance as they would use if God only were present to hear. They will not be laboring to impress others by their singing, and hence artificial representation will hold a very subordinate place in their regard.

Not only is musical expression often carried to excess, but, for want of a correct judgment of what ought to be expressed, it is often *misplaced and false*. Not the pervading sentiment of the hymn or stanza is expressed, but only its phraseology. Words are dramatized intensely, while thoughts are, apparently, almost unperceived. In singing such couplets as the following —

"The vital savor of his name
Restores their fainting breath;" —

"To chase the shades of death away,
And bid the sinner live;" —

"Our quickening souls awake and rise
From the long sleep of death;" —

"Ever will he be thy stay,
Though the heavens shall melt away;" —

"He will gird thee by his power,
In the weary, fainting hour;" —

the chief object with many choirs is, not to represent the lively sentiments which these couplets contain, but very carefully to paint the phrases, "fainting breath," "shades of death," "sleep of death," "melt away," "weary, fainting hour."

Who has not noticed the effect upon some choirs of such words as "death," and "grave," even when the stanza in which they occur is of a jubilant character; — as in the lines —

> "He makes me triumph over death,
> And saves me from the grave"?

Appropriateness, in singing these lines, is thought to require the voices to falter upon such words. In singing the stanza —

> "This is the grace that lives and sings,
> When faith and hope shall cease;
> 'T is this shall strike our joyful strings
> In realms of endless peace" —

it is not uncommon for the second line of the stanza to be sung "diminuendo" throughout, because the word "cease" is at the end of it. The stops of the organ are, one by one, thrust back, the voices gradually suppressed, till in the middle of the stanza there is a general cessation. Doubtless the discontinuance of faith and hope may be expressed in this way, but the writer of the hymn would much prefer that our expression should relate to the grace which does *not* cease with faith and hope, but forever "lives and sings." How often do choirs drop suddenly from full voice almost to "pianissimo" when they would express the word "peace"; — as in the stanza —

"The saints shall flourish in his days,
Dressed in the robes of joy and praise;

Peace, like a river, from his throne
Shall flow to nations yet unknown"!

or in the lines —

"Defend me from each threatening ill;
Control the waves; say, '*Peace! be still!*'"

We have heard a choir endeavor to express a feeling of sadness at the thought of the end of time, in singing the words —

"His worship and his fear shall last,
Till hours and years and time be past."

We have heard a choir attempt to paint the full meaning of the word "mourn," in the line —

"Cease, ye pilgrims! cease to mourn."

If the same choir had sung the line —

"No groans shall mingle with the songs,"

doubtless the "groans" would have been heard.

Such efforts to "express" words and phrases in singing are trivial, to say the least. Sometimes they are ludicrous. And it is very common for the appropriate impression of a hymn to be sensibly impaired by them, even if its prevailing spirit is not positively misrepresented.

If the singing is regarded as an act of worship, the congregation will not desire *long organ interludes* between the stanzas. Interludes are, in themselves, an evil. They break the continuity of the hymn and delay its progress. When the hymn is of a highly emotional character, containing the language of devotion throughout, its several parts so closely connected in thought, that the entire effusion emanates, apparently, from a single glow of devout affection, as, for example, the hymn of Bernard, "Jesus! the very thought of thee," or the hymn of Palmer, "Jesus! these eyes have never seen That radiant form of thine,"—its repeated interruption by an interlude following each stanza, is a violence to which the hymn should never be subjected. To separate a prayer into paragraphs by intercalated strains of music, would be a parallel case.

Occasional interludes may be needed, to give singers a few moments for taking breath. The time which would be occupied in playing a single line of the tune, is amply sufficient for this purpose. For the organist to play longer than that, when the worshippers are kept standing to hear him, is to fatigue more than to relieve them. With suitable tunes, tunes which are quick-moving and not too high, two interludes in a psalm of six common metre stanzas ought to be considered sufficient; and, as a general rule, there should be no more interludes than are positively needed for relief from fatigue.

The interludes which are used should be such in character, as to preserve the impression which the hymn and tune are fitted to produce. The organist, beside being master of his instrument, should be a man of quick sensibilities and a devout mind. His heart should warm at the fire which kindled the fervor of the hymn. He should be in full sympathy with both hymn and tune, and should know how to express that sympathy. In giving out the tune, he should play nothing but the identical chords and progressions, note for note, of which the tune consists. Between the stanzas, he should play nothing that is frivolous in character or secular in its associations. He should not confuse the minds of the people by taking up a different movement from that in which the tune is sung. He should not keep them waiting for him to change the stops. He should not harp upon fancy stops, or loiter and play seesaw with the swell. He should not fall into a musical reverie, and play in such a vague and dreamy way that, when the singing is resumed, there will be a general feeling of uncertainty about the time. He should not play in a dilatory or hesitating way, as though he were either indifferent or at a loss. He should feel that the time which he is using is valuable; that the congregation are standing in act of solemn worship, and that with such an instrument as he has in charge with which to help and lead them, they may reasonably expect him to be serious and in earnest. He need not play without taste, or without elegance; but he should have a meaning in what he plays, and he should express it with promptness, distinctness, and precision. If, then, his playing is one in spirit with what is sung, and if the energy of a warmly sympathetic emotion is infused into it, the evil of interludes will be greatly mitigated.

A good organist will endeavor to avoid *monotony* in his interludes. He will usually step a little aside from the beaten path of the tune which he has been playing, into some neighboring and related key, not by harsh and pedantic transition, but by such gentle and ingenious modulation as we hear in the playing of thorough-bred organists. He will seek variety in his *cadences*,— sometimes resorting to the half cadence, and sometimes closing upon the dominant of the relative minor. The delicate avoidance, by these or any similar methods, of the perpetually recurring common cadence, will be most grateful to the ear.

Still the interlude is an evil, and it should be, as far as possible, dispensed with. It stands in the way of an *accumulation* of devout interest, as the singing of the hymn progresses.

Sixthly, the success of congregational singing will depend very much upon the use of suitable tunes. The tunes must be *simple, natural, and easy to sing*.

By this it is not meant that they should be tame and monotonous, or in any respect inferior as compositions. Certainly it is not meant that they should be so utterly destitute of character as are a large part of the tunes which have recently come into use; much less that they should violate any of the laws of musical science. A tune may be simple, and yet possessed of sterling merit, as Dundee and the Old Hundredth. It may be simple, and yet classic in its whole style and structure, and conformed to the most rigid rules of scientific progression in both melody and harmony, as Tallis and Phuvah. It may be simple, and yet capable of all the awakening and elevating, or subduing and impressive effects which are intended in the hymn with which it is used. A tune may be simple, and yet afford, in both melody and harmony, a pleasing variety. When a tune is all this, and possesses at the same time an individuality to which every line and every strain contributes, and which would be instantly disturbed by the removal of one of the lines, and the substitution of a new one not clearly and logically one in thought and spirit with the other three, we have the perfection of a tune. And it must be seen to be no easy task to furnish, within the narrow compass of four lines, a tune which shall possess both unity and variety, and still keep within the bounds of simplicity and naturalness.

By simplicity in a tune is meant plainness, or freedom from artificial ornament. Music, as an art, claims the attention of a worshipping assembly just so far as it may assist devotion, and no further. All those highly-wrought artistic effects which are intended to captivate the ear and divert attention to themselves, are to be avoided.

We will specify a few things, in our ordinary church psalmody, which seem to us to be at variance with simplicity.

First, *an excessive use of dotted notes.* These notes are often valuable in giving expression to spirited hymns, and often, words of several syllables may be uttered more gracefully by the use of them; but, in general, they produce a jerking effect, which is undignified, disturbs the movement, and annoys the performer. A rest, instead of a dot, is still worse. The voices are brought to a sudden pause, to start again upon a short note, at the hazard of having no two voices start together. Nevertheless, the tunes with dotted notes are usually popular. Witness Arlington, Zion, Cowper, Ariel, Rock of Ages. But they are seldom well sung on account of the difficulty of keeping the proper time.

Secondly, *an excessive use of ties and suspensions.* These are generally a mere musical dalliance standing in the way of a straight-forward and manly utterance of praise. They belong properly to weak and sentimental music. Witness Shirland.

Thirdly, *dots and ties united*, as in the tunes Antigua, and St. Martin's. To require the voice to change its pitch two or three times on a single vowel, is certainly no help to devotion, and it causes needless delay. And the performance of the three tied notes, the first one being dotted, is almost uniformly bad. The second note of the three is seldom articulated distinctly, but only slid over in passing from the first note to the third, just as one who is careless of his speech slides over the second syllable of the word *government*, without attempting to pronounce it.

Fourthly, *fugues, duets, and solos*. These can hardly be supposed to answer any higher end in psalmody than to humor an idle fancy, and foster the vanity of the performer.

Fifthly, *triplets*. Triplets, in such a tune as China, are absurd. They impart an air of gayety, to say the least, to Brattle Street. In the old tune Portugal, they are guilty of positive levity.

Sixthly, *the use of a supplementary line in the composition of the tune*, by which it becomes necessary to repeat one of the lines of every stanza which is sung in it. The tune-maker knows that his tune is to be sung in a stanza of four lines only, but he does not succeed in making his musical thought complete in the short space of four lines, and he therefore adds a line. The composer who writes five lines of notes for every four lines of words, either lacks the power of concise writing, or he intentionally exalts the tune above the hymn.

All these musical conceits which have now been indicated are a hinderance rather than a help to the spirit of devotion, and very often they may be regarded as a confession, on the part of the composer, that his tune is an inferior one. He perceives the want of any real merit in it, and then tries to compensate for this by some pretty conceit thrown in here and there, and by something striking in his rhythm. We often discover in literary composition a painful effort after intensity of style. It is shown by a redundance of adjectives, superlatives, and striking phrases, which are the more multiplied wherever the page lacks weight and vigor of thought. Such is the labor of the tune-maker whose material consists chiefly of dots, ties, suspensions, triplets, rests, fugues, syncopations, solos, duets, and the use of supplementary lines.

A tune for the congregation must be *natural* as well as simple. It must be the opposite of whatever is forced and far-fetched. The remark often made, upon hearing a new tune, that "it sounds familiar, and resembles some other tune that we have heard," is sometimes more complimentary to the composer than it was intended to be. The love of originality in young composers, if they have not positive genius, too often leads to the production of cheap oddities and eccentricities, entertaining at first to lovers of mere novelty, but really as unworthy of the countenance of a sober criticism as they are unfit for the solemn service of the house of God.

But, what is more to our present purpose, these novelties in music discourage and bewilder a large class of worshippers, who can sing only as they lean upon other voices. Tunes intended for the congregation should be so natural in the progression of the notes as to invite the confidence of the unpractised and timid, many of whom, now silent through fear, would, by a proper style of tune, be encouraged to cast their voices upon the general current of song, not doubting that they would be borne along safely upon its even, steady, and majestic flow.

A tune for the congregation must be *easy to sing*. It must not be so high or so low as to tax severely the voices, or so slow as to fatigue them, and prevent a vigorous and well-sustained performance of five or six stanzas. There must be in the treble or leading part a clearly-defined melody, readily discovered by the ear, pleasing and inviting to the voice. This is really indispensable; for if those voices which are led more by the ear than by the eye (and they are not few), attempt to sing a proper choir tune in which the melody is adroitly distributed among the four parts, they will be quickly confused and put to silence.

The melody should consist mostly of *small intervals*. If large ones are used, they should be natural, and should occur in such relations as to be easily measured by the voice. The Old Hundredth is a good tune in this respect, having only one large interval, and that a fifth. We are not to expect vocal exploits by the congregation, and they would be quite out of place if we could have them. Those venturesome leaps of the voice across the chasm of strange intervals, like the distance from A flat up to F in the tune Rest, reminds one of a passage in Uncle Tom's Cabin, in which the Ohio is crossed by hazardous leaps upon floating pieces of ice. If they are well done, we are left in wonderment; and until they are well done we are trembling for the performers.

The melody should, as a general thing, be *continuous and smoothly flowing*. It should not cease, and give way to monotone, as it must when repeated tones are used, like those in the second line of the Old Hundredth, in the first and second lines of Meribah, and in all tunes written in the chanting style. Repeated tones are monotonous, and they are not usually sung in good time.

One of the best examples of a *smoothly flowing melody* is seen in the tune Phuvah. Contrast this with the tune Christmas in E flat, ascribed to Handel. Who could hesitate in choosing between these two for the use of a large congregation? The leading impression of good congregational singing is not beautiful, or sprightly, or wild, or fantastic, but *grand*. It is like what we feel in standing on the bank of a large river, with smooth surface and a steady, uniform progress. There are eddies and rapids and falls, and we enjoy all these, but they are only occasional; the general course of the stream is smoothly and majestically onward, its broad bed dropping its level by almost imperceptible gradations toward the sea. Here is a path for ships; and such a path the congregation must have, for the congregation is something more than a skiff; and the stream of melody which floats it should be like a river near the sea, and not like a mountain brook.

A model tune for the congregation would unquestionably be written in *common time*. The objection to triple time arises from its slowness, and failure of ordinary singers to sustain, properly, the first two parts of the measure, when they are united either in a single note or by two tied notes. Ravenscroft's collection of a hundred and fifty psalm tunes contained only five tunes in triple measure. "The triple measure," says the Rev Mr. Havergal, "requires skilful vocalists. It requires a degree of sustaining power which crude singers know nothing about." Any one may perceive the truth of this remark in the singing of such tunes as Abridge, Barby, Balerma, Howard, Rothwell. Often have we heard the old tune Mear, in triple measure, sung in such a manner that one could hardly tell whether it was intended to be sung in triple time or common time. There are other forms of triple measure, however, one of which is represented by Hebron, and another by the Italian Hymn, which are not open to the objections here specified.

Tunes in common time, *having the initial and terminal notes of each line long, and all the rest short*, present the best possible rhythmic form for the congregation. This is the ancient form of the Old Hundredth, St. Anns, Tallis, and the whole class of old tunes which these represent, but which have been much changed and sung for two or three generations past in notes of equal length, and all of them long. The labor of singing them in this manner, when more than three or four stanzas were to be sung, has always been tiresome. For this reason, the tunes have, as a class, fallen in great measure into disuse. Excellent as they are acknowledged to be, they are avoided on account of their slowness. Even the Old Hundredth, of which it is said that it would be difficult to find a parish in England or Scotland (and we might add, or in America) in which it is not known and admired, is not sung often. It is reserved for great occasions, on which there are voices enough to sustain a slow movement, and for the doxology, which has but one stanza. Many a feebler tune does more service than the Old Hundredth. But, "*originally*," says Mr. Havergal, "this tune was regarded as the liveliest and most cheerful in the whole psalter. *Now*, it is sung in a heavy, drawling manner; and so inveterate is this custom, that we do not seem to see how inconsistent it is with the jubilant character of the psalm." Again, he remarks, "The old singers sang at a greater speed than modern singers. A dozen verses, reduced to six by a double tune, formed a very moderate portion for one occasion. *The modern drawl* makes four single verses quite long enough."

Let the question be asked, whether there is really any good reason for being four or five times as long in singing a hymn, as we are in a proper and impressive reading of it? The mind takes in the meaning of the hymn as rapidly as the hymn is ordinarily read, and if a great deal more time is allowed by the tune, the mind becomes listless, the tones languid, and the act of praise inanimate and dull. "It were to be wished," said Dr. Watts, "that we might not dwell so long on every note, and produce the same syllables to such a tiresome extent, with a constant uniformity of time, which disguises the music, and puts the singers quite out of breath; whereas, if the method of singing were but reformed to a greater speed of pronunciation, we might often enjoy the pleasure of a longer psalm with less expense of time and breath, and our psalmody would be *more agreeable to that of the ancient churches*, more intelligible to others, and more delightful to ourselves."

By restoring the tunes, to which Dr. Watts here refers, to their old rhythmic form, in which they may be sung about twice as fast as we have been accustomed to sing them, they may be brought into frequent use, and become, as they surely must, the most serviceable and satisfactory tunes which congregations can use. Long hymns may be used in them without fatigue, and without the mutilation of the hymns by the omission of stanzas. The words will be uttered with greater distinctness, and the singing, while it will be marked with increased animation, will not incur the charge of lightness. The long initial and terminal notes will preserve its dignity. "This old notation," says an English organist, "is earnestly recommended, for the reason that when the first and last notes of each strain are longer than the others, the tune may be sung with considerable spirit without being divested of one particle of its solemnity." It is pleasant to know that "this old notation" belongs exclusively to psalmody, and has no secular associations whatever.

Tunes for the congregation should be *characterized by strength*. They should be like the large timbers which are used in the bottom of a frame, capable of bearing all the pressure that can be put upon them. Without attempting to show by any analysis what the strength of a tune is, it will be safe to say that the Old Hundredth, Dundee, St. Anns, Monmouth, Windsor, Canterbury, Tallis, Phuvah, Bava, are strong tunes. By looking at their structure, we may derive profitable suggestions in regard to the style of tune which is most suitable for a congregation. It is worthy of notice that strength of musical thought, in these examples, assumes, as it naturally would, a very simple garb of expression. They are perfectly plain tunes. They admirably illustrate the simplicity which has already been defined. They have no dots, ties, suspensions, or duets. They present a strictly syllabic union of words with notes. They have no more lines than are required by the metres in which they are written. They are in common time. The melodies consist mostly of short intervals. Their melodic compass is so moderate, that it is easy for the voices that sing them to bring out their strength; and the same may be said of their being in common time rather than in triple time. Their rhythmic notation, as it originally stood, was that of the long and short notes, already described, of which Mr. Havergal says, "it is generically the old form, *the traditional one, and the only one which all singers feel to be natural.*"

It will by no means be maintained that a tune cannot be strong, or suitable for a congregation, without being rigidly adjusted to the pattern here presented. But the union of strength and simplicity, in tunes of such acknowledged excellence, is a significant fact, and is sufficient for a practical suggestion.

Tunes for the congregation should be *spirited.* What Charnock says against "frozen and benumbed frames," in the worship of God, may very properly be applied to singing his praise. He says: "Dulness is against the light of nature. I do not remember that the heathen ever offered a snail to any of their false deities, nor an ass, but to Priapus, their unclean idol; but the Persians sacrificed to the sun a horse, a swift and generous creature. God provided against those in the law, commanding an ass's firstling, the offering of a sluggish creature, to be redeemed or his neck broke; but by no means to be offered to him."

Again, quoting the verse, "This is the day which the Lord hath made; we will be glad and rejoice in it;" he adds, "A lumpish frame becomes not a day and a duty that hath so noble and spiritual a mark upon it." "There is a joy when the comforts of God are dropped into the soul as oil upon the wheel, which, indeed, makes the faculties move with more speed and activity in his service, like the chariots of Ammi-Nadib."

May it not be said with truth that the wheels of our musical chariots need oiling? While the act of praising God in song is in its nature the most joyous service that belongs to our public worship, there is in many of our churches scarcely a fault that so much needs correction as that of a dull and spiritless performance. The hymns are sung with such "drowsy powers," that the "hosannas languish" and the "devotion dies." And this fault arises in great measure from the kind of tunes which are sung. They are either too slow, or they are weak, or they are empty and characterless.

In a collection of tunes for the congregation, there should be *variety*. The harp of the human sensibilities has a great number of strings, and each string is capable of many tones. The music which is provided for this harp to play should go through a wide range of expression, or it will dishonor the capacity of this noble instrument. While the great majority of the tunes should be suited to express the cheerful emotions, the collection would be sadly deficient without a frequent use of the *minor key*.

The rich resources of this tender musical scale have been greatly underrated, and greatly neglected. This is owing partly to the want of musical culture, partly to the want of refined and delicate sensibility, partly to the habit of associating minor tunes only with sad and funereal occasions, and partly, also, to the want of that deep religious experience which teaches what it is to cry unto God out of the depths of penitence, of spiritual desertion, and of irrepressible longing.

Music is like a magnetic needle. The major and minor scales are its positive and negative poles. And there is in the mind a sort of musical polarity corresponding to these poles, but changeful, and differently affected at different times by the presence of either of them. At one time it attracts what at another time it repels. The resounding strains of Zion could not be sung in Babylon. And there are seasons of darkness and of spiritual captivity in the experience of many a Christian, when a bright and gleeful song is "as vinegar upon nitre." The rich minor tune is the song with which a heavy heart is in quickest sympathy.

But the range of the minor key is not limited to mournful and pathetic expression : it extends to all the softened and subdued feelings which belong to Christian experience. Many hymns that are prayers, are most appropriately sung in it. Humility and confession belong to it. Reverence before the infinite Majesty is very impressively uttered by it. Nor have we exhausted its powers even then; for, while it is eminently fitted to express all the *lowly* attitudes of the mind, it is by no means to be confined to them.

Upon this point there is great and gross misapprehension. It is a common impression that there is a weakness in this key, which unfits it for use except when the soul is bowed down and bereft of strength. It has served us so often at such times, that we think it can do nothing else. But, in truth, it has a strength and dignity which do not yield to the major by one particle. It is not vivacious, and not naturally cheerful, but neither is it always sad. It is sedate, thoughtful, majestic. It has its tremulous plaint and its sympathizing wail; but open its deeper registers, and you hear successions and combinations of tone, whose grandeur lifts the soul. It can stoop to soothe us in our troubles, or it can open its broad wing and rise with us to the loftiest forms of adoration. The highest sublimity often seeks its aid, and is at home amid its solemn chords, like proud keels in the bosom of swelling waves.

§ 13. *Illustrations of the preceding Remarks.*

The tunes in the Sabbath Hymn and Tune Book, appear to have been prepared with a steady eye toward the principles which we have now laid down. It has not fully adopted these principles, but it has made a decided advance towards them.

Probably it has advanced far enough in this direction for the present; quite as far as will be appreciated by congregations whose taste has been exclusively formed upon the prevailing choir tunes. What we have to say in commendation of this book will be spoken of its *leading characteristics*, and not of every individual tune in it; for evidently there are tunes here which were not introduced upon their merits, but merely because of the popular demand for them. On the whole, however, the book furnishes many illustrations of the principles which we have endeavored to advocate.

1. It demonstrates that there can be for the people a collection of simple, easy tunes which are, nevertheless, *in the highest degree respectable as musical compositions.* See, for examples, the following list:—Alpheus, Sidney, Holbein, St. Michael, St. Nicholas, Kepler, Nilo, Barrow, Holland, Strand, Pekin, Elbe, Wall, Deal, St. Nicolai, Arnon, Tiber, Kelvin, Monmouth, Huron, Bingham, Erfurt, Phuvah, Blois, Theon, Butler, Lyne, Bethany, Agnol, Brent, Stanley, Galena, Dunfermline, Sherman, Nazareth, Berry, Beckford, Canonbury, Bonn. These are tunes whose merits will not be called in question. Though generally simple, they are scientific in their structure, and will stand the ordeal of musical criticism. Quite a number of old and familiar tunes, of equal merit, are not included in this list.

2. Eminently characteristic of this book are the *strength and spirit* of its tunes. These are their marked and leading traits. While nothing is light or gay, or secular and undignified in them, they have an awakening and inspiriting quality which eminently fits them for the service of praise. The following are examples:— Owen, Theon, Welt, Paul, Kepler, Field, Marden, Ryle, Mamre, White, Hull, Roland, Mead, Erskine, Beckford, Alfred, Alford, Otley, Fleet-Street, May, Wayne, Goodwin, Longwood, Cooper, Orion, Tyng, Bedford, Durham. Some of these are muscular and bold. There is another class, not less enlivening in their influence, perhaps, than these, but characterized rather by a bright and joyous tone, as— Kitto, Wales, Tully, Oak, Kelvin, St. Nicolai, Knight. In this enumeration, mention is made chiefly of new tunes, as the old ones are already known. The predominance of such tunes as these in this collection will

infuse a new spirit into our psalmody, wherever the book is used. It will awaken a new interest in the singing, as a part of worship, and will incline scores of persons to sing whose voices would never be heard in such tunes as Barby, Blendon, Shirland, Park-Street, Stonefield. We shall have strains more like what might have been struck from the impassioned harp of David, when he said, " My lips shall greatly rejoice when I sing unto thee;" "I will offer in his tabernacle sacrifices of joy."

3. There is a good proportion of *tunes in the minor key* in this book. They are about forty in number, and some of them are used twice. They are of rare excellence. They will help the spirit of devotion, and will exert a refining influence. For good examples of minors, see Agnol, Lyne, Bingham, Strand, Stanley, Brent, Hereford, Stello, Calvary, Noel, Vane, Tyne, Cole, Wall, Elliot, Galena, Malva, Canonbury, Akland. Strand is a tune whose beautiful melody is made very effective by unisonous singing.

4. A somewhat new feature of this book is the frequent use of *double tunes*. In these tunes, two stanzas are sung in immediate connection with each other, without any pause between them, and without any interlude. An increased animation in singing will be a consequence of this; and as the tunes are quick-moving, long hymns may be sung in them, without abridgment, and with less repetition of the same strains of music than in single tunes. For good double tunes, see Alfred, Agnol, Rayford, Rayner, Roland, Kepler, Deal, Byrd, Bendon, Ormond, Glen, Cole, Malta, Grove, Malva.

5. Great pains has been taken in this work to provide

pleasing melodies. We doubt whether Dr. Mason has ever, in any of his previous publications, devoted so much care to this point. It appears to have been a motto with him, " *The melody is the tune.*" He has endeavored to furnish melodies which could stand, as such, independently of the other parts; and he has presented them in such bold relief, that those who have an ear, even if they cannot sing by note, will easily discover them and follow their lead. Repeated tones, in which there can be no melody, are generally avoided, and tunes in the chanting style (with but one or two exceptions) have been omitted.

The *bass*, standing next in importance to the leading melody, has received special attention, and has been enlivened with more melody than basses usually contain. In consequence of this, the two remaining parts have a narrower function to perform, and many who now sing them will prefer to sing upon the treble,—a thing which, in congregational singing, is not only admissible, but greatly to be desired. Alterations will be found in the bass of several old tunes, as Canterbury, Nuremburg, Dedham, Arlington, Wilmot, Sicily, Stephens, Lanesboro', Hebron, Dover. The object of this is evidently twofold. First, that the harmony may be more complete when the treble and bass only are sung; and second, that the bass may always be kept below the treble, although the treble be sung an octave below its pitch, as is the case when it is sung by men's voices. For an example of this, see the small notes in the bass of Hamburg.

6. *The large number of tunes in sextuple measure*, is another peculiarity of this book. Respectable tunes in this movement are usually so popular, that they need

but little commendation to bring them into favorable notice. The following are good examples of this class: — Bethany, Holland, Alvan, Anley, Maitland, Ortonville, Ware, Bartow, Abville, Ell, Ray, Rayford. Aston, Holtham, Malta, Bonar, Bayton, Calbra.

7. There is an unusual *variety* of tunes in this collection. This was to be expected as a legitimate result of the plan of the work, which required the appropriate musical expression of all the shades of religious feeling contained in so large a collection of hymns. If there is variety in the hymns, and if there is appropriateness in the adaptation of tunes to them, then there must be variety in the tunes. This variety is found in the proportion of *old and new* tunes, in the supply of *minor* tunes, in the departments of *melody, harmony,* and *rhythm,* and in the very unusual number of *metrical forms,* many of which have never before appeared in our books of psalmody. The harmonies are rich, ecclesiastical, and in all respects the best. They show the results of life-long study. If, for reasons already stated, there is, and ought to be, but a small number of tunes in the slower forms of triple measure, this lack is compensated by a large· number of excellent tunes in sextuple measure. It is true that the old notation, already described, occurs very often, as it certainly should; but, notwithstanding this, the rhythmical varieties are great, and some of them are quite new. Of course a greater variety might have been obtained by a liberal admission of all those faults of style to which we have above referred as at variance with true simplicity, and by resorting to such musical spicery and condiment as perverted appetites crave. We should then have a medley rather than a variety,

and should be keeping alive that unhealthy and prurient taste, which so much needs to be held in check. When it is considered how severe a taste has presided over the introduction of tunes into this collection, and how many cheap and factitious methods of catching the ear have been sternly rejected, it is matter of surprise that the collection furnishes a variety so large and rich. The result shows that the most ample resources must have been at hand in its preparation, and the most indefatigable industry exercised upon them.

A first glance at the tunes might lead to the supposition that there is too much *sameness;* but on further examination it will be found that this can have reference only to the eye, or the notation, and not to the ear. The tunes are written mostly in black notes, in order to encourage a more rapid performance. If half of them had been written in white notes, the desired variety would have appeared to the eye, while the effect upon the ear would have been the same as now.

But probably the impression of their sameness has arisen from their simplicity, and from the very frequent use of that ancient rhythmic notation, on the merits of which we have already enlarged. .This notation occurs so much oftener in this book than in any other now in use among us, that it constitutes one of the most noticeable peculiarities of the work. Being new to us, it attracts attention unduly, and often, doubtless, to such a degree that *the essential character* of the tunes, lying in their melodies and harmonies, is unperceived. As the rhythmic form is of course the same in every tune in which it is used, there is, to a superficial judgment, an appearance of sameness in the tunes as a class, whatever richness of variety there may be in their melodies and harmonies. But the rhythm is only the drapery of the tune. It is to the tune itself, what verse is to thought, a mode of expression. It may be changed, and often is changed, without affecting the identity of the tune.- In the tune Evan, for example, one may choose common time, and another sextuple time, but the tune is the same in either dress. Dundee, St. Anns, and all such tunes in common time might be made to put on the rhythmical dress of Hebron. Their essential merit would not be affected by the change.

But there is probably a slight prejudice in some minds against the restoration of this ancient rhythm, for the reason that it changes the movement to which they have always been accustomed in old and standard tunes. This prejudice is very natural, and was cherished but a few years ago by those who are now zealous advocates of what, in every rational view of it, must appear the best possible rhythmical form for the congregation, and what so high an authority as Mr. Havergal pronounces to be " the only one which *all singers* feel to be natural." It is the belief of the writer of these pages, that the charge of sameness in the tunes of the Sabbath Hymn and Tune Book has arisen *mainly* from the restoration of this ancient rhythm. If this be true, the charge will not long continue to be made, for it is found that the old notation, after a very short acquaintance with it, is felt to be in every respect superior to what has been so aptly termed " the modern drawl."

8. Some of the tunes, if considered merely as musical compositions, may be regarded as unsatisfactory, or as

destitute of an artistic interest. But it must be remembered that they are designed to be ecclesiastical and congregational in their character. They are, therefore, characterized by a noble simplicity, an admirable fitness for the purposes of devotion, and a most commendable adaptation to the musical capacity of the great majority of singers; and that they are as musically rich and varied as they could be consistently with simplicity, devotion, and successful congregational use. Actual use *by the congregation* is to be the test of their worth. This is the only proper criterion by which to judge them. A few voices using them at the social fireside may not discover their value. They are made for the great congregation, and for a multitude of voices; and when a multitude of voices are heard upon them with such "loud noise" and "joyful noise" as the psalmist desired, when, in addition to all the force of vocal and instrumental chorus which could be gathered, he called upon the sea to roar with all its fulness, it will be seen that the simplest and strongest tunes are not only the best for devotional effect, but that under such a weight of intonation they are the most satisfying to the ear.

Tunes less simple than these could not be sung by the people generally, while such tunes as these may, with suitable painstaking, be sung everywhere. The tunes which the Reformers introduced were such as the Old Hundredth and Monmouth, in the very form, rhythmically, in which they now appear in the Sabbath Hymn and Tune Book, and the people *did sing them* — sang them in the churches and schools, in the streets and fields. We have only to imitate the example of the Reformers in regard to the kind of tune which we set before the people, in order to be as successful in congregational song, other things being equal, as they were.

Those tunes in the Sabbath Hymn and Tune Book which constitute its chief peculiarity, resemble more nearly the tunes which were used by the Reformers, than those of any other collection within our knowledge. The bold thought, the earnest piety, the martyr-like courage and strength of will, which produced and pushed forward the Reformation in the face of the papal world, found its musical expression in those strong and simple structures which could, and sometimes did, bear the roll of thousands of voices in unison. And it is known that these tunes produced the taste, in England, in the early part of the sixteenth century, for music of that simple, solid character, which distinguishes what is known as the School of English Church Music, the purest and highest type of a genuine ecclesiastical style which has ever existed. That style of sacred song with which are connected the immortal names of Tye, Tallis, Farrant, Byrd, Morley, and Orlando Gibbons, whose works are classics, and "who laid the foundation on which are built the stupendous choruses of Handel's oratorios," may be said to have had its birth in the glow of Luther's heart and the strength of Luther's thought. It was a style which found congenial soil in the English national character. It was consistent with its manly strength. And every step which is taken, by the compilers of our collections of church music, toward a return to that style, from the weaker, the secular, the sentimental styles which the foreign and worldly tastes of southern Europe have furnished, should be hailed with gratitude and delight. It has been supposed that whatever bears the name of

such composers as Haydn and Mozart is fit for the
Sabbath and the sanctuary; and our books of psalmody
have been filled with extracts from the masses of such
composers, written in operatic style, and for papal ears
that were too worldly to enjoy the noble strains of their
own Palestrina. These extracts with which our tune-
books have been flooded are neither ecclesiastical nor
English, and they should be rejected just as fast as the
public taste can be educated to something better.
Protestant churches should be as far from the Papal
church in the character of their songs, as they are in
ritual and creed.

A renowned English scholar and musician, Dr.
Crotch, has spoken so ably and so truthfully upon this
point, that we cannot forbear calling in his testimony.
He says:

" The psalms used and composed by the Reformers,
and those by their immediate successors in this kingdom, together with those made in imitation of these
pure sacred strains, are alone worthy of study; while
all the Magdalen and Foundling Hymns, with psalms
made out of songs, glees, quartets, in drawling, whin-
ing, minuet-like strains, with two or three notes to each
syllable, full of modern and chromatic discords, should
be denounced and utterly abolished.

"As long as the pure sublime style, the style peculiarly suited to the church service, was cherished, which
was only to about the middle of the seventeenth
century, we consider the ecclesiastical style to be in a
state of perfection; but it has been gradually and im-
perceptibly losing its character ever since. Improvements have, indeed, been made in the contexture of

the score, in the flow of melody, in the accentuation and expression of words, in the beauty of the solo, and the delicacy of the accompaniment, but these are not indications of the sublime; church music, therefore, is on the decline. The remedy is obvious. *Let the young composer study the productions of the sixteenth and seventeenth centuries in order to acquire the true church style*, which should always be sublime and scientific. But I must caution him that he will probably be disappointed at first hearing them. He will meet with critics and writers who assert that whatever does not produce effect cannot be worthy of our admiration; but the sublime, in every art, though less attractive at first, is most deserving of regard. *For this quality does not strike and surprise, dazzle and amuse, but it elevates and expands the mind*, filling it with awe and wonder, not always suddenly, but in proportion to the study bestowed upon it. The more it is known, the more it will be understood, approved, admired, venerated, — I might almost say, adored."

9. The tunes in the Sabbath Hymn and Tune Book are *suitable for children*. They have simplicity, vivacity, variety, and pleasing melodies; and their chaste and church-like character qualifies them to exert a much-needed influence in the formation of a correct taste. In many of our Sabbath schools, the musical taste of the children is formed upon models which are far enough from being either sacred or classic. In the preparation of the thousands of Sabbath school tune-books which have been scattered throughout the land, the great object seems to have been to provide music which would *please the children*. If teachers

and superintendents are remonstrated with for using such airs as Hail Columbia, the Marseilles Hymn, and even well-known convivial and drinking songs, and "negro songs," they reply that "the children like them;" and this seems to be thought a sufficient reason for introducing them.

"The past connection of these airs with secular words is not the only, nor always the greatest objection to them. *They are not adapted to the expression of sacred words, and are unfit for use as sacred music.* The evil accomplished is one that extends through the whole life of the children; for tastes and ideas formed in childhood are not easily changed in later years; they get wrong impressions as to the uses of music in church; the distinction between music which has for its object the mere gratification of the senses, and that which has a sacred purpose, is utterly destroyed. It is not strange that, under such circumstances there should be so strong a tendency in our sacred song to degenerate into a mere pastime. We hear it used as a pastime in childhood, and come to regard this as its proper use. It is quite likely that children may not as eagerly engage in proper church music as they do in the jigs, ditties, and negro songs which are now so much used in Sabbath schools, but if properly trained they will like more appropriate music, and as they grow older, their tastes being properly formed, they will have a true idea and enjoyment of genuine church music; that is, of music appropriately used for the expression of religious thought and feeling. It is not a question of what children like best, but of what is best for them. We are not condemning the use of lively, cheerful music in Sabbath schools or in church. On the contrary, the drawling way in which many admirable tunes, as the Old Hundredth, for instance, are too often sung, is a great evil, and has done much to drive them out of use. When we are expressing in song cheerful feelings, secular or sacred, the music must correspond, or it will be inappropriate; but there is a fitness of things, and there are many airs, and these very popular, which are not adapted to the expression of any religious feeling whatever, joyful or sad.

" Generally it is better that the same tunes should be used in the Sabbath school, which are used in the religious services of the church with which it is connected. The children are thus prepared to take their part with the great congregation, and the identity of the songs they use with those used in the more formal worship has also a good influence upon them. If these tunes are proper ones, and are properly sung, they will be interesting and cheerful; there will not be difficulty on this score; but, even should there be, it is better to sacrifice something in this way than in matters of more importance; better that the music should be less attractive than that its attraction should be evil.

" We are sure that many of these Sabbath school tune-books are accomplishing great evil to the cause of church music. It is not wonderful that children so educated should look for mere musical excitement and diversion in church music when they arrive at maturer years, instead of aiming at anything like religious benefit."

10. The Sabbath Hymn and Tune Book exhibits a striking *appropriateness in the adaptation of hymns to tunes.* Evidently the great burden of labor in the im-

mediate preparation of the book has fallen upon this department. To adjust twelve hundred and ninety hymns to tunes appropriately, that is, with discernment of the real character of each hymn, and of the musical notation which it requires for its most effective utterance in song, was no light undertaking. It was a work requiring long experience and sound judgment. It has received the benefit of both; and the result shows a remarkable appropriateness, felicity, and oneness of spirit between hymn and tune. That there was need of this labor to be performed by one who was competent to do it, let the unfit selection of tunes which we notice in our churches almost every Sabbath answer. Week after week the best hymns in use are suffering the violence of being yoked with tunes with which they can have no manner of sympathy. Often the tune does not appear to be selected with any reference at all to the hymn, any further than to have it of the right metre. The choir leader consults merely his own musical likings, or the mood of mind in which he happens to be. If he likes tunes of the dainty and sentimental sort best, we shall hear them upon all occasions. We have in mind a *pretty* tune, usually, and very appropriately, sung to the words —

> " By cool Siloam's shady rill
> How sweet the lily grows
> How sweet the breath, beneath the hill,
> Of Sharon's dewy rose."

It is not long since we heard this tune sung, by a very respectable choir near Boston, to the hymn —

"Keep silence all created things,
And wait your Maker's nod;
My soul stands trembling while she sings
The honors of her God.

"Life, death, and hell, and worlds unknown,
Hang on his firm decree;
He sits on no precarious throne,
Nor borrows leave to be."

In regard to the matter of adaptation, as it appears in the Sabbath Hymn and Tune Book, we notice several things.

First. — Care has been taken not to violate old associations. There are many instances in which a particular hymn has become associated, by long usage, with a particular tune. The hymn always suggests the tune, and the tune the hymn. In such cases, both will generally be found upon the same page in this book.

For example, the hymn, "All hail the power of Jesus' name," to the tune Coronation. The hymn, "How pleased and blessed was I," to the tune Dalston. The hymn, "Rise, my soul, and stretch thy wings," to the tune Amsterdam. "Ye tribes of Adam join," to Lenox. "Come, sound his praise abroad," to Silver Street. "Your harps, ye trembling saints," to Olmutz. "Majestic sweetness sits enthroned," to Ortonville. "On the mountain's top appearing," to Zion. "There is a fountain filled with blood," to Cowper. "Thus far the Lord hath led me on," to Hebron. "Broad is the road that leads to death," to Windham. "Oh thou, to whom all creatures bow," to St. Martin's. "My soul, be on thy guard," to Laban. "Come, thou

Almighty King," to Italian Hymn. " The voice of free grace," to Scotland. "Early, my God, without delay," to Lanesboro'.

In all the above instances, and doubtless many others, the hymn and tune will be found together in this book. If, however, we turn to the tune Wells, we shall find that it has been separated from the hymn, " Life is the time to serve the Lord," to which it has so long been sung. The reason is obvious. The character of the tune Wells is lively, joyous, bold ; and the last stanza of this hymn is wholly unsuitable for such a tune —

> " There are no acts of pardon passed
> In the cold grave to which we haste;
> But darkness, death, and long despair,
> Reign in eternal silence there."

Second. — It is noticeable that hymns suitable for occasions of special interest, such as Ordination, Dedication, Joining the Church, Baptism, and the Lord's Supper, are set to the most familiar old tunes, such as Peterboro', St. Martin's, Dundee, Ward, Downs. Notice the hymns to which these tunes are set, upon pages 183, 381, 233, 45, 165.

Third. — An interesting connection is established, in this book, between old versions of the psalms and the oldest tunes. The book commences with the Old Hundredth, itself more than three hundred years old, and upon the same page with it stand the three most noted versions of the One Hundredth Psalm : first, that of Sternhold and Hopkins, "All people that on earth do dwell," which are the first English words with which the tune was ever sung, and which are nearly as old as the tune; then, the version of Tate and Brady, about half as old, " With one consent, let all the earth;" then, the version of Watts, " Ye nations round the earth rejoice."

On the next page is a minor, as old as the Old Hundredth, to an old version of the Eighty-fourth Psalm, by Milton, " How lovely are thy dwellings fair." On the next page is the old tune Canterbury, to a hymn from Tate and Brady. The fine old Scotch tune, Dunfermline, stands with the Scotch version of the Twenty-third Psalm, " The Lord's my Shepherd, I'll not want," to which it was often sung in the time of John Knox. Both hymn and tune are, therefore, more than three hundred years old. Upon the forty-ninth page is the tune Canon, being the original form of the tune now known in many books as Tallis's Evening Hymn. This tune is about three hundred years old, and is set to hymns by Bishop Kenn. The Thirty-fourth Psalm, from Tate and Brady, commencing, " Through all the changing scenes of life," is set to the stalwart old tune St. Ann's.

Tate and Brady's version of the Sixty-fifth Psalm, " For thee, O God, our constant praise," is set to the tune Bava, which is one of the old Genevan tunes known to have been in common use by the Pilgrims in 1620. Monmouth is restored to its original form as composed by Luther, and stands upon the same page with his hymn, " Great God, what do I see and hear." Lewin, on page 350, to the 404th hymn, is the tune to which this hymn has long been sung in Germany. On the 115th page are two hymns from the Latin, to an old Roman minor, all of which must be several centuries old. Christmas, on page 112, is an English Christmas carol, seven or eight hundred years old. It has been sung two hundred years in England to the words, " While shepherds watched their flocks by night."

Fourth. — There is an adaptation of tunes to peculiarities of structure in particular hymns, which is worthy of notice. See pages 366, 244, 262, 199, 139, 110, where, in one or more of the hymns, the uniform repetition of the closing line or lines in every stanza requires a corresponding " refrain " in the music. The effect of this is intensive. See the tune Walford, where the music provides for a jubilant expression of the words —

" The year of jubilee is come,
Return, ye ransomed sinners, home."

The same effect in " Shining Shore " is already well known.

In the tune Ellard, page 259, there is a special adaptation in the last line. Clayton, page 311, gives forcible expression to the repeated line in the hymn. Owen, page 74, has a special adaptation to the 339th hymn, in the very strong musical emphasis of the last line. The last line of every stanza contains the burden of the hymn, and to this the music corresponds. The boldness of the octave interval contributes largely to this effect. See, also, the very spirited tune Welt, page 350, to hymn 573. Olden, page 224, has a special adaptation to hymns 292 and 298, in the impressive utterance which is given to the first three syllables of every stanza. Notice, also, that this special adaptation is not allowed to mar the unity of the tune as a whole.

The third line is introduced with the same rhythmic form as the first line, and thus the proper balance of the tune is preserved.

On pages 146 and 318, the emphatic commencement of each stanza in several of the hymns is well expressed by the first four notes of the tunes Berne and Ray. On page 218, Dixon has a still more striking adaptation to the 649th hymn.

In some instances careful provision has been made for the appropriate utterance of difficult words: as the word "Gethsemane," in the tune Morley, on page 163, and the word "crucified," in the tune Worth, page 216. The voice is allowed to move only a semitone in the utterance of these words, and thus not only an easy utterance, but a subdued and tender expression is given in singing.

Fifth. — There will be found an agreement between the hymns and the tunes, *as to the general spirit and impression of each.* Each hymn seems to have been studied, its true emotional character discerned, and such music provided for it as would best aid its expression. Coldly descriptive or didactic hymns, if there are such, have not been wafted upon the wings of sextuple time; nor are hymns of direct address to God made to trip off in a brisk, chanting style, like the words, " Thou dear Redeemer, dying Lamb," to Hussitan Chant.

For a good specimen of general adaptation, see the vividly descriptive hymn, " The Lord our God is full of might," to the tune Ocean, page 76. The energy of all the hymns on page 74 is finely illustrated in the tune Owen. Mossley, page 388, breathes the same spirit of contentment which dictated Madame Guyon's 140th hymn. Nilo, page 164, has a gentleness of character which seems to have grown out of the 541st hymn, and is a beautiful expression of it. The method of barring, employed in this and some other tunes in this book is new. The effect of it is peculiar. It gives a variety in the measure which cannot be obtained by that which is found in such tunes as Hebron, Rockingham, etc. Preston, page 266, is evidently intended for Bonar's hymn, 906, and is an excellent adaptation. The same may be said of Elbe, page 140, to the 434th hymn. Theon, page 131, expresses the 1225th hymn with almost martial vigor. The same may be said of Marden, page 393, to hymn 1022; and of White, page 283, in its connection with the 896th hymn, and, indeed, with all the hymns on the page. Pekin, Dennis, Hereford, Zeta, Severn, Mamre, Tully, Kent, Vail, are all good adaptations to the hymns connected with them. See, also, Ware, page 288, to the 61st hymn; Elton, page 188, to hymn 538; Knight, page 269, to hymn 264; Paul, page 396, to hymn 993; Galena, page 273, to hymn 1147; Epsom, page 123, to the hymns under it, and especially to the first one. Elliot, page 352, to the hymn, "Just as I am, without one plea," has been commended by the English authoress of this favorite hymn as the best of the many musical adaptations which have been furnished for it. Leslie, page 194, in even time and in the minor key, seems to be the appropriate expression of a narrative hymn, whose sentiment is that of penitential gratitude —

" I was a wandering sheep,
I did not love the fold."

Deal, page 32, in the style of the old English madrigals, has a sweetly meandering melody, and is happily united with Montgomery's hymn —

> " Glad was my heart to hear
> My old companions say."

Both hymn and tune express the content of a pious soul when in the house of God " With friends and brethren dear." Keeble, page 79, is far better for the hymn, " Brightest and best," than the old tune Folsom. The first note in the last line of Folsom is wholly impracticable.

Portuguese Hymn, page 270, a good tune for congregational singing and a general favorite, is adapted to several good hymns, so that it may be often used. Roland, page 296, has the same rhythmic form as Coronation. It has all the spirit of that celebrated tune without its faults. It is not too high, does not compel us to sing the last half of every stanza twice, and does not trifle with quavers.

We would call attention to an important principle of adaptation seen on the 193d page in the connection of the tune Kelvin with the 419th hymn. The hymn and tune are closely related in character. A sunny cheerfulness pervades them both. The hymn takes its root in the text, " I am with you alway." It is an exhilarating thought that in all our toil and trouble, in all our darkness and loneliness, Christ is with us. Of course we are to bear this toil and trouble, and to experience this darkness and loneliness, but that is not the leading thought in the hymn. The leading thought is, that Christ is with us. That is its key-note. That is what animated the mind of the author when he wrote it. Now, if in singing this hymn our minds are not in the same posture of delight at the thought of Christ's supporting presence, our musical rendering will be false, and the true impression of the hymn lost. But what kind of performance do we hear from most of our choirs in a hymn of this kind? We hear almost nothing that expresses the prevailing sentiment of the hymn. The choir seem hardly to have raised any question as to what that sentiment is. Their strength is to be laid out on particular words and phrases. They see in the hymn the words, "sadness," "dark and drear," "storm is sweeping," "lonely valley," "chilling stream," and they take the greatest pains to express these phrases, and to make them as dreary as possible, without an apparent thought of Christ's being with us in all to banish our "sadness," and to make the valley anything but "lonely." Such a performance is a mere playing upon words, while it misses or ignores the real import of the hymn, and instead of helping its proper impression, injures it. There is no doubt that many choirs would deliberately select a doleful tune for this hymn, judging from the words "sadness" and "lonely valley," that such a tune was required. And here is a sufficient reason, if there were no other, why we should have a book for use in public worship in which hymns and tunes are appropriately united.

11. The Sabbath Hymn and Tune Book omits tunes which are not adapted to congregational song. Doubtless many persons will miss from this collection *certain favorite old tunes*, which they would wish to see. To lovers of psalmody there are usually a few such tunes, without which no collection is, in their view, complete.

As the hope of pleasing all would be vain, since no two persons would make the same selection for a book of this kind, it becomes necessary that principles, rather than individual preferences, should determine the admission of the tunes. The regard in which we hold a favorite tune is not always based upon any intelligent estimate of its value. That may be the best of tunes to us, which, when subjected to the test either of a musical analysis or of actual use, is demonstrated to be totally unfit for the congregation. It is remarkable what power there is in certain much admired hymns to introduce into favor very objectionable tunes, and delude us into the belief that the tunes are as good as the hymns. The popularity of the old tune Jordan is a remarkable illustration of the power of the hymn, " There is a land of pure delight." The tune Stephens would have been as much admired as Brattle Street, if it had always been sung to the hymn, " While thee I seek, protecting power." Naomi owes much of its popularity to the words, " Father whate'er of earthly bliss." The hymn, " Why do we mourn departing friends," if sung in a season of affliction, would attach one to a worse tune than China. Cowper is far from being a perfect tune, but we seldom think of its defects when singing the words, " There is a fountain filled with blood." " Rock of Ages " furnishes another similar example. If we may be deceived in regard to the real merits of tunes thus associated, and if they have faults which are a serious obstacle to success in congregational singing, should we not willingly, for the sake of so worthy a cause, allow them to be dropped ?

No one person should select the tunes for so wide a use as this book contemplates, in the exercise of his own unaided judgment. Dr. Mason is probably as well qualified to do this as any one; but his selection, in this case, was made with the help of a hundred lists of tunes, prepared in as many different sections of the country, and representing what were considered, in those respective districts, the most approved and serviceable tunes in use. By these lists he was guided, and it is probable that the selection he has made comes as near to meeting the public want, in its widest extent, as any selection of respectable and suitable tunes could do.

12. *Brief statement of Rules for Congregational Singing.*

For the sake of presenting compactly the principal heads of remark contained in the latter part of this chapter, bearing upon what are believed to be the best methods of conducting congregational song, we have gathered these heads into the subjoined table of practical Rules.

(1.) The congregation should *stand* when they sing.

(2.) They should rise, simultaneously and promptly, when the organist, in giving out the tune, has reached the beginning of the last line.

(3.) They should stand, in the usual attitude of worship, facing the pulpit.

(4.) If the help of a choir of singers, well disposed toward congregational singing, can be secured, they may be of great service in leading the congregation. But if the congregation are not led by a choir, they should be led by a precentor.

(5.) The organ and the choir or precentor should be

in front of the congregation, near the pulpit, and on the same level with the pews.

(6.) Children should be instructed in singing, at home and in the schools, and should be encouraged to sing with the congregation.

(7.) The greater part of the congregation, male and female, should sing upon the treble of the tunes. It is indispensable that there be men's voices on this part.

(8.) Let the hymns and tunes that are used be made familiar by frequent rehearsals, both in public and in families.

(9.) Use any given hymn always with the same tune.

(10.) Use a book in which the hymn and tune are upon one page.

(11.) Let the singing be in steady uniform time from the beginning to the end of the hymn, without any noticeable acceleration or slackening of the time.

(12.) Let there be no forced pauses for the observance of punctuation, nor any needless delay at the end of the lines.

(13.) Let there be no labored effort after "expression," by means of frequent and sudden changes from soft to loud and the reverse, or by the swelling and tapering of the voice, or by studied accentuation.

(14.) The connection of the hymn should not be broken by organ interludes, or needless, long pauses.

(15.) The singing of a familiar hymn will often be more spirited if the reading of it from the pulpit is omitted.

(16.) Use tunes that are strictly congregational in their structure. But, until these are learned, it may be advisable to use such choir tunes, judiciously selected, as are already familiar.

WARREN F. DRAPER,
PUBLISHER AND BOOKSELLER,
ANDOVER, MASS.

Publishes and offers for Sale the following, which will be sent post paid on receipt of the sum named.

GUERICKE'S CHURCH HISTORY. Translated by W. G. T. SHEDD, Brown Professor in Andover Theological Seminary. 438 pp. 8vo. $2.25.

This volume includes the period of the ANCIENT CHURCH (the first six centuries, A. C.) or the Apostolic and Patristic Church.

We regard Professor Shedd's version, now under notice, as a happy specimen of the TRANS-FUSION rather than a TRANSLATION, which many of the German treatises should receive. The style of his version is far superior to that of the original.— [Bib. Sacra, Jan. 1858.

DISCOURSES AND ESSAYS. By PROF. W. G. T. SHEDD. 271 pp. 12mo. 85 cts.

Few clearer and more penetrating minds can be found in our country than that of Prof. Shedd. And besides, he writes with a chaste and sturdy eloquence, transparent as crystal; so that if he goes DEEP, we love to follow him. If the mind gets dull, or dry, or ungovernable, put it to grappling with these masterly productions. — [Congregational Herald, Chicago.

The striking sincerity, vigor, and learning of this volume will be admired even by those readers who cannot go with the author in all his opinions. Whatever debate the philosophical tendencies of the book may challenge, its literary ability and moral spirit will be commended everywhere. — *New Englander.*

These discourses are al marked by profound thought and perspicuity of sentiment. — *Princeton Review.*

LECTURES UPON THE PHILOSOPHY OF HISTORY. By PROF. W. G. T. SHEDD. 128 pp. 12mo. 60 cents.

CONTENTS. — The abstract Idea of History.— The Nature and Definition of Secular History. — The Nature and Definition of Church History. — The Verifying Test in Church History.

The style of these Lectures has striking merits. The author chooses his words with rare skill and taste, from an ample vocabulary, and writes with strength and refreshing simplicity. The Philosophy of Realism, in application to history and historical theology, is advocated by vigorous reasoning, and made intelligible by original and felicitous illustrations. — *New Englander.*

Professor Shedd has already achieved a high reputation for the union of philosophic insight with genuine scholarship, of depth and clearness of thought with force and elegance of style, and for profound views of sin and grace, cherished not merely on theoretical, but still more on moral and experimental grounds. — *Princeton Review.*

OUTLINES OF A SYSTEMATIC RHETORIC. From the German of DR. FRANCIS THEREMIN, by WILLIAM G. T. SHEDD. Third and Revised Edition, with an Introductory Essay by the translator. pp. 216. 12mo. 75 cts.

This is a work of much solid value. It is adapted to advanced students, and can be read and reread with advantage by professed public speakers, however accomplished they may be in the important art of persuasion. This edition is an improvement upon the other, containing a new introductory essay, illustrating the leading position of the work, and a series of questions adapting it to the use of the student. — *Boston Recorder.*

It is not a work of surface suggestions, but of thorough and philosophic analysis, and, as such, is of great value to the student, and especially to him who habitually addresses men on the most important themes. — *Congregational Quarterly.*

The Introductory Essay which Professor Shedd has prefixed to this valuable Treatise, is elaborate, vigorous, impressive. It excites the mind not only to thought, but also to the expression of thought, to inward and outward activity. The whole volume is characterized by freshness and originality of remark, a purity and earnestness of moral feeling. — *Bib. Sacra,* 1859.

BIBLIOTHECA SACRA AND BIBLICAL REPOSITORY.
E. A. PARK and S. H. TAYLOR, Editors. Published at Andover on the first of January, April, July and October.

Each number contains about 225 pages, making a volume of 900 pages yearly. This work is larger, by more than 100 pages per volume than any other religious quarterly in the country.

This Review is edited by Prof. E. A. Park, of the Theological Seminary, and S. H. Taylor, LL. D., of Phillips Academy, Andover. Among its regular contributors, are eminent scholars connected with various theological and collegiate institutions of the United States. Its pages will be enriched by such contributions from Foreign Missionaries in the East as may illustrate the Biblical Record ; and also by such essays from distinguished naturalists as may elucidate the agreement between Science and Religion. It is the organ of no clique or party, but aims to exhibit the broad scriptural views of truth, and to cherish a catholic spirit among the conflicting schools of evangelical divines.

"Questions of philosophy and the analysis of language, of Biblical and literary criticism, of the constitution and life of the Church of Christ, of practical morality and evangelical religion, of biblical geography and the interpretation of prophecy, and the relation of Science to Religion, together with ample literary intelligence, both foreign and domestic,"— these make up the matter of each number, and cannot fail to interest Christian Scholars, Clergymen and Laymen.

Terms. — $4.00 per annum. A discount of 25 per cent. will be made to those who pay STRICTLY IN ADVANCE, and receive the numbers directly from the office of publication, postage UNPAID. When supplied by agents, $3,50, in advance ; otherwise $4.00.

Postage. — The postage is five cents per number, or twenty cents per year, to any part of the United States.

TESTIMONY OF THE PRESS.

The articles, treating of interesting themes useful to the general scholar as well as the theologian, fully sustain the very high character of this quarterly, which, restricted to no sect, and broad in its range of thought and instruction, has commended itself to the best minds in our own and foreign lands. [Boston Courier.

This, as is well known, is the great religious Quarterly of New England, if not of the country, and is held in high estimation in England and Germany as the principal organ of biblical and philological criticism in the English language.

This work as now conducted, deserves a large and generous patronage from clergymen of all denominations. [Puritan Recorder.

No Parish is either poor or rich enough to be able to do without its benefit to its pastor. [Congregationalist.

INDEX TO THE BIBLIOTHECA SACRA AND BIBLICAL
REPOSITORY, Volumes 1 to 13 (from 1844 to 1856.) Containing an Index of Subjects and Authors, a Topical Index, and a list of Scripture Texts. Paper covers, $1.75; cloth, $2.00; half goat, $2.50.

BIBLICAL REPOSITORY, First Series, comprising the twelve volumes from the commencement of the work to 1838. The first four volumes contain each four numbers ; the succeeding eight volumes, two numbers each. A few sets only remain.

The Biblical Repository was commenced at Andover, in 1831. The present series of the Bibliotheca Sacra was commenced in 1844. The two periodicals were united in 1851. The volume of the combined periodicals for the present year (1858) is the forty-sixth of the Biblical Repository and the fifteenth of the Bibliotheca Sacra.

VIEW OF ANDOVER. A finely executed Lithographic View of Andover, on a sheet 18 by 24 inches, exclusive of the margin.

The sheet contains a view of the Town from the west, and an enlarged delineation of the Literary Institutions in the border. It will be sent by mail, post paid, on receipt of $1,25.

www.ingramcontent.com/pod-product-compliance
Lightning Source LLC
Chambersburg PA
CBHW051733300426
44115CB00007B/540